THREE QUESTIONS FOR SIXTY-FIVE COMPOSERS

THREE QUESTIONS FOR SIXTY-FIVE COMPOSERS

Bálint András Varga

UNIVERSITY OF ROCHESTER PRESS

First published 2011
Second printing 2015

University of Rochester Press
668 Mt. Hope Avenue, Rochester, NY 14620, USA
www.urpress.com
and Boydell & Brewer Limited
PO Box 9, Woodbridge, Suffolk IP12 3DF, UK
www.boydellandbrewer.com

ISBN-13: 978-1-58046-379-9
ISSN: 1071-9989

Library of Congress Cataloging-in-Publication Data

Varga, Bálint András.
[3 kérdés, 82 zeneszerző. English]
Three questions for sixty-five composers / Bálint András Varga.
p. cm. — (Eastman studies in music, 1071-9989 ; v. 85)
Includes index.
ISBN 978-1-58046-379-9 (hardcover) 1. Composers—Interviews.
I. Title.
ML390.A1113 2011
780.92'2—dc22

2010045369

A catalogue record for this title is available from the British Library.

For Friedrich Cerha,
Georg Friedrich Haas,
and
Johannes Maria Staud

CONTENTS

PREFACE TO THE ENGLISH-LANGUAGE EDITION

This book is proof that composers, whether they are compatriots or live far apart, whether they belong to the same generation or are (grand)parents and (grand)children in the closely knit family of creative musicians, listen to each other. It is as simple as that.

Before submitting the manuscript in 1986 to Editio Musica Budapest, the Hungarian state music publisher where my job was the promotion of contemporary Hungarian composers, I made an attempt at a graphic demonstration of the intricate web of interrelationships: who has influenced whom, what influences reach over several generations, creating a family tree, so to speak, of composers or of compositions. Needless to say, I failed, probably not just because of lacking talent in the visual arts.

The genealogical table of contemporary music is so complex as to defy illustration. I hope these interviews will nevertheless help the reader to trace creative influences over the decades. In addition, the composers' statements should give an idea of the working of their minds within the areas defined by the questions. (For the three questions, please see the preface to the Hungarian edition.)

This book, then, is about musical genealogy and aspects of the psychology of musical creativity.

In addition, the interviews highlight the role of politics in the development (or stagnation) of the arts such as music; they demonstrate the resourcefulness of those deprived of but hungry for information, in a successful effort to find loopholes; they also highlight the tremendous significance of the radio as a provider of inspiration. Nowadays when radio stations are starved of financial resources and tend to ignore minority interests (which contemporary music no doubt represents), the statements of many composers regarding the fundamental role music broadcasts have played in their lives ought to make editors stop to ponder whether they are doing the right thing.

Now, close to the end of the first decade of the twenty-first century, with many of the composers dead, the answers to the three questions have acquired the status of documents of the recent past. I have nevertheless decided to pare down the number of interviews originally published in Hungarian from eighty-two to sixty-one. I have left out those whose names and music would not be known on an international scale and whose replies contained no element of novelty which would have added to the picture.

Four composers have been added, raising their number to sixty-five: on realizing that Austrian music received inadequate representation in the first edition, I have approached representatives of three generations: Friedrich Cerha (1926), Georg Friedrich Haas (1953), and Johannes Maria Staud (1974). I have also dedicated the book to them, as a sign of my esteem for their music and my gratitude for many years of wonderful cooperation, which enriched my stint with Universal Edition (UE). As I was about to submit the manuscript to the publisher, the long-lost cassette of my interview with Alfred Schnittke, recorded at the Aldeburgh Festival in the late 1980s, surfaced unexpectedly. This is its first publication.

In the mid-1990s, that is, about a decade after the appearance of the Hungarian edition, I decided to confront composers with the views they expressed in the late 1970s–early 1980s, to see if they wished to revise them in any way. Many of them complied, as indicated by the date(s) appended to the interviews. In preparing the material for the English-language edition in 2009–10, I got in touch with the composers once again to bring their answers up to date. As a result of these revisions, *Three Questions for Sixty-Five Composers* has become an altogether different book from the Hungarian original.

On rereading the text after so many years, memories were conjured up which I felt needed recording. Hence the short introductions to some of the conversations. They are rather lightweight, very subjective sketches which I hope will round out the portraits drawn by the interviews. Where there were no personal recollections to draw upon, I have provided some factual information.

Bálint András Varga
July 2010

PREFACE TO THE HUNGARIAN EDITION (1986)

The Three Questions

1. *Have you had an experience similar to Witold Lutosławski's: he heard John Cage's* Second Piano Concerto *on the radio—an encounter which changed his musical thinking and ushered in a new creative period, the first result of which was his* Jeux vénitiens (1960–61).

2. *A composer is surrounded by sounds. Do they influence you and are they in any way of significance for your compositional work?*

3. *How far can one speak of a personal style and where does self-repetition begin?*

Eighty-two composers have undertaken to reply to the same three questions. Masters and pupils, pioneers and followers, allies and adversaries. Comrades. Each and every one of them heir to the same tradition, except for the youngest, themselves predecessors who have enriched tradition for the new generations to draw upon.

In becoming composers, they have woven further the infinitely varied carpet of music history, in keeping with inherited rules, but changing, modifying, refining the method of selecting and knotting together the yarns. The carpet is there, spread out for all of them to see; each is free to learn from the others, whether the classics or contemporaries.

That is what the first question is about: having taken a seat at the loom, what has served as inspiration—the carpet woven in the past or those currently engaged in weaving it? And having arrived at a personal method, have they been able or willing to modify it, following the realization, sometimes through a revelation, that there are other ways as well?

It was Witold Lutosławski who called my attention to the possibility of a revelation. He had only heard on the radio a few minutes of a composition he had not known before (the second piano concerto by John Cage) and, all of a sudden, it opened up new vistas—for him hitherto uncharted territories. That experience changed once and for all the Polish composer's musical thinking.

It was that astounding confession that in subsequent years induced me to try to find out whether other composers had had similar experiences when listening to a piece of music.

I wanted a reply to the thrilling question as to what complex interplay of influences had shaped the music history of the past decades.

The eighty-two replies shed light on even more than that. They help us to understand the psychology of creation and the multifarious impulses—the rays of the sun seen through the foliage of a tree, a scent or recognition of the musical structure of a film—which can indirectly inspire a composer. We learn that a composer could wait for years before taking a decisive step in a particular direction, simply because he or she lacked the courage to do so—and then hit upon a kindred trait in a musical work or a painting which served as encouragement to openly embrace the new. With the help of replies we can discover the primary source of a phenomenon—such as a painting which unleashes a chain reaction covering several continents. And we realize that with the appearance of radio and recordings, frontiers and geographical distance have lost their erstwhile significance.

Replies to the first question also remind us of the extent to which history and politics can have a bearing on the dissemination of music-related information. Irrespective of the political system, they can restrict the flow of information and create an analogous situation, say, during the years of World War II in the United States or Hungary in the fifties.

Composers were interviewed who, after 1957/58, exerted a fruitful influence on the thinking of their Hungarian colleagues, and because they also reported on their own formative impressions, we can further trace the genealogy of contemporary Hungarian music. The contributions by Hungarian composers outline the music history of the past decades, the veritable shock caused by hearing new music in Warsaw, Darmstadt, Rome, or Vienna, the experience of live performances of Western music, experience which liberated some, shook others, evoked rejection, or led to the decision to start again from scratch. There followed the digestion of influences and finally the development of an individual musical idiom, the "return to paradise lost."

Replies to the second question also tell us a great deal about the psychology of creation. A composer is surrounded by sounds—the basic material with which he works. Are the acoustic phenomena of the outside world—the natural and the urban environment—of any relevance?

From the composer who paints sound images created purely by his imagination on the canvas of silence through musicians who consciously absorb the sounds of nature or the noise of machines to artists writing electronic sounds—the range is wide and includes innumerable variations.

Once again, we are supplied with data about the well-known fact that the antennae of a sensitive nervous system pick up anything—light, colors, emotions evoked by an encounter, even signals of their own bodies—which can lead to musical ideas. Beyond all that, a recurring sonorous experience serves as inspiration irrespective of style and national or generational background—the pealing of bells—which inspires the fantasy of composers and influences their emotions.

The third question stemmed from the many years I had spent in publishing contemporary music. It was rooted in the disappointment-cum-annoyance I felt when a new work I had looked forward to with so much curiosity and anticipation turned out to be but a repetition of features I knew all too well from previous compositions. I often questioned the very raison d'être of pieces which to my mind were lacking in new traits—ideas that clamored for release from the workshop. I missed the surprise, the unheard-of element which I could then have welcomed each time I was listening to the work again.

My impatience would more often than not give way to sober realization. I turned to music history for examples: after all, Bach, Mozart, Beethoven, and other great masters also had recurring features in their music, which ensured that their listeners could identify them. Apparently, they also repeated themselves—repeated *something*—which we recognize as their style.

What is, then, the difference between personal style and self-repetition—where does one end and the other begin? Where is the border between them? That was the third question.

Whether they admitted it or not, this was the question that proved for composers the hardest nut to crack. It forced them to look into themselves, and some of them actually preferred to turn for analysis to their ancestors (Vivaldi, Bach, Mozart, and Stravinsky being the examples most often cited) rather than to their own work. Some composers, however, proved disarmingly honest and expressed many original ideas which would often mutually contradict one another.

Ever since formulating this question, I have realized that it could be applied to *any* creative activity, and in a broader sense, to any human manifestation. Visiting the one-man show of a painter's work or reading a volume of short stories by a writer, or even spending a longer time together with a friend or an acquaintance, the same question emerges in the back of my mind. It is a question relating to the richness of invention, of personality, the recharging or depletion of "batteries"—indeed, their presence or absence.

The first two questions, too, can be applied to other arts. Everyone is exposed to influences that can continue to work as long as one lives—influences that may modify the way one looks at the world. Everyone has his or her own way of coming to terms with these impressions which can be of similar significance for painters, sculptors, or writers as for composers. The same three questions ought to be put to them as well.

I only met about half of the eighty-two composers in person, the rest received my questions in the mail. Personal meetings led to genuine conversations where the number of questions went well beyond the three basic ones. The interviews were recorded, transcribed, arranged in a readable form, and returned to the composers for checking. The scripts were either sent back by return post (Boulez, Stockhausen, Ligeti) or I had to wait for them for years (Kagel, Birtwistle)—or indeed, for all the reminders, no reply was forthcoming (Nono).

I am sad that Messiaen is missing from the list: as one of the most significant composers in the second half of the twentieth century as well as a teacher of Boulez, Stockhausen, Kurtág, and many others, he was a key figure whose replies would have given the book added weight.

I am also disappointed that some composers did not feel like elaborating on their replies (Hans Werner Henze, Dieter Schnebel, Henri Pousseur, and others). Most of them, however, were happy to help and even if the end result may not bear comparison with live interviews, they add up to pithier contributions than those by composers who had no time for the genre of the interview.

It was thrilling to prepare this imaginary roundtable conference by composers from all over the world. Collecting the material took about eight years and proved particularly exciting when contrasting commentaries emerged which involved composers such as Earle Brown, Morton Feldman, John Cage, or Witold Lutosławski.

Some people are of the opinion that statements by composers need not be taken all too seriously. Let their works speak for them. I, for myself, regard these statements as irreplaceable documents, and since I have not been blessed with the gift of creativity, I am happy to play the role of amanuensis.

Bálint András Varga
April 1985

One

GILBERT AMY (1936)

Twenty-seven years after our interview in the composer's home, very little lingers on in the way of personal recollections. I was picked up at the railroad station by Mme Amy in her rather ramshackle Renault 5 and driven to their house. There, I was received by the composer with genuine hospitality. He had none of the air of the "master"; rather, I was struck by his modesty and disarming simplicity.

The interview itself proved ideal for the purposes of this book in that the composer could cite several examples of the way some of the milestones of new music history exerted a direct influence on his own efforts.

Early on in his career, Amy was regarded as a talented pupil of Boulez's, implying perhaps a failure to develop a personality of his own. In later years, however, the individual traits of his music made those of his teacher recede into the background. As Paul Griffiths puts it: Amy "has travelled a great distance from the Boulezism of his 20s to the spacious works of his 50s and 60s, maturity with him bringing a wider awareness and also a greater sense of perplexity."[1]

I.

I believe every composer shares the experience reported by Lutosławski at one point in his career. I am surprised how late in his life he encountered it.

I was twenty years old when I first heard music by composers of the Second Viennese School; also some more recent pieces. The lessons I drew from them determined the way I wrote music. Later too, I heard works which may not have made me want to imitate them, but they encouraged me to take over some of their technical means. Such was Stockhausen's *Gruppen* for three orchestras or some of Boulez's compositions.

A composition may exert a lasting influence if it is rooted in tradition but also brings something new and creates a synthesis of the two. For instance, in *Gruppen*, Stockhausen does not change the instrumentation of the orchestra, he works with the forces we all know from the concert hall. On the other hand, he devised a new spatial arrangement and a notation which have nothing to do with the traditional symphony orchestra. The instruments sound in the usual manner but we hear them differently

1. Paul Griffiths, *The Penguin Companion to Classical Music* (London: Penguin, 2004), 21.

because of the novel arrangement. I regard it as a significant achievement for Stockhausen to have found the adequate notation for the piece.

I heard *Pli selon pli* and *Marteau sans maître* before *Gruppen* and was gripped in both by the fact that they did not move music toward chaos but showed the way toward a new kind of organization. I heard *Marteau* in 1955 when I was nineteen years old and a year later I wrote my *Cantate brève* in which I attempted to digest that experience. It was premiered at Donaueschingen in 1957. Just as Boulez's composition, mine, too, was written for a singing voice, as well as marimba and flute. The experience with *Gruppen* led to *Antiphonie* for two orchestras (composed in 1961/62 and premiered in 1965). I do not think it is a good piece but it provided an occasion for me to experiment with the technique of writing for an orchestra "blown up" into two units. Ten years later, in 1971, I returned to the double orchestra where I succeeded in realizing what I had unsuccessfully tried to do in *Antiphonie* and other pieces. Incidentally, in the 1960s, other composers were also experimenting with the possibilities offered by placing instrumental groups in various points of the hall, it was in a way in the air at that time.

II.

I read an interesting book recently, written by the Canadian composer R. Murray Schafer. In *The New Soundscape* he studied the quality and quantity of the sounding world of several cities. The book made me realize how many different sounds had disappeared from my life once and for all—sounds I used to hear once in a while in my youth, which was after all not so long ago. As a child, you could still hear street vendors, for instance, with their characteristic cries to attract attention. Singers also came to our courtyard. The honking of cars was not yet prohibited.

I do not think I am a naturalist composer. I was never motivated to render the rumbling of the sea, the blowing of the wind, or to imitate the rhythm of raindrops. I never felt like going through with that exercise. Still, if I listen to an old piece of mine which I more or less forgot, I am surprised to discover sound colors which came about not as a result of an abstract organization of sounds but emerged almost like conjuring up a particular natural sound. The explanation must be that subconsciously, I am influenced by the sounds of the environment. It is as if a little computer were at work in my brain which processes and transforms the information coming from an outside source and which influences my pen while [I am] composing. Those who have a superficial knowledge of my music, often comment that they can hear sounds of nature in it. —It could be, I do not know—I would reply. While at work on a piece, I never think of nature.

I have little time for electronic and electroacoustic music, but two or three years ago I did write a multimedia piece based on Arthur Rimbaud's poem *Une saison en enfer.* It meant that I had to spend some time in a studio. The piece is scored for solo voice, choruses, instruments, and electronics. While at work, I realized that what I was actually trying to achieve was to bring electronic sounds closer to natural ones, while natural sounds—the piano, the singing voice—I tried to bring closer to artificial sonorities. When the two met, there arose an interesting ambivalence—a sensuous, almost natural sound.

What I was actually out to do was to arrive at the border between the two kinds of sonority and I realized that that border area was also to be found in nature. Under certain circumstances such is the sound of the wind or of an airplane in the distance, the hubbub of a city or the noise of masses of people. These phenomena are difficult to analyze, especially if we take a sample of them. They are neither natural nor artificial—perhaps they are cosmic.

III.

It is impossible to talk about oneself. The composer may analyze the processes he has used, he may elaborate on the methods he is applying in the work he is currently engaged in, but that is about all he can undertake to do. At least, that is how I see it.

To answer your question, I can tell you how I proceed from one piece to the next and how I try to avoid repeating myself.

I never take an old work to fashion a new one out of it. I may produce several variations of a particular composition but that is something different. While at work, I wish to create something specific.

It has never occurred to me to repeat a procedure that proved itself in the past. I consciously strive to always do something different. Of course, a composer will have developed a particular technique, a certain manner of manipulation which—if you are lucky—can add up to a style.

You may address the question to me: —Amy, your latest piece is nothing but a copy of the one you wrote two years ago. Why don't you renew yourself? —If that is the impression my new work gave you, I am surely to blame. One thing is certain: once I have discovered that I am repeating myself, I become bored and the piece holds no interest for me any longer. I believe each of my compositions has its own, specific material, emotional and energy charge, which differ from those of the previous and the subsequent pieces. In other words, even if I may not claim with absolute certainty that I never repeat myself, I do not consciously make that mistake.

1983

Two

MILTON BABBITT (1916–2011)

The composer's early years were marked by what may have struck the outsider as a hesitation between two professions: those of a mathematician and a composer. He showed a precocious interest in and talent for both, proceeding to study and then to teach them at universities.

Milton Babbitt is one of the pioneers of serial and electronic music; he played an important role in the development of the synthesizer and was one of the founders of the Columbia Princeton Electronic Music Studio.

According to Paul Griffiths, his "music has crystalline intelligence, charming humour and repose, which it maintains despite, very often, a great deal of activity. In lectures and theoretical articles he has been a vigorous proponent of serialism, and his works do not disguise the fact. But they take the battles as won, and clothe the labour in grace."[2]

Babbitt's replies came in two letters, on January 19 and March 11, 1983. I forget why he made the remark in parentheses in the very first sentence, but I am including it for it might throw light on his personality and his self-assessment in the world of music. The replies are, I find, unique in their inspiration by mathematical logic, certainly as far as composers featured in this book are concerned.

Thank you very much for your flattering inquiry; I am honored to have been thought (if only afterthought) of in this regard, and to be included among such eminent thinkers about music.

I.

By international coincidence, I just heard Lutosławski repeat this story at dinner last night, and again—to a group of students—at the Juilliard School this afternoon.[3]

I am probably as voraciously selfish in my mode of listening to music as any other composer. However unaware one may be at any given moment of that disposition, one is always listening to music for what it suggests, intimates, and initiates for you, as a composer. But perhaps it reveals something, or more than something, of how I listen and how—and why—I compose, that no mere moment in a work has ever had that effect upon me, but the processes I, often suddenly, infer in a work, have. As I have revealed elsewhere, as a child, playing

2. Griffiths, *Penguin Companion to Classical Music*, 44.

3. Please see the first question on page xi or, to read the story as the Polish composer related it, see page 162.

clarinet in a band, modes of musical connection that I never had imagined revealed themselves to me in the *Oberon* overture. Soon thereafter, my hearing of the Brahms's Second Symphony made me vividly aware of references across movements of so extensive a work. And the most recent such striking experience was at the premiere of the Violin Concerto of Schoenberg, where the very opening of the first movement revealed possibilities of personal extensions to me, which, by the end of the first movement, would have changed my life, had it not already been changed by his Fourth String Quartet.

II.

I am not aware that the sounds—including the verbal—of the outside world have had any direct or explicit effect on my composition. I am accustomed to having to compose under a strained variety of practical conditions, but the different external noises of those ambiences have had no discernible influence. I prefer to compose in a room whose quiet is disturbed only by the, relatively, nonmusical noises of a game, preferably football, on the television.

III.

I never use the word "style" voluntarily, and when obliged to, do so only with full, inhibiting awareness of the amount of serious, sophisticated thought that has been devoted to the issue, if such it is, by qualified thinkers, and of the complex methodological problems involved. Too often, the concept produces a cataloguing of communal commonplaces, or of persistent idiosyncrasies, most dangerously to a viewing of the works as a statistical sample from a musical population, rather than a singular, individuated composition to which one wishes to bring as few analytical and normative a prioris and as many alternative construals as possible.

But, however defined and applied, style is a term of "supervenience," for it would be preposterous, even contradictory to assert that "two works are identical except with respect to their style." Style, then, is not a separable, primitive attribute, but a compound of characteristics. It is, thus, determined by the choice of pertinent attributes; it is the consequence of an ontological decision with regard to "what there is" in a work, or works, or "music." Therefore, any two works, by a suitable ontological choice, could be deemed stylistically identical, or by another ontological choice, stylistically disjoint. Nothing less than every "possible" characteristic of work can define the "style" of a work, taken as a thing in itself, without presuppositions as to stylistic definers.

As a composer, I am not concerned with "my style," for the composer whose works share the greatest number of "reasonable" characteristics may be said to be stylistically most consistent, and if those shared characteristics share the least with other works of, say, the past, then he is described as stylistically most "original" and "singular." In the former case, he repeats himself; in the latter, by attempting to write music which avoids what music ever before has been, he is as much a victim of the past as the composer who insists upon writing music only as it has been before.

But as a necessarily constrained human being, my works must possess properties in common; man makes the style.

Second letter:

Thank you very much for giving me the opportunity to clarify and amplify my comments. Just as it was not a single moment in the Schoenberg Fourth Quartet which profoundly affected me, it was not just a single insight which it provided me. The very opening measures of the work, in the first violin, demonstrated the use of registral deployment to define a relation between hexachordal collections which influences the work in a variety of persuasive ways, ranging from local counterpoint (creating aggregates) to the overall progression of total movements. The very first measure, in just the disposition of the three notes of the second violin, reveals a replication in the six notes instrumentally and registrally projected by the two violins, of the discrete hexachords of the set, interpreted by the first violin of those opening measures, the first of so many instances of "imaging."

Or, for instance, the third movement displayed a well-defined durational rhythm of aggregates. Pitch adjacencies of the opening statement become the contrapuntal simultaneities of two lines both derived from that opening line, and combinatorially related to one another. And I could continue on, as to the significant function of not just the hexachords, but the tetrachords and trichords of the set, in delineating and preparing pitch areas of various series forms, and thus serving constantly and continuously to recollect and intimate, to recall and predict, thus providing the listener's memory with the means of eventually entifying the work as a unified totality, an "all of a piece" of music. In sum, the Schoenberg Fourth Quartet suggested to me so much of the reach and richness of reference, the depth and scope of relatedness that the twelve-tone conception offers for personal extension and expression.

As for "supervenient": a supervenient term is one which describes a compound of "primitive" properties, which is—accordingly—an abbreviate definition, whose "meaning" one has a right to have explicated by a revealing of the constituent single attributes. "Beautiful," for instance, is—at best—a supervenient term, for it would be obviously absurd to assert that two compositions are identical except that one is "beautiful" and the other not; but it is easily possible to assert and imagine that two compositions are identical except, for example, for their pitches, or dynamics, or temporal values, etc., which are singular properties, or predicates.

1983

Three

SÁNDOR BALASSA (1935)

For most of the nineteen years I spent with Editio Musica Budapest (EMB) promoting contemporary Hungarian music in the world (1971–90), Sándor Balassa and I were friends.

I had heard from an acquaintance at Hungarian Radio that Balassa, who was employed by the same institution as music producer, composed in his free time and his pieces were quite good. I remember meeting him one day in front of the radio headquarters, dressed in his drab clothes, with a worn briefcase in his hand. "I hear you compose," I said to him. "Yes," he said, modestly, with a shrug of his shoulders.

That is how it started. As soon as I had heard a piece of his, I was bowled over and from then on did my very best to make him known in and outside Hungary. A number of prestigious performances and commissions followed: Pierre Boulez conducted Balassa's Iris *on February 6, 1976, (a date I shall never forget) with the BBC Symphony Orchestra in London. Also featured were Ligeti's* Lontano *and Bartók's* Duke Bluebeard's Castle *(with Siegmund Nimsgern and the best Judit I have heard to date: Tatiana Troyanos). Through my good acquaintance with Aaron Copland, I got Balassa a commission from the Koussevitzky Foundation. There followed requests from Boston and the BBC Philharmonic Orchestra. His operas and ensemble pieces also received performances. Over the years, Sándor Balassa became a composer to reckon with; he rose to prominence in Hungary and received some of the highest government decorations. He came frequently to my home and I visited him a number of times in his house at Budakeszi, just outside Budapest.*

I warmed to his personality—I found him genuine, sensitive, and modest. I was also attracted by his closeness to nature as well as by his naiveté. Two memories come to mind, both connected with our visit to London (the first one for him), to do with the Hungarian concert of the BBC Symphony Orchestra. I took him for a walk in the city and when we came to Westminster Abbey and the Houses of Parliament, I noticed he had tears in his eyes. He was simply overwhelmed by the experience of seeing those monuments at close quarters. One day we stepped out of our hotel (King's Hotel, it was called, in a narrow sidestreet near Hyde Park, owned by aged Hungarian ladies). He noticed a wounded pigeon lying on the street—still alive but clearly past help. He picked it up and, to end its suffering, smashed it with tremendous power against the sidewalk. I was lost for words, quite shaken, and once again, I saw that he was quietly crying.

However, things were in a state of flux, both in Balassa's music and Hungarian political life. I could not come to terms with aspects of his orchestral work The Chant of Glarus*—a piece reflecting his love of the Swiss Alps. I told him so, he was displeased. It was the first time we had had a disagreement.*

Now that I have checked the date of that composition—it was written in 1978—I am uncertain whether in fact we were friends for most *of my time with EMB. Clearly, at a distance of nearly thirty years, events (outside and inside) change perspective. In any case, the fact remains that our friendship petered out slowly, primarily for political reasons. As Hungary was edging toward the year 1989 when communism collapsed and political parties appeared on the scene, the notion of extreme right became a daily reality. Much to my consternation, Balassa drifted in that direction. I became very emotional about that (I remember our last conversation at the end of which* I *was on the verge of tears) and soon we lost contact, especially after I had left Hungary in January 1991, initially for a stint in Berlin.*

We did talk once on the phone in 2009 and I asked him for a CD of his latest works. He sent me one by return post—four orchestral compositions, all recent, recorded and released at his expense. They show a naive concern for Magyar culture and the Magyar past, which he apparently idealizes and hankers after. All four pieces are alike, as if he were trying to hammer home the same idées fixes over and over again. I tried to be honest in my comments without hurting his feelings but my letter has remained unanswered.

In any case, Sándor Balassa consented to read our old interview again and confirmed that his convictions had not changed over the past decades.

I.

At various times in my life, especially during the years of study, I was deeply impressed by composers of the past. Again and again I would heave a sigh: if only I could also write music like that!

However, when I was composing, grappling with the material, the world would be shut out. Time and again, during a concert, I could not concentrate on what was being played because the sounding presence of my own music inside me isolated me from the acoustic environment.

As far as contemporary music was concerned, Takemitsu's orchestral piece *Coral Island* was a source of inspiration: I heard it on the radio in the 1960s. Its beauty evoked quite an emotional commotion; all of a sudden I felt a brotherly fellowship with its author. The experience stayed with me for years, it also helped [me] to find my own voice and tempered my solitude, my sense of confinement. (The hollow and aggressive, conservative European avant-garde of the time put me off). I am sorry that Takemitsu did not continue on the path he had embarked on.

Even if you did not have an experience comparable to Lutosławski's, Verdi's Il trovatore *did give a direction to the outburst of all your impulses that were clamoring for release. I do believe, though, that the significance of your encounter with the film version of the opera had something of the dimension of the Polish composer's Cage experience.*

That encounter had the effect of a veritable explosion! It was not only an encounter with Verdi but also the first time in my life that I glimpsed "Art." It not only transformed me, it also started me off on the thorny path toward becoming an artist. It confirmed my faith in my future as a composer. Next to Verdi, other composers also influenced me: Bach, Mozart, Beethoven, Mussorgsky, Kodály, Debussy, Puccini, and Stravinsky. It was not primarily their style that impressed me. The techniques, the technologies of music production never interested me to the extent that I would have become anyone's *follower*. It was the spiritual and intellectual radiance of those masters that gripped me and called forth in me the ability to respond to greatness and quality.

II.

The outside world has always talked to me.

I was fascinated by thunderstorms, showers with a scent all their own when you could *feel* the mushrooms grow faster, the evening twilight with its cricket orchestra. I heard the scream of tree trunks split in the freezing cold and the happy song of the lark floating above.

The sounds of the mountains and the waters are primal sources of the structure of my hearing. At fourteen, I was a watchman on top of the church tower at Komádi.[4] I would spend the summer nights up there. The bells pealed every hour beneath me and I blew the horn toward the four cardinal points of the globe letting the firemen know that I was awake. The stirring of the village in slumber underneath, the soft stillness of the tent of stars above: an unforgettable fullness of harmony. Looking back, I can now understand how happy I was then. It was all like in a fairy tale.

It is that fairy tale that I would like to turn into music.

The inorganic noise of machines, indeed all the noise that floods us unbidden has an effect on me quite unlike the sounds of nature: they annihilate me. The noises of the city, the din of the factories: acoustic pollution; harmful for me and all living beings—unbearable.

It is to find a life in a quiet place that I have moved to Budakeszi. A large proportion of mankind today are town dwellers with their hearing deteriorating. In this situation, musical sounds are all the more valuable. Their artistic and biological effect is of a higher order. In olden times, when Handel or Liszt were living, the post horn or the sound of the village smithy's anvil could be perceived as pleasant and inviting. Handcraft still had a human face and had the power of building communities. The sound of our world is foul and ugly. Listening to machine-made music with the volume turned up harms our health.

---

4. Town in eastern Hungary, with some six thousand inhabitants.

Sounds of the outside world can be identified in your music. In Tabulae *it is the throbbing of the human heart, in the* Chant of Glarus *the calls of the young deer you found in the forest near Budakeszi.*

My music is nourished by sounds of the environment but it transfigures the raw material taken from nature, it lifts it into a human dimension where it changes its material and spirit without severing its link to its sources. As music is not part of the forest, so are the sounds of the woods, as concrete reality, not part of music. The forum created by art is a place where man can meet himself and the cosmos. The signal sounding there is addressed to man and tells him of totality.

Your Requiem *incorporates the voice of masses of people. If you had not told me in an earlier conversation, it would never have occurred to me that the rhythmic cries at a soccer match inspired a particular passage.*

Yes, that passage is in the third movement. When I was composing the piece, I could hear the voices of the fans as they were egging on their club, the FTC, the nearby stadium [see fig. 1].[5] They used a diminution—and that was precisely what I needed at that point. I lifted that idiom as a matter of course from the soccer stadium and put it in my score.

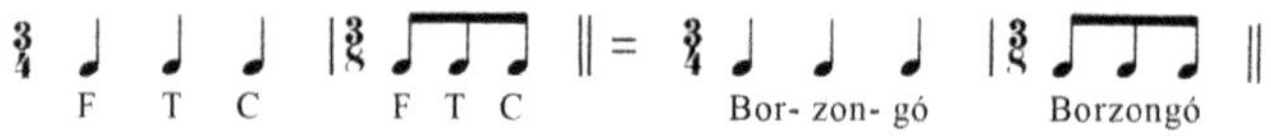

F T C F T C = Bor- zon- gó Borzongó

Figure 1. Sándor Balassa received his inspiration through the window from the People's Stadium near his home. FTC are the initials of a popular soccer team in Hungary.

III.

To my mind, Bach would be angry if he knew that the first volume of the *Wohltemperiertes Klavier* is performed nowadays at a single concert. The twenty-four preludes and fugues were not meant as a recital program. Or, just imagine a huge concert with 300 concerti grossi by Vivaldi played one after the other. I think, if he had to listen to it, the composer himself would have a breakdown.

A composer does not work for a complete edition of his music. He strews his pieces in time and space. If a Vivaldi concerto is programmed next to Mozart and Bruckner, nobody would be thinking that the other 299 were composed in the same spirit.

A composition consists of changing and permanent ingredients, present in a particular proportion. The changing moments appear as a result of the composer's development, his progress in time, the enrichment of his knowledge, both acquired and inherited.

5. FTC stands for Ferencvárosi Torna Club. Ferencváros is the name of a Budapest district, and *torna* means "gymnastics."

The artist, while changing his subject, tells of this and that—what he has experienced and dreamed of in the course of his life.

The permanent and repeated moments are manifested through the author's personality and his limitations. The fact that his subjects are communicated by him, means that we see through his eyes, we experience his works filtered through his personality.

The composer renews himself all the time and remains the same nevertheless. He struggles to re-create himself day by day, but strives also to link the changes to the values he has already created in the past.

The fact that your personality is given and is relatively permanent is not a question of volition. No one can leap over his own shadow. Those wise enough will not even try. Stravinsky changed his style many times, but he remained himself—that is, he was always composing the same. On his own evidence, Mozart could compose in sixteen different styles. Today, we hear his oeuvre as unified.

Has this question ever occupied your mind?

I do have a tendency to renew myself. It is so much part of my nature that I cannot even tell a joke twice in the same way.

This predilection for change is present in everyone, to different degrees. The variations of folk songs, the creation of innumerable versions, the need *not to do the same* and *not to do it the same way* springs from that source. While the ability to change evolved from the primeval requirement to adapt to the environment, the urge to preserve, to repeat what has proved itself in the past was born out of the instinct of self-preservation. We use the most important words more often than the other ones, we eat basic foods day by day. Natural cycles, the periodic repetition of aspects of our lives are all stereotypes that have become biological necessities.

The same must apply to the arts as well. If I regard something as important, why shouldn't I repeat it several times. For instance, if I want to alert passengers that their train is approaching a ravine and the rails have been removed, I will shout until they can hear me.

I also want to tell people to remain faithful to their youthful ideals. Why should I only do so just once? The fact that modernist music has lost the sympathy of listeners is due in part to its renunciation of the principle of repetition. Look, I am no linguist. I have no intention of inventing new languages. I would like to communicate something in the language we have, so that my message should reach its addressees. My main concern is for them to understand me.

If I do not concentrate on the principal voice, I will end up being the main obstacle of rendering my music effective. If, for instance, I were to tell the words of warning to those approaching the ravine backward only to avoid repetition, caught in the thrill of creating a new means of communication, I should be left alone with my triumph, watching people as they perish.

1982/85

Four

LUCIANO BERIO (1925–2003)

When I think of Luciano Berio, the first thing that comes to my mind is my desperate search for the rue Thorigny in Paris, late one evening in November 1978. I went out of my way (a phrase particular apt in this context) to be punctual but the street proved hopelessly elusive, even though I had a map in hand. More often than not, the narrow streets appeared to be nameless, with no plate to help me find my bearings; they were also deserted, with no one to ask. Then, as if by magic, I found myself standing right there.

Berio had been reluctant to take time for an interview (one of the very first conversations I conducted for this book), for he was in the middle of composing his opera La vera storia. *In the event, we talked—I am tempted to say—"at the foot" of the giant score which was lying open on his desk.*

By 1978 I had only thought of two of the three questions and it was not until March 1980 that I was able to pose the third one, in an underground room of IRCAM, the institution founded by Pierre Boulez, where Berio was briefly at the head of one of the departments.[6] *He was tired, tense, and in a bad mood, having had an accident which caused him to limp. The interview was a short one—which is why he revised it two years later.*

The longest period we spent together was in January 1981 at his home in Tuscany. The village of Radicondoli is typical of the region in that it is built on a hilltop. Outside it, rather further down the slope, at a distance of roughly a kilometer, stands Berio's house "Il Colombaio." I spent five days there, put up in the guesthouse, a converted stable, to conduct a book-length conversation with the composer, published in time for a portrait concert at the Budapest new music festival in October of the same year.

Berio was putting finishing touches to La vera storia *but devoted eleven hours to talking about his life and music, usually in the evenings. If he was ready to go to bed, he did not hesitate to yawn right in the middle of my question; there was nothing for it but to switch off my tape recorder.*

One day, his young wife Talia came with the alarming news that someone who looked rather suspect to her, was approaching the house. Berio opened a drawer of his desk, produced a small revolver, and took up a position near the window, to see what the man was up to. In the event, the man walked past the house and out of view but the episode brought home to me the danger the Berio family (with two baby sons) was facing in living in an isolated house outside the village.

---

6. IRCAM stands for Institut de Recherche et Coordination Acoustique/Musique.

On the other hand, it was wonderfully quiet and ideal for work, not to speak of the beauty of the countryside. Once the morning mist had lifted, distant villages loomed in the distance—castle-like, with tall, elongated houses. If I turned round, I appeared to be looking at the same settlement, as if brought near with a telescope. Farther off, invisible to the eye, lay Siena, Florence, and San Gimignano.

On the eve of my departure, Berio treated me to a farewell dinner. He grilled a chicken in his fireplace, cut it up so that each of us had exactly the same portion—but then put the best pieces from his plate on mine. He also opened the last but one bottle of a rare Swiss wine and was in the best of spirits.

Berio was a man who enjoyed life to the full. His was a healthy musicality, if such a juxtaposition is acceptable. If he had any crises as a composer, he did not let on. He was perfectly aware of what he was worth and in his professional life, expected to be treated with due reverence. "I know I make things difficult for me"—he told me in my UE office—"but I think I have arrived at a stage in my career where I am in a position to demand."

Perhaps one more detail which has stuck in my mind. I first heard his Concerto for Two Pianos and Orchestra *(1972/73) in Milan, some time in the early 1990s. I was swept off my feet and told Berio so.*

"This is one of your very best pieces!" His reaction caught me by surprise. For a few seconds he pretended he had not heard it, then, in true Italian fashion, joined his fingertips together and moved his lower arm up and down a number of times. Talia interpreted for him: he was quite aware of the concerto's merits but also of those of many other works which were at least as good. To single out the concerto was wholly irrelevant. I learned my lesson.

I.

To me it is a strange question because it ultimately implies that a musician can compose works as if they were objects. More or less beautiful or interesting, but objects that can influence, or can be suddenly influenced by other objects. I don't believe that a musician can fall from his horse—like St. Paul on his way to Damascus—and come under the spell of a sudden revelation that changes his creative life completely. I believe that musical creativity is a complex and long-sustained process and that accomplished works are the signals of that process. Of course, the creative process has many different roots—but I think that real influences can occur only at a much higher or deeper level: for instance, as an organic interaction among different cultural areas (think of Bartók) or as a confrontation with—and as transformation of—natural models (think of Paul Klee).

Also in folk tradition "painters" and "musicians" have always been influenced by nature—because of their need of imitating it—but in a way that their visual or sound results imply a necessarily simplified vision of nature.

For them nature is a magical or dangerous dimension or a purely utilitarian one. We could say that in the so-called primitive art the result tends to be simpler than the natural model while in cultivated art—that is, an art aware of itself—the result tends to be more complex than the model and, of course, more analytical. Actually, the model is often only a pretext and it disappears in the web of references (technical, historical, expressive, social) in which it has been absorbed. A meaningful and expressive musical "object" is a terribly complex fact: we should be able to place it also in a historical continuity that has its own laws and not, simply, in a sequence of sudden stimuli and sudden reactions to those stimuli. This is why I think that real influences can only occur on the level of ideas rather than as a reaction to isolated events. Ideas, unless you are a child, are as hard as rocks: they are not too sensitive to accidents or chance.

II.

Personally, I am not interested in sound as such. If you work with electronic music, for instance, you know that it is quite easy to invent new sounds or to imitate natural sounds. I am only interested in sounds that are the result of a musical process. Neither am I influenced, as far as I know, by the noises of the outside world. But I must admit that, at least conceptually, I am attracted to the sounds of the sea, always the same and always different, while musically I am totally indifferent to birds, car horns, and insects. Natural acoustical models, as I was saying before, can be a pretext, occasionally, that has to be absorbed and quickly forgotten in a responsible creative process.

How about silence?

Silence is a feature of sound, as stillness is a feature of movement and death is the ultimate feature of life. Silence is not an absolute, it is a relative idea and it exists only in terms of an opposition. Even perceptually, absolute silence does not exist just as there is no absolute black. Musically, silence is always inhabited, always full. Silence is a quality, emotionally, conceptually, and even physically. If you go into an anechoic room the least you can hear is the pulse of your bloodstream. What is interesting is to invent sound qualities that take the place of silence. In order to do this in a meaningful way you must establish hierarchies of sound densities.

Can you give me an example in your own music?

In my Concerto for Two Pianos or *Coro* I establish different harmonic levels of different complexity. The simplest one—that is the most transparent and the most "distant"—takes the place of silence. If you have three simultaneous levels of development—one very present and articulated, one less articulated and more neutral, and a third level rather static and on a completely different time scale—you can call this last level "silence." Like a painter who puts gray on his canvas, then he has different colors and different articulations of forms. The gray you see in the background is "silence" but still, gray is gray, it is not nothing. When you close your eyes, you see the gray of the retina rather than a dead black. The idea of silence is relative and takes place according to the hierarchies you create in your sound structure.

How about general pause? Does it play any part in your music?

No! It was important in music where time was metrically and rhythmically measured. It was a dramatic and even functional gesture; often humorous as in the finale of Haydn's Symphony No. 90, C major, where the GP is made of four empty measures.

III.

Style is quite an ambiguous concept that emerged in musical vocabulary in rather modern times. I agree completely with Schoenberg who held that the idea of style has little to do with the process of music. Of course, if you want, style is connected with anything we do. You can take it for granted that if I walk from here to the door I will do it in my own style. If I write anything, verbal expression will have the imprint of my own style. But that has little to do with the content of what I am saying. I have the feeling that those who talk of their own individual styles are dead. That is why I cannot answer your question.

1978/80/82

Five

SIR HARRISON BIRTWISTLE (1934)

We first met some forty years ago, at the Dartington International Summer School in Devon, England. The place was spectacular. The late fourteenth-century Dartington Hall stands in its own grounds, which include a tiltyard and a walled garden. The Summer School was in those years directed by Sir William Glock (1908–2000), legendary BBC Controller of Music whose passionate advocacy of contemporary composers changed the corporation's music policy and the profile of the Proms of which he was artistic director.

True to form, the Summer School had several young composers on its staff. It was among a group of them sitting on the lawn that I first caught sight of Birtwistle, John Tavener, and others. Whether Peter Maxwell Davies was with them I can no longer recall: Harry's and Max's friendship was crumbling, since they were about to part company as joint heads of the ensemble Pierrot Players (later to be christened the Fires of London).

The first impression one gained of Birtwistle (and this may not have changed since) was of a reserved, unsmiling man who appeared to be pondering ideas which did not seem to be giving him much pleasure. "He is rather dour," I heard people say.

On closer acquaintance, of course, you realize that he is anything but. A kind-hearted and vulnerable man with a warmly resonant, musical voice, Birtwistle is, like any creative person, anxious for his works to find wide acceptance but is just as committed to preserving his integrity. He knows full well that his idiom is not immediately appealing to the uninitiated ("It would be no problem for me to write music easy on the ear," he told me at the Lucerne Festival where he was featured composer on the occasion of his seventieth birthday in 2004. He added that he quite consciously stuck nevertheless to the language he felt his own).

We were talking at the end of the interval, about to take our places, to listen to one of his major orchestral compositions, Earth Dances (1985/86). *It is a monumental block of primeval power and unless conducted with thorough knowledge of all the score's intricacies, the music tends to overpower the listener. The Lucerne performance was not ideal I thought, and it was not until Markus Stenz directed it with the Concertgebouw Orchestra in Amsterdam a few years later that I felt: at long last* Earth Dances *has been done justice to. Demanding scores do have their perils.*

I.

Do you mean after I considered I had a style? If I look back over the past, say, fifteen years, I detect no radical change of direction. My preoccupations seem to me to be the same as they always were—but influence is a funny thing. I think there are two kinds—one conscious and the other subconscious. The conscious influences are not concerned with a particular composer, but more often with points of detail, and not necessarily in first-rate pieces. If you were to ask a cross-section of established composers, obviously a lot of the same names will crop up.

Sometimes something like a point of notation in a student work might solve a particular problem. There have been times, however, when a certain piece of music, by its directness, has unlocked certain things in an oblique way.

Often when I am listening to music, there are details which excite me, like points of departure which I identity with and could take into other directions. Not necessarily someone else's music, but even my own. I had this experience recently listening to Dunstable motets. I suddenly imagined a new direction which music could take. Or when we were listening to *Silbury Air* the other day, a direction suggested itself that seemed to me superior to the one that I had chosen. It seemed absolutely clear what I should have done, or could have done, but then again you forget the decision that you made at the time of doing what you did anyway.

Does it induce you to go back to old pieces and rewrite them?

No, because I consider the context arrived at and the moment of decision unique, even sacred. You never arrive at that point again. That is why I hear things in my music and I can't think why I made the decision to do what I did.

In composing, there are two opposites working in me at the same time, even contradictory. One which is concerned with highly formalized ideas and the other to do with improvisation and intuition. One being played against the other. I would only rework things to make them clearer. But what I call "moves" interest me a great deal: how music moves from one point to another.

Not long ago, I was introducing an audience to my orchestral piece *The Triumph of Time,* which was being played with Brahms's Second Symphony. I found myself talking more about Brahms than myself because I found he had better examples, or maybe simply because there is a distance, but he certainly creates contexts for things to happen, and then never does what you think he is going to. The moves are oblique if you like, but perhaps that is the essence of a lot of great music. I don't know.

Could you elaborate on this?

Music by nature is linear, it exists in timespans, and in timespans there are rhythms which obey what I would call a natural progression. A natural order of things which we have come to understand in terms of music. I suppose it could loosely be called "language," the way that time speaks. In the process of composition you can actually go along with the current, and let the thing just happen so that it fulfils all the natural ambitions in a traditional way.

(Brahms is more interesting for me than Mahler. Mahler often only inflates the symphonic form, just increases its scale whereas Brahms changes its meaning. Also in this aspect I notice in a lot of contemporary music that the composer is striving for a complexity but that complexity is merely local and vertical and rather more intricate than complex, and while the material is modern the linear aspect is often overly simple.)

I am interested in taking things in other directions but at the same time creating a form which is cohesive and not simply quirkish or eccentric, but in creating situations in which I can do the opposite to what you might expect. It is essentially a dramatic idea, concerned with the juxtaposition of material. Something which I got from Paul Klee.

Do you mean that music has to surprise?

Not necessarily, but a lot of music that I admire does, and continues to do so even on repeated hearings, when the surprise is expected. I have been very struck by the juxtaposition of material in Bach, in Beethoven's string quartets, and in a very different sort of way, Haydn, particularly in the string quartets he does remarkable things.

Also in the development sections of his piano sonatas.

Absolutely, the piano sonatas! They are some of the wildest pieces ever made. They certainly never do what you think they are going to. Haydn's material is never quite as straightforward as it seems on the surface, but I think you hear it in context to the ordinary, so that the surprise is in a sense constantly there.

II.

I was brought up in the countryside. I am much more consciously turned on by color. Sound only interferes. I cannot say I am aware of being influenced by it.

But to come back to the sorts of influences that I talked about in the first question—I thought about this a couple of years ago.

I was brought up in a small town in Lancashire. I was taught the clarinet. I was a clarinet player. When I was fourteen or fifteen I played in the local theater, a fourth-rate music hall. We played arrangements of popular music which were originally for a bigger combination than we had. We were only four or five. Consequently there was always an imbalance. The complete harmony was not always there. What we were given was a short score. There was a bass player, a violin, a piano, and me. Out of that you made up the arrangement as you went along. That sound that I was part of I think has had a great influence.

It was not an orchestration as we would understand it, say in Debussy, a fusing of instruments, but rather the opposite, where the absolute identity of the instrument is maintained, even when playing in unison. A sort of instrumental role-playing in which it is not a matter of fusing but of keeping them absolutely separate. The sound of these instruments has, I know, been a major subconscious decision maker.

In what way has color played a role? You have also mentioned smell in the past as being important for you.

Color and light! I have identified with painters much, much more than with any composer. This comes back again to your first question: the things that have given me the right to do what I have done, or have given me the courage, if you like, to take those shortcuts that Lutosławski has been talking about—for that is what it really is, a Caesarean section, you cut it out, you simply say why don't I just go there? Well, it is the same thing with painters.

I have found with painting that I have suddenly thought you can see the courage, you can see the directness—and I have done it. Piero della Francesca, I would think, is one of the strangest painters—I think of his juxtapositions . . . it also connects with the second question, how he makes moves, why certain decisions are taken. What it adds up to is a sort of very precise classical geometry of juxtapositions of objects which I think remarkable. They create an enigma, a mystery, a very strange world which is about the subject yet not about the subject, it is about areas and not about areas. It is to do with this same thing of moves—why did he make some of those decisions that he made? Yet, if you could put it down to a formula, it would be academic.

Color is like orchestration, if you like. You can't divorce color from a picture, it is part of it. You cannot divorce orchestration from a composition.

I just find smell very evocative, in a purely Proustian sense. Like taste. I do not know if it has anything to do with music but it seems to me to be a very potent recaller of material. Smell is something . . . I smelt something the other day that I hadn't smelt for forty years: the smell of a dairy. The sour smell of slightly stale milk—no matter how you clean the place you can never get rid of it. I went to a farm and I smelt this and it was amazing—it was my childhood . . .

But do you get any musical ideas from smells?

No.

III.

Do you know what Auden said about this? An artist spends ten years imitating other people and the rest of his life imitating himself.

First of all, I do not see composition anymore as a question of ideas. Because ideas are ten a penny. If we sit down now for the next five minutes, I can give you forty ideas for compositions which I could write. I would have to choose which one I do but I could do it. I am not short of ideas—it is very easy.

Originality, in a sense, is not difficult. It is what brings about situations—very radical things—like the process of why Jackson Pollock arrived at the point where he thought he should drip paint. Or the four-minute silence of Cage. Those are radical things. We can think of things equally original if we want to. It is not simply a matter of doing that. It is coming back to a lot of the things we have been talking about—context, where you are.

The way that my music works—it is like there are many threads. If you can imagine levels. Certain of these levels are coming into being and certain levels are dying. Like the process of evolution in life. That sounds rather phony but you will understand the analogy. There are certain preoccupations which in one piece are just the germ of an idea, there are certain things which are very bright, and certain things which are the residue of something which is already becoming extinct. So there are all those processes and if you have to take a sample of them at a certain point, at that point what is up front and what is in the foreground of the material, is what I am composing at the moment. Sometimes I will take one aspect of something and very clearly make what I would call an occasional piece, simply subject that technique or that idea, if you like, to that process and simply do that. I do that more and more. They are really like my sketches, they are about one thing, they are for two instruments, let us say, or one instrument, and they do that specific thing, nothing else.

They are a commentary on something. When I feel that in a piece I haven't done as much as I could with an idea, but I do not want to write a piece which is to do with a lot of things, I want to do just that one thing. I think Bach did that, too, not that I am making any judgment about me and Bach. But I am sure that's what he did.

1983/85

Six

PIERRE BOULEZ (1925)

When Pierre Boulez brought his Residentie Orchestra of the Hague to Budapest in March 1968, I had already heard his name, though none of his compositions. It had a classical ring to it, even a patina, which means that I must have come across it repeatedly for a number of years.

It was natural for me, then, to take a tape recorder to his concert at the Erkel Theater (a hall of notoriously poor acoustics). I turned up in the artist's room during the interval and he was quite happy to reply to my questions, even though he might just as well have preferred to take some rest.

The program looked like this:

Webern: Five Pieces for string orchestra, Op. 5
Boulez: Éclat
Webern: Symphony Op. 21
Bartók: Music for Strings, Percussion and Celesta

It proved far too hard a nut to crack for many people in the audience, including myself. Webern was in those years hardly known in Hungary; even Bartók's music posed difficulties for the ordinary music lover. Éclat *brought a message from a world we did not know even existed.*

I did not hesitate to confess to Boulez the many question marks in my head and was struck by his unassuming and friendly response, the understanding he showed for my perplexity, and his readiness to explain what he "meant" by composing Éclat. *While maintaining that music could not be expressed in words, he agreed to what he termed "translating" the piece without attempting to spell out its "content."*

He said: "In this little piece I wished to write contemplative music—one which has no direction or perceptible development. The subject itself does not develop—the basic feature of the music is its timbre. This applies in particular to the main group of instruments, the sound quality of which cannot be modified. When they play together, a new kind of sound arises: improvisation affects the sonority directly. That is why I say that this music has no direction. I cannot tell you more—even this much is far too prosaic, far too vulgar. I could perhaps liken Éclat *to the behavior of fish in an aquarium. They hover motionless for a long time—all we can see is the slow gliding of colors. Then, all of a sudden, they take fright at something and flit like an arrow. This music is also like that. A mixture of contemplation without any direction and gravity as well as lightning-like swift movement in a particular direction."*

In response to a comment I made, Boulez was willing to elaborate: "I would want listeners to initially respond to the timbre. The colors of Éclat *are velvety and pleasant to the ear, they are devoid of any aggression. However, it could indeed be perplexing that you do not know where the piece begins and where it ends. This is a result of the fact that, as I said, the music has no direction. The reaction of the musicians in the orchestra was particularly interesting for me. In the beginning, they also felt completely lost. Later however—so they told me—they enjoyed playing the music, which is half based on improvisation, more than the performance of works where they had to concentrate on metric ensemble playing."*

Needless to say, Éclat *presents no challenge today anymore, in any case for those at home in contemporary music. One just sits and savors the beauty of the piece.*

In 1968, then, Boulez's name was familiar to someone like me—uninitiated as yet in new music but with a genuine interest in music in general. When György Kurtág had left Budapest for Paris in 1957 on a year's study trip, he resolved to compose a work during his stay and show the score to Boulez. In the end, he left without anything to show (and, in consequence, decided not to meet the composer in person)—but it is remarkable that Boulez in his early thirties should have possessed that much authority for a Hungarian composer who had been cut off from the West for decades. As Kurtág has confessed to me, he had not heard a note of Boulez's music but was aware of his standing. "He was the absolute star!" as he put it. Ligeti had told him about his experiences in Darmstadt but even earlier, in 1956, at the first Bartók Festival to have been mounted in Budapest since World War II, he met some musicians from Romania who were avowed "Boulezists." While in Paris, he was a regular visitor to the salon of the Russian painter Ida Karskaya where he would meet Richard Rodney Bennett and Susan Bradshaw. Both of them former pupils of Boulez, they continued to be his admirers. It was in the home of Karskaya's son, Michel, that Kurtág first heard Marteau sans maître. *And, of course, Kurtág would attend Boulez's concerts with the Domaine Musicale, which proved to be "tremendously important."*

If you have read the interview with Morton Feldman in this book, you will see that for some American composers Boulez was the *major representative of European music, they challenged him and respected him and perhaps also wanted to impress him.*

Indeed, I believe that Pierre Boulez has achieved everything any creative artist can ever hope to achieve: he has become a symbol. He stands for postwar European music, combining as he does composing, conducting, teaching, writing on music and art (he has published a remarkable book on Paul Klee), and founding institutions such as IRCAM and the Ensemble Intercontemporain.

Boulez has been around in international musical life for sixty years. He is also—for me—something of a biological miracle. Ever since I first met him, I have witnessed his inexhaustible energy. He may have aged since 1968, but he is as busy as ever and is apparently never tired. We at Universal Edition invited him one day to a typical Viennese pub, a Heuriger, *and after a full day's work some of us were ready to go to bed around midnight. Boulez, by far the oldest of us all, who had also had rehearsals during the day, was as lively as ever. When he noticed that we were looking stealthily at our watches, he looked at his and commented: "What's the matter, it is still early!" Eventually, he let us go home.*

It would be understandable if one felt rather overawed in his presence: he is after all living music history. But Boulez is good at putting people at ease. On one occasion, he told me "I am always friendly," from which I have deduced that courteousness (perhaps a synonym in this case for friendliness) is a conscious choice of social behavior on his part—one to which he has kept all these decades. Of course, courteousness is also a means of keeping aloof, of maintaining a certain distance. For all our long-standing acquaintance, I cannot claim to know him well. My association with his publisher, Universal Edition, has failed to bring us any closer: he commands such authority worldwide that promotion of his music, in the traditional sense of the word, is simply out of place, it is almost an absurdity: he does not need it. Also, because sadly, he is always short of time as far as composing is concerned; new pieces take a long time to leave his desk. A world premiere by Pierre Boulez is a rare event and hence a sensation.

Since that first interview in 1968, he has given me several more, such as the one below. In 1998, he took time to check it and make some changes, in his characteristically tiny but clearly legible handwriting.

I.

Yes. You listen to some music and you immediately think of what you can extract from it for your own use. From that moment, you are no longer listening to that piece—you concentrate on the problem that has occurred to you.

For instance?

I was listening to a work by Morton Feldman. It does not matter which one. Of course, I was perfectly aware of the fact that I was listening to the event more than the music itself, but then, at that moment, the idea of *Éclat* came to my mind. Under the influence of Feldman's piece I realized that one could compose music with short cells, even single chords, which come from nothing and disappear into nothing. I had long planned to write something with instruments suitable for that, but the idea itself cropped up at that time.

While listening to *Mode de valeurs et d'intensités* by Messiaen, I felt that its structure was too rigid for my taste. After all, you cannot build a piece on the repetition of the same pitches even in a different order. But at the very first hearing, I immediately realized the consequences of loosening up the factors which are absolutely tied in the piece. With Messiaen, a certain dynamics, intensity, and duration are linked to a single note. For instance, in a given scale every E♭ in a given register has exactly the same duration, dynamics, intensity, and so on. In other words, in a fixed succession of pitches there exists only one kind of E♭, whereas I was interested in making those ties variable. That was when I wrote the first book of *Structures.*

II.

Half and half. Sometimes I am interested in the sounds of the outside world, sometimes I am not. Of course, you cannot literally transcribe the sounds of the environment into music. Sounds surround us, they are part of the environment which also surrounds us and we select from them what is necessary. The process of selection is one which I cannot describe. It depends on the level of interest at any particular moment—whether I wish to absorb the sounds or not.

That is all I can say: it depends so much on what I happen to be doing at the moment. Of course, a particularly striking sound may attract my attention even though I am "closed" to sounds at that time.

III.

I think everybody has at least a desire to renew himself. One is at the same time bound to the world one has established for oneself. The difficulty lies in how to leave that world without destroying it and in having a definite goal toward which to proceed.

I can give you two examples from the previous generation: Webern and Stravinsky.

Webern is easy to follow, for his development was rather slow and continuous. There are certain constant features in his music: brevity, dynamic range, paucity of instruments, and the desire to express his ideas in a highly concentrated manner. These traits recur in practically every one of his compositions. At the same time, his style developed considerably, from a kind of free style characterized by romantic expression, toward a constructivist, Mondrian-like style. It is a development which could not be foreseen at the beginning but which was very logical in the end. He tried to express his truth bit by bit.

In the case of Stravinsky, on the other hand, he gave a lot out of himself at the very beginning and then tried to discover new territories. In reality, he chose models in the past and adjusted his personal features to them. During his life, everybody was saying: how marvelous, the way Stravinsky can renew his style. But over a long period he was putting on new masks rather than renewing certain aspects of his personality. He was not the only one to do that at that moment of our century. It was one of the first appearances of what one can call "historicism."

Just as you cannot change the color of your eyes, a composer has his gestures which remain with him from beginning to end. That is what gives his personal touch. The dramatic gestures of Beethoven are the same in his earliest works as they are in his last compositions, but his personality underwent such an important evolution that those gestures became much more significant. And they had more impact at the end than at the beginning.

These gestures are, in my opinion, the marks of creative personality. As the years go by, the composer develops their efficiency and then, as he gets into his work, he makes them more to the point. That is the right way of renewal.

Actually, it is not so much a question of renewal as one of development and discovery of himself. I do not like the word "renewal," it does not mean much to me. It implies more or less that you change your skin like a snake! But you have to probe deeper and deeper in your personality and discover things of which you were not aware before. They are not new, they were always there but you did not know of them. It is this self-discovery which is important and not the desire to do something new all the time. The latter endeavor is very superficial.

That reminds me of what you told me about Notations *in Budapest in 1978: that in returning to the early piano pieces, you discovered many things in them which were there but until then you had not realized their existence.*

Yes, that process is very characteristic of me. From that point of view, I am very introspective.

Does this problem often exercise your mind?

Always, always. Especially now that I have something like thirty years of creativity behind me.

1978/80/98

Seven

ATTILA BOZAY (1939–99)

At the "Pagoda," as Hungarian Radio's café is called, on account of the shape of its glass-and-metal entrance hall, I would often see a smiling young man, rather short of stature, with his hair combed in what was then, in the mid-1960s, considered a modern style. He was two years my senior, that is, around twenty-seven at the time, and as he says in our interview, he did "office work" at the radio—I am not quite sure what exactly it may have been. We were to be introduced in 1971 or so, after I had joined Editio Musica Budapest (EMB) to promote the works of Hungarian composers: until the fall of communism, EMB was the only publisher of its kind in the country and as a result, its job was to take on pieces by every composer worthy of the name.

Bozay had a pronounced country accent, his vowels in particular had a timbre which had an unusual ring to them for my urban ears. He was a shy young man: on one occasion he confessed that he could not bring himself to ask a question a third time. If he had missed the reply, he might repeat the question, but he would rather say thank you and leave than admit that he had again failed to understand the person's answer.

As many of his colleagues, Bozay went out of his way to be "up to date" in his idiom. His chamber compositions in particular, such as Formazioni *for cello solo or* Two Movements *for oboe and piano posed what counted at the time as tremendous technical difficulties. In fact, it was for Heinz Holliger to prove that the oboe work was playable and he kept it on his repertoire for some time. When I first heard the cello piece, I was completely out of my depth, I had no idea what to listen for and rather watched what appeared to be a more or less hopeless struggle of the cellist with his instrument. Years later, when I was better versed in contemporary music, I had no trouble following Bozay's train of thought and learned to appreciate the work.*

After Bozay had taught himself to play the Hungarian folk instrument, the zither, and composed his Improvisations *for the instrument alone, I helped him obtain invitations to several festivals in Western Europe. I drove him to Graz, for instance, a city in Austria not far from the Hungarian border, and lost count of the cigarettes he smoked one after the other during the five-hour drive.*

Yes, Bozay had a self-destructive strain. Years later he was drinking more than was good for him and, rather like Sándor Balassa, as he changed his musical style, his political views also came to the surface. Or was it the other way around? The avant-garde was passé; Bozay turned toward a rigorously classical idiom in which he wrote chamber music such as piano and cello sonatas. With one-party rule gone in 1989, he was appointed director of the National Philharmonia, which initially kept its monopoly as the *Hungarian concert organization. In his new position (which he did not keep for long), Bozay assumed a stiff, aloof air, losing his endearing freshness and sincerity of old. Probably he felt he needed to put on a mask, which may have covered his face but did not fit.*

At one point, he had a heart attack. "You just lie there and fear for your life," he confessed. When we last met, at an opera premiere in Budapest, his smile was once again boyish and frank. A second heart attack killed him, a month after his sixtieth birthday. There were a number of speeches at his burial, the last one by a prim-looking lady no one knew: she paid her respects on behalf of a religious community whose members claimed to be followers of pre-Christian Hungarians, a kind of shamanistic faith. Apparently, Attila Bozay had gone whole hog.

I.

I have not had an identical or even a similar experience.

True, the masters of the Viennese School—Schoenberg, Berg, Webern—had a very strong influence. In 1957–58, at the Academy of Music, my colleagues and I listened with keen interest to the few worn LPs and tapes which we could organize for ourselves.

We then proceeded to discuss what we had heard. Some liked the music, some did not, others expressed a liking for one piece or another. As far as I was concerned: an unknown world opened up for me, for the music had been more or less forbidden in Hungary. Twentieth-century music I had access to included compositions by Bartók and Kodály, a few pieces by Honegger, even fewer by Stravinsky, in addition to the older generation of Hungarian composers: Ferenc Szabó, Endre Szervánszky, Ferenc Farkas, Pál Járdányi, György Ránki, and others.

Understandably enough, I had no style of my own at that stage. I was writing little pieces in a variety of styles, but I was always having a hard time with the idiom I had inherited, or rather, acquired, from the previous generation. As an adolescent, I produced many pieces which were conventional as far as their form was concerned, they imitated certain neoclassical or neofolkloristic patterns, but their harmonic world drew its inspiration from elsewhere. I was looking for more chromatic melodic turns, more chromatic, more altered harmonies. The problem was that it was all rather confused and in questionable taste. I used the Debussyian chord of the ninth, its slightly jazzy variations, augmented chords, here and there a sharper dissonance. I wanted a sound world different from tonality but could not yet organize it.

That is why the music of the Viennese masters impressed me so much: they helped me tremendously to organize tones and I was of course also interested in their novel treatment of intervals, harmonies, and timbres.

The twelve-tone technique provided me with a compositional method for many years, one which ensured a greater stylistic unity. It taught me to work with tones and to go beyond the mere notation of the sounds found on the piano without first of all having a clear idea of what I was going to do with them. The technique made for discipline, similarly to the Palestrina style which I was also fond of. I think the simultaneous presence of strict rules and freedom is very important for me. Strict rules paralyze me but liberty perhaps even more: it makes me unbridled and undisciplined.

The *Reihe* technique only served me to organize tones, I never wrote serial music because I was attached to the Hungarian school as far as form and rhythm were concerned. In other words, the rhythm and form of my music stemmed from one world while my intervals and harmonies from another. I feel this duality is present to this day.

Beyond listening to records and tapes, did you take time to analyze the scores as well?

I did not see many scores and I only looked at them while listening to the records. I analyzed perhaps one or two works. I did not really need to: I had learned the basic notions before hearing the compositions. I also received some guidance from Professor Farkas and I did not think I needed more, for I did not wish to engage in complicated operations with the row.

Why do you think that the encounter with the Second Viennese School had nothing in common with Lutosławski's Cage experience?

For one thing, because Lutosławski was by then a mature composer whereas I was only nineteen years old. For another, I continued to compose tonal or modal compositions, with a little bit of chromaticism, pieces which had a free structure: dodecaphony was not my exclusive method.

It was only later, after graduating from the academy, that I looked at what I had written, in an attempt to assess what may have been of any value of the copious production of the previous five years. I found that the dodecaphonic compositions that had given me so much trouble and turned out to be uneven did have more or less successful sections or even movements which were worth returning to with a view to salvaging them. At the same time, however impeccable my examination pieces may have been, I found them bland. (Perhaps because I did not find them "modern" enough. To be up to date was a magic word in the 1960s, even for the older generation of composers.)

I fashioned my Opus 1 out of five violin duets and six piano pieces: I revised two of the violin duets and one piano piece and turned them into *Three Violin Duets.* Opus 2, *Episodi,* was meant right from the start for bassoon and piano; it also had a version for bassoon and chamber orchestra. Eventually, I stuck to the original idea, but the printed score was at least its third version. I also revised my String Trio, Op. 3, while leaving its instrumentation unchanged. I regarded it as an important work and I have not changed my opinion to this day because I feel that in that piece working with the technique came quite naturally to me. *Bagatelles,* Op. 4, for piano was the last of the revised academy compositions; I left *Paperslips,* Op. 5,[7] as it was. True, it is not dodecaphonic. Still, the intervals and timbres of the second (and perhaps also the third) movement bear traces of my dodecaphonic studies. In my vocal compositions, I was always cautious in working with dodecaphony. Two of the three movements of the song cycle *Cries,* Op. 8[8], were dodecaphonic, the third one was not.

My dodecaphonic period lasted from 1958 until 1965 but its influence continued in the years to come: the techniques and constructional procedures applied in the 1970s took account of the twelve tones, though differently from before.

Did you encounter similarly important experiences later on which, like dodecaphony, gave you guidance for a number of years?

Quite a few compositions made a deep impression but by that time I had calmed down and developed a method which later influences could not undermine. Perhaps aleatorism struck me stronger than any other but I forget which piece.

I used aleatorism, for instance, in my Zither Concerto, Op. 24; the encounter of zither and cimbalom in *Mirror* is also aleatoric, even though the material is not. The folk-song montage *Variations,* Op. 29 for orchestra, as well as a children's song montage are also aleatoric in character.

Did the years dedicated to composing your opera[9] change or modify your idiom?

Procedures emerged to the surface which in former years (perhaps because of too much proximity or lack of independence) I had only been able to apply in a cliché-like or derivative manner. I have mentioned Bartók, Kodály, Debussy, Stravinsky, but I could also cite Britten and Prokofiev. I have now been able to rid myself of their stifling influence and I believe I can use this language in my own way or at least in a manner which I feel is authentic.

In the opera, too, I apply a method of construction which is not twelve-tone but nine- and ten-tone and is heir to that technique. There is no row, but there is a sound system where I can now freely play with the tones, I no longer hesitate to draw on other twentieth-century trends, especially certain characteristic features of the first half of the century, without fearing that I might be imitating them.

---

7. For soprano, clarinet, and violoncello.

8. For tenor, violin, violoncello, clarinet, horn, and piano.

9. *Csongor és Tünde,* Op. 31.

II.

I think I am a composer who hears from within. I try to create my sound material from inside myself. It does occur, however, that the sounds and sonorities of certain compositions do affect me and can set in train sound processes in my mind.

The noises of the outside world tend to disturb and irritate me. Still, having listened to some contemporary pieces which address themselves to concrete musical material or its transformations, or even under the influence of electronic works, I grow for a short time sensitive to noises of the outside world, I can hear the sounds of the street or nature as music. We had three dogs in the neighborhood, and on one occasion they barked at the same time. I listened to it with fascination for a few minutes, observing the rhythm of their coming closer to each other, sometimes barking almost—or even completely—simultaneously.

I have experimented with a few pieces where noise was preponderant. Such is the Improvisation No. 2, Op. 27,[10] for instance, where the string instruments play practically no traditional tones, except for the flageolets of the first and last movements. In my String Quartet No. 2, Op. 21, too, there is a movement made up exclusively of the players drumming on the body of the instruments or playing *sul ponticello.*

In your Zither Concerto, the wind players produce some amusing animal sounds—perhaps your statement that you only hear from within should be taken with a pinch of salt.

Perhaps I was wrong. After all, in the fourth movement of Improvisation No. 2, I play on the mouthpiece of the recorder and everyone identifies the result as birdsong. But it is one thing to imitate birds and another going to bed in the early hours of the morning and not being able to sleep for the infernal twittering. I love the sounds of the night when I am walking in the city. I had such experiences mainly at the time when I was working at Hungarian Radio. I did office work all day, then I composed and went home at dawn.

Did you compose at the radio?

Yes. In studios. Memories of those nocturnal walks live on in the notturnos of the first *Pezzo sinfonico*, Op. 13, mixed with memories of Parisian nights. The notturno with its allusion to Gregorian chant recalls the image of Notre Dame; children's songs were incorporated after seeing a ball that had landed in the bush; a little child had perhaps looked for it in vain. It was once again at night, I was dead tired and was making my way home. After hard work till the small hours, the sight of the ball filled me with incredible warmth. I felt so lighthearted that the experience accompanied me to Paris (where I composed the *Pezzo sinfonico*).

---

10. For recorders and string trio.

Summing up: I have sometimes, as a result of a conscious decision, drawn on outside influences in a piece, in a highly abstract way, or at least giving it a musical form. It appears as though such influences have also left traces in my music without my realizing it—I was never aware of it and certainly did not make an issue out of it.

III.

I cannot answer this question because—for better or for worse—the danger of self-repetition has never been a threat. My problem has been, rather, to be writing too many different pieces. I have been accused of eclecticism, something that I minded very much because my goal was to arrive at a unified style which was at the same time rich and varied.

With more than twenty years of composition behind me, I do feel that there very well are characteristic traits in my music. Returning features appear in a spiral: after a lapse of several years, a problem would come to the fore once again, to be addressed on a larger apparatus and a higher level.

For instance, the last movement of *Series,* Op. 19,[11] is based on the chordal arrangement of all-interval rows. I wrote it in 1970. Six years later, the same question was exercising my mind in the second *Pezzo sinfonico,* Op. 25.[12] I played with intervals in the piano piece *Intervalli,* Op. 15, of 1969, and also in the first movement of the String Quartet, Op. 21, no. 2, composed two years later.

I can only compose if I feel I am trying out something new. If in retrospect I find that it rhymes with something I wrote in the past, I am very pleased. However, I never decide in advance such correspondences, it is not for me to be consciously progressing in small steps. It has happened in the past that, led by a desire to forcefully create a new style, I attempted to make a new piece out of an older one—but I failed. The second *Pezzo* turned out to be wholly different from the first one and the third one will possibly be something else once again.

I wonder what I am going to compose after the opera. Now that I have completed it, I shall obviously take a rest—but when I start work again, am I going to return to an earlier style? I do not think so. Out of curiosity, in the intervals in between orchestrating the opera, I have improvised something on the piano and I found I was back again in my old clichés. I felt that I had reached a dead end.

---

11. For chamber ensemble.

12. For orchestra.

I have some children's choruses in the making. Their style may have something in common with a children's chorus in the opera. The genre itself is new, I never composed for children's voices in the past.

As you can see, I have no idea which way I am going to turn. I am almost certain that I am not going to repeat myself. I do not know how much longer I can afford to be roaming about. I am forty-five years old—shall I be able to do something new till the end of my life? Liszt succeeded in doing so, with me it is not so sure.

On the face of it, it is easier to explore new territories all the time. It also appears to be superficial because it is a horizontal rather than vertical activity. At the same time, it is extremely exhausting because one is never in harmony with oneself. Again and again, I have to find something new where I can temporarily feel at home—while I am composing a piece. Perhaps that is why I have been able to conserve my relative youth—but it is of course just a semblance.

It could be true that I do not go deep enough in exploring a problem, even if it would be worth dedicating several years to solving it. That is the question I shall be facing in the future.

1984

Eight

EARLE BROWN (1926–2002)

The interview with Earle Brown tells the attentive reader rather a lot about the composer's personality. It could of course be just my subjective interpretation. At the time Brown came into his own as a creative personality, in the early 1950s, composers were motivated by the ambition to invent genuinely new music which went far beyond the prewar achievements of their older colleagues such as Arnold Schoenberg. If they hit upon a feature which appeared to have no precedence in music history, they strove to have it "patented" as their intellectual property.

In talking to Earle Brown, I had the impression that he needed the universal acceptance of his authorship of his new notational system and conducting techniques to buttress his self-esteem. Perhaps he felt that time was running out, that his claim to fame was proving tenuous, with his friends and colleagues of the New York Group, John Cage and Morton Feldman in particular, having an international following while he, Brown, apparently had none. Perhaps I was less conscious of this in 1984 when we did the interview than in the late 1990s when he came to Vienna to lecture to students at the university and it was obvious that his health was deteriorating. Time is ruthless but it is also inscrutable. Perhaps it will decide to relegate Earle's music to the footnotes of music history but it may just as well ensure that his oeuvre will enjoy a comeback—not for its novelty, which will have faded, but for its intrinsic value.

I.

I'm not sure if Lutosławski "learned his notation system" from me, as Feldman said, but it is very likely that he saw it and was influenced by it sometime between my development of it in 1952 and whenever it was that he first used "proportional notation" and/or my "open-form" scoring and conducting techniques. If you know my *FOLIO* (1952/53) (published by AMP Schirmer), you know that it contains what I believe to be the first use of proportional notation, open-form, graphic scores, what I called "time notation" (to differentiate it from metric notation), etc.

David Tudor took *FOLIO* and other works of mine, Cage, and Feldman to Darmstadt in 1953 or 1954. Our works and methods were a very great surprise to the Europeans and had a tremendous influence from that point on. Boulez saw my *FOLIO* and other open-form works of mine in 1952, on his first trip to New York. He liked my pre-*FOLIO* work very much (Schillinger-inspired twelve-tone serial works) and later helped me very much in Europe. At that time Boulez could not accept the "freedom" that I gave to the conductors or musicians to make spontaneous variations on the form and structure of my composed musical materials. His response to *FOLIO* was that WE COMPOSERS must control everything and make all of those decisions. He did not understand my aesthetic thinking and follow my influences from painting and sculpture (Pollock and Calder) and my generally "open" American mind. I had played much jazz and believed strongly in the ART inherent in responsible spontaneous shaping and performing processes.

I feel that the first large and significant truly open-form work after my "experiments" in *FOLIO* is my *TWENTY-FIVE PAGES* (1953), for one to twenty-five pianos. Tudor took this to Darmstadt also. It is really the work that influenced Stockhausen's Piano Piece XI and Boulez's Third Piano Sonata. A lot of European musicologists do not seem to know of my *TWENTY-FIVE PAGES* and I frequently see statements that the S. and B. works are the first open-form works.

This is distinctly not true given the existence of *FOLIO* and *TWENTY-FIVE PAGES* and the fact that they were in Darmstadt in 1953 or 1954. (Tudor's first visit must be looked up in the Darmstadt archives and/or I must confirm it with him.)

Given the above, it seems likely that Lutosławski would have been influenced by my work. Cage was not doing open-form or improvisational works in 1952 or 1953. He himself says that his first "indeterminate" work was in 1957 or 1958.

I insist that my work is not "chance music." I have used some "statistical distribution" techniques (Schillinger influence as well as my background in mathematics) but never "chance" techniques. In almost every case I compose (subjectively) the sound materials that are later subject to "open-form" potential, as I describe the rules and possible ways of activating the open-form process. In the spontaneous (or prearranged) variations of the musical "events," as I conceived open form, it is not done by chance, but on the contrary, by informed and conscious CHOICE! on the part of the conductor or musician. It is a very complex matrix of interlocking responsibilities that I create, in and for the work.

Now to your three questions:

In regard to Lutosławski's statement, I have not had a similar experience with other composers' music, except perhaps with seeing and hearing the Ives *Concord Sonata* in approximately 1946. As I have said, my similar experience of "realizing that I could compose music differently," came primarily from the powerful effect on me of the work of Jackson Pollock and Alexander Calder, who, as you know, both did radical things to how we think about making and experiencing ART. The "mobiles" of Calder led me to "open form"; I originally called *FOLIO* and my other early works "mobile scores." Europe later called it "open form." The "improvisational" "drip" techniques of Pollock led me to the conducting techniques I developed for DECEMBER *1952* (in *FOLIO*) and *AVAILABLE FORMS I* (1960/61) for eighteen instruments: the spontaneous signaling, superimposing, and forming through conducting the open-form works has been compared by others—and I was conscious of it—to "painting" with sound and is also like "sculpting" the sound into its final form in each performance—obviously different in each performance, but always utilizing only the musical materials (events) that I have composed for that work. In the case of DECEMBER *1952*, which is a graphic score, not only the form but also the content is "open." Clearly, all of this came about, and I was able to assimilate, develop, and extend these influences, through my background in jazz—its "open" and spontaneous nature.

II.

I am open and responsive to the sounds of everyday life—wind, rain, birds, motors, the sound of leaves on trees, the sound of walking in the woods—and have been influenced by them. There are many sounds in my tape and orchestral works that were influenced by such sounds, but almost always produced on instruments or groups of instruments. I think that I was the first (or one of the first) to use instrumental-orchestral sounds such as blowing only wind (no pitches) through instruments in "melodic" ways (rising and falling wind sound which I first heard in a jazz clarinet solo by Jimmy Giuffre), the clicking of keys, playing *arco* and *pizzicato* on the "wrong" side of string instruments, bridge (playing "beyond" the bridge, etc.), as well as extremely dense, close-spaced, extremely fast articulation in groups of instruments or on keyboards. These things I consider to be "normal" extensions of instrumental sounds. I do not use or like the striking of nonpercussion instruments or the disassembling and "distorting" of the basic nature of instruments.

III.

An individual style is to follow one's own instincts and poetry and do exactly what one must do regardless of what anyone else is doing or what anyone thinks of what you are doing.

The Calder and Pollock influences hit me around 1947 but it took me until 1951–52 to discover how to bring the "poetry" of their work into music: not to imitate their work—there is no way to do in TIME (music) what they do in SPACE (painting and sculpture)—but their innovations in how we make and experience art can be translated into the art of sound and performance. At least I thought it could be and it resulted in *FOLIO*, *TWENTY-FIVE PAGES* and *AVAILABLE FORMS I* and *II*, and other works. *FOLIO* was really the beginning of my personal style and I think that it has developed, but remains a very personal "poetics." I really also think that although that revolutionary way of thinking had a very large effect and influence on all music and "performance art" since that time, my music remains a very personal style—I believe. Self-repetition begins when one's imagination and invention run dry. The basic nature of my aesthetic commitment and instinct has not changed since *FOLIO* (1952), but I have transformed and developed my expression of it considerably since then.

There is one other thing about the Lutosławski quote and history. He is probably right about hearing the Cage Piano Concerto and its effect on him. It is unclear, however, what he heard. There is a Cage Concerto for Prepared Piano and Chamber Orchestra from 1951 which has nothing to do with "open form" as far as I know, and is in conventional notation (according to John himself). There is also a Concert for Piano and Orchestra from 1957–58, which can be played in different arrangements of the orchestra materials and uses many different "invented" notations. Which did L. hear?

Another matter: my *AVAILABLE FORMS I* was first performed at Darmstadt in 1961 and I believe it to be the first fully "open-form" work for orchestra. (As above, I had been working in "open form" since 1952 for pianos and other groups.) I saw L. recently and he claims not to have been in Darmstadt in 1961 but I have a distinct memory of having been introduced to him right after the performance of *AV. I.* (He must know better than I where he was in 1961!)

Curious, however, because I have a recording of L. on which he is quoted as saying very much what your quote of him says, except that he says that it was seeing and hearing Cage in Darmstadt in 1961 that changed his life . . . !

Two things: Cage was not in Darmstadt in 1961 . . . I was with *AVAILABLE FORMS I.*

L. says on this record that he was in Darmstadt in 1961. So was he influenced by Cage or by me??? (I think by both of us at different times in different ways, but his music is far closer to my way than it is to John's (truly chance) music.

I'm not trying to argue anything and don't want to start a major controversy but these contrasting quotes and remembrances are really fascinating. If you can solve the mystery I would very much like to hear about it. All quotes and memories are subject to failure so we may never know. I know what I've done where and when, I think! as far as reported here, at least.

I'm sure that I was not influenced by L., at least not before 1961. I didn't know anything of him before that, but again, in my memory of things.

I hope that this is not far more than you wish to know about Earle Brown. When I do get to writing to you I really run on.

1984

Here is an extract from Witold Lutosławski's letter to me, of December 12, 1984:

> Now the Feldman–Earle Brown affair: (1) I have never been in Darmstadt, (2) I have heard the *2nd Piano-Concerto* of Cage through the radio in 1960 and then started to compose *Jeux vénitiens* in which the notation was my own invention, (3) I have never seen any score of Earle Brown. I heard his *Available Forms* in 1962 in Tanglewood, Massachusetts, and then I was introduced to him. At that time I was already composing *Three Poems of Henri Michaux*. So I don't think I have really been influenced by Earle Brown's music although I wouldn't mind! So I don't think there is mystery in the whole affair.

Nine

SYLVANO BUSSOTTI (1931)

In the years devoted to collecting material for this book, approaching Sylvano Bussotti was a matter of course: his name was almost on a par with Berio's and Donatoni's. His replies arrived on a single sheet of paper, written in hand (see fig. 2), and while I sensed an impatience about them, they also revealed a fascinating, original personality I would have been happy to meet in person.

Twenty-seven years on, impatience seems to have prevailed: he chose not to reply to my letter inviting him to look at the text again.

Bussotti is an all-around artist: composer, poet, painter, designer, choreographer, sculptor, photographer, opera and film director. He has also led festivals (such as the Puccini Festival and the concert section of the Venice Biennale) and established his own production company, "Bussottioperaballet," which ran a festival in Genazzano. For a time, Bussotti was also director of the Teatro La Fenice in Venice. In old age, he seems to have scaled down his activities.

I am going to try and reply briefly to the three questions.

I.

Three composers have influenced me—listening to their music as much as their personal acquaintance:

Luigi Dallapiccola, when I was fourteen
Pierre Boulez, when I was twenty-four
John Cage, when I was twenty-six

I attended the world premieres of some of their works—*Il Prigioniero* (Dallapiccola), *Le marteau sans maître* and *Doubles* (Boulez), and *Variations* (Cage). *All my works* composed at the time bear the imprint of those compositions.

II.

I do not exclude the outside world while composing. The so-called "sounds," including "noises of everyday life" do not influence me much, nor do they inspire me. (Inspiration, as you are no doubt aware, is a rather moot notion. I am sometimes inspired by human beings but never by phenomena, and phonetics only to a certain extent.) A "creator" is influenced more than anything by musical culture.

III.

Self-repetition is to my mind primarily a biological characteristic of man rather than of composers. It does not emerge, it is *there* because we are born with it. Style is a retrospective category mostly assessed by critics *a posteriori* often without considering the deep sense of musical creation. However, as a mirror of myself, my personal style or conscious self-repetition are inimitably mine.

1983

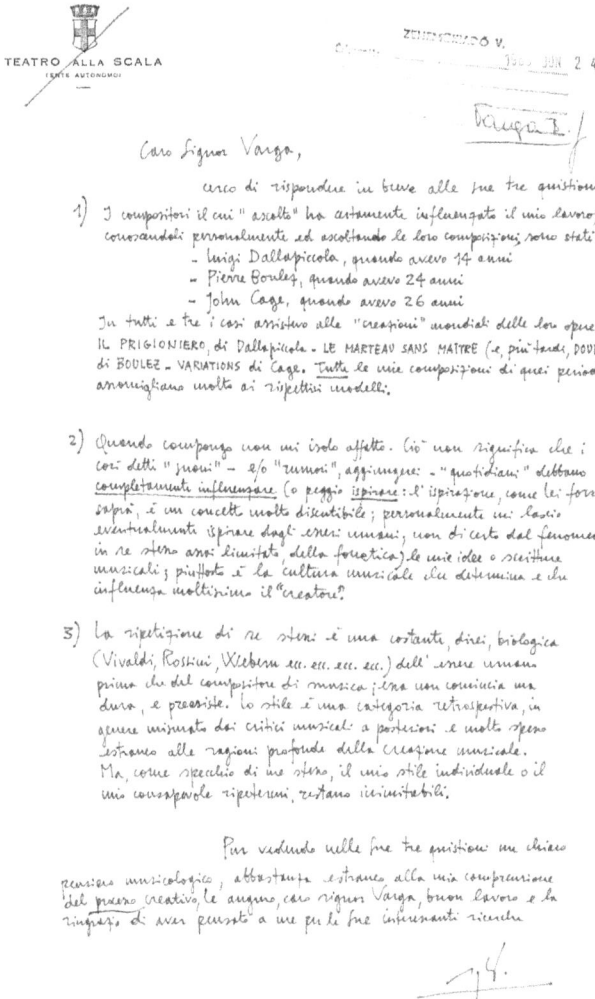

TEATRO ALLA SCALA
(ENTE AUTONOMO)

Varga I.

Caro Signor Varga,

cerco di rispondere in breve alle sue tre questioni.

1) I compositori il cui "ascolto" ha certamente influenzato il mio lavoro; conoscendoli personalmente ed ascoltando le loro composizioni, sono stati:
- Luigi Dallapiccola, quando avevo 14 anni
- Pierre Boulez, quando avevo 24 anni
- John Cage, quando avevo 26 anni

In tutti e tre i casi assistevo alle "creazioni" mondiali delle loro opere: IL PRIGIONIERO, di Dallapiccola - LE MARTEAU SANS MAITRE (e, più tardi, DOUBLES) di BOULEZ - VARIATIONS di Cage. Tutte le mie composizioni di quei periodi assomigliano molto ai rispettivi modelli.

2) Quando compongo non mi isolo affatto. Ciò non significa che i così detti "suoni" - e/o "rumori", aggiungere: - "quotidiani" debbano completamente influenzare (o peggio ispirare: l'ispirazione, come lei forse saprà, è un concetto molto discutibile; personalmente mi lascio eventualmente ispirare dagli esseri umani, non di certo dal fenomeno, in se stesso assai limitato, della fonetica) le mie idee o scritture musicali; piuttosto è la cultura musicale che determina e che influenza moltissimo il "creatore".

3) La ripetizione di se stessi è una costante, direi, biologica (Vivaldi, Rossini, Webern ecc. ecc. ecc. ecc.) dell'essere umano prima che del compositore di musica; essa non comincia ma dura, e preesiste. Lo stile è una categoria retrospettiva, in genere misurato dai critici musicali a posteriori e molto spesso estraneo alle ragioni profonde della creazione musicale. Ma, come specchio di me stesso, il mio stile individuale o il mio consapevole ripetermi, restano inimitabili.

Pur vedendo nelle sue tre questioni un chiaro pensiero musicologico, abbastanza estraneo alla mia comprensione del processo creativo, le auguro, caro signor Varga, buon lavoro e la ringrazio di aver pensato a me per le sue interessanti ricerche

S. B.

Figure 2. Sylvano Bussotti's replies came in a handwritten letter, in his native Italian. Reproduced by kind permission of the Bálint András Varga Collection, Akademie der Künste, Berlin.

Ten

JOHN CAGE (1912–92)

The Warsaw Autumn Festival was for many years Eastern Europe's only access to music from the West. It was a crack in the Iron Curtain through which composers in the communist countries could obtain information of vital significance for their work.

For me, it offered a unique opportunity to meet composers such as John Cage, Iannis Xenakis, or Jean Barraqué and performers such as Cathy Berberian. In my luggage, I always had a tape recorder with me, just in case.

In 1972, Merce Cunningham and his ballet company were guests of the festival; they danced to Cage's Cheap Imitation *played on the piano by the composer himself. Before the performance, I set out in the backstage labyrinth of the Drama Theater, in search of Cage. I opened a door at random—and there he was sitting at a table, a prophet-like apparition with his full beard, tousled hair, and a weary, lifeless look in his eyes. He agreed to meet me after the show, stood up, and disappeared.*

The interview we recorded in Warsaw appeared in Hungarian in a collection of interviews in 1979. When I conceived of the three-questions book around 1978, Cage was one of the first composers I approached. He answered under the "message" rather than "reply" heading of his printed "note-o-gram" in what appeared to me to be a tantalizingly terse fashion (see fig. 3).

Twelve years later in his New York apartment, he struck me as an altogether different person, easy to talk to, less of a seer but still anxious to express his thoughts in the most lucid manner. (You will find our interview appended to the conversation with Morton Feldman.)

We met a third time in 1989 at London's Almeida Theatre, scene of one of the portrait concerts devoted to György Kurtág's music. He sat in the first row and I asked him what he had made of Kurtág's compositions. Cage hesitated for a second and said: "I am glad to have heard them." An incomparably noncommittal reply; I did not press him further.

I.

The white paintings (not painted white, just unpainted canvasses) of Robert Rauschenberg gave me the courage to make *4'33"*, my silent piece, which I had thought of 4 years earlier but had not actually composed. Also the first graph sketches of Morton Feldman prompted me to develop compositional means involving chance operations (*Music of Changes*).

II.

The noises around me *are 4'33"*. I try in my work not to interrupt that.

III.

I am not concerned with a personal style or "self-expression" (nor was Thoreau). I hope through my work to change myself ("self-alteration"), to open my mind to possibilities outside of it.

1980

When asked to amplify his replies, Cage answered:

My answers were brief on purpose and as explicit as I care to make them. Amplification can be made one way or another by the reader. If I send you details they (my answers) will simply be less useful in the society.

NOTE-O-GRAM®
© THE DRAWING BOARD • BOX 505 • DALLAS, TEXAS

JOHN CAGE
101 WEST 18 STREET (5B) • NEW YORK, NEW YORK 10011

MESSAGE | REPLY

TO Bálint András Varga
1053 Budapest
Károlyi utca 5
HUNGARY

DATE May 1, 1980

1. The white paintings (not painted white, just unpainted canvasses) of Robert Rauschenberg gave me the courage to make 4'33", my silent piece, which I had thought of 4 years earlier but had not actually composed. Also the first graph sketches of Morton Feldman prompted me to develop compositional means involving chance operations (Music of Changes).
2. The noises around me are 4'33". I try in my work not to interrupt that.
3. I am not concerned with a personal style or "self-expression" (nor was Thoreau). I hope through my work to change myself ("self-alteration"), to open my mind to possibilities outside of it.

With best wishes,
John Cage

BY

DATE

SIGNED

Form N-873® The Drawing Board, Inc., Box 505, Dallas, Texas

INSTRUCTIONS TO SENDER:
1. KEEP YELLOW COPY. 2. SEND WHITE AND PINK COPIES WITH CARBON INTACT.

INSTRUCTIONS TO RECEIVER:
1. WRITE REPLY. 2. DETACH STUB, KEEP PINK COPY, RETURN WHITE COPY TO SENDER.

Figure 3. Cage used a printed form for his correspondence. Its size made for terseness. Reproduced by kind permission of the Bálint András Varga Collection, Akademie der Künste, Berlin.

Eleven

ELLIOTT CARTER (1908–2012)

An exact contemporary of Olivier Messiaen, Elliott Carter is thankfully still with us, providing a living link to the first decades of the twentieth century.

As a pupil of Nadia Boulanger in Paris as of 1932, he may well have heard Ravel play the piano (he was to write a moving obituary upon the French composer's death in 1937 for Modern Music, *a magazine for which he had begun to contribute articles beginning in 1936). His summaries of the New York concert seasons in the late 1930s afford a telling glimpse of performances of music which was then new (such as Webern's recent arrangement of Schubert's German Dances of 1824), by composers who were still active and counted as his older contemporaries: beyond Webern also Bartók and, most significantly, Charles Ives. In the book he sent me (see below), he marked several articles in the collection of his writings published in 1977 by Indiana University Press—articles from the 1930s onward, all to do with the music of Ives.*

I first encountered a work by Carter in Budapest in the 1970s when Charles Rosen played his Piano Concerto with the BBC Symphony Orchestra conducted by Pierre Boulez. I was rather nonplussed by what I heard but was nevertheless aware of its being a substantial and significant piece of music.

In subsequent years I continued to hear compositions by Elliott Carter at infrequent intervals and my impressions never changed: I found them too abstract to move me but always interesting as an intellectual challenge. The change came as late as 2007 or so when the orchestral piece Soundings, *composed when Carter was well into his nineties, fascinated me with its mellowness and echoes of traditional inflections.*

I was in London in the late 1980s, attending a concert which had John Cage in the audience. In the intermission, I accompanied a friend to his car, to find Elliott Carter getting out of one parked right next to it. On greeting him, I suggested he might want to meet Cage, who was conveniently nearby in the concert hall and was perplexed by the vehemence of his rejection: no, he was busy, he had an appointment to keep. Back in the hall, I told the American pianist Yvar Mikhashoff (1941–93) of my exchange with Carter. He explained that the two composers were practically not on speaking terms, even though they lived quite near to each other. Cage would have been happy to break the ice but Carter would not budge. I was reminded of Stravinsky and Schoenberg in Los Angeles who had also preferred to keep aloof. With Cage, four years Carter's junior, gone, all chance of a rapprochement is lost once and for all.

I.

The hearing of *Le Sacre du printemps*, Ives's *Concord Sonata*, Varèse's *Intégrales* and *Hyperprism*, Berg's *Wozzeck*, Schoenberg's *Pierrot* and *Glückliche Hand* in the mid-twenties in New York interested me so much in music that I decided to become a composer. I had found that older music did not attract me during those years and it was only much later that I found it of any interest.

Around 1949, I programmed the first performances of Ives's *Central Park in the Dark* and *The Unanswered Question* at Columbia University. They had interested me at that time because of the concept of stratification of different kinds of music—which I had been thinking about for several years—as in my Cello Sonata. This, combined with a hearing in Mexico City of the first of the *Player Piano Studies* of Conlon Nancarrow, who had been a friend for a number of years, helped to crystallize the concepts which have appeared in my music ever since 1950. (Starting with the First String Quartet: it quotes a theme of Ives and one of Nancarrow because, as I said in my program note, these two composers suggested both in their music and in personal contact ideas which I developed in that score. Of course, at that time this meant very little to anybody since both were nearly unknown. Now . . .)

Around 1927, polyrhythms I found in Scriabin, Ives, and others fascinated me, but it was not until 1948 that I found a way of using them that satisfied me.

II.

Since my music is concerned with all sides of life—sounds, actions, human relationships—motions (visual, audible, visceral, and psychological) form the basis of my musical thinking. Poetry has had a considerable influence on many of my works—Lucretius on my Double Concerto, St. John Perse's *Vents* on my Concerto for Orchestra, Hart Crane's poems on my *Symphony of Three Orchestras*, not to mention my four song cycles and other vocal works.

III.

Each of my works is an adventure into a new conceptual, expressive, and musical domain which I have not yet explored. Their style is not something consciously thought about, but is a reflection of the expressive and musical intention. To work out a series of stylistic devices and then use them as formulae bores me as a prospect and it bores me in others who do it. Self-repetition is to me a sign of fatigue.

1982/96

In March 1985, I received the following letter from Mr. Carter:

"Rather than answer your many interesting recent questions I am sending you a copy of the book *The Writings of Elliott Carter.* In it you will find four large articles about Charles Ives describing my meeting with him as a boy, and our correspondence some of which was carried on through Mrs Ives (which includes a discussion of whether to consider the performances I arranged for in 1946 of *CENTRAL PARK IN THE DARK* and *THE UNANSWERED QUESTION* as first performances or not) (pp. 341–42). Discussions of his 4th Symphony written before the work was first performed in its entirety appear in 'The Rhythmic Basis of American Music' (1955) as well as a discussion in the same article of Nancarrow (p. 160). The matter of stratification, polyrhythm, metric modulation in my own music is discussed at length in 'Music and the Time Screen,' p. 343 and in other places, in the book. I think you will find answers to all your questions either in this or in the book by David Schiff, *The Music of Elliott Carter* (Eulenburg Books, London). In my writings there is also a brief note on Ligeti (p. 168) written while I still wrote for the newspapers.

The plan of your proposed book seems interesting and I hope you have the best of luck with it. It is courageous of you to include something about an American composer—for all of us have had a very hard time penetrating European indifference to our work."

Twelve

FRIEDRICH CERHA (1926)

Friedrich Cerha is something of a national institution in Austria. Over the past half century, his name has become synonymous with contemporary music—its creation, performance, teaching, and analysis.

In a pioneering effort in what was at the time an archconservative environment, he founded (together with Kurt Schwertsik) the ensemble "die reihe" in 1958 and has conducted numerous world and national premieres (of works by Cage, Boulez, Ligeti, and others) over the past decades. Between 1960 and 1997, he appeared with some of the world's leading orchestras, including the Berlin Philharmonic, the Cleveland Orchestra, and the Concertgebouw as well as in opera houses in Berlin, Munich, and Buenos Aires.

Cerha has also been invited by Austria's top new music group, Klangforum and by the ORF Symphony Orchestra to conduct his own works in addition to a varied repertoire.

As a professor of composition, Cerha has had considerable success with pupils such as Georg Friedrich Haas who have since established themselves as composers of the middle generation.

Friedrich Cerha is highly articulate in his writings on music. His program notes on his own compositions reflect an analytical mind and a capacity for looking at his creative process dispassionately. The same is true of the epochal work of reconstruction he did on the third act of Alban Berg's Lulu *(1962–78): he has released an "Arbeitsbericht," a work report, recording in detail what Berg left behind and how he went about reconstructing the material. The complete* Lulu *has since become a staple of opera houses the world over.*

Cerha is a quiet, reserved man with a wonderful sense of humor and remarkable talent as a public speaker. In private, he tends to be taciturn and either lets his wife, Gertraud, do the talking or utters a few words in response to a question or remark. One has to spend quite a long time in his company to see him smile or even laugh out loud and to realize how funny he can be.

The symbiosis of Gertraud and Friedrich Cerha is now something of a legend. Mrs. Cerha, whose tiny frame conceals an absolutely formidable energy, is an indefatigable but not uncritical advocate not only of Cerha's music, but of the contemporary music scene as a whole, with a series of in-depth articles and lectures on it in and outside Austria. The two regularly turn up for new music concerts at the Wiener Konzerthaus where they have seats reserved for them. Their presence is reassuring: the Cerhas are there, all's well with the world.

If a work by Cerha was being featured, he would appear on stage to receive the audience's tribute of stormy applause, pointing with a now well-known gesture to the musicians: they were the ones who deserved recognition.

I.

There has been no comparable experience or event in my development as a composer. I can identify works—from Wagner's *Rienzi*-Ouverture and Richard Strauss' *Salome* that I heard at twelve and thirteen resp.—which made a tremendous impact. I can also name others which I enjoyed playing on the violin at the same age, or indeed later, I performed as a conductor with particular pleasure and frequency. There are compositions I love (such as Stravinsky's *The Soldier's Tale* or the Serenade Op. 24 by Schoenberg) and there are pieces, like Boulez's *Marteau sans maître*, which I admire. Nevertheless, I would ascribe no creative influence to any of them. A comprehensive list would strike one as being extremely varied.

Undoubtedly, my musical activities are marked by the prominent role played by my preoccupation with the Viennese School. After the world premiere of my performing version of the third act of Alban Berg's *Lulu*, my whole work as a composer began to be seen in that light. In response, I can say that expressive, broad melodic and harmonic arches characterize already the slow movement of my Violin Sonata No. 1 of 1946, written at a time when I had not heard a note by Berg. Emotionally charged developments mark even my serial compositions, much to the surprise of Nono. It is their dramatic impact which distinguishes my texture compositions (*Klangkompositionen*) of around 1960 from apparently similar pieces, such as Ligeti's *Atmosphères*.

My work on *Lulu* did not start until after I had conceived those compositions. But even in passages with a stronger kinship to that musical idiom, any "espressivo" is often attributed (just as in the case of Wolfgang Rihm) to a particular tradition usually identified with Mahler or Berg. In any case: it is not a question of any direct influence by those two composers. It could be that one of the basic roots of their music also happens to constitute a primary element of my own which of course also possesses facets of a wholly different kind.

Although my music has nothing in common with Cage's, I did study his work rather thoroughly, and the manner in which he notated the results of chance operations may have inspired the proportional notation I used in an attempt to convey my musical ideas in compositions like *Fasce* (1959–74) and *Spiegel* (1960–61) in ways which appeared to me to be the most rational and precise.

In November 1959, I conducted the second European performance of his Piano Concerto (1958) with David Tudor as soloist and the ensemble "die reihe" playing. Indeed, I like much of Cage's music, especially his works for prepared piano, the String Quartet or *Sonatas and Interludes* and was lucky enough to be able to prepare a concert with him and to make music together. I was moved by the earnestness and precision of his approach, for instance in measuring distances in the *Variations*, although it was "only" to lead to the realization of chance manipulations. I felt a kinship in his attention for "things," in finding a purpose in dealing with them.

II.

I devote attention to the way the world sounds. My fantasy responds to birdcalls, breakers, the gurgling of water in brooks, the rustling of leaves in the wind, the crackling of fire, the snapping of tree branches in the forest at night, but also to short-wave noises or the sound of passing vehicles. They will of course appear stylized and are not always directly or easily recognizable in the music but once hinted at, they will be perceived as such.

For me, *Spiegel III* is a genuinely Mediterranean "sea piece" and in my compositions of the past fifty years there have been passages where silence, stylized as a series of static *pianissimo* chords, is pierced through by brief, nature-like sounds. They make a concrete appearance, in different guises, whenever I am working at night. Incidentally, Ligeti discerned and discussed a similar passage in my harpsichord concerto *Relazioni fragili* (1957).

III.

Self-repetition and style are, to my mind, neither synonymous notions nor a pair of opposites. As pointed out earlier, curiosity impelled me already as a student to discover as much as possible in music and thereby also a great variety of musical ideas. After a period of "purist" compositions such as *Mouvements* (1959–60), *Fasce,* and *Spiegel,* where, around 1960, I conquered for myself an idiom free of formulations stemming from our traditions, I sought once again variety as a possible artistic quality, in pieces like *Exercises* (1962–68), the basis of the stage work *Netzwerk* (1978–80). It was my goal to reach it through complex musical organisms. In setting out on that path, I would sometimes change my "style" abruptly (in an effort to make certain spheres of ideas accessible for my purposes), as a result going against the predominant stylistic precepts of the time.

It has always been important for me (in those years particularly so) to make sure I did not repeat myself as a composer. It was not until I reached an advanced age that I became fully aware of the fact that through varying long established ways of musical thinking, one's fantasy can be fired and new constellations can come about as well.

As far as the relationship between style and quality is concerned: what is it that constitutes Stravinsky's "style?" And: did Picasso have a style at all? In any case, I have always abhorred the supposed need to develop a manner whereby my "artistic personality" can be readily identified—something that applies nowadays particularly to the fine arts and is often mistaken for "style."

2010

Thirteen

GEORGE CRUMB (1929)

I never met George Crumb; he was kind enough to reply to my questions in writing (see fig. 4). At the time I approached him, he was one of the most popular American composers in Europe. His Eleven Echoes of Autumn *(1966),* Ancient Voices of Children *(1970), and* Black Angels *(1970), in particular, were staple fares on concert programs. While in recent years I have not been seeing his name much in print, a quick search on Google produces 526,000 visits to his site, and 55,700 to* Black Angels *alone. Thankfully, interest in his music is still very much alive.*

His reply to the first question shows a rare awareness of influences which have shaped his thinking. The rest of the text, too, presents him as a tone poet (to translate a German synonym for "composer," which appears to me apt in describing George Crumb) with a sober and objective attitude to his art.

I.

In my own case, I must say I have been very much influenced by turn of the century composers Claude Debussy and Gustav Mahler. I am quite sure my music sounds nothing like the music of either of those composers and yet I think the influence is something of the order you are suggesting in your question. There is certainly something evocative in the music of these composers and this has suggested obliquely a certain kind of music to me.

In regard to the influence of Debussy and Mahler on my music, I could itemize the following special features:

1. Mahler's use of long pedal tones (as in the beginning of his first Symphony); in my music I would cite the last page of my "Night of the Four Moons" or, again, my use of long drones in "Songs, Drones, and Refrains of Death."
2. Mahler's predilection for the genre of "Night Music" (as in his Seventh Symphony) and his use of birdsong (in several works); I would mention my "Night Music I" and Four Nocturnes and also my frequent use of bird-song motifs.
3. Mahler's extremely slow tempos in certain movements (last movements of Symphonies #3 and #9, for example), which suggest a "suspension of time"; I have used something similar in several works (e.g., in "Eleven Echoes of Autumn").

4. As direct references to Mahler, I would cite the final song of my "Ancient Voices of Children," which contains a motif similar to one used by Mahler in "Der Abschied" movement "Das Lied von der Erde."

In regard to Debussy, I would mention:

1. The whole tone scale, which I use frequently.
2. The impressionist piano idiom based on much use of the damper pedal. My usual writing for piano requires the damper pedal to be depressed throughout!
3. Debussy's use of Eastern materials (Pagodes, from Estampes). I would similarly borrow from the Orient: the use of the sitar and tablas in my "Lux Aeterna," [and] Tibetan prayer stones in "Night of the Four Moons." Also my melodic materials sometimes suggest the Orient (certain scale types, certain kinds of timbral and ornamental articulations).

I would say, too, that of the classical twentieth-century composers probably Bartók and Webern have been the most influential. I think in this case, however, the influence is much more direct, in other words, not oblique. For example, Bartók's music has suggested certain pitch cells, let us say, or certain rhythmic motifs to me and I have assimilated these things in my own music. And with respect to Webern, the influence probably has to do with timbre, and texture—as I say, these are more direct influences.

II.

First of all, I should say my music has been very much influenced by sounds of nature: the sounds of wind, of birds, and especially of insects, which I think was an influence of Bartók, since again Bartók invented insect music as we know it.

Beyond this, a composer can also be influenced by the acoustic in which he has grown up as a child. In my case, I grew up in West Virginia in an Appalachian river valley, with its reverberant, echoing acoustic, and I think my music reflects this particular sound world.

III.

Your third question is the most difficult one for me. First of all, I would say very generally that I do not think it possible to create a style unless there is a certain carryover from one work to the next. In other words, I feel that one can't reinvent music with each new work. There are simply some things which are part of one's personality—you could refer to fingerprints.

All of the great composers of the past had immediately recognizable fingerprints. With a more recent composer like Stravinsky, for example, even though he is referred to as having changed style many times, what strikes me about his music over his whole lifetime is its consistency.

Again, there are certain stylistic traits, technical procedures—in short, fingerprints, I would say again—that occur in Stravinsky's music of all periods.

I know nowadays we have a sense that time is rushing by so quickly and there is this feeling that a style cannot remain valid for more than ten years or more than five years or maybe more than one year. Perhaps this is something new in our culture in general: this sense of an accelerated movement and the fact that we must always question our basic premises. I think, however, that we can overreact in this direction.

I feel that—as I said a few moments back—the important thing is to create a style and unless enough carries over from one work to the next, the listener has no clear image of the composer's profile. As a matter of fact, I think the listener would be confused. There has to be some internal consistency, in my view. Of earlier composers a remarkable example would be Johannes Brahms, who, in this respect, was able late in life to go back and revise his early B-Major Piano Trio. Much of it was entirely rewritten, I gather, yet it is miraculous that a composer virtually at the end of his career could become involved in something that was a very youthful work. This could be an extreme example of stylistic consistency. I think even Beethoven would find it difficult to revise Opus 1 or Opus 2, let us say, in the year 1825. But even in Beethoven there are consistent stylistic traits that go through all the periods.

I think there is a tendency nowadays for composers to not trust their basic impulse. I have always felt that each composer has a certain finite number of basic types which exist in his mind since childhood and I am not sure that he enlarges the number very much. I think if he tries to deny these basic expressive types, he is doing violence to himself as an artist. It would be psychologically impossible to reinvent music with every work.

1980/83/read and approved in 2009

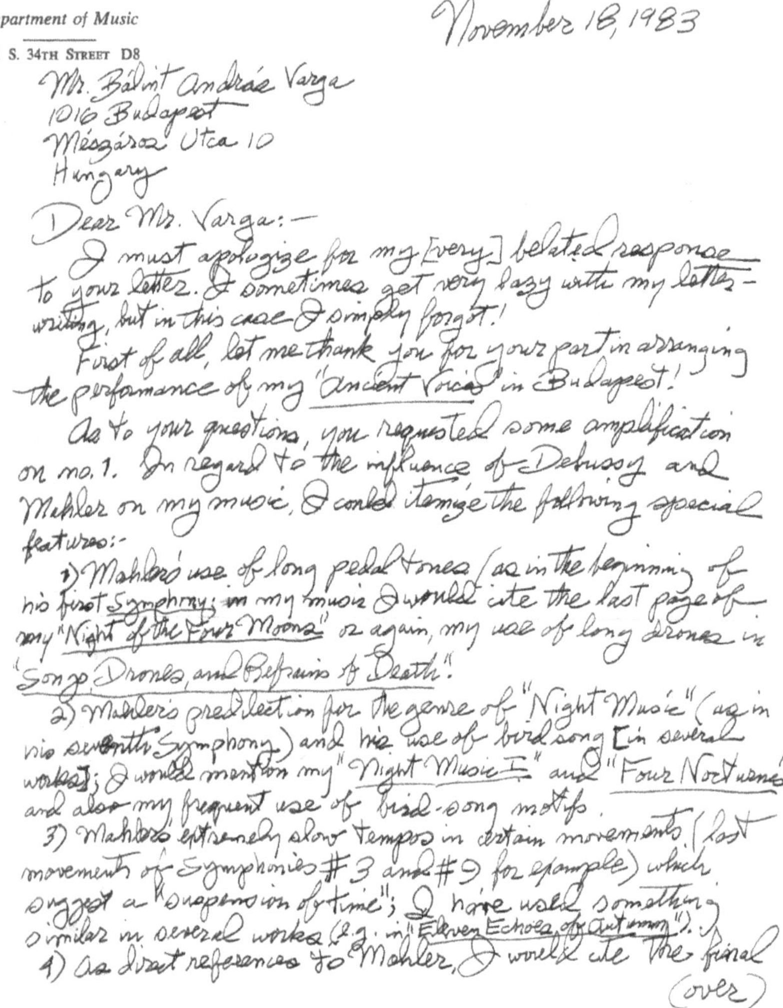

UNIVERSITY *of* PENNSYLVANIA

PHILADELPHIA 19104-3861

Department of Music

201 S. 34TH STREET D8

November 18, 1983

Mr. Bálint András Varga
1016 Budapest
Mészáros Utca 10
Hungary

Dear Mr. Varga:—

I must apologize for my [very] belated response to your letter. I sometimes get very lazy with my letter-writing, but in this case I simply forgot!

First of all, let me thank you for your part in arranging the performance of my "Ancient Voices" in Budapest!

As to your questions, you requested some amplification on no. 1. In regard to the influence of Debussy and Mahler on my music, I could itemize the following special features:-

1) Mahler's use of long pedal tones (as in the beginning of his first Symphony; in my music I would cite the last page of my "Night of the Four Moons" or again, my use of long drones in "Songs, Drones, and Refrains of Death".

2) Mahler's predilection for the genre of "Night Music" (as in his seventh Symphony) and his use of bird song [in several works]; I would mention my "Night Music I" and "Four Nocturnes" and also my frequent use of bird-song motifs.

3) Mahler's extremely slow tempos in certain movements (last movements of Symphonies #3 and #9 for example) which suggest a "suspension of time"; I have used something similar in several works (e.g. in "Eleven Echoes of Autumn").

4) As direct references to Mahler, I would cite the final

(over)

Figure 4. Letter from George Crumb. Reproduced by kind permission of the Bálint András Varga Collection, Akademie der Künste, Berlin.

song of my "Ancient Voices of Children" which contains a motif similar to one used by Mahler in "der Abschied" movement "Das Lied von der Erde".

In regard to Debussy, I would mention: —

1) the whole tone scale, which I use frequently.
2) the impressionist piano idiom based on much use of the damper pedal. My usual writing for piano requires the damper pedal to be depressed throughout!
3) Debussy's use of Eastern materials [Pagodes, from Estampes]; I would similarly borrow from the Orient: the use of the sitar and tablas in my "Lux Aeterna", Tibetan prayer stones in "Night of the Four Moons". Also my melodic materials sometimes suggest the Orient (certain scale types, certain kinds of timbral and ornamental articulations.

I hope that these additional comments will serve your purpose!

I wish you all best success with your book!

Most cordially,

George Crumb

Figure 4. *(concluded)*

Fourteen

SIR PETER MAXWELL DAVIES (1934)

Max and I met in Budapest around 1968. He was a rebellious young man at the time, very antiestablishment, proud of his working-class background and with a streak of Puck in him. Narrow-mindedness, snobbishness, petty-bourgeois Weltanschauung *provoked his sardonic sense of humor and he had tremendous fun thumbing his nose at people who he thought deserved it. When he was touring Australia with his ensemble, for instance, he had the impression that his hosts had no idea of music whatsoever. So he introduced his musicians saying "This is Mr. Brahms, this is Ms. Mozart," and so on. It was not until much later that the penny dropped.*

I was Max's guest in London a number of times and he took me to concerts—such as Stravinsky's Agon. *The music was rather beyond me at the time but I noted his elation, I saw his knowing smile as if he was conducting an intriguing dialogue with the composer.*

I also heard/saw some of Max's own music theater pieces, which fascinated me: Eight Songs for a Mad King *(1969) and* Vesalii Icones *(1969). I have since seen several more of his chamber operas and believe they are his real forte, more so than his orchestra and chamber pieces, which have made less of a mark on an international scale.*

I was in London at the time the ensemble Max was running together with Harrison Birtwistle, the Pierrot Players, was renamed, following Birtwistle's departure, "The Fires of London." Max came home one day, quite thrilled about it all. "Home" reminds me of his apartment in Fitzroy Square, which was filled with medieval timber furniture. I remember a table, in particular, almost black with age, with a delightful smell of old oak and matching, if rather narrow, benches. From Hungary he had brought with him a Madonna with Child, a wonderful piece of naive folk art.

Max's penchant for the arts of the Middle Ages was demonstrated also by his choice of subject for his first opera Taverner, *his subsequent music theater pieces such as* The Martyrdom of St. Magnus, *his love of music by Purcell, Gesualdo, and others, which he arranged for The Fires.*

He was very generous, inviting me to the Dartington summer courses and even enrolling me in a course for creative writing in Wales, which proved a disaster: if I had ever deluded myself that I had any talent for writing fiction, I was disabused of it after the first session. I was also Max's guest in Edinburgh, in 1970 I think, where I was introduced to Henze, whose opera Elegy for Young Lovers *featured on the festival program. After the performance, I made the faux pas of telling Henze how very German I thought his music was. He did not seem to appreciate my remark and*

I was quickly enlightened that he wished to sever his contacts with the country of his birth, he simply did not like to be identified as German.

Forty years have passed since. Max was knighted in 1987 and was appointed Master of the Queen's Musick in 2004. You could not be more establishment than that. Observing his career from afar, I have the impression that international recognition has not come his way but his brilliant and original chamber operas have made it into the repertoire.

I.

I think that kind of experience came for me when I was quite young, when I heard for the first time Bartók's Concerto for Orchestra. I must have been twelve at the time. I happened to be listening to the Third Programme of which I was an addict (it was the only source of sanity and sense in that working-class environment and the rather dreadful school environment).

I remember turning on and landing in the middle of the concerto and realizing that an orchestra could be used in a way that could parallel certain thinking processes which I could not define in any other way but which I was already actively involved in, moving toward some kind of possibility of expression which I did not in fact realize in physical sound terms until probably two years later, when I was fourteen. But that was certainly a turning point, and probably the biggest.

I remember another one which was earlier than that—one of those visionary experiences where you actually realize how music works. I do not know if it had anything to do with the actual piece I was listening to, although I think ideas associated with that piece had a great deal to do with it.

I must have been eleven or so, listening to *The Planets* by Gustav Holst. I had very little experience in music. I do not think I had even heard an orchestra live. My parents were out at the cinema and I was listening to the radio and out came this piece. I was intrigued by it all. In the course of it, I had a vision of a kind of cosmic clock—it is the only way that I can describe it. It was a three-dimensional object that filled the whole universe. It had circles within circles, moving in relation to each other. It had pendulums. I could describe it in great detail but what that visionary experience, inspired by *The Planets,* told me in a very direct way was: This is a reflection of the whole cosmos, this is music and you have to learn how to relate the two things. I could not put it in words then but the vision occasioned by that piece determined my whole thinking about music. I realized that music had to work with the precision of that cosmic clock.

Did you compose before?

Of course, I was composing all the time. I have probably got two of the pieces that I wrote about the age of eight; I chucked them all out when I was about fourteen.

Does listening to a piece today inspire you in any way?

Yes, it does indeed. But very often it is not a contemporary piece but an old one. I do not see the difference between music from this century and music from another century, in many ways. Of course, there are differences but I can be equally inspired by one or the other.

When I was at college and university, the whole phenomenon of medieval music, plainsong going right up to music of the Renaissance hit me and took me and I worked with that. That was cumulatively over a period of a year, I suppose—one of those turning-point experiences and it has probably influenced every note I have written.

Pierrot lunaire was another work of key significance. I knew it from the score from student days but only heard it live for the first time in 1961, at the Cheltenham Festival. The work influenced me in two ways: (1) I enjoyed and hoped to be able to employ differently but relatedly its knife-edge balancing act on the outer rims of tonality—the tensions created by that were definitely exploitable in terms of my own language, and (2) the theatrical presentation of the first performance, where the reciter/singer was costumed as Pierrot, and the instrumentalists were invisible to the audience—an embryonic music-theater situation which has shone through my own *Eight Songs for a Mad King, Miss Donnithorne's Maggot,* and others more remotely descended from the Schoenberg/Giraud model.

At first I found the Schoenberg technically difficult, hard to understand the composer's mind, his selection processes, and so on but conducting the work hundreds of times and systematically analyzing it gave me insights which have been most fruitful—an instruction about organized freedom.

II.

Sounds influence me very much, positively and negatively. When I lived in the south of England and when I lived in Italy, America, and Australia, I have been in cities or in parts of the country where there is a traffic noise even if it is from a mile away—and worst of all, those days, airplane noise. Very often military airplanes which swoop down low—they have an effect on your ears with their blasts of white noise, of blinding light in your eyes. It makes your ears not function, you shrivel your listening functions and they just cannot work at all, after that kind of blasting. These days when I travel by jet plane I find my ears do not function properly. Last time when I flew to Aberdeen to change planes, I had trouble with my right ear—I could not hear anything through that ear for about three days after that.

Any sounds you are fond of?

The sound which I find inspiring is usually a very small one. I think a prerequisite for enjoyment and appreciating and working with that sound is that certain other sounds be blocked out. I do not find any inspiration whatever in traffic noise. That is why I came to live here in Orkney, because at Rackwick there is no mechanical noise except for very occasional airplanes and an occasional fishing boat in the bay.

But there, when I have been home for a few days, at least you can hear the wind, you can hear the sea, you can almost call it an Aeolian harp of the sound of the waves crashing against the bottom of the cliff, being carried on the wind and setting up overtones depending on the cliff face—it is very hard rock face. One has a very interesting sound spectrum there to live with, apart from that noise, all the natural noises of birds and seals and very small mammals which you learn to listen to and to recognize their sounds, and the insects. That would not have happened if I were within reach of traffic noise, and those sounds have been a very positive influence on my work.

Of course, in a concert hall situation, where you have electricity and mains noise (in this country, it is an out-of-tune G) and you have sounds of traffic coming in which they always do and you have the sounds of the air-conditioning system which is worse, you cannot physically expect an audience to tune in to sounds as small as that. But you can, through your writing at a much more vulgar, gross kind of volume, try to convey something of what those very minute and concentrated sounds can mean.

III.

I suspect self-repetition begins when you start thinking what your personal style is. Because if you start thinking about it too much, it is probably going to become mannered because you will start wanting to preserve it, to make it evident that this is your personal style. And, if it becomes mannered, the necessity for those gestures is probably going to evaporate. You are going to repeat gestures which have lost their force.

I think there is a big difference between mannerism and style. But if you ponder style in relation to your own work too much instead of actually pondering the problem of composition and what it is all about and what you are doing, to try to relate your work to experience facing the problem for itself, not in relation to what you have done before, and if you try to do something different in every new work, I think it is probably going to be much more positive, and I think, ironically, if you ignore questions of style—if you have got any style—and you go and try to renew yourself and do something new all the time, then that style is going to be there. I suspect it is a preoccupation for musicologists and people who come after, if they are going to be interested at all, of which there is no guarantee, and it is for them to decide whether what a composer has written, has got a thread going through it which you can define as his personal style.

I think it is a very romantic tendency, in the worst possible way, to be as in-looking as that and be worried whether what you are doing is consistent with your own style, as it has hitherto been defined. Every new work modifies that and with the advent of every new work what your style is has to be redefined. At least I hope so, I hope it is a continuously developing thing. I know that I am particularly open to criticism here because I have written works in all sorts of styles and I will continue to do so. But I do begin to suspect that there is a common thread even through the most disparate things. I cannot define it. If I could, I might stop writing.

1980, approved 1997

Fifteen

EDISON DENISOV (1929–96)

When Tikhon Khrennikov, general secretary of the Union of Soviet Composers, visited Budapest, it fell to me to interview him for Hungarian Radio. I was perfectly aware that I was talking to a figure of unparalleled power in Soviet cultural life, a hard-liner, one who was sly enough to keep his position regardless of who happened to be boss in the Kremlin, from Stalin through Khrushchev to Brezhnev. Born in 1913 (a contemporary of Witold Lutosławski), he was appointed to head the Union of Soviet Composers in 1948 and only relinquished the post in 1991 when the Soviet Union collapsed. He died at the age of ninety-four, in 2007.

I was bold enough to provoke him by citing the names of Soviet composers I knew were refusing to toe the party line. Alfred Schnittke and Edison Denisov were among them. I shall never forget Khrennikov's reply, nor the tone of his voice: "These composers are not typical examples of true Soviet artists. They do not represent what we regard as genuinely Soviet music. You should rather hear Tishchenko . . ." and he listed a few more names I can no longer remember.

In other words, Denisov was under a cloud. The conditions under which he was forced to work can be guessed, thanks to reminiscences published by Mstislav Rostropovich and countless others who either managed to defect or had no other choice but to stay in the Soviet Union.

When I met Denisov in Moscow in the late 1970s, life for the cultural opposition had grown somewhat easier. He was allowed, for instance, to publish his compositions in Hungary and even in Austria. I remember seeing him in the company of a director of Universal Edition who wanted to talk to him about the opera L'Ecume des jours, *based on the eponymous novel by Boris Vian (1920–59). I think he was pleased to meet us, coming as we did from a part of Europe he may have admired for its freedom. He was quiet and soft-spoken but there was no mistaking his self-confidence.*

Despite the thaw in his country, he engaged the services of an acquaintance to deliver the script of his replies by hand.

I.

If in art one comes upon a phenomenon for the first time, one which may not be of any importance in itself but which does represent something new, it is bound to leave a trace, just as anything else that crops up in the course of one's life. Artists respond to such a phenomenon in accordance with their personality—how exactly, is impossible to foretell.

I prefer ideas that emerge imperceptibly, often as a result of long internal processes, to those borrowed from others. Borrowing is of course the easier way. Nowadays when composers are inundated with commissions with pressing deadlines, many of them resort to that method. With regard to the public, it is not difficult to pass off on them the spurious as genuine. Today, those artists have success who absorb alien ideas into their own means of expression and present them in an easily comprehensible form. Compositions are wanted that meet with momentary interest, only to vanish once and for all.

In all the fields of art, the fake ousts genuine works of value—something that has been happening for years. Their creators bluff without compunction. They conceal bluff quite consciously behind literary declarations to make sure no one notices that the emperor has no clothes on.

In the history of art, there has never been such a quick succession of "trends" and "currents" as in the past decades. This tempo outdoes even that of the 1920s.

Today, it is easier for anyone to become an "artist" because any sense of responsibility is gone. There is a growing demand for painting devoid of painting, for literature lacking any of the traditional values and in music, too, they seek the kind with a total lack of spiritual content, the basis of musical material.

There are, of course, some talented artists who bandy about brilliant or surprising ideas—often they succeed in making a transitory impression. Coming across such works can even be of use, for they jostle one out of one's idleness and give one's fantasy a prod. An influence like that is mostly good for a single use only, but it may unexpectedly give a genuine artist new compositional ideas.

In my case, the gestation of a work takes longer than committing it to paper. Sometimes, the original idea undergoes far-reaching transformations during the course of work—often as a result of some outside influence (also of a musical nature). A chance encounter can modify our train of thought. Contemporary music has not had such an influence on me, but painting—and more rarely, literature—all the more. Still, I want ideas to come from myself rather than from any outside source.

As far as possible, I endeavor to keep track of what composers I think highly of are up to: Boulez, Xenakis, Ligeti, Nono, Lutosławski, Crumb, and others. I never take over anything from them, but I analyze some of their compositions (for instance, Boulez's *Mallarmé Improvisations,* Ligeti's *Lontano,* or Nono's *Ha venido*) in order to understand the organizing principle of the musical material.

II.

We are moving further and further away from nature. Our sounding environment offers no help for composers to create works of genuine value.

Of course, film music or incidental music for plays does not exclude the use of so-called nonmusical sounds. "Props-music" often demands the application of such means, for it must become an integral part of the production, it cannot be a self-standing constituent. In my incidental music for Lyubimov's productions at the Taganka Theatre, I have often had recourse to musical noise, especially in *The Master and Margarita* and *Crime and Punishment.* I have also written distorted *Gebrauchsmusik,* for Yuri Trifonov's *House on the Embankment* as well as a program dedicated to poems by Mayakovsky. In absolute music, however, such means must not gain the upper hand—it would necessarily lead to a lowering of standards so that the composition would become decoration for a nonexistent spectacle. Decoration does not carry any real information. Such is the case with diverse nonmusical sonorities, ranging from clusters to concrete sounds. The primary carrier of information is intonation, that is, not the artificially created intonation of neo-Romanticism (more precisely: pseudo-Romanticism), but one that is born naturally—living intonation.

I employ mobile clusters in several compositions. The first such work was *Peinture* (1970) for orchestra. Those are, however, no blocks of sound put together on the basis of some logical consideration. Rather, they are concatenations of melodies with related intonation, melodies that unfold on the basis of autonomous logic, which form rather complex sound mixtures. Timbre acquires an important role, filled out by the hidden lives of melodic voices.

I have only written one piece which is based exclusively on the sounds of living nature: *The Song of Birds* (1969) for prepared piano and tape. Apart from the material played by the soloist and some electronic passages, the music is made up solely of a montage of birdsong. I like this piece to this day, perhaps because its basic material—birdsong—is no dead, mechanical or electronic montage of sounds, but is sensitive, deeply musical material.

For some time now, I have been unable to work in a city environment: noises disturb concentration and destroy the fragile, living organism that is being born in me. Over the past ten–fifteen years I could only compose in the brief periods when I had left the city and was all by myself. The best ideas came to me during long walks in the forest (or skiing in winter), or in the summer, rowing to the middle of a lake. While at work on a composition, it is more important for me to make direct contact with living nature than to exclude sounds around me. In works written under such circumstances, I have never made an attempt to imitate the sounds of nature—it was important for me to feel the surrounding world. I wrote my long, soft piano piece *Signes en blanc* in the middle of Lake Ladoga, in the summer of 1974. I rowed to the middle every evening, admired the breathtaking beauty of nature, the ever-changing colors of sunsets in the North. I think that is what I needed at that time. I agree with Debussy: in his view, the sight of sunsets is more useful for a composer than listening to Beethoven's *Pastoral Symphony*.

During work I never listen to any music (with the exception of Mozart) and do not open any contemporary score (especially those of a related genre).

I believe that music ought to be born just as naturally as any living being, independently from fashion. It is best when it is born at a time when we feel as though we were but tools in the hands of another, higher will.

III.

In our age when one new "school" and "trend" crops up after another, it is particularly important for us to guard our personality and ignore changes of value in the music market. A genuine artist possesses a scale of values of his own, one which is in perfect harmony with his personality. Stravinsky and Picasso had exceptional careers; most artists, once they have found their own personal style, do not change radically their means of expression. At the same time, a composer who has mastered the technique of composition and has found a style which matches his personality, will also sense that he possesses the freedom of expression. Anything else depends on his spiritual charge and the traits of his personality.

Life can create situations where the artist has no time to prepare innerly for a new work and to elaborate it thoroughly. Then he has no other choice but to draw on technical solutions which have proved themselves in the past: to repeat himself. In the long run, a genuine artist cannot find satisfaction in such a way of life. The time will come when he turns down prestigious commissions and only listens to his inner voice. It will guide him to the sole possible path leading to solitude, an unknown world full of closed doors. Behind the doors, there lie unsuspected treasures which only become visible for the true Master. Such are the most important moments in life.

1984

Sixteen

HENRI DUTILLEUX (1916–2013)

In 1983, I spent a few weeks in Paris on a French government scholarship to meet some of the major composers living in the city and record interviews with them for the three-questions project. My mastery of the language was shaky to say the least but I was helped by an interpreter. Her presence gave me confidence but I only asked her to translate when I did not understand a particular word or sentence. I was anxious not to interrupt the interview if I could help it. This explains why the conversations with French composers are mostly monologues; I only asked questions when absolutely necessary, since the three basic ones were known anyway.

A contemporary of Milton Babbitt, Henri Dutilleux has chosen a different path in that his music is rooted in the tradition of twentieth-century French music, mainly Debussy, Ravel, and Roussel. His output is not large but what he has produced in the way of orchestral music is played with some regularity, especially Timbres, espace, mouvement ou "La nuit etoilée" *(1977/78) and the cello concerto* Tout un monde lointain *(1967/70).*

I.

No, frankly, I do not think that my evolution would have ever been determined by the shock caused by listening to any particular composition. Of course, since reaching the age when I was able to write music, that is, since I was fifteen, there have been some works which have impressed me a great deal, but my style has developed gradually, without any reverses, I should think.

I must say: on hearing *Pierrot lunaire*, I met with a world which struck me as wholly alien and new, unrelated to anything else. All in all, I think I must have felt very much like musicians well before my time (like Stravinsky or Ravel) when they encountered *Pierrot lunaire* for the first time: it was for me, just as it must have been for them, a veritable mirage.

As it was indeed also for Dallapiccola and Puccini.

Indeed. If we think of the musicians of the Second Viennese School, the pupils of Schoenberg, like Berg (especially *Wozzeck* which impressed me no end), possessed an idiom that influenced me through its novelty. Webern also, but in a different fashion: it was, I think, his rarefied sound world and the rarefied form of his music that left a trace on my thinking.

For me, the rupture that World War II brought with it was obviously of decisive significance. Before the war, I had written a few pieces which I have since suppressed. World events induced me to think. For quite a long time I actually stopped writing music. I tried to find myself, to find my style. And a great deal of music that I had not heard because I was too young—such as works by Schoenberg, Bartók, Stravinsky, and quite a few more—appeared on my horizon, all at the same time. Of course, I had heard *Le Sacre du printemps* and *Les Noces* between the two world wars. But after the liberation, we were flooded by music we had not known before. All of it appeared simultaneously, thanks especially to radio broadcasts. Composers were programmed who had been prohibited, like Schoenberg, or French musicians like Darius Milhaud and many more who had been blacklisted during the Occupation.

This abundance of new music proved almost too much, coming as it did all at the same time. Young musicians who were still far too impressionable to diverse influences, ran the risk of becoming eclectic. That is why I decided not to compose at all. I did not produce anything but it does not mean that I did not continue to work.

Musicians who were even younger, those born around 1925, found themselves in a slightly different situation. I mean composers like Boulez, Luciano Berio, Stockhausen, Luigi Nono, and other French musicians like Serge Nigg. They were still studying after the war. That explains why they showed such an immediate interest in the Second Viennese School and serial techniques—to a certain extent in order to escape Messiaen's influence. Some of them were obsessed by Messiaen's musical language, something which he himself saw the dangers of.

Which of your compositions would you describe as the first "Dutilleux?"

The first one was no doubt my Symphony No. 1 (1951)—it came rather late. A few years before, I had composed a *Sonate pour piano* (1946/48) which was a work of transition. Those two compositions satisfied me as having an orientation rather different from the spirit of "French fashion." (*Dutilleux said the last two words in English.*) Incidentally, my very first pieces were quite short and were written under the influence of French musicians of the generation of Florent Schmitt, Maurice Ravel, and Paul Dukas.

I can say that it was really my *Sonate pour piano* where I realized what I sought to do at that moment. It is quite a sizable piece and has pages which I like to this day for their density. There are others which I like less, also in my First Symphony, for they still bear signs of immaturity. Completed three years after the *Sonate,* I have tender feelings toward it as for a child one does not wish to disown. However, it was *Métaboles* (1962/64), a work written much later, where I succeeded in fully realizing myself in music. That is also what many other musicians think of the piece, those who belong to a different school, no doubt because some of the elements used are often applied by serialists as well, a particular organization of the sound material and even of "musical time."

At a certain period, the one we talked about just now, between 1945 and 1960, dodecaphonic music was all the rage. I was several times on the jury of the International Society for Contemporary Music. Most of my fellow jury members were interested exclusively in works composed according to the doctrines of serialism. A new sort of tyranny, really, and a new academicism.

Of the 100 or so scores that we examined, I can say that perhaps two-thirds would have sounded exactly the same. I was at the time rather ostracized by the serialist clan but at the same time I was intrigued by their attitude, especially by their music, and I felt obliged to take a critical look at what I was doing.

As you see, it is very difficult for me to define in a spontaneous and concise fashion just what my aesthetic orientation was at any given time. Looking back, I can determine where I am much better—that is the privilege of old age.

Personally, I have always been anxious to keep in touch with musicians whose idiom was wholly different from mine, also those who had nothing to do with the institutions of official music education. I have gone out of my way to meet musicians from Central Europe who had settled in France and who were older than me, like Marcel Mihalovici. I had occasion to listen to some of his works which I would never have known had it not been for our personal contact.

Also, I heard many concerts of the Domaine Musicale. I never rejected the compositions they played, I was always curious to see what novelties there were to discover.

However, there is never enough time. That is what one is the shortest of—a difficulty touching on the question of the musicians' social status: how can they succeed in expressing their ideas in an epoch like ours? How can they make a living? Right now, I can live on my music, on my income as a composer, but until I was fifty-five or sixty years old I could not afford it, I had no other choice but to try and make ends meet by having a job on the side. But that is another question—one that has never been solved in any country and at any time.

II.

The sounds of Nature are of great significance for me. I am strongly attracted by its various manifestations—sounds and colors.

On the other hand, I hail from a region where the carillon is very popular. There are many of them in the belfries of Flanders, something that left its mark on my youth. As a child, I was fascinated by their sound. Those played in Belgium and Holland have a particularly beautiful sonority, typical of the region.

However, all that has been transformed in my music. It has helped to stimulate my composition, but differently from Messiaen for whom the song of birds had such a basic importance. Birds are important for me as well, but unlike Messiaen I am no ornithologist. In my music, it is often as if a lark were gliding in the distance with its song transformed.

Of course, it is very well possible that a new work can be born out of an impression like that, yes, certainly. But emotional shocks can also originate elsewhere, such as in literature or sculpture. For instance, when Rostropovich commissioned my cello concerto *Tout un monde lointain,* I was inspired by reading some poems by Baudelaire, such as *La chevelure* in the volume *Les fleurs du mal.* Not only do his poems serve as inspiration but so do his prose poems as well and indeed everything he wrote on art in general. It is Baudelaire's universe that has impressed me, in its totality.

An even more recent composition was inspired by a painting by Van Gogh in the Museum of Modern Art in New York: the *Starry Night.* This picture gives the impression of mobility and at the same time of stellar space. It is absolutely extraordinary. There again, it evoked an emotional shock. Those are very strong impulses indeed. As you can see, poetry has played a role on the one hand, and painting on the other.

What is the title of this composition?

It is called *Timbres, espace, mouvement ou "La nuit étoilée."*

But sometimes the ideas are strictly abstract without having anything to do with literature or sculpture. That is often the case with music. You do not necessarily need support, what is important is emotion. This impulse can come from something one has read or a film one has seen—great films directed by great artists. I must say I love the theater and the cinema.

Some significant film directors have nourished my thinking: Bergman, Fellini, and some others, like Jean Renoir in France. I take pleasure in observing the mechanism of construction, the structure (for instance, flashbacks).

Have you written any film music?

Yes, but that is an altogether different question. When I was young, I wrote music for films to make some money, also as a kind of drill for me to learn to work fast. I would not wish to compose music like that today.

I would love to have established contact with some really good directors who would have enriched my spirit. Sadly, I never had occasion to do so, except once, with Jean Grémillion, an important artist. He enjoys a high reputation in the French film world but he never had the success he would have deserved, nor the financial assistance he would have needed.

No, my interests lie elsewhere. What interests me in a film is the work of art in time and the work of art structured like a musical composition. Bergman, for instance, has such films, such as *Wild Strawberries,* so do Wajda or Losey—all their films are composed with a great deal of rigor, also of course with imagination, and you can profit from that. Their films were organized according to principles which are related to musical composition. The same is true, to a certain extent, of architecture.

III.

In my view, an artist expresses a certain number of strong ideas which are exclusively his and which he repeats tirelessly but in different ways. It is also important, however, to strive for renewal.

Has the question of self-repetition ever exercised your mind?

No, I shouldn't say so.

But you do have an individual style, so that one can identify any piece of yours.

That is not for me to say. . . . Some people, some friends do tell me that they can recognize my music. So much the better, but you would embarrass me no end if you were to ask me now to improvise something on the piano in my style. I could not produce a caricature of myself. I could imitate certain other composers, perhaps. Recently, one said to me: I have heard a piece on the radio and did not know who it was by. I listened on and eventually thought: "That must be Dutilleux." I hear comments like that quite frequently.

I believe there are certain traits which remain constant. With the passage of time, I recognize them quite clearly. I can identify them, I can name those constant features and also say in which aspect of my work they can be found.

That is interesting, by the way, because for the author they are mostly unconscious. Looking back, one realizes which particular characteristics become prominent and constitute a style.

On the other hand, if one fails to look for the new, something that has never been heard before, if one makes do with the idea that occurs to one without working on it, one runs the risk of loquacity. That is actually the difference between composition and improvisation. We know that Chopin improvised at the piano for a very long time and the composition assumed its final shape after a great deal of effort.

The same is true of composers who only worked at the piano, such as Stravinsky or Ravel. Apparently, however, it did not suffice for them as a tool. As far as I am concerned, I use the instrument less nowadays—perhaps less and less as the years go by.

But actually, I have the temperament of a harmonist and for me, harmonic language always has a reason. I believe you cannot simply eliminate this notion and pretend that this element has lost its raison d'être. Indeed, I am convinced that it is of great significance. I often say that you must have a harmonic conscience as you have a rhythmic or a contrapuntal conscience. Nowadays, musicians with a certain creative talent completely ignore the harmonic aspect. That is why they end up writing banal music, commonplace.

Such negligence leads to a lack of balance which always astounds me. Just imagine a Picasso who could not draw!

I do understand what Stravinsky meant when he declared that harmony, considered from a traditional point of view, had a brilliant but brief history and that its domain could no longer be explored or exploited. But Stravinsky himself never lost, rather on the contrary, what I call a "harmonic conscience."

1983/96

Seventeen

PÉTER EÖTVÖS (1944)

In 1964 or so, my father, who was financial director of a Budapest theater, told me about a young man of twenty who could be relied upon to compose music at a moment's notice for any play with the greatest ease. My father was terribly impressed by Péter Eötvös and arranged for us to meet. Péter visited me at home and I was in turn impressed by his calm, his self-assurance, his maturity: although three years his senior, I felt much younger and certainly far less sure of myself.

We have been in touch ever since, although I cannot claim to be a close friend. I have kept memories of certain episodes most of which are so distant as to appear dreamlike.

For instance, standing near the headquarters of WDR, the West German Radio, in Cologne, and Péter complaining that his association with Stockhausen was so time-consuming that he hardly ever came to composing even though that was his actual goal in life. He felt he was unable to organize his schedule so as to set aside periods for his creative work. That must have been in the early 1970s; ten years later when we conducted the conversation below, he was still in the throes of a frustrating struggle for time to compose. It was not until he married his present wife, Mari Mezei, that his life became organized with iron discipline. The result is there for all to see: one opera after another emerges from his studio (including the phenomenally successful Three Sisters *of 1998) apart from works for orchestra and chamber music.*

Another scrap of memory is linked to rehearsals for the world premiere of György Kurtág's . . . quasi una fantasia . . . *Op. 27, no. 1*[13] *for piano and instruments arranged in space. The time was October 1988 and the venue the Berlin Philharmonie's wonderful chamber hall, which had actually inspired Kurtág to write the piece. The soloist was Zoltán Kocsis, the Ensemble Modern was playing. After an ethereal first movement, which consists of slowly descending scales on the piano with ever so soft, hallucinatory tones coming from suspended cymbals, gongs, tam-tams, mouth organs, and other instruments from all over the hall, the music abruptly changes tempo and turns into a headlong flight as if the orchestra were persecuting the pianist. A fiendishly difficult score, which Péter Eötvös went on rehearsing with his usual calm and authority, until at one point he asked the musicians to join him on stage. And there he said something I had not heard from a conductor before: he admitted he had reached a dead point, he did not know what else to rehearse, he gave up. The problem was, of course, coordination between the solo instrument and the musicians dispersed in space at different levels, given the crazy speed of the music and the changing role of the piano, now submerged in the ensemble, now taking over*

13. The work is dedicated to Zoltán Kocsis and Péter Eötvös.

the lead. Péter's face was worn. As I learned later, he had received disturbing news from his family, but with tremendous self-discipline he carried on and brought the composition to resounding success.

More than twenty years later, even student ensembles take the second movement in their stride. This is a recurring phenomenon: a difficult score seems to shed its pitfalls with the passage of time.

Back in the 1970s, I visited Péter in his then home, a former farm among the bucolic hills near Cologne. There I met his Chinese wife, the pianist Pi Hsien-chen and his baby daughter (in the meantime herself mother of a child with her Kurdish husband), and heard him play the piano. Well over thirty years later, I have not forgotten his amazing mastery of the instrument, his poetic touch. Vaguely, I also remember a visit to nearby Kürten, Stockhausen's house—a building of pioneering architecture with an atmosphere where I felt wholly out of my depth. I do not think I said a word beyond greeting the composer, I just listened to the two of them talk, not as master and pupil but as equals.

In the past, I detected a certain tension beneath Péter's apparent calm. Nowadays, it seems to have evaporated and has been replaced by the serenity and infectious sense of humor of one who is securely en route to achieve what he set out to do in life.

I.

The first major experiences that leave a lasting impression on one's mind occur in childhood. I decided at the age of four to become a composer. Between the ages of six and fourteen, I came under the influence of Bartók more than anybody else; he served as the foundation, the point of reference for my thinking. The basic works included *Mandarin, Bluebeard, Music for Strings, Percussion and Celesta, Night Music,* and the *Sonata for two pianos and percussion.*

From 1958, that is, when I was fourteen, I took a keen interest in electronic music: that is where I best found my bearings.

How did you have access to electronic music in Budapest in 1958?

Rudolf Maros would bring recordings from Darmstadt; János Viski, too, had some interesting tapes at home.[14] In Budapest there was always a way to find the things you wanted. In the early 1960s, then, the situation took a turn for the better. I remember, for example, Dr. László Végh, a physician, composer, translator, and writer who regularly organized semilegal listening sessions in his house. There was an avant-garde group interested in contemporary music and its members found the means to keep abreast of the latest developments.

---

14. Rudolf Maros (1917–82), Hungarian composer. János Viski (1906–61), Hungarian composer, professor of composition at the Budapest Academy of Music.

After 1962, I composed quite a few electronic pieces for short films, drawing on the rudimentary equipment I had at my disposal.

When in 1966 I moved to Cologne—home of one of the best electronic music studios—I was fully up to date, there was nothing to catch up with.

Still, could you name a few works?

Compositions by Stockhausen: *Studie* I and II, *Gesang der Jünglinge*, *Gruppen* (at the Budapest Academy of Music, I had prepared a piano reduction for three pianos, twelve hands). I was not yet familiar with *Kontakte* even though that was the most important electronic work of those years. I copied Boulez's two *Improvisation sur Mallarmé* by hand because the scores were not yet available. Actually, it is not so much the individual pieces that count—much rather, their combined bulk.

I played the piano part of the instrumental version of *Kontakte* in concert some twenty-five times; right now I am preparing the orchestration of *Studie II* for the BBC Symphony Orchestra.[15] This occupation has brought back childhood memories, it has conjured up an incredibly colorful world with its memories of color, light, sound, and smell.

In this case, then, it is not my music that has been influenced by another composer but my whole being.

Incidentally, while we are talking of influences, that of jazz has been of considerable significance: it is the only kind of music that relaxes me. It eases any physical and psychological stress; I could listen to it anytime.

What I want more than anything: to be able to address myself to my own music. Sadly, I do not have sufficient time for that. I would need longer periods at a stretch: if I only have two days, I cannot even begin to think. Each interruption has such a drastic effect that whatever may have been born in two days, would fade away by next time. I would need to start from scratch.

You have nevertheless composed quite a few pieces. What major influences would you single out?

It would be difficult to give you any concrete examples. I wrote a piano piece in 1961: I called it *Kozmosz*. It has traces of the influence of Webern, Bartók (*Night Music*), but even more importantly, Gagarin's space flight; in fact, that was what triggered off the compositional process. It included a great many elements of electronic music, transposed onto the piano.

My madrigals were influenced by Gesualdo. As far as my chamber music is concerned, I cannot discern any influence there.

Not even Stockhausen's?

No. I wrote what came from within, something which is obviously an amalgam of many different influences. Music has been of less importance than painting, sculpture, architecture, or walks in the forest. It is the

15. Comment by Péter Eötvös in 2009: "This plan never materialized."

technical aspect of composition that has had relevance: if others have found a solution to a particular problem, I did not have to invest time in experimenting with it. Even so, there are so many questions left one has to find the answer to.

Still on fine arts: when I was fourteen or so, Klee and Henry Moore held more interest for me than any sort of music.

I take it that these influences have a bearing on your music in an indirect manner—on form or part-writing.

Indeed, on both. As far as form is concerned, Ligeti and I talked about it recently. I told him that for me, musical form was like an object. Musical works appear to me like objects in their spatial dimensions. I sense them as blocks, a boulder or, say, a feather. In reading a score, I do not necessarily start at the beginning. I might first look at the ending and slowly turn the pages backward. I can experience it the same way as if I had started on page one. There is an image in my mind of this block in front of me and I can chart it in any direction at all. It suffices for me to address myself to a single detail and through it develop an idea of the rest. Given a certain amount of experience, you can grasp a fifty-page score at a single glance.

In composing, I first have a sense of the density, the mass of the piece. Similarly to a sculptor, I first have to decide whether to use wood, tissue, or stone.

Conducting is similar. I do not think in processes; rather, I am out to establish my bearings in the block. The sounding material is a kind of mass for me, with a velocity, streaming, tension of its own. For me, there are no "melodies" or "harmonies"; I do not respond to them. Harmonies present themselves as densities. That is also how my memory works. I find it difficult to learn a score by heart; I ceaselessly reread all scores.

You mentioned having drawn on technical solutions found by others. Can you name a few examples?

I cannot remember having consciously borrowed anything from other composers.

You singled out Webern and Bartók as having influenced your Kozmosz.

Certain elements do occur. My *Sequences of the Wind* has no precedent in music history but if it does remind one of anything, then it would be Japanese ceremonial music. My choral piece *Endless Eight* is also devoid of any influences, except perhaps for a scrap of Steve Reich-memory who appealed to me at the time. However, while I accept his way of composing, I could certainly not accept the same from myself—with me, it turns into its opposite. In other words, influences can undergo a transformation. But it is best if one influences oneself.

For me, composing does not mean inventing something. The pieces that I write *exist* already, I only have to notate them. I then spend several years cleaning them, "nurturing" the written material with a view to making the score as simple and clear as possible. In other words, to ensure the score is unequivocal. Now that I have been conducting a great deal, I have learned many practical things. The compositions stay the same but I have realized that there are many ways of communicating them to the performers.

II.

Music is sonority. Its basic ingredient can be anything that sounds, between noise and silence. However, sound by itself is not yet music. Sounds become music if they are bound by "musical" interrelationships. Basically, composition is the creation and discovery of these connections. Since music-making is a fundamentally human activity, the sounding world only becomes music if our mind has discerned an underlying structure to it.

For example, street noise is not music but if I were to cut out a section from it which lasts, let us say, seven seconds beginning with the honking of a car, continuing with street noise, and ending with the bell of a tram, that is a three-part musical unit.

Cage's piano piece *4'33"* is an example of the opposite. It is silence in three movements, lasting four minutes and thirty-three seconds. That is music, too. In my own *Mese* (Fairy Tale) the reciting of Hungarian folk tales becomes music, whereas in my *Tücsökzene* (Cricket Music) the singing of crickets is transformed into a composition.

I am citing those extreme examples to make it clear: whatever one commonly calls "musical sound" (usually that of instruments and of the singing voice), is only a narrow segment of music's basic material.

For me, the notion of sound exists in two kinds of process. One is the process of *contraction and expansion* with regard to the frequency range audible for our ears, from the broadband noise (that of jets or the sound of cymbals) via sounds of a narrower range, the frequency of which is easier to define (the ringing of an anvil, the sound of a vibraphone) back to the broad frequency of silence (of the forest, the silence or noise of our inner hearing).

The other process is more of a speculative nature but it is, to my mind, the basis of musical thinking. You could call it *the condensing of time*. Since sounds are oscillations, each oscillation, each repetition in time can become "sound." Let us start with an extremely slow repetition, such as the New Year. If I were to speed it up twelvefold, I get an oscillation lasting a month. If I speed that up thirtyfold, it becomes a day. That, speeded up twenty-fourfold, results in an oscillation lasting an hour. I speed that up again by sixty and the oscillation lasts one minute which still cannot be perceived by our ear but it can be grasped as a form, such as a musical form. Speeded up yet again by sixty, I get an oscillation of one second which is perceptible as meter. If that is speeded up sixteenfold, we hear it as the lowest audible sound, sixteen oscillations by the second, *16 Hertz.* From then onward until about sixteen thousand Hertz we perceive the oscillations, the repetition of time, as audible sounds. This game with time can be continued ad infinitum, in the direction of slowing down or speeding up.

From a compositional point of view, this thought process boils down to a *unit* derived from *time* as an abstract notion which creates a connection between form, rhythm, sounds, and timbre. Stockhausen's *Kontakte* I mentioned earlier, is a fundamental example of this way of thinking and my own *Elektrokrónika* of 1972 is another example, developed a stage further.

Lately, I have been preoccupied with spatial acoustics; I have found several sounds which are neither noise nor silence, they have no definable pitch but only create a sensation of space.

May I now remind you of the actual question: do the sounds of the outside world affect you in any way?

This is something two-directional. The outside world does appear in my music but I, too, create the outside world. I can only conceive of this as a concatenation. Whatever we put down in writing is the manifestation of the outside world. I am but a transformer in this process. Whatever I produce affects another composer and so forth. Beethoven was influenced by whatever outside influence it may have been; he composed his string quartets; they influence me and become something different which in its turn will also exert an influence. This is a concatenation, nothing else.

Why do you fall back on the sound of the wind in its concrete reality in your Sequences of the Wind*?*

I do not think of it as concrete at all. It is precisely the neutrality of the sound that is important for me: it has no definable pitch. I could just as well have opted for something else but that is all I could think of when I needed a sound which served my purpose. It could be transposed to anything else, its function would remain the same. Recently, it occurred to me to compose it for chamber ensemble. I would dispense with the wind, its role would be taken over by instruments—it is just that I would need many instruments to reach that broader frequency band. In the original version it was the simplest thing to do to get someone to produce a SSSSSHHHHH-sound with his mouth. It could also have been created with filters and noise generator but that would have been lifeless and would have required too much effort. Nothing is easier [than] to get someone to stand there and do SSSSSSHHHHHH . . .

III.

I have been reading a volume of essays by Busoni published in 1906. He writes he was always being reproached for his habit of arranging works by other composers. Bach, he argues, was an "arranger" of his own music: he was composing the same thing day by day, for decades, with no essential changes whatsoever.

I might add to that: every composer writes the same thing all his life and within the same historical period they all write the same music also.

Basically, everything is self-repetition. That is the basis of our lives, everyone does and says the same thing, looks or smells or hears the same way—and yet always differently.

I do not find anything wrong with self-repetition. For some, it is of vital importance to repeat themselves. Some creative people change direction with no difficulty at all—such as Picasso. This is a question of vitality: he moves faster, his life has a faster pulsation, in other words, he covers certain phases within a shorter period of time than others. Some people would need five hundred years to go along a particular path and there are Petőfis,[16] Mozarts, and Schuberts who arrive at the end of their road at thirty, having covered a distance that would take others three times as many years.

As far as I am concerned: sadly, I do not compose every day, I do not write series of pieces. As a result, I have the impression that my works differ from one another rather considerably. If I could compose with any regularity, my method would probably have evolved differently.

1983/2009

16. Sándor Petőfi (1823–49), great Hungarian lyrical poet.

Eighteen

MORTON FELDMAN (1926–87)

During the eight years of collecting material for this book (1978–85), it became something of an obsession for me to seize whatever opportunity presented itself to interview composers of international standing. I forget how I learned of Morton Feldman's impending visit to Vienna. In any case, it proved quite easy to organize an appointment and I duly turned up in the Austrian cellist's house where the composer was staying. I drove there from Budapest with the three questions and not much else on my mind.

For I must plead guilty to having known precious little at the time about Feldman and his music. All I knew was that he was considered an important composer and that was enough for me to reach for my microphone. It will not be difficult to imagine my acute embarrassment in meeting this unique man face to face. I felt hopelessly European, hopelessly bourgeois, hopelessly underinformed. However, I made a brave effort to conceal my uneasiness and to conduct a conversation with Feldman as if it were the most natural thing in the world.

By 1983 when Feldman and I met in a leafy suburb of Vienna, I had had some experience with interviewing composers; my conversations with Lutosławski, Xenakis, and Berio had already been published. But in their case, I had had no difficulty following their train of thought; I was at home with the way they reacted to my questions. Feldman, on the other hand, seemed to have come from another planet (as indeed Cage had done when I first met him in Warsaw in 1972). In replying, he would let his thoughts and associations roam freely—with me always behind, doing my best to keep pace. As you will see, at one point I gave up: for try as I might, I could detect no connection at all between what he was saying and my question that he was supposed to be answering. It turned out that he had forgotten all about it. (As I was to learn later, it was not unusual for him to let the thread drop.)

For all his self-assurance, I had the impression that he was fighting a duel with invisible adversaries, that he was out to defend his music and his philosophy, that he had something of an inferiority complex with regard to European music and European culture, that he was calling everybody's bluff who was not an ardent admirer. He challenged me, too, by telling me, almost with childish pride, of his recent compositions, which were extraordinarily long; I had the impression he was testing my reaction. I cannot recall how I responded but I am sure I felt I would be unable to concentrate on a string quartet for six hours.

Subjectively, I feel that his pleasurable surprise on learning that his music had had some influence on Pierre Boulez was a sign of what I took to be his insecurity—that he set great store by recognition coming from the French composer. Perhaps he shared this with Earle Brown: in October 1999, Brown sent me a set of interviews he had given to Olivier Delaigue ("Earle Brown and France") and jotted on a yellow

Post-it note: "Dear Bálint, I thought that this would interest you—don't show it to Pierre! (just kidding). Warm regards, Earle."

With regard to Feldman's comment on Boulez ("we do not really like each other"—see below), I remember sitting next to Boulez in Paris at a concert conducted by Michael Gielen. Feldman's For Chorus and Orchestra I and II *were featured on the program. While I was listening, fascinated by this highly original music, Boulez was fidgeting in his seat, protesting against passages which in his view did not make any sense. I realized I was witnessing a conflict of two original musical minds but could not help enjoying what I was hearing.*

In any case, I do feel that this conversation with Morton Feldman gives you an idea of what he was like as a person and what motivated him in writing his unique music.

Boulez says he was inspired by one of your pieces to compose Éclat*—I said before switching on the tape recorder. Feldman was visibly intrigued.*

"Did he really say that? Interesting, for we do not really like each other." Then he smiled and added:

"So Earle Brown was right after all. He had spent some time in Paris and when he came home, he said to me: 'Boulez has been listening to your music!' And I laughed. I didn't take it seriously, so it's interesting that Boulez should have mentioned it."

I.

When I first met John Cage and I came to his apartment to visit, he was analyzing Webern's Opus 21.

When was that?

In late 1950. And I said: "What're you doing?" And he said: "I'm analyzing, come, let's do it together!" So we sat down and did it together. And one of the things that disturbed me about European or American mainstream music was the antecedent and consequent building blocks for the continuity of the music—you know, even in Webern, tra-**ra**, tra-**ra**—the symmetry. That's what disturbs me in Boulez.

I never knew Satie. John Cage and I went over his music (*Socrate*)—in terms of the asymmetric rhythmic structure. I never knew it existed. It was a tremendous influence in the sense of how beautiful music sounded no longer involved with that particular type of . . . that you don't need that kind of relationship in constructing music.

So I'd say that my musical insights came from music—not from hearing any piece, but from studying. I was a very good student, like Boulez was a good student. The only thing is, being American, I was more open.

When you analyzed Webern's Opus 21 with Cage, was it the first time you had encountered that piece?

Yes. There were no scores in America.

How come?

When I was growing up during the war and I might say even a year after the war . . . naturally there were scores for those that were involved in that world with scores, but for just a young student, you could not buy them in the music stores, there were no recordings of Webern. In fact, someone at high school with me went to the library and copied out his Five Pieces for String Quartet. I still have it. He photostated it and we all took a copy. So that was my first introduction to Webern, with my fellow-student's handwriting. It was a real discovery.

It is very interesting: the relationship of Webern to both Europe and America. I think that young people like myself in America and young people in Europe discovered Webern to some degree at the same time. It had a tremendous impact on Cage and me. Tremendous!

The only difference is: we had a different kind of balance. We had Varèse in New York rather than Messiaen in Paris. We had a better composer than Leibowitz: Stefan Wolpe. He was my teacher. I don't think Messiaen is a strong composer. Varèse is, I feel, a little stronger. We also had Milton Babbitt, very important, who actually serialized all the elements, before Messiaen. An elegant composer, a brilliant, funny, witty, erudite man.

So the artistic atmosphere in New York was, I think, a little more open and a little more inventive and a little more pragmatic than in Paris. It allowed for a different kind of exploration, it allowed for a synthesis of Webern and Satie, which would be unthinkable in Europe. It would be like synthesizing Hauer and Webern. Unthinkable! It's still unthinkable (*laughs*).

Let us get back to that visit with Cage when you joined him in analyzing Webern. You said you had not been struck by its symmetry. Was that the only feature of the music that evoked any reaction from you?

I was not impressed by the construction. I played Bach, I could not get excited (*laughs*).

So there was nothing that impressed you.

I didn't like the fact that the instruments were picked out to demonstrate the law. And its simultaneity. I didn't like instruments used for that reason. I didn't like instruments used subordinate to a hierarchical situation. That was the thing that struck me.

To return to the original question: would you say that Webern's negative influence or Varèse's positive influence induced in you a new way of thinking about music?

It's not a new way of thinking—it's a new country. And the new country might be the desert, it might be the North Pole. You see, what bothered me also in Webern, was the metamorphosis of pitch into interval. Like a sex change. You go to Copenhagen with a pitch and come back with an interval (*laughs*). In fact, in a recent piece that is going to be done with

Frankfurt Radio, a violin concerto, I have three cadenzas. And the cadenzas are all just the intervals, three rows from Webern's certain late pieces are quoted in my rhythm. Nobody knows this but I used it because the piece was too pitchy, and I wanted to get into intervals. And I decided, why write intervals, they exist like found objects. So I used the Webern rows as found objects, very good intervallic rows.

Which Webern works?

The first Cantata, the Concerto—I don't remember now, it's not important. Because I do not want to write intervals, but I thought that piece needed a more intervallic logic, a distraction where you hear the intervallic rather than the pitch-oriented situation. Which is to some degree where my music is: it is in between the pitch and the interval.

It's a strange world. You cannot systematize it. Because by pitch I don't mean necessarily key, but I mean it's very much where it is at that time, it's not drawing to another intervallic situation. There is no polarity.

I don't want to seem polemical against Europe. Europe always gets excited when it discovers the new. Lutosławski's excitement was when he discovered modernity. My excitement was that I discovered that which already existed: Satie. So my excitement was the opposite. Everybody took it for granted, nobody took it seriously but with it was a way of breathing, a way of shaping which was very, very important for me. So it was Satie, in terms of the flexibility of the shape and it was Varèse for the directness of the sound which I, as a young person, found very important.

Which of your compositions would you single out as the result of those influences?

I think my early *Extensions* for violin and piano, *Three Pieces* for piano, pieces for two pianos got involved with a different kind of shaping and no longer involved with symmetrical shaping.

Now let me read to you from Cage's reply to my first question: "Also the first graph sketches of Morton Feldman prompted me to develop compositional means involving chance operations (*Music of Changes*)." *He would not elaborate on exactly what he meant. Will you explain in what way your graph sketches may have influenced him?*

I think in only one way: the possibility of the existence of music without cause and effect.[17] Because there was no connection between what he and I did. Mine always remained aleatoric. In other words, when it was finished, it did not solidify. You had to put it back in a bottle, it was liquid, you see (*laughs*). His chance operations were already fixed. What he really did was to use chance operations for an already existing category. Cage's early music is really a synthesis of Boulez and me.[18]

17. See Cage's comment at the end of the interview.

18. Ibid.

You know, there was a marvelous exchange of letters with him. He met Boulez as a young man. He met Boulez and me almost at the same time. They were close. The letters were never published[19]—Boulez sent him diagrams of the serialization of all the elements.[20]

That was what John Cage did in the early chance pieces. He serialized, by ways of chance, all the parameters. Where I helped is that he saw that on a chain, there is no longer any need for cause and effect.

Did Cage influence you at all?

I am always embarrassed by this question. His admiration for me influenced me.

You mean that you had a like-minded person who encouraged you, who stood behind you.

That was magnificent. Wonderful. I don't think anything would have happened with me without meeting Cage. Just *meeting* him was the biggest influence on my life.

He says we talked a lot about music. I don't remember talking a lot about music. I remember talking a lot about painters because we were meeting all the new great painters who were in America at that time.

Another influence Cage mentions in his reply is Robert Rauschenberg and his white paintings, which gave him the courage to do 4'33". Did you have any such experience with the visual arts?

Oh yes! Visual arts helped me get music out of the middle register.

Will you elaborate?

Because they are all over. All the registers were like *alles zusammen.* Like in Pollock. It is all over. There was not a subdivision of focus. European music was like a river, like the Danube I saw from the plane when I came. It had a nice focus. Beautifully middle. Beethoven extended it, he made the middle bigger. Webern made it a little bigger, but it was "big" almost like organ music. A little more room in there. But it was not really big-big. It was not all over. Painting helped me not to define registration.

What influenced John Cage in Rauschenberg was an answer to a philosophical question about life and art. Robert Rauschenberg is exactly my age. And brilliant. He said something that was very influential to a lot of young artists at that time. I think this is the influence of Rauschenberg, with his white paintings, to Cage. He said that he does not want either life or art. He wants something in between. A very influential statement: neither life nor art but something in between. And Cage would see this beautiful white thing in the shadows of the environment. He lived in a

19. The correspondence, edited by Jean-Jacques Nattiez, was first published in Switzerland 1990 as *Pierre Boulez/John Cage: Correspondance et documents* (Winterthur: Amadeus Verlag).

20. See Cage's comments at the end of the interview.

very beautiful apartment, Cage, and he saw where art and the outside environment could collage. Not interfere with each other. That was the philosophical metaphor about doing something with the music, too.[21] A very interesting period.

For me, the problem of music is that it has too much to do with music. And it becomes a lecture. One of the things that is influencing me now is that I am asking the question: Is music an art form or does it only have to do with music forms? John Cage is only involved with music forms. In other words, the discovery and the exploration of music is, in a sense, within the material. That there is nothing there behind the material. So in that sense, John Cage is not a mystic.

Don't you think that his music exudes an atmosphere and in doing so, it communicates something beyond the music, it communicates a way of thinking?

I think his music is a fantastic protagonist. I think it asks a lot of questions. I think it's the atmosphere of asking questions.

Whereas yours?

The atmosphere of answering them (*laughs*).

In that case, one must envy you: you seem to have the answers. Few people can claim that.

Only for my music. Only. You see, that's another problem: I don't feel that it's a community. I could never listen to a piece of Boulez and get some insight from the piece. I could listen to a piece of Boulez and could say to him what I said once to Ligeti, who I like very much, we are very good friends, and I said to him: "György, you are too gifted to write European music" (*laughs*). I think the tragedy of Ligeti is, in a sense, that his imagination is one place and his background and tradition are fighting both. I really meant what I said. I said it humorously, but I thought if he could have been just less involved—where he would use the didactic element of research in a more casual way like I have used it. Where the didactic element in Ives does not become the subject as it does with Ligeti and Boulez.

II.

Sounds do not surround you.

There are sounds right now.

I don't hear them.

You don't hear them?

No.

What sounds do *you hear?*

---

21. See Cage's comment at the end of the interview.

Nothing. I hear them but they are indigenous. In a place that builds modern buildings—do you hear the drilling that's going on? It is absolutely like having a lion in a jungle. I mean it is indigenous to the landscape. It would be interesting if you would hear an Islamic chant. What's happening here? OPEC, OPEC! (*Vienna is the headquarters of the Organization of Petroleum Exporting Countries*). In other words: I hear it like everyone else but it is not a source of . . .

. . . inspiration.

It's not a source of anything. Most of the time I think of it as pollution. Noise pollution.

How about the sounds of nature, such as the wind, birds, and so on?

I have no contact with them. They don't interest me at all. I can live very well without them.

So in composing, the sounds always come from within.

Yes, only when I am composing. Otherwise, you are crazy. I don't go around hearing sounds. Some people do! Stockhausen, I am sure, is one of them.

Lutosławski's initial response was similar to yours. A few years later, he admitted that in preparing his Novelette *for rehearsal, that is, when he had to learn the score as if it were a piece by a different composer, he realized that he had put in, without knowing, a birdsong that he had heard in Oslo. Also, in conducting* Jeux vénitiens, *he spotted the traces of birdsong in the flutes.*

I'd rather that he would be more aware that the notation is Earle Brown, that would be more realistic than hearing a bird in Oslo.[22]

Shall I tell you a story about Mrs. Lutosławski? I met her recently in California, we had a festival together. We were having coffee and she told me the first time she had heard a piece of mine in Warsaw. Somebody had told her that the piece she was going to hear, didn't have a loud note in it. She said, that's impossible. She said that she gets frightened easily. As she was sitting and listening to the music, she was holding on to the chair, waiting for a loud note (*laughs*) . . .

. . . which never came. Actually, why do you keep the dynamic level of your music soft?

Instead of asking why it is soft, you should ask why isn't it loud.

Why isn't it loud, then?

Because when it's loud, you can't hear the sound. You hear its attack. Then you don't hear the sound, only in its decay. And I think that's essentially what impressed Boulez. That he heard a sound, not an attack, emerging and disappearing without attack and decay, almost like an electronic medium.

---

22. See also comments by Earle Brown and Witold Lutosławski.

Also, you have to remember that loud and soft is an aspect of differentiation. And my music is more like a kind of monologue that does not need exclamation point, colon, it does not need . . .

An interior monologue, you mean? Because a monologue can very well do with exclamation marks and colons . . .

. . . not in Beckett. People who imitate him and have no punctuation . . . there is always something interfering visually. The sentences are wrong, the words are wrong, there is an interference with the continuity of the eye. So you can always tell very bad stream of consciousness.

Whereas with Joyce or Beckett, there is nothing to interfere, and you never lose your place. A big influence: the lack of punctuation in literature. The lack of differentiation of space in New York painting.

You know that marvelous remark of Disraeli? Unfortunately, he was not a good writer, but if he was a great writer, it would have been a wonderful remark. They asked him why did he begin to write novels. He said because there was nothing to read (*laughs*). I felt very much like that in terms of contemporary music. I was not really happy with it. It became like a Rorschach test.

I'd say that now, maybe because I am a professor and I am teaching young people, so I am listening to music more than when I was as a young person, I am more interested in music now than when I was young.

I've become very, very interested in Stravinsky. I never admitted to his genius. And I'd say that Stravinsky now is influencing me, only because his nondevelopmental aspect was a sense of trying to make a continuity really without the kind of Germanic cause and effect. So I appreciate it now, I appreciate making moves. Stravinsky almost invented the moment form, of making moves from one thing to another, rather than having the organic, stylistic continuity of Boulez or Cage, for that matter. Cage does not make moves. Xenakis makes moves once in a while. The only one that makes moves is Stravinsky. Satie did not make moves but he made marvelous moves from a certain type of *pianissimo* to a *fortissimo*. Almost like an echo.

Late in life, I've become sympathetic to Stravinsky and I play more of his music in my seminars than Webern or Schoenberg.

Which period?

Recently, I spent a lot of time on *Les Noces*, for a lot of reasons. All the great Stravinsky.

There is a marvelous John Cage and Stravinsky story. Cage became very close to Stravinsky in the last years before Stravinsky's death. Cage told me, he was having a conversation with Stravinsky and Stravinsky asked him who had influenced him as a young man. He did not know too much about Cage's history—that he had studied with Schoenberg. So Cage told him about it and said the music of Schoenberg had influenced him. Stravinsky was hurt and he said: "And my music? Why didn't my music influence you?" And Cage said: "Because it was not chromatic." And Stravinsky said: "But my music *is* chromatic, why is it everybody thought my music was not chromatic?"[23] (*laughs*).

What I am doing now in many of my seminars is discussing the chromatic moves in Stravinsky which are marvelous. They are very easy, just half a step or something.

I am also involved with Stravinsky because of my concern about instruments. That instruments can in a sense do more than tell the story of the music's hierarchical organization.

And by that I mean Stravinsky has memorable instrumental imagery. There is not one instrumental moment in all of Schoenberg's work that one remembers. Maybe the second violin part of the harmonics in the Fourth String Quartet. Maybe the fourths in the double basses in the Chamber Symphony. But other than that, there is no instrumental imagery. There is no instrumental imagery in Cage, there is none, really, in Ligeti. There is no instrumental imagery in Bartók, unless it's descriptive. There is no instrumental imagery in Lutosławski, there is no instrumental imagery in anybody. But there is instrumental imagery in Stravinsky. Varèse—almost. Not good enough. *Intégrales*—one moment.

Will you define what you mean by instrumental imagery?

My music.

III.

Stravinsky referred to Mozart as the "divine cliché."

This is a very, very serious problem. Every country has it. I have asked this question all over. A variation of this question.

What music travels? I'm sure there is music in Hungary that only travels from one section of Budapest to another. And if it goes across the river, it's great in Buda, but in Pest . . . (*laughs*).

This is a very, very important question.

The question is political. It has nothing to do with Hungary because it also goes for Canada. By "political," I am not trying to talk about East and West. I am not talking about capitalism or communism. By "political," I mean that a personal music cannot . . .

It's very hard to get the nuance here, in this remark. I don't feel that music could rise beyond the . . .

By "political," maybe I mean "cultural," "historical," because there's no difference whether a country could have been . . . I feel that music must rise . . .

---

23. See Cage's comment at the end of the interview.

I think it's finished. Let's start this question all over again.

I think what's killing the world is nationalism. And I think it's killed off music, too. It killed off Stockhausen with a Prussian approach, it killed off Boulez with a French elegance, it killed off Cage with a pragmatic attitude (because America is pragmatic). It killed off Italy with its self-indulgence, its Baroque, Rococo, overfed music. It killed off English music with the pompous landscape.

And I think just as nationalism is killing off countries . . . Nationalism is very good, say, for the first four years of a country.

Are you sure you are replying to my question?

You know, I forgot your question.

Up to what point can we speak of a personal style and where does self-repetition begin?

Many people feel that if they hear one piece of mine, they heard it all. Yet all Rembrandts are more or less the same. All Giottos are more or less the same.

You are not hurt when people make this remark? Perhaps you agree?

About my music? I don't agree. It means they are not listening.

All Proust is the same. Kafka is the same. Everything is the same. All gardens in Vienna are the same.

Why is it people expect music to be so different? I'll tell you why. Because people get very bored, they can't listen to music. They can't listen to music. I give a lecture sometimes and I will play a beautiful melody of Mozart, say, from a concerto, and then I'll play the chords underneath. And to some degree, the chords underneath are more beautiful than the melody. Nobody hears the chords. Nobody. They just hear the tip of the iceberg, as we would say. That's the problem.

My problem is that I want all my pieces to be the same but I haven't got the discipline to make it the same. By the "same" I mean that it travels the same ground all the time. The minute you have an extra instrument in the same style, everything changes. It's the *context* [of] how to listen to my music. One has to listen to my music on the variety of the vertical and not on the variety of how the construction or the dramatic element of the linear, directional . . .

It's a moral thing, it's like the Tower of Babel. I more or less agree with Kafka when he said, we already know everything.

I think it has to do with my concentration. And I think it also has to do with exactly what *are* phenomena? I like to tell my students and remind them that the theory of the origin of species by Darwin was based on a very modest little bird and the beaks. But the bird came from his own district of England. It did not come from some exotic animal which Karlheinz Stockhausen hunted up—he goes out into the musical jungle and wants to bring back some animal with six arms. Really, it's true.

Boulez is very typical French. Like Cousteau who goes underwater and looks at the fish, the crazy fish . . . Messiaen, too, likes the exotic. We call it slumming. It's like years ago people used to go up to Harlem to see the young black people dance. Slumming. And the French always like to go to the Orient. André Malraux, you know. *Man's Fate.*[24] China, the Chinese revolution, you know. Exotic places. Only in exotic places can things happen.

Whereas your attitude is?

Stay home.

Stay home, and?

Work very hard (*laughs*).

The one that explains what I am really talking about is Kierkegaard. He doesn't like the artist, because the artist is changing all the time. He doesn't trust them. He doesn't like the ethical man too much. He is always moralizing. He likes the religious man, because the religious man has only one mood. And I believe that too. I believe when my work arrives at one mood, it's as if I am praying. Which is another remark of Kafka's: art as prayer. To get closer to that thing that one is praying to.

Again, one would have to define what you mean by prayer in this context.

Prayer is getting close to that which does not exist. It is very much what I feel when I work.

To attempt the impossible, really.

To attempt the impossible, by concentration. Rather than looking for it. But this is the whole subject of Proust: not to look for the experience in the object but to look to the experience in ourselves. What is so fantastic about the whole moral of Proust is that the beginning of his book is very idealistic. He is reading Ruskin, he is learning how to have an aesthetic point of view and as life goes on, all that disappears.

I feel that this is true of most composers. Too many notions about aesthetic, too many notions about music and no understanding of themselves in relation to music.

Sometimes, though, it would be disastrous to get close to oneself.

1983

In 1984, I visited John Cage in his New York apartment, to confront him with some of Morton Feldman's statements.

I.

What in fact influenced you in Feldman's early graphic sketches?

It was a clear statement of there being a range of possibilities and that any element in that range would be satisfactory in response to a question or in response to a demand. If one wanted one sound, then within the

24. Reference to André Malraux's novel *La condition humaine* (1933).

range of his graph music, you see, where you have, say, the number 2 and you want two sounds that are in the middle range, any two will do.

I think implicit in my use of chance operations is the fact that any one of the answers will be satisfactory.

II.

Was your early music a synthesis of Boulez and Feldman?

That is mysterious. I don't know exactly what he means. Because when you say Boulez, there are many things that come to mind and when you say Feldman, equally, many things come to mind.

To my mind, at the moment, is the notion that Morton Feldman could have been thinking that there was something systematic in the work of Boulez and he likes to think of himself as a poet who has nothing to do with system. And I think he likes to think of me as someone who has to do with system because he thinks of the use of chance operations as a relation to a system. I disagree with him there. I think that chance operations are not a system but are a utility.

III.

On the correspondence with Boulez:

I met Boulez in the late forties in Paris and I was instrumental with publishers in getting his works published for the first time. Then, as a result, he gave me the manuscript of the Second Piano Sonata, which I have put in the collection that I have formed at Northwestern University. And now, at that university, is our correspondence. So that if you wanted to see it, you could.

Boulez has asked that it not be published until we are both not living. I think it's unfortunate that that's the case because it was an interesting exchange of ideas. What was particularly interesting to me was that we came to an impasse and the result was that what had been an exchange of ideas became no longer an exchange of ideas because Boulez refused my thoroughgoing use of chance operations. Even though he was willing, because of the importance for him of the work of Mallarmé, and he discovered in the posthumous work of Mallarmé which is called *Le Livre*, Mallarmé's deep involvement with chance operations. So it was at that point that it was necessary for him to establish a rightness of the use of chance operations as opposed to a wrong use of chance operations. My use, of course, was the wrong one, but his was the right one. That was what he wished to show in his article called "Aléa." So that the word "aleatoric" was invented by Boulez to describe the proper use of chance operations.

I never use the word "aleatoric" in connection with my work—I always use something about chance operations and, more specifically, I Ching chance operations.

IV.

On the influence of Rauschenberg:

I think I had already had such ideas as far as the fusing of life and art went and they came to me from my study of Zen Buddhism with Suzuki. I had also thought of the silent piece two years before I wrote it. And the reason I did not write it when I thought of it was because I was aware that many people would take it as a joke and not seriously.

That was why, when I saw the empty paintings of Rauschenberg, that I was prepared to have, as it were, a partner in this serious departure from conventions. The French would call it *démarche.* In other words, I don't think I was influenced by him—I was encouraged in something that I was already convinced about individually.

V.

On the dialogue with Stravinsky:

The story is partly true, but it's changed, it is a variation of the truth.

When I was young, I made a survey of contemporary music. It was during the depression and I made that survey also in order to give lectures to housewives. That was how I made my living. Well, after making the survey, I came to the conclusion that I preferred the music of Schoenberg to that of Stravinsky because it opened more doors toward what seemed to me to be the future. I particularly did not like the neoclassicism of Stravinsky. I responded as everybody else did to his ballets, they were so vigorous and through the folk material so lively, but the idea of Schoenberg's music opened doors without saying what should go through the doors (*laughs*).

I only had one conversation with him and the reason I had it was because he had admired my performance of the Devil in *L'histoire du soldat.* I was the Devil, Elliott Carter was the Soldier, and Aaron Copland was the Narrator. Everyone said we were very well cast (*laughs*).

So I went to see Stravinsky and he, of course, was very entertaining because he was so intelligent. I explained to him that I had, as a young man, decided in favor of Schoenberg and not in favor of him. As a result, I had studied with Schoenberg. And he said why, and I said because it seemed to me the chromaticism was very important. And he said: "But my music is chromatic, too!"

Then he explained that the reason he did not like Schoenberg's music was because it was not modern. I was struck by that because in a sense he was right. When Schoenberg was teaching, he would take four notes and he would say: "Bach did this with these notes, Beethoven did this, Brahms did this and then, speaking of himself in the third person, he would say 'and

Schoenberg did this.'" So he thought of himself directly in line. Whereas Stravinsky thought of himself as having made a break with the past. And of course I felt that way too and felt more friendly toward Stravinsky. However, I still think I made the right decision in studying with Schoenberg rather than someone connected with Stravinsky, and I think Stravinsky's own actions [support that]: in late life he began to neoclassicize—if not Schoenberg—Webern.

Nineteen

LUKAS FOSS (1922–2009)

"Dear dedicated (to the cause) Mr. Varga"—Lukas Foss wrote me on an aerogram, on June 1, 1979 (see fig. 5). "And thank you for your persistence." Yes, I was persistent, otherwise the three-questions book would never have come into being. And with Lukas Foss I needed to be stubborn, for he was so busy conducting that while at home, he never had any time to write. He continued to send me aerograms, scribbled onboard planes that were taking him to yet another concert, or in hotel rooms. On June 1, 1979, he was en route to South Korea; in 1982 when he did eventually reply to my questions, he happened to be in the Embassy Hotel in Kansas City. "I came across your letter of September 30," he wrote me on November 22, "just as I left for a tour. Not wishing to keep you waiting for an answer, allow me to jot down a few sentences in reply."

Here are his "loose, improvised jottings":

I.

No—I have never had Lutosławski's experience—or, to put it another way—that is the experience I have whenever I hear other music. If it is music I love, it gives me ideas: how to apply some of my own ideas to what I have just heard. It is like a love-relationship. You immerse yourself in a love and you find yourself.

In my *Baroque Variations*—notably No. 2, the Scarlatti one (Nonesuch record)—I turn other music into dreams of mine.

When I listen to music I do not care for (sometimes my colleagues') I say to myself: "wait a moment—why didn't he do it this way, or that way, it could have been wonderful"—then I feel that I have discovered something like a scientist who thinks of a "better way" (to solve a problem).

II.

Sounds, noises (such as "white noise" that has no "human" associations) mean nothing to me. Music is sound + noises, but it is not born out of sounds and noises, it is born out of silence. It is sounds and noises that have meaning. Would meaningless chatter suggest a poem to a poet? No. Sounds with meaning don't come from sounds void of meaning. Of course ocean waves suggested music to Debussy, birdsongs to Messiaen, but that is because ocean waves and birdsongs have a meaning for us. The former suggests "yearning" (*Sehnsucht*), the latter "innocence" . . . etc.

III.

Style is personality. Self-repetition begins when you become your own "connoisseur"; then you become vain, and either out of vanity, conceit, or laziness you repeat. Painters do it out of business acumen. They sell their style, their "idiom." One gets caught up in "image building"—which is a twentieth-century disease. If you worry about your "image," you will not develop. If you develop, you will not repeat.

In his letter of December 21, 1982, Foss added:

The change in my musical language came about via my teaching at UCLA, Los Angeles. In the early 50s, at the time when the word "aleatoric" had not yet permeated our musical jargon, I started the first "Improvisation Ensemble" in order to help my students free themselves from the tyranny of the printed note. Our early improvisations sounded like written (tonal) music badly remembered. Little did I know then that my venture into improvisation would change me more than my students. It turned me into an experimental composer. Namely, one day I thought: if our improvisations sound like written music badly remembered, what would be the kind of improvisation that would be fresh, original, and thrive on the chance aspect? With that question I opened the whole Pandora's box of modern music.

1982/97

Nov 22 82

Dear Mr. Varga

I came across your letter of Sept 30 just as I left for a tour. Not wishing to keep you waiting for an answer, allow me to jot down a few sentences in reply. (The tape will have to wait till I have a chance to make one)

1.) No - I have never had Lutoslawsky's experience — or, to put it another way — that is the experience I have <u>whenever</u> I hear other music. If it is music I love, it gives me ideas: how to apply some of my own ideas to what I have just heard. It is like a love-relationship. In my Baroque Variations — notably No 2 the Scarlatti one (Nonesuch record) I turn other music into dreams of mine. When I listen to music I do <u>not</u> care for - (sometimes my colleague's) I say to myself: "wait a moment - why didn't he do it this way, or that way, it could have been wonderful - then I feel that I have discovered something like a scientist who thinks of "a better way" — (to solve a problem).

The prestige hotel of downtown Kansas City

1215 Wyandotte Street, Kansas City, Missouri 64105 (816) 471-1333

Figure 5. Letter from Lukas Foss. Reproduced by kind permission of the Bálint András Varga Collection, Akademie der Künste, Berlin.

2) Sounds – noises mean nothing to me. Music is sounds + noises, but it is not born out of sounds and noises, it is born out of silence. It is sounds and noises that have meaning. Would meaningless chatter suggest a poem to a poet? No. Sounds with meaning don't come from sounds void of meaning. Of course ocean waves suggested music to Debussy bird songs to Messiaen, but that is because ocean waves and birdsongs <u>have</u> a meaning for us. The former suggests "yearning" (Sehnsucht) the latter "innocence"--- etc.

3) Style is personality. Self repetition begins when you become your own 'connaisseur'; then you become vain, and either out of vanity, conceit or laziness you repeat. Painters do it out of business-acumen. They sell their style, their "idiom". One gets caught up in 'image building' – which is a 20th century desease. If you worry about your 'image' you will not develop. If you develop you will not repeat.

Hope these loose improvised jottings help you toward your worthwhile project.

Ever sincerely

Lukas Foss

Figure 5. *(concluded)*

Twenty

ALBERTO GINASTERA (1916–83)

The Argentine composer was sixty-five years old when I met him in Budapest but he looked considerably older. He spoke slowly and haltingly, perhaps because he found it difficult to express his ideas in English. His wife, the cellist Aurora Natola-Ginastera (who had played the world premiere of Ginastera's Second Cello Concerto that very year, in Buenos Aires) was sitting next to us, watching over her husband with a motherly, anxious look in her eyes. Perhaps he was no longer in good health: he died two years after our interview. He would like to have checked the transcript of the conversation—sadly, he passed away before he could have done so.

I.

An aspect of a work by another composer may set my fantasy in motion: I imagine the way I would approach it. This is of common occurrence among composers. I think this is one explanation for the presence of so many different styles in contemporary music, in contrast with the past.

When I was young, Bartók and Berg influenced me in this way. What struck me about Bartók was the way he incorporated imaginary folk music in his *Music for Strings, Percussion, and Celesta* as well as in his string quartets. Something similar is present in my own string quartet as well. When I was feeling my way toward dodecaphony, I was gripped by the expressive power of Berg's music. My first opera, *Don Rodrigo,* bears traces of the influence of *Wozzeck,* especially in its structure, in the use of closed forms.

Lutosławski's style did indeed undergo a radical transformation. My own development toward a personal idiom was much slower. Today, we have one thing in common: a kind of extended tonality. It characterizes his double concerto for oboe, harp, and strings, just as my piano sonata which I completed recently. In both pieces, you will find a new folklore. In his case, it is the polonaise. This particular work of his did not influence me: I heard it on the radio on the day I completed my sonata.

Changes in musical structure are to be found the world over. Composers like Lutosławski, Dutilleux, Petrassi, myself, and others are moving toward a much clearer kind of music. My new cello concerto, for instance, may not be easy but it is very pure music.

II.

Sounds of the outside world do not influence me much but it does happen that they attract my interest. For instance, during a recent visit to Puerto Rico, I heard the song of a frog called *coqui*. This animal is indigenous to Puerto Rico, it cannot be found anywhere else. If you ever happen to visit that country, you are bound to hear its characteristic sound. I have put it in the second movement of my cello concerto: it is present in the glissando of the violins and the xylophone. The concerto happens to be very South American, not only because of its themes—the whole work has a South American air about it.

In other pieces, I was influenced by the sounds of the South American forest. I did not use any concrete sounds—I composed those that emerged in me under their influence.

III.

My music has been analyzed by many critics. They have found individual features of which I was not conscious but I was aware of their presence in a subjective manner. Such as, for instance, its marked rhythm which appears in my first work for the piano, *Panambi*, and is also present in my latest compositions, the cello concerto and the piano sonata. Second: its lyric character and the sweeping melodies influenced by South American landscapes—the pampas, the plains. Third: the use of percussion to which I owe the friendship of Varèse.

In conclusion, to return for a moment to your first question: I composed my first ballet under the influence of Stravinsky and Ravel, where one of the native dances is accompanied exclusively by percussion. When I flew to the United States on a Guggenheim Scholarship in 1945, this piece was conducted by Erich Kleiber with the NBC orchestra. Varèse was in the audience. I did not know his music, neither had I heard anything by Messiaen, but I had seen Milhaud's *Les Coéphores* which also has a scene for voice and percussion. It was my passion for percussion instruments that led to the *Cantata para América mágica* for soprano, a large percussion orchestra and two pianos, a setting of ancient, pre-Columbian texts.

1981

Twenty-One

KAREL GOEYVAERTS (1923–93)

The date of his birth and his choice of profession more or less determined Karel Goeyvaerts's path. He was bound to mix with Stockhausen and Co. in Darmstadt where, like Stockhausen, he heard and was bowled over by Messiaen's Mode de valeurs et d'intensités. *Like Stockhausen, he studied with the French composer in Paris and, under his influence as well as Webern's, he composed a sonata for two pianos (1950–51) which has kept his name alive. Goeyvaerts's claim to fame is his having written the first totally serial work; he and Stockhausen performed it in Darmstadt and created quite a sensation. Significantly, the sonata bears the title "Nummer 1." There followed several compositions taking the numbering further, Nummers 5 and 7 being electronic pieces produced at the WDR Studio in Cologne (1953 and 1955, respectively). In later years, Goeyvaerts wrote five compositions, which he called* Litanies, *their instrumentation varying from solo to orchestra. His final work was the opera* Aquarius *(1983–93).*

The Belgian composer replied to my questions in English.

I.

No similar experience has occurred to me. Since I was very young, I was interested in the music of living composers. I listened to very much new music and I am sure this has influenced my way of thinking, but there has never been an important turn on my way. If Webern's music influenced me much since the late 1940s, this occurred gradually, when studying his music more and more. In 1950/51 I wrote the first totally serial work of music which certainly had to do with Webern, but was already a big step ahead.

II.

I think it is not possible not to be influenced by the sounds of everyday life. Although when I am composing, I prefer to be in a quiet atmosphere. Milhaud could compose with street noises around him. They even seemed to stimulate him. But like most other composers (I guess), I prefer to transpose the sound world of everyday life into musical patterns when I am sufficiently far [away] to abstract it from reality.

III.

Individual style comes spontaneously and is not to be looked for. It is the result of a genuine and new musical idea. Every composer should refrain from composing whenever such an idea is lacking. In such a case, he is likely to do over again what has been done before, either by other composers or by himself. A rich idea may yield several works, every one of them being a further development of it. As soon as this possibility of further development is exhausted, it is better to stop with it and wait for another idea to be carried out.

1982/83

Twenty-Two

SOFIA GUBAIDULINA (1931)

With Edison Denisov and Alfred Schnittke, Sofia Gubaidulina was a black sheep of Soviet cultural life. Her position was aggravated by her faith and a mystical approach to music, evidenced by her replies to my questions.

When I contacted her, she was still living in the Soviet Union; by the time we met, briefly, in the 1990s, she had settled in Germany. I think it must have been at a concert in Innsbruck, Austria, that I went up to her, instinctively slowing down my steps, softening my voice and bending my back. It is not that she looked frail: she has a round baby face, pretty even in her sixties. It was the vulnerability in her eyes that made me hesitate about whether I should go ahead and introduce myself. She struck me as extremely shy, anxious to protect her privacy. When I did address her, it was her publisher, sitting next to her, who replied; Gubaidulina looked almost frightened and I beat a hasty retreat.

I was full of admiration for her wonderfully intense violin concerto Offertorium *(1980–86), which had taken my breath away when I heard it on the radio, with Gidon Kremer as soloist.*

For many years I did not know much else but was aware of her fascinatingly mixed background, which no doubt influenced her outlook: one of her grandfathers was a mullah, her father was a Tartar (in fact, she was born at Chistopol in Tatarstan), her mother had Russian, Polish, and Jewish blood. No wonder she is on record as saying "I am the place where East meets West."

Sofia Gubajdulina was kind enough to revise her contribution for a publication of the Academy of Fine Arts, Berlin. Her Russian text was translated into German by Hans-Ulrich Duffek, director of the composer's publisher, Sikorski.

Your questions have induced me to ponder on these things which are actually self-evident. In reality, however, they turn out to be extraordinarily complex—especially the third question. But let us consider them one after the other.

I.

It has never happened in my life that the encounter with a work by another composer would have made me realize that I could compose basically in a different way. I have, however, often observed how a piece that was being played would be spun on in my head differently from the way it was actually being performed. This double hearing of music is a peculiar state of mind. It frightens me.

II.

As a rule, the sounds of the outside world disturb me. If I happen to be in good physical condition, I can switch off quite easily and concentrate on my inner ear.

It has occurred just once that the sounds of the outside world fascinated me. I was sitting in a room with the lights dimmed, there was no trace of music. I heard the noise of children playing in the street. I realized that the shouts and exchanges of words were in fact of a musical nature—that they could actually be composed or could become part of an instrumental or vocal texture. Sounds like that easily evoke logical musical ideas. I had no recording equipment with me, otherwise I would have translated those ideas into practice.

III.

The phenomenon of repetition as a mark of individual style could best be described through the example of a medieval scribe writing a liturgical text. Some features of his handwriting—the idiosyncratic slant of his letters, the way he presses his quill on to the paper and adorns the letters, depending on the sharpness of his quill (*stilus*)—are bound to add up to a system of repetitions of expressive qualities. The similarity of the repeated strokes articulates the overall image of the text. To this perfectly normal (structural) significance is added a further aspect which is perceived far quicker (see the following diagram):

. . . .

- - - - - -

Above the quantity of material elements (letters, text) a (dotted) level of structure has been set which refers to the repeated strokes.

In a work of art there comes about, once in a while, an entire pyramid of such articulations:

.

. .

. . .

. . . . .

- - - - - - - -

And finally, the entire quantity of the idiosyncrasies of a written work (i.e., a manuscript) can be reduced to a single principle, whereby the time required by the perception of the text appears to be condensed, so to speak.

That is precisely the transformation of time which differentiates a work of art from a simple piece of communication. For here, the material quantity (of the letters, words, events) is overcome and a unity (spirit) will be reached.

To the extent that the scribe of the spiritual text comprehends the events described in the paper roll he has been entrusted to copy, he finds himself in an exceptional state which has been defined by many religious writers as "the sojourn of the soul in the spirit."

The process of the transformation of time and the rise to the top of the pyramid with the help of the particular expressive qualities of his writing which characterize exclusively this scribe, have been evoked by a wholly different kind of oscillations. This is where the element of fire has a role to play. Here, there are no repetitions even though many expressive qualities are repeated.

If the consciousness of the creative person eschews this process of the transformation of time and concentrates exclusively on the production of particular means of expression, these means will be quickly objectivized and will become an instrument which informs of his own state of mind, rather than one which has the goal of serving as the "sojourn in the spirit." In that case, the repetitions of such particular means of expression are bound to be perceived as self-repetitions. For there reigns no longer fire but a thing. You can only inform of a thing just once. Any repetition would be superfluous and unnecessary.

1984/2006

Twenty-Three

GEORG FRIEDRICH HAAS (1953)

Georg Friedrich Haas was born in Graz, a city in the east of Austria, but spent his childhood in the mountainous province of Vorarlberg, on the Swiss border. The landscape and the atmosphere of the place have left a lasting impression on his personality.

The atmosphere was marked not so much by natural beauty in the accepted sense of the word. Rather, Haas experienced the mountains as a menace; he felt closed in by the narrow valley where the sun rarely penetrated. Nature for him represented a dark force.

The composer adds: "Just as important for me was the experience of being an outsider: unlike my younger siblings, I never learned to speak the local Alemannic dialect. Also, I was a Protestant in a predominantly Catholic society."

Haas has not had an easy time of it as a composer. He speaks openly of the years of "total failure" in trying to make his mark—another experience to leave its imprint on his development, aggravating his pessimistic leanings. Success, when it did gradually emerge, only mitigated his pessimism but could never wholly eliminate it.

It is no wonder, then, that night, darkness, and the loss of illusions should have played such an important role in his oeuvre (such as his Hölderlin-opera Nacht *(Night), 1995/98). It was not until quite recently that his music has been illuminated by light.*

*Light effects, as integral components of a range of his compositions, have featured prominently for quite some time now, designed by artists especially for the music. (*in vain, *2000, and particularly* Hyperion, *a Concerto for Light and Orchestra, 2006). However, light as opposed to darkness first emerged as late as 2006 in* Sayaka *for percussion and accordion as well as in the piano trio* Ins Licht *(Into the Light), 2007, written for the farewell concert marking my retirement from Universal Edition.*

Georg Friedrich Haas is known and respected internationally as a highly sensitive and imaginative researcher into the inner world of sound. Most of his works (with the notable exception of the Violin Concerto, 1998) make use of microtonality, which the composer has subjected to thorough examination in the wake of Ivan Wyschnegradsky and Alois Hába. He has taught courses and lectured on the subject in several countries; in 1999 he was invited by the Salzburg Festival to give a talk under the title "Beyond the Twelve Semitones," with the subtitle "Attempt at a Synopsis of Microtonal Composition Techniques." In the last paragraph, he writes:

"'Micro-' counts as 'tonality' only in contrast with 'normal tonality' in its role as a system of reference. Where this system of reference has become obsolete, the notion of 'microtonality' has been replaced by the free decision of the individual composer in his use of pitch as his material."

"I am not really comfortable with being pigeonholed as a 'microtonal composer.' Primarily, I am a composer, free to use the means needed for my music. There is no ideology regarding 'pure' intonation, either as Pythagorean number mysticism or as a notion of 'Nature' determined by trivial physics. I am a composer, not a microtonalist."

In each new work, Haas enters uncharted territory, but his music is firmly rooted in tradition. His profound admiration for Schubert has found moving expression in his Torso *of 1999/2001, an orchestration of the incomplete piano sonata in C major, D. 840, an image of the tragic figure of Franz Schubert. Haas paid respect to Mozart not only in his* . . . sodaß ich's hernach mit einem Blick gleichsam wie ein schönes Bild . . . im Geist übersehe,[25] *composed for string orchestra in 1990/91, but also in* Sieben Klangräume,[26] *2005, meant to be interspersed with movements of Mozart's* Requiem *fragment (that is, divested of the supplements provided by his pupils). In* Blumenstück *(Flower Piece), 2000, for chorus, bass tuba, and string quintet, one hears echoes of Beethoven (perhaps never intended by the composer). In the Concerto for Violoncello and Orchestra, 2003/4, the solo instrument quotes a motif from Franz Schreker's opera* Der ferne Klang *("O Vater, dein trauriges Erbe").*[27] *Commissioned by the Gewandhausorchester Leipzig, Haas's latest work for orchestra (*Traum in des Sommers Nacht,[28] *2009) is a tribute to Mendelssohn, drawing on motifs from works of that composer, masterfully woven into Haas's own music.*

The Cello Concerto, just as Wer, wenn ich schriee, hörte mich . . . ,[29] *1999, for percussion and ensemble, reflect Haas's political commitment and his bitter realization of his helplessness as a composer: there is no way his music could serve to better the world. The percussion concerto was written at the time of the Balkan war; when Haas heard airplanes flying overhead carrying their deadly burden, he asked himself whether anyone could hear him, if he were to cry out in protest against the war. The Cello Concerto begins with a scream in unbearable pain, followed by a section where the drumbeat conjures up the march rhythm of the Prussian army: a plea against fascism.*

I.

I cannot recall a particular musical composition which would have brought about a fundamental change in my musical thinking. Rather than having a single encounter with a "key work," I have had many such encounters.

25. So that afterward I can take it in my spirit, like a beautiful picture.
26. Seven Sound Spaces.
27. The Distant Sound (O Father, your sad legacy).
28. Dream in the Summer's Night.
29. Who could hear me if I were to cry.

I grew up in a mountain village. However impressive the landscape may have been as it changed from season to season, life there in the 1950s and 1960s was largely cut off from cultural developments in the world outside. It was visited by skiers in winter and hikers in summer—that was about it. Thanks to my parents' record collection I had access to music by classical and early romantic composers (basically from Mozart to Mendelssohn).

That music opened a window onto different worlds. Worlds different from the one into which I felt I had been thrust. Later, it would serve as an Archimedean point through which I could fundamentally transform those worlds (as far as I was concerned).

I came in touch with new music at school. Gerold Amann, a dedicated pedagogue (I think highly of him also as a composer), confronted his seventeen-year-old pupils with Ligeti's *Volumina*, Berio's *Sequenza* for trombone, and Penderecki's *Lukas Passion* a few years after their world premieres. It was then that I conceived an affection for the music of György Ligeti.

My first encounter with the music of John Cage was rather unusual: I heard *Sonatas and Interludes* (for prepared piano) on the radio. I was doing my military service and had my headphones on—after 22.00, that is, when the junk music which we had been forced to listen to all day was at long last switched off and we were supposed to be asleep. Cage showed up the possibility (albeit Utopian for a soldier like myself) of intervening in a given instrumental setup and transforming it based on individual criteria.

(I cannot here go into all the pivotal works of music history which influenced me during my music studies, however important those influences may have been.)

Ivan Wyschnegradsky's "espaces non-octaviants" (non-octaviating spaces) may not be a composition, "merely" a textural principle. Still—this principle has exerted a decisive influence on my musical thinking: networks of intervals which stretch over the entire audible space and extend (virtually) into the no longer audible realm (ultra- and infrasound). The octave loses in the process the function it possessed up to that point in music history.

Giacinto Scelsi: in listening to a concert at the Graz Musikprotokoll festival that was devoted exclusively to his compositions and lasted several hours, I realized that he shaped sonority "as such," purely as a sounding process, evolving instant by instant. Those apparently freely flowing spaces where the difference in the richness of beat in more or less neighboring tones creates a depth and an intensity which for me, up to that moment, had been "unheard of," gripped me—I sensed the necessity to take up in my work where Scelsi had left off.

Creative processes are sometimes set in train by verbal statements by composers which may have rather an intriguing relationship with the compositions to which they refer. I remember a fascinating lecture by Tristan

Murail in Darmstadt: the orchestral work which was subsequently performed was markedly different from what I had expected on the strength of the lecture. I realized much later that the pieces which correspond to what I had expected from Murail would need to be composed by myself.

In the early 1980s, the Graz composer Hermann Markus Pressl wrote an impressive, straightforwardly structured vocal work which he called *Asralda.* The piece is based on the contrast between temperament (tritone A–E♭) and the overtone series (fifth D–A). That contrast has been stylized in the title, an artificial word, composed of "Asraphael" (= spiritual principle, = tempering, = A–E♭) and "Esmeralda" (= sensory principle, = overtone series, = D–A). The ideological, slightly esoteric background did not interest me in the least. However, the contrast between temperament (in my case mostly tritone-fifth and tritone-fourth chords) and the overtone series was to exercise my mind in many of my compositions over the next thirty years. Also: at the end of *Asralda,* the singers leave the hall and sing from outside—the same happens in my opera *Nacht* (but in contrast with Pressl, in my piece the instruments in the hall and the one singer who stayed behind produce a counterpoint: a desperate cry with which the opera comes to an end). There are also features I took over unconsciously: in the opera *Nacht* the singers outside the hall sing in conclusion a repeated D', the instruments an E♭'—that those very same pitches occur in Pressl's piece struck me after all these years just a few days ago.

It is by no means merely impeccably executed compositions that provide one with important ideas. In some of my compositions, the bass tone of an overtone chord of pure intonation is clouded over by a dense microtonal cluster. That sound owes its inspiration to discussing a composition by a pupil of mine in Graz in the 1990s. The piece itself was so poor that I had to give it the lowest mark.

The Salzburg Mozarteum used to house an Institute of Ecmelic Music (the term referred primarily to twelve-tone microtonality). In the 1980s and early 1990s, the Institute organized symposia on subjects to do with microtonality. I attended them on a regular basis. The symposia were rather bizarre events with absurd and silly compositions and concepts. They attempted to justify their existence solely by the fact that they used tones beyond tempered tuning. The Institute was headed by a composer who only addressed himself to microtonality shortly before his appointment to be Professor of "Basic Musical Research." A colleague of his, likewise an Austrian professor, was a pianist (he earned his living as an accompanist). He concentrated his efforts on working out chord charts which he was kind enough to place at the disposal of interested composers (thank God no one availed himself of his offer . . .).

However, it was at those symposia that I learned most of what I know about microtonality. I was taught what to avoid and invested a great deal of my time in pondering how to make sense out of the nonsense to which I had been subjected.

I repeat: it was not one encounter with one piece of music which transformed my musical idiom but many encounters. The list is incomplete. If I were to write this text tomorrow, I would possibly mention other names and other encounters as well.

Summing up:

Again and again, in listening to (new) music, I wonder how it could be done otherwise. Again and again, my attention would turn from the piece just heard to apply the conclusions I drew from it to the music I am currently working on.

Drawing on what you have heard in your own creative process and reflecting on solutions found by other composers are, to my mind, an integral part of a composer's craft.

II.

I rarely absorb in my music sounds and sound processes that I hear in the outside world.

However, the fascination exercised on me by the overtone chord is undoubtedly rooted in its technological origin: I grew up in the vicinity of a power plant. The transformer station—an eerie place with innumerable cables and insulators—emits a constant overtone chord. Memories from my early childhood of electric machines which produced similar sounds may also play a role.

Two examples of my own music occur to me on the spur of the moment, with the conscious use of sounds of the environment: *Fragment* for twenty-nine speaking voices (1978) and String Quartet No. 2 (1998). In both pieces, I incorporated the sound of a refrigerator.

I believe, however, that ideas regarding form are influenced by sound experiences (and time experiences). I assume that the turning up and fading out of sounds take their cue from how the sounds of planes (or of bees) change as they fly by—possibly also of cars that pass by. Different sound sources may also be involved, such as the breathing noises of two or more persons.

I think it does not make much sense to record with pencil in hand (or with a microphone) a protocol of such movements. I listen within myself and seek the right time. Where this "right time" has its origin, is of marginal interest.

Speech rhythm is also important—the rhythm of German with Austrian accent which I speak. My melodic structures are largely derived from that speech rhythm. I do not mean any concrete spoken text which will then be transferred to music (as Janáček would do). I experimented with that just once, in one of the *Fantasies* for clarinet and viola (1982). I failed. Since then, I have composed "abstract" speech melodies with an expression of (for me) clear outlines. As if one would hear someone speak on the other side of a wall: one recognizes the melody but understands no word.

III.

It does not take long to reply to this question: I do whatever I feel to be right.

I do not worry about returning to the material of older pieces. For nearly two decades, I composed basically with only two chords. And I have not yet exhausted all the possibilities inherent in the relationship between them.

I am convinced: if I really do what I want to do, I will never repeat myself. For it is highly unlikely that I want exactly the same today as I did three months ago (not only in music . . .).

2010

Twenty-Four

HANS WERNER HENZE (1926–2012)

Henze is one of the major opera composers of the twentieth century. His Boulevard Solitude *(1950–74),* König Hirsch *(1953–56),* Elegy for Young Lovers *(1959–87),* The Young Lord *(1964),* The English Cat *(1980–90),* L'Upupa *(2000–2003), and others regularly feature on the programs of German (and sometimes also of Austrian) opera houses. I realize that to express an opinion on Hans Werner Henze based solely on my few personal encounters with him, which go back decades, would be grossly unjust. The same goes for his music: I do not know enough of it for me to form a considered judgment. All I can do is to record my disappointment at his decision not to elaborate on the replies he sent me in 1983.*

I.

I have not had a similar experience but music by other composers does often influence mine: Machaut and Bach, Monteverdi and Verdi, C. M. von Weber and Alban Berg. This is a continuous dialogue conducted over centuries and that is also what nourishes my musical thinking, that is what my music is born from, and that is to which it owes its characteristic features.

II.

Birdsong, the variety of noises, the wind in nooks of houses and in the foliage of trees, vibrations of the human voice which can be magical but also unbearable, the sound of instruments—I need all that for composing, they are part of my consciousness. The noise of machines, the swears and lies of those in power, the screams of the sufferers, the tortured, the oppressed have induced me to render my music expressive and easy to understand; to resist horror through strict form.

III.

Self-repetition occurs when the artist takes himself too seriously and ritualizes whatever he may have achieved; when he forgets about modesty, his curiosity ebbs away and he becomes useless.

1983

Twenty-Five

KLAUS HUBER (1924)

We met in Paris in 1983 rather by chance, an opportunity I seized so as to add our interview to the three-questions book. I forget whether I subsequently sent Klaus Huber the German transcript, but in the 1990s, when I thought it would be interesting to confront composers with their views expressed in the early 1980s, I did post him the text. Sadly, Professor Huber dragged his feet. We would meet twice a year: in April at the Witten Festival of New Chamber Music and in October at the Donaueschingen Festival. I had to realize eventually that while there was a will, there was apparently no way. I was ready to give up when the German publisher MusikTexte commissioned the Swiss musicologist Max Nyffeler, a former pupil of Huber, to put together a volume of his writings and interviews.

Max Nyffeler succeeded in persuading the composer to revise the text which duly appeared in the book Umgepflügte Zeit. Schriften und Gespräche[30] *in 1999. Below, you will find my translation of the conversation as published in that volume. The editor devised a title for the text: "Coming to Terms with Man's Isolation."*

I would like to add that no interview has ever shattered me to the extent this one did, with Professor Huber recalling the scream uttered by his wife as she committed suicide by jumping out of the window. His apparent matter-of-factness in recounting it only added to the devastating effect. I was also shocked by his experiences as a soldier in the Swiss army, infected as it was by Nazi ideology. As a Hungarian, I was moved by his association with Stefi Geyer (1888–1956), the object of Bartók's unrequited love and dedicatee of the first violin concerto of 1907/8. Also, by the fact that Professor Huber attended the world premiere of the Sonata for Two Pianos And Percussion *in Basel, on January 16, 1938—he must be one of the last surviving listeners of that historic concert.*

I.

I could not single out a composer whose concept would have evoked such a fundamental change in my thinking. I hope it is a permanent process. It is not a question of experiencing a big shock once in your life and from then on composing differently, thereby being spared of any further shocks.

It was rather late in life that I became acquainted with avant-garde music in any depth. It was late for my age because Zurich, where I was studying,

30. Max Nyffeler, ed., *Umgepflügte Zeit: Schriften und Gespräche* [Replowed time: writings and conversations] (Cologne: MusikTexte, 1999).

was rather provincial at that time. I was, you see, a school teacher until my twenty-second year. It was then that I decided to study music, for all the doubts I may have had in my mind. To begin with, I took violin lessons from Stefi Geyer for two or three years. The musicality of this woman, the way she approached music, were a revelation to me. At the same time, I was also studying with my godfather, the composer Willy Burkhard. That was also an important experience even though I would not say it was a sudden revelation: I had known his music ever since I was a young boy.

Let us go further back. At the age of fourteen, I attended the world premiere in Basel of Bartók's Sonata for two pianos and percussion, with the composer and his wife at the piano. I am very grateful to my father for taking me with him because I am sure I would never have gone of my own incentive. That concert was a wonderful experience of my childhood but one which I did not of course digest in any conscious manner. I could imagine that it may have triggered my love for Bartók and may have strengthened my wish to approach music in no narrow, dogmatic way.

Another shock of those years—I was still a boy—was a performance in Basel of Alban Berg's Violin Concerto [played] by Adolf Busch. Also, Willy Burkhard's great oratorio *Das Gesicht Jesajas*, premiered by Paul Sacher.

Those were perhaps the three things that emotionally strengthened my resolve, although I had been used to writing music as a relatively small child.

Of decisive significance proved the concert organized by the ISCM [International Society for Contemporary Music] in Zurich in 1955 to mark the tenth anniversary of Webern's death. Willi Reich was there, also Erich Schmid, a Swiss conductor and a pupil of Schoenberg. That was when I first heard any music by Webern. It may have led to a breakthrough similar to Lutosławski's encounter with Cage, for it awakened me to the fact that it was possible to compose differently from the way my teacher had taught me.

I was writing for a time rather introverted and intimate pieces and attempted to find somehow a personal idiom between Bartók and Webern. I developed highly marginal possibilities of serial music without having any idea of relevant efforts in the early 1950s. Boulez has said that the uninformed composer is like a cuckoo: he lays his eggs in alien nests. Perhaps I could not quite steer clear of that danger. Still, in actual fact, I never laid my eggs in foreign nests: the chamber cantata *Des Engels Anredung an die Seele* (1957, to words by Georg Albini) for tenor and small ensemble (flute, clarinet, horn, harp) was rather different—I would once again say marginal.

It was decisive for me to have a vocal point of departure, something which could not at that time be taken for granted. I turned toward mystical texts of the late Baroque (Albini lived between 1659 and 1714), also in *Auf die ruhige Nachtzeit* (1958), another chamber cantata for soprano, flute, and string trio (to words by Katharina Regina von Greiffenberg, 1633–94).

Then followed an attempt to free myself, in an oratorio to words by Augustine which kept me busy from 1958 until around 1964. It was one of those pieces which failed to adhere to the prevalent music aesthetic of those years. It continues to be played once in a while and I think you can still gain by listening to it today.

The first serial score which made a strong impact on me was Stockhausen's *Kontra-Punkte;* studying it thoroughly opened up new aspects. In the 1950s, soon after the "collision" with Webern's oeuvre which I then gradually absorbed, I became acquainted with the latest compositions in Donaueschingen: *Livre pour quatuor* by Pierre Boulez, a wind quintet by Henri Pousseur, and I remember in particular (I have to own up to it now) John Cage's *34'46.776"* for two prepared pianos which he premiered himself, together with David Tudor, in Donaueschingen in 1954. The futuristic intention, the will to free himself completely from a predetermined form, made a deep impression on me at that time.

I would like to tell you an anecdote at this point: the exact duration was printed in the program, as if it was part of the title: thirty-four minutes and a few seconds and tenths of seconds. Some of my Swiss friends started their stopwatches, ready to believe in the metaphysical miracle of the composer's sense of time, for when the piece ended, they had exactly the same duration on their watches. What they apparently did not realize: Cage and Tudor also had their stopwatches.

There was a dedicated musician and writer on music, Walter Fabian, who invited Cage to Zurich. Evidently, the Tonhalle in the city center was not free, so they rented a hall in a suburb, at Helvetia Square, where Cage and Tudor repeated the concert. It was followed by a discussion, and the middle-class audience which contributed typically bourgeois arguments to the polemic, intimidated me. One also drank beer and there was a gentleman who thumped on the table and said he wanted to hear David Tudor play Mozart's *Sonata facile*—if Tudor refused, he would not believe that Tudor could play the piano at all. It was an unusually cheap polemic, people sitting in the front were smiling. I realized, not as a Zurich resident but one coming from Bern, how very provincial we were.

Cage encouraged my idea that there was also a speculative aspect to music and he influenced my thinking about musical time. Soon afterward, I started to work with chance in my own way, with dice and the like—although you cannot find any traces of it in the actual music. I still have recourse to that practice once in a while: to achieve an open distribution of means, I set in train, for instance, a chance process with the help of Markov chains.

With regard to Pousseur, I conducted a debate in letters with the Zurich music critic Fritz Muggler who was a great admirer of the Belgian composer. I defended the *Livre pour quatuor* against Pousseur's wind quintet which I found at the time too Webernesque. I may have been wrong but it did seem to me that Boulez had succeeded in opening up new aspects of music. I found his composition more innovative and also more musical with regard to his treatment of the instruments; for me, the form was extraordinarily inspiring.

Those were very strong impressions of the time. I cannot report on everything that dated from later years but I would like to mention Bernd Alois Zimmermann whom I sadly did not get to know well, but whose work confirmed my own endeavors in a particular way. His music is anything but "musique pure." He wrote extraordinarily complex scores equal to the pluralist spirit of the time, the pluralism in our culture. He is perhaps the composer to whom I feel closest although I also responded very strongly to Ives—the Symphony No. 4 and other works—in the early 1970s.

In Freiburg, we devoted two terms to studying the oeuvre of Charles Ives. Some of my pupils, such as Wolfgang Rihm or Ulrich Gasser, instrumented Lieder of his and we put on a big, composed Ives concert under the title "Calcium Light Night" (borrowing it from one of his pieces for chamber orchestra).

Back to Zimmermann: of course his opera *Die Soldaten* but also *Antiphonen* for viola and ensemble and other pieces as well, such as *Présence,* the "ballet blanc" for piano trio which I still regard as a work of genius, with all its quotations—Zimmermann confronted me with the problem of multilayered music, also from a stylistic point of view.

In 1970/71, I wrote a piece for violin and a small orchestra of thirty-six musicians: *Tempora.* There, I addressed myself to the problem of quotation, in that I used quotations of quotations. One takes a rhythm, a conventional rhythm which turns out to have also been used by Mozart in his G-Minor Symphony. If you extract it, it is but a conventional rhythm. I have used two of such Mozartian rhythms and a West Swiss conductor refused to premiere the work because he was of the opinion that I had messed up Mozart.

That is also how I came to terms with Ives. The idea of "musique pure" became for me, thanks to the revelations of Cage, Ives, and Zimmermann, totally absurd.

II.

I commented on that a little bit when I told you of my concept of space and time which evolved in me ever stronger, perhaps in different pieces in a different manner. In the provinces, in Zurich, I lived in a rather quiet environment. Still, around 1968, when I was teaching in Basel and was informed of the unrest in Zurich by one of my pupils who was directly affected, Max Nyffeler, but also through personal experience, the idea of pure art which keeps its distance from the real world as far as its content is concerned and aims at achieving an aesthetically perfect artifact, appeared to me increasingly irrelevant.

In a range of compositions I worked with concrete alien materials, in an associative manner: the rattling of chains, marching troops, like in the repression-music of the oratorio *Erniedrigt—Geknechtet—Verlassen—Verachtet* . . . , memories of Nazi songs . . . I quoted fragments of a marching song which I myself had had to sing in the Swiss army in 1945, that is, after the war, in the recruit school: "Bis an den Feind schleich ich mich ran und zünde meine Handgranate an." (I creep right up to the enemy and ignite my hand grenade.) I used to protest against that singing business and had to suffer reprisals as a result. Oddly enough, we had a fascist aftermath in the army; in the recruit school I had many relevant experiences.

Let us now look at the question from a different angle. White noise is supposed to be perfection itself. For me, however, the pink or light-blue noise of the woods is far more perfect than the electronic reproduction of all the pitches, like electronic white noise. That is perhaps also the reason why I am to a certain extent averse to electronically generated music. For me, the sounding environment is enormously important, especially noises. The resonances of what is happening are essential for the communicative and signal-like character of my music.

And then, there are sounds as expressions of human life which for me are almost of obsessive significance—such as screams. I do not mean the primeval scream in the psychoanalytical sense of the word, but the human scream—when many people are screaming or just one. The scream of birth, the scream of death. It is something that is pursuing me all the time so that I am forced again and again to compose it. Also, falling, falling down, shattering.

There are private experiences behind it: the suicide of my first wife who sprang out of the window. At the time I thought I would never be able to work again, I was devastated. It may well have transformed my musical thinking completely. After it happened, all music appeared to me to be false and far removed from the reality, the cruelty of life. Far removed from art as artifact, as something artificial which had nothing to do with the hardship of life. I felt I had to start completely anew.

From then on, I have looked differently at the premises of life, different values have assumed significance. Even today, I can easily forget that I am a composer. I am not preoccupied with the fact that I am a composer, I create music and music is the world. Rather, I am conscious of the fact that I, as a human being, am here for a humane purpose, one which ought to be central to my existence, and that I could at some future point in time stop composing and teaching and something else might take precedence.

That has also changed my attitude to religion. Earlier, my religiosity tended to be conservative, perhaps with a touch of mysticism. In fact, I do find that there is a difference between deep mysticism like that of Juan de la Cruz and the devoutness of the Church. Mystics have been more often than not heretics who were in conflict with the Church and exerted a revolutionizing influence. Just think of nature mystics such as Francis of Assisi or Ernesto Cardenal of Nicaragua today whose poems I admire and who has become one of Latin America's most combative poets.

However, I withdrew at the time into the inwardness of religion which was destroyed through that experience in the autumn of 1958, so that today, I could no longer claim to be able to say what is faith or religion.

I could add that any art which concentrates exclusively on man, where the individual is supposed to be the navel of the world, appears to me to be highly questionable. It is against this background that you have to view my love of the Far East and certain ideas of Zen, primarily of Japanese Zen Buddhism. I see a link there with the depth of particular European mystics. For me, it helps to come to terms with the isolation of man within [the] cosmos—something I attempt to highlight through the means of music. These problems cannot of course be solved directly with the help of music. Escape has no real chance, for man remains a prisoner of himself.

III.

I believe the music market forces a sort of self-stylization upon composers, whether or not they are aware of it. Those who can be instantly identified through their scores as well as the sounding result of their scores appear to have more public success. They become something of a brand product which sells better.

That may be polemical but I do believe you have to make this point once. I believe many composers have possibly become inured to pressure from outside so that they no longer realize to what extent they are reacting to commercial pressure while writing. However, that is surely not the only cause of self-stylization. Another one appears to me to be that a composer needs to have faith in himself and he can achieve this the more he has staked off his domain. A personal style helps to acquire more security.

Let me illustrate this with an image. However small the domain may be that a composer can call his own—if he is capable of fortifying it sufficiently, intellectually and argumentatively, while defining all other music in a lucid manner, in relation to his domain, only letting any other music in, so to speak, as long as it reinforces his terrain, then he can construct an aesthetic and stylistic fortress which he is in a position to defend. On the other hand, composers who are open and do not fear to question their own style, are obviously far less secure.

Well, those were some general observations. As far as I am concerned, I find it essential for a composer not to be afraid of insecurity. He ought not to build a fortress in defense of his terrain but should repeatedly subject his style to a critical scrutiny. After all, he is part of the social and political processes of our age and he must react to them. The processes of our time put a question mark over so much, that no music, even "great" music, may ignore it. Premises can shift completely within a period of five years.

I have never asked myself how I could arrive at self-stylization or at a personal style—rather the opposite. When I began to compose, I developed a certain intimate, introverted, perhaps even very straightforward style. Some commentaries expressed the opinion that I had a sort of clarified style one only achieves with age and things like that. In a broadcast, Hansjörg Pauli expressed the view that I might not live much longer.

My development has perhaps taken me in the opposite direction from other composers, that is, I have broken out of a relatively narrow style and extended my terrain more and more. I have exposed myself to insecurity and have repeatedly attempted to revoke the finality of what I had completed.

There is another aspect as well: the pressure to produce new works. If you want to live from composing, you are always fighting against deadlines and may well get bogged down in certain repetitive compositional processes. One has hardly any time to leave a particular compositional or methodological solution behind. Having delivered a new piece, one has to address oneself right away to the next commission.

Some composers from the Far East have taught me how to cope with that problem. I am thinking in particular of Yori-Aki Matsudaira, the son of Yoritsune Matsudaira. We met in Stockholm in 1966, when I heard a little piece of his which impressed me a great deal. I asked him what else he had composed and he said he had only written four pieces. He gave me their titles and instrumentations and did not seem in the least embarrassed by his low output, however unusual it may be nowadays. Among the great composers whom I knew well, only Dallapiccola, Lutosławski, and Luigi Nono managed to protect their independence from market forces. I would also add György Kurtág. I hope he will also succeed in keeping clear of the treadmill.

1983/99

Twenty-Six

ZOLTÁN JENEY (1943)

When he cofounded the Budapest New Music Studio at the age of twenty-seven (for more details on the studio, please see László Sáry, chapter fifty), Zoltán Jeney was something of a rebel. He rebelled against officialdom, the all-pervasive ideology of the party and the kind of music he was expected to compose. He had been allowed to breathe some fresh air in Rome where he studied with Goffredo Petrassi in 1967/68. Today, he is an establishment figure: head of the Department of Composition at the Budapest Music University and winner of several major prizes awarded by the Hungarian government for artistic merit.

Of the former composers of the New Music Studio, he is perhaps the most cerebral in his approach to composition. It follows that his works are rather abstract in character, with processes carried through to their logical ending before another process is allowed to get under way. This fundamental feature does not wholly apply to Jeney's chef d'oeuvre, much admired in Hungary: Halotti szertartás *(Funeral Rites), a large-scale oratorio composed between 1987 and 2005, a setting of Latin, Hebrew, Greek, and Old Slavic texts as well as twentieth-century Hungarian and Italian poetry. The world premiere on October 22, 2005, under Zoltán Kocsis was a major triumph.*

I.

> *Dieses Buch wird vielleicht nur der verstehen, der die Gedanken, die darin ausgedrückt sind—oder doch ähnliche Gedanken—schon selbst einmal gedacht hat.*
>
> [This book will perhaps be understood only by those who have had the same—or similar—ideas in the past.]
>
> —Ludwig Wittgenstein, *Tractatus logico-philosophicus,*

I think Wittgenstein's statement is true beyond his own book also on a more general level. For instance, it is valid for interpreting and understanding musical phenomena as well. To my mind, it provides the only way for us to understand Lutosławski's case: his encounter with Cage's piano concerto made him conscious of a change in a certain direction that was already taking place in his mind.

My own inverse case also bears out Wittgenstein, perhaps even more unequivocally. In 1964, at the Warsaw Autumn Festival, I saw Merce Cunningham's ballet to music by John Cage. The choreography appealed to me just as little as did the music. In fact, the latter irritated me no end. Since I did not like the production, I wasted no more thought on it, I more or less forgot all about it. I banished it from my consciousness, so to speak. Years later, in 1971, it emerged all of a sudden once again and to my surprise I found that my memory of it was wholly positive: I remembered the ballet as fascinating and the music (apart from the fooling around of musicians working with Cage) incredibly exciting and inspirational. This reevaluation of my memory happened without my hearing any other work by Cage in the meantime or seeing Cunningham's ballet again. It was that new experience that motivated me to subject Cage's oeuvre to a thorough study.

Apart from that, I cannot remember any revelation which would have radically changed my thinking as a composer. I can of course report on musical experiences without which no composer (no musician) can embark on a career (and which in retrospect may appear to have been signposts marking a direction one takes or serve as [an] explanation for particular choices); also on composers whose oeuvre engaged my attention for a longer period or to which I used to attach more importance at a given time, but I am by no means sure that they exerted more influence on me in every case than other factors which remained hidden.

Also, the factors which affect musical thinking are not exclusively positive or even of a musical nature, just as compositional (musical) activity cannot be separated from other manifestations of a personality. As a result, in order to be able to report on the influences that have formed one it is not sufficient to know oneself well—as far as humanly possible—but one ought to have a dual ego one of which could at any given moment in one's life keep tabs on what is taking place in the other.

Given our biological makeup, this is clearly impossible. Even Schoenberg who to my knowledge went furthest in self-observation as a composer and in 1931 made a detailed list, almost like an inventory, of those who had influenced him and in what way, wrote in 1950: "My technique and style have not been developed by a conscious procedure" and "I have not had a chance to observe the development of my personality." Nevertheless I believe that these diverging statements do not contradict one another, rather, they are complementary: in our final perplexity regarding creation, our best guides are all the same the real and imagined influences and kinships as seen and stated by the composers, provided we are aware that we have mostly to do with hints rather than with connections which could strictly be interpreted as causes and effects.

As far as I am concerned, in my childhood I admired Verdi. Then, around the age of eleven, when I started to compose, my paragons were Beethoven, Chopin, and Liszt. At fourteen, the beginning of my compositional studies proper, the encounter with Liszt's late works and Bartók's *Mikrokosmos* pointed me to the way where continuity (continuous change) appears to have been more characteristic than abrupt change. Needless to say, I came under a great many influences—something I did not resist, for I became conscious of the fact that I would not regard art as a field of intentional originality. The decisive question regarding a composition remains one and the same whether it shows traces of "outside influence" or seems to be "wholly original": whether its (heterogeneous or homogeneous) elements between them are capable of rising to the level of a new order.

My thinking as a composer was formed after Bartók (but never against him) by Schoenberg and later by Webern. In the mid-1960s I welcomed the music and the theoretical writings of Boulez in the belief that they could contribute to the integration of the diverging currents of contemporary music—something I regarded as particularly important at the time. However, when I set out to draw the consequences of that thinking for my own work, I had to realize that Boulez's methodology was valid almost exclusively for his own compositions, either because the idea of a "unified world language of music" was for the time being an illusion, or because the method itself was not suitable for bringing about integration. (Today—following the failure of integrational methods devised with varying scopes and validity—I am of the opinion that it is mainly because of the first reason that no single endeavor can achieve the desired result, however coherent the method may appear to be.) That recognition—while it did not question the significance of Boulez as a composer—also meant that I succeeded in ridding myself of the inner compulsion which I suppose never became a conscious goal and which against my will would have wished to circumscribe the tradition which would have had to be regarded as exclusively valid.

Then, around 1970–72, I felt that I had to rethink the basic musical notions for myself and to help me, I would need to concern myself with musical tradition in the widest sense of the word—that is, those aspects of it to which I had access and which I could absorb. From then on, depending on the aspect which happened to be uppermost on my mind—I could make several lists, existing side by side, of composers and compositions which were of the greatest significance for me. Instead of actually making those lists which would be bound to be fortuitous anyway, I would like to single out two factors which I am convinced have continuously influenced my musical thinking and my work as a composer even though I would not be able to assess the extent and the content of that influence: one is my work in the Budapest New Music Studio which I cofounded in 1970, the other is the range of lessons that I drew for myself from Albert Simon's[31] unique musical analyses.

"On revient toujours"—as Schoenberg put it. The only composer in my childhood whose work I knew thoroughly, even though in a single genre, was Mozart and his piano sonatas. The fact that I nevertheless did not take my cue from him in my first attempts at writing music was due—I think today—to my immaturity. For quite some time now, it would make me infinitely happy if I could truthfully claim that he is influencing my work, however modestly—if the admiration I feel for his music would somehow be identifiable in my own compositions.

II.

I am interested in all existing sounds, those that I know and those I have not yet come across; just as I am interested in any kind of research into making sounds that have not existed in the past. (What I have in mind primarily are sounds produced by computers, through additive synthesis [as yet mainly in theory]: sounds of any overtone structure can be produced and transformed into one another.) I regard it as particularly important that all sounds at our disposal should be acceptable and usable in music. I have therefore quite consciously developed my readiness to be open to such sounds.

However, this theory—while it undoubtedly determines the range and directions of my compositional activity—rarely appears in the actual works in a direct and tangible manner. This is because the process of composition cannot but be an activity which filters, selects, and organizes the material (= the domain of sound phenomena covered by the work in progress) from a particular aspect. This activity is influenced and sometimes even determined by subconscious and other processes and forces beyond our control, each time in a different proportion and in a way which defies analysis.

31. Albert Simon (1926–2000) was a Hungarian conductor. A legendary figure, he was admired not so much for his concerts but for his rehearsals, which set a high standard of musical integrity. He insisted on a faithful adherence to the score and a level of performance that more or less proved unattainable for his orchestra made up of students of the Budapest Academy of Music.

III.

> *Evitate il mestiere! Fate che tutto sia un principio, come se non vi fosse mai stato un principio!*
>
> [Avoid craftsmanship! Make sure that everything should be a beginning, as if there had never been a beginning!]
>
> —Ferruccio Busoni

He who wrote the above in 1911 was probably one of the most cultivated musicians of all time. He never denied the significance of knowledge—on the contrary!—but as a result he was also aware (as was Schoenberg) that creative activity in the strict sense of the word was unimaginable without inspiration because in the latter's absence, even the highest degree of *métier* only sufficed to produce stereotypes (cf. *opera seria* in the second half of the eighteenth century). The presence of inspiration, on the other hand, ensured that even literal repetition would not be tantamount to "self-repetition." Bach, for instance, could not be accused of it even when he lifted movements from existing works and placed them in a new one. However, inspiration only works in the presence of knowledge. I would even go so far as to claim that the larger the knowledge about craft and about its material, the greater the degree of inspiration *could* be (if it can be measured at all). Because inspiration is, as it were, knowledge without knowledge—in any case, subconscious knowledge. If it were conscious, it would not be what it is. This fact reminds one yet again of the existing but not definable border beyond which the essence of artistic activity can only be divined.

The question itself can only be posed against the background of the contemporary concept of art, willy-nilly mirroring its confusion. In the absence of unequivocal points of reference, "personal style" and "originality" have been promoted to become the highest criteria, even though these are even in the primary meaning of those words only accessories of great works. In addition, originality today is only recognized if it appears as a "personal" flourish of a material which is already known in some way and is in general use, without drawing any particular lesson from it. (Genuinely original composers, such as Varèse or Satie, had no success.) It is however not the artist's job to be constantly examining the differences of his work from others or to be intentionally different from them, but to make sure he knows his material thoroughly and to fulfill the function so precisely formulated by Klee: "The artist is the trunk of the tree. . . . In his role as tree-trunk he does nothing else but collect and transmit what he has sucked from the depths. He does not serve, nor does he reign; he transmits—that's all." (So steht er an der Stelle des Stammes. . . . Und er tut an der ihm zugewiesenen Stelle beim Stamme doch gar nichts anderes, als aus der Tiefe Kommendes zu sammeln und weiterzuleiten. Weder dienen noch herrschen, nur vermitteln.)

1985

Twenty-Seven

MAURICIO KAGEL (1931–2008)

"Kagel was not the sort of person one would have expected to die"—a nonsensical remark, perhaps, but those who met the composer, however briefly, would no doubt see what the anonymous author may have meant.

In his music, Mauricio Kagel poked fun at accepted notions and figures of music history. The very title of Mirum *for tuba has a tongue-in-cheek quality, as does* Variationen ohne Fuge *for large orchestra, especially the full title, which goes like this:* Variationen ohne Fuge über die "Variationen und Fuge," über ein Thema von Händel für Klavier op. 24 von Johannes Brahms (1861–62). *In English:* Variations without Fugue on the "Variations and Fugue" on a Theme by Handel for Piano, Op. 24, by Johannes Brahms (1861–62). *The piece has Brahms and Handel make a personal appearance in period costume. I am particularly fond of the title* "Unguis incarnatus est," *which has a devoutly liturgical and irrevocably final air about it—when in fact all it means is "ingrown toe nails." (Composed in 1972, it is "for piano and . . .") In his* La trahison orale *(1981/83), he even went as far as to invoke the Devil. Why did he succumb to Death?*

Kagel was someone who seemed entirely sure of himself, as if he had never been plagued by self-doubt, as if he had been perfectly conscious of his place in music history. While most of his colleagues usually display pleasure on receiving a favorable comment on a composition, Kagel would simply agree with you and say "Yes, it is one of my best works." I remember expressing genuine admiration for his Die Stücke der Windrose *(1988/93) for salon orchestra, an extract from which he conducted in Vienna's Wiener Konzerthaus. He nodded, the serious expression on his face unchanging, and concurred. So he should have, I suppose: why pretend to be grateful for recognition when he knew it was his due?*

An addict to sincerity, I decided not to shake his hand following the Austrian premiere of his Sankt-Bach-Passion *(1981/85)—I would have found his self-assurance jarring.*

I.

Reading books on music has always been more of an immediate inspiration to compose than listening itself. I can still remember an episode that happened back in Argentina:

I was probably around sixteen years old. The summer vacation was over and I resumed my attempts at composing. I had to realize, however, that the weeks spent in nature had not been conducive to an intellectual activity like composition. I could not concentrate; all I had in my head were crystal-clear images of high mountains and the dark blue water of a lake. If I closed my eyes, the Andes appeared as an album of picture post-cards, multiplying freely to form collages.

There was nothing for it but to put work aside and start on a book on Monteverdi. I was particularly fascinated by the chapter treating of the transition of madrigal to opera. I became so excited by the process whereby absolute music was adapted to the concrete reality of the stage—in other words, the triumph of the urge of sensual visualization which is so characteristic of the subject of madrigals—that soon enough I had to stop reading and return to composition.

That was probably the first time that I was confronted with the development of a musical genre, which rid me of the passive form of reception. In any case, it was then that I began to understand that the best tradition of our musical past is always modern—and in no way sacrosanct. "Stile antico" only existed if it was already a thing of the past at the time of its emergence and was of mediocre quality. Monteverdi, on the other hand, is contemporary music to this day; it was in his honor that I composed, in 1965, *Musik für Renaissance-Instrumente* (Music for Renaissance Instruments).

The fact that music had existed before I myself started to compose has always been a bonus for my own work. It has not so much to do with an acoustic tradition. Rather, it is linked to the tradition of composing which makes it possible for people to put together sounds and noises. For me as a young man, it was precisely the existence of music written by *others* that justified my wish to become a composer. I have noticed time and time again that the reading of composers' biographies as well as musicological studies have inspired my creativity.

I wrote one of my first independent works in the early 1950s, immediately upon reading a description of Vinteuil's Violin Sonata in Proust's *A la recherche du temps perdu*. It fascinated me to invent music "from hearsay," partly because the creative fantasy could always fall back upon the book that had given rise to it. On the other hand, the invention could unfold without any restriction. It was quite a shock for me to realize that contact with extramusical phenomena, in this case literature, enabled me to develop my own musical idiom. The motif in the case of Vinteuil's *blanche sonate* was actually not music itself but the suggestion of the *petite phrase*—it was all about composing a melody which, corresponding to its varied descriptions, could also work inductively.

I did not know at the time that Proust had modeled Vinteuil's piece on César Franck's Sonata for violin and piano. Of course, specialists are still at loggerheads over this point. An alternative possibility could have been that—just as with the other key musical work of the novel, the *Septet*—a range of models were absorbed into one. No wonder that the notion of *souvenirs involontaires* played such a basic role in the conception of Proust's *moments musicaux.*

Incidentally, in *La Trahison Orale* (The Oral Treason, 1981/83), my musical epos on the devil, I reused my youthful piece for violin and piano. Thirty years on, this section bears the number 27.

It happens, too, that in writing about music by other composers, I sense a heightened need to write music myself. Perhaps this is the sincerest form of objectivity rooted in subjectivity. In any case, this definition could be true of many events and analyses that occur in the world of music. The purported validity of an analysis could be in the eyes of a composer of transitory nature, since the aptness of the result can change if the aesthetic position of the composer takes another direction. The fact that the past is a ceaseless supplier of arguments for the present also means—if one interprets the principle of reciprocity with poetic license—that the present constantly anticipates the future.

Do you have any other pieces which owe their existence to literary works?

Tremens (1973), for instance, which I wrote after a stay at a university clinic where I took drugs under medical control. This happened in 1961, after I had read the classical opium literature of the nineteenth and early twentieth centuries: Thomas de Quincey, Baudelaire, Cocteau, Huxley. I met Henri Michaux in the early 1960s and was gripped by his books and his exploration of the center of the *ego.* I found our conversations extraordinary, for he strove for a perfect symbiosis of art and life and had by then attained the existence of a guru, living as he did the secluded life of a hermit. He was a guru of the only genuine sort, one who no longer needed proselytizers. Nothing commercial, no sect, no clothes of a special kind, no propagation of a Message, no industrial reproduction of benevolence, bliss, or transcendental spirit. Simply to be there and subject oneself to a study which was as precise as possible without being a burden to others. I could no doubt write an essay on my visits to Michaux. He was living in Paris in hermetic isolation and one really had the impression that one was conversing with his voice while his body was absent. It was the triumph of sensitivity over bodily frailty. Originally, I had meant to work on *Tremens* together with Michaux but a classical cooperation—in the sense of an *aller et retour* of ideas and materials—was not possible for a number of reasons. I decided therefore to use the protocol of my stay at the clinic as a literary basis. In fact, I forced myself to repeat what Michaux himself had done in his own research with mescaline and LSD.

Has the music of other composers inspired you in any way?

Not so much the music as the attitude and the biography of other composers have been essential. For instance, the fact that good composers have usually been stubborn and most of them still are. Composing means looking into yourself all the time—something which requires perseverance and hard work. The example of other composers gives me strength and the renewed wish to go on being stubborn, to continue my adventures.

A certain stubbornness is necessary for the composer to withstand all the dangers that lurk on him. I hardly ever accept a commission with a deadline in the following season—I want to have at least three years at my disposal. Although I work nonstop, I refuse to let myself be destroyed by the need to rush. Also, I only write pieces which deeply interest me. Those two simple measures have helped to develop a strategy to keep me fresh. In my profession, being continuously interested is of elementary significance and must therefore be part of an attitude.

II.

I am not inspired by the sounds of the environment in a strictly musical sense. If the noise level becomes too high, I do react with my adrenalin. The only thing I need and listen to is stillness. As a composer, I respond to every acoustic phenomenon with heightened sensitivity. Silence thus becomes just as audible as its opposite and helps me to invent music. Gadgets in the environment have not modified the way I compose but have decidedly expanded the number of sound sources at my disposal. Pieces like *Acustica*, *Der Schall* (The Sound), *Tactil*, *Privat*, *Zwei-Mann-Orchester* (Two-Men-Orchestra), or *Unter Strom* (Under Current) are products of a fruitful exploration of the acoustic habitat which surrounds us all. It may well be a piece of private utopia but I do believe that these compositions have exerted quite an important influence on the relevant scenes of new music. In music therapy, in the production and development of instruments for children of preschool age, in music education, the impulses coming from my ideas have reached ever wider circles. This gives me pleasure, for the new-music ghetto is indeed a little cut off from real life—it would otherwise be imprisoned in an ivory tower.

III.

These are two difficult and complex questions. Self-repetition begins, perhaps, where one is no longer consciously aware of it. One writes and writes, it is all going swimmingly, without any hitches, because one can fall back upon a stock of models that one has amassed. I am, I believe, known for the variety of my compositions. Variety here is the outcome of a permanent thinking process: you take steps in a *similar* direction, but drawing on highly diverse means. It is wrong to imagine that you permanently have to enter new territory; it can even be detrimental if the new arises as a result of a strained or cramped effort. Music history is full of relevant examples. Also of those of an opposite kind where originality has remained hidden in such an inconspicuous manner that these works do not grow old.

I believe that you have to carefully differentiate between repetition, style, and trait. Mozart was a genius never mind the fact that you can immediately recognize his music or indeed that you can miss the correct Koechel number by one or two. In a way, the order in which his pieces were written within particular periods of time is exchangeable. The same is true of Bach. There are, however, composers who are also easy to recognize—which is a pity because their music becomes as a result less interesting. Our ears often make biased judgments. If some works of a particular composer did not appeal to us in the past, from then on we listen to his works with a negative "experience," we tend to reject them out of hand.

Mozart is a good example of a high degree of redundancy carried by a kind of musical idiom which actually necessitated repetition—this had a clarifying significance. He did not take long to develop the elements of his style, they were pretty soon there and then he addressed himself to varying them. There arose an apparently endless stylistic repetition, but at the same time also an incredible richness of musical forms. Redundancy, then, is the actual formal system which allows the unfolding of the material.

What I am getting at is this: in the history of musical idioms there have been styles where repetition has led to unnecessary lengths. And there have been others which through repetition have become that much more valuable. The advocates of Anton Bruckner will not hesitate to find arguments in favor of his "heavenly lengths"—arguments which should prove the necessity of that kind of rhetoric. Some will be speaking of formal symmetry, also of proportions, others will qualify the duration of the symphonies without which the climaxes could never have risen to such heights.

As you see, we are all in a position to change our preconceived ideas under the influence of aural psychology, music history, or music criticism. Listening to music is simultaneously listening to the history of music. Both have the same source: interpretation.

1983/85

Twenty-Eight

GEORG KATZER (1935)

When I visited Georg Katzer in a small town near East Berlin in 1983, neither of us realized that the German Democratic Republic (GDR)—indeed, the Hungarian People's Republic where I came from and the whole so-called socialist camp including the Soviet Union itself—had but six more years to exist. Katzer welcomed me not only because I had been sent by Hungarian Radio to do a program on contemporary music in the GDR and he was pleased that his music would be broadcast in Budapest, but also because for people in East Germany, Hungary was almost a Western country. We were allies in the Warsaw Pact, we were bound together by the ties of eternal and inseparable friendship as the official party slogan went, but the powers that be in Berlin made it difficult for East German citizens to visit the People's Republic of Hungary. For good reason: it was on Hungarian soil that families and friends from both halves of Germany could meet. Travel from the East to the Federal Republic was all but impossible.

For all the rigidity of the German communist system and the stifling atmosphere that manifested itself the moment one left the plane at Berlin's Schönefeld Airport—features that were far less present in Hungary—we also had a great deal in common. I found that I could unwind much faster with someone from the GDR than someone from the other side of the border because we shared the same destiny, we spoke each other's language. While Hungary was not divided into two halves, there was nevertheless a kind of Western Hungary: all the expatriates who had fled in the late 1940s, in the wake of the revolution in 1956 or in later years, on a visit to the West from which they did not return. For all of us, the West meant personal freedom, the freedom to express one's opinion, higher living standards, a more humane way of life.

Some East German composers were lucky enough to have a publisher in the West. Paul-Heinz Dittrich, for instance, was taken up by Universal Edition in Vienna. That meant that his scores reached the Federal Republic and they were performed for political reasons, independently of their quality (not that he was a poor composer). If, however, a composer succeeded in obtaining an exit visa to settle in the West, he had to realize pretty soon that as an ordinary citizen of the Federal Republic, his person (and his music) ceased to be of any interest. Tilo Medek comes to mind: as far as I know, he fairly soon stopped composing altogether. There were also some who continued to thrive after the fall of the Berlin Wall—such as Siegfried Matthus. His operas and orchestral works went on receiving sporadic performances and he was appointed artistic director of a small festival.

To go back to that gray autumn day at Zeuthen near Berlin: Georg Katzer extended a warm welcome to me and in addition to giving me an interview for Hungarian Radio, he also promised to send his replies to my three questions in writing. (We continued to meet at Donaueschingen annually, right up to 2007 when I retired from Universal Edition. In recent years, he has been even quieter than in the 1980s and claimed to be happy with performances of his compositions, though he had nearly stopped writing large-scale works and concentrated on chamber music.)

After a lapse of twenty-six years, Katzer read his text of 1983 again in 2009 and decided to leave it unchanged. "It is a document of the times," he wrote. So it is.

I.

I have not had a sound experience that would have led to a radical change in my musical thinking. On the other hand, it does happen quite often that in listening to music from the loudspeaker or in a concert hall I hear something entirely different from what is being played around me—either as a counterproposal or correction. The strongest ideas come to me not while listening to masterpieces: the reaction described above would be questionable or even impossible, because of the music's power of conviction. My imagination takes off on its flight if there are promising ideas in a work which fail to unfold in a cogent fashion. That is the most frequent case with living music. Perfect masterpieces are just as exceptional as essays lacking in ideas altogether. The current concert repertoire is misleading because music history is more than the few compositions which overshadow—justly or otherwise—the innumerable pieces that have fallen into oblivion. To put it briefly: I respond to masterpieces as a listener. Works that are less than impeccable awake the composer in me, while boring music leaves me cold both as a listener and as a composer.

Well then, while I have not been "enlightened" from one second to the next on hearing a piece of music, I have of course had thought-provoking experiences every now and again—encounters with works by other composers. I owe the most important stimulus to the music of Lutosławski.

My first composition, a string quartet, bears the impact of Bartók's quartets. Not much later, my *Streichermusik I* (1971), reflects the result of a different kind of thinking which can be traced back to my studies of Lutosławski's *Jeux vénitiens*. In that work, Lutosławski had succeeded in ridding himself of Bartók's influence, thanks to a different model of organization. I was fascinated by the floating meter of the music and I hoped that in applying it in my own work, I could loosen my own rhythmic and metric construction. As a consequence, I began by discarding all my various speculations regarding the organization of time and in the pieces I wrote next there cropped up traces of "limited aleatoricism."

Later, I received encouragement from Ligeti (*Aventures*) and Dieter Schnebel (*Glossolalie*), in that they showed me the path in a direction which might (perhaps) evoke the interest of a (supposedly) wider public with the help of introverted chamber music. That led to a few works in the genre of instrumental theater, for instance *Szene für Kammerensemble* after Goethe-Eckermann.

Right now I am working on a flute concerto. Its first movement is based primarily on the rhythmic impulse. Prior to that, I wrote a study (it has never been published), where I experimented with a very subjective interpretation of minimal music. Once again, I was gripped by the simple numeric relationships inherent in rhythm. Not so much the machinelike, motory pulsation but the sensory and intellectual thrill that comes from "built-in" mistakes. It induced me to study yet again some early works by Stravinsky, with the aim of becoming sensitive to pulsating and unsettled time-continuity.

Recently, I heard *Harmonica* by Lachenmann. It may well be that this experience has also stimulated me in an as yet unpredictable way and will bear fruit in the years to come.

II.

Noise-related sounds are present in my music. Some of my electronic pieces in particular are based on noise. My instrumental works of the past few years also make extensive use of it.

While I am sitting and typing away, I can hear—my typewriter; somebody is playing the piano (is that music or noise?); a car is passing by and birds are chirping outside my window; a train is rattling in the distance; a shout is heard; the refrigerator switches on; somebody is hammering; a pigeon is cooing. All that is happening simultaneously and seemingly without any system, or rather, as part of a system which is too complex for us to grasp. In recent years, I have made several attempts at organizing such sound fields in my music. For all that, I do not believe in the sheer imitation of the sounds of the environment and of their grammar—in any case, I do not regard them as an exclusive source. An aesthetic like that owes much to the mediation of other works of art which represent for the artist a highly specific and very important layer of reality. Conquering noise for music is the achievement of several generations of composers (among the ancestors, one would need to start with Ives at the latest). It has to do with the all-encompassing mechanization of the environment: we are all aware of its acoustic consequences. The emancipation of the musical material happened at the same time. Are we to regard it as pure chance? In my opinion, we have to tame this new acoustic environment with the help of the aesthetic discovery of noise. If we imitate it cheerfully, it will no longer appear menacing, it will be easier to put up with.

III.

A personal style manifests in a general form the salient features of a composer's diction. Let us think of Stravinsky: for all the fundamental changes in his way of writing, there remained certain permanent characteristics, such as pronounced rhythms, the terseness of formulation, the economy of means, the elimination of romantic expression, the unpredictability of details while the work as a whole remained transparent, the ceaseless balancing between motoric continuity and discontinuity, and so on. Such general traits should stem from the composer's way of thinking and his gestures of movement. In music, the expression of such traits always entails the transgression of some norm. Personal style is therefore deviation from the generally obligatory, in other words, a specific interpretation of the technique of composition.

Such specific features can also become a trademark; once it's there, it becomes easy for radio, television, publishers, and the music press to communicate between the work and the audience. If the composer succumbs to the dictates of his trademark, he runs the risk of quoting himself, that is, of exhausting his own music through its exploitation. That is how style becomes a mannerism. Preclassical composers were not exposed to such dangers: they did not need to look at their own work as self-realization at any cost. (Although there was no other way for masterpieces to be born. If a composer had paid his homage to God differently, it would have been regarded as sacrilege.) With the appearance of the music market, however, the laws of the market became applicable to art as well and those laws relate back to the producer of art objects. He cannot but stick to his trademark which has proved to sell well. That is why self-repetition is a very real danger for established composers. Their artistic integrity can be measured by the extent to which they can steer clear of that danger.

I have committed that crime two or three times myself. Have paid for it, too: I have always been disappointed by the outcome of rehashing an older, successful piece.

To my mind, an artist need not worry about finding his own style. I think it would be detrimental. Style is born out of the desire to express oneself and it cannot be limited to standard pawned articles. Behind a quasi-synthetic personal style produced lightly there lies no face but a mask.

Listening to my very first piece was a frightening experience: I was faced with the recognition that somebody else—namely Bartók—was speaking from my music. It made me for a long time sensitive against imitating outside influences, taking over preexisting means of expression without giving them a thought. Lutosławski I approached more analytically, focusing on the tools he had used to arrive at particular results rather than on their emotional impact. For all that, Lutosławski left a trace on my scores, no doubt as a result of my unqualified admiration for the composer of *Jeux vénitiens.* My later compositions, too, are not without the influence of encountering other music. As I said earlier, *Szene für Kammerensemble* or *De musica* would have assumed a different shape had it not been for the enlightening experience of Ligeti's *Aventures* and *Nouvelles aventures.* Not that I felt close to their style: my starting point was a different aesthetic concept. I admired them—but at a distance. To this day, that is how I approach any other music that thrills me: Ligeti's *Horn Trio* or Xenakis's string quartet *Tetras.* I can only remain faithful to my style if I conduct a dialogue with the works of others. That is my guarantee against the danger of my style stiffening into mannerism. Whether I take over something from other styles does not worry me all that much.

1983

Twenty-Nine

ERNST KRENEK (1900–1991)

At eighty-two, Krenek did not really feel like investing time into answering my questions. His reply was friendly but negative: he was too busy with composing, and, at his age, I could not expect him to take time off to contribute to my project. He returned my questionnaire and wrote in hand "sometimes" after the first question, "no" after the second, and the following short comment after the third one: "I attempt not to repeat myself in my compositions. Whether basic traits can nevertheless be identified as being common to them all, constituting a personal style—this is subconscious, just as our handwriting."

I was cheeky enough to cite the example of a number of composers who had responded favorably to my request, although they were equally busy. Krenek eventually gave in and sent the following rather brief replies (in English). Little did I know then that ten years later I would be promoting his music published with Universal Edition and would have a great deal to do with his devoted widow, Gladys.

I am sorry I failed to draw him out on his widely differing stylistic periods—for instance, whether his decision to convert to dodecaphony had been due in any way to a revelation similar to Lutosławski's Cage experience.

I.

As to [question] I, I remember only these few cases for consideration: in the second movement of my Piano Sonata, Op. 59 (1928), I tried to apply the same trick that Schubert used in the last movement of his *B-Flat Major Trio* by transforming the 2/4 of the main theme into the 3/2 of the second without changing the tempo of the quarternotes. I did the same thing by using the tempo of the quarternotes of the *March* (4/4) in the 3/2 section of the second idea. Incidentally, he did the same thing in one of the late *Three Piano Pieces*, which I don't have handy.

Obviously, the whole cycle of the *Reisebuch aus den österreichischen Alpen*[32] is influenced by Schubert, as well as various details of period construction in several works of the period 1925–30.

Then I also remember that in my orchestral work *Eleven Transparencies*, Op. 142, in No. 10 ("Upon hearing the call from far away") I was "inspired"

32. Composed in 1929 for voice and piano, to the composer's own text. Eight of the twenty songs were arranged by Krenek for medium voice and orchestra in 1973.

by Delius's *Upon hearing the first cuckoo in spring,* a lovely, haunting piece that was playing for years over the radio as theme song to conclude an evening broadcast.

Finally, in my choral work *Lamentatio Jeremiae Prophetae,* Op. 92 (1942), I was influenced by the general character of Johannes Ockeghem's music, not by any particular details.

II.

I am unable to remember ever having been "inspired" by outside sounds (bird calls, waterfalls, traffic, or whatever) nor by visual elements (paintings, or the like); if at all, perhaps by literary associations, but I could not quote any examples.

III.

I have expressed myself in various styles, or manners of writing (which has been held against me), but I think that in all of them there are subconscious mannerisms that may be traced through all of my works regardless of differences of style, just as a person's handwriting shows constant characteristic elements throughout his life.

1982

Thirty

LADISLAV KUPKOVIC (1936)

In his late twenties, Ladislav Kupkovic was one of the leading avant-garde composers in Slovakia. He conducted the Philharmonic Orchestra, founded a new music ensemble in 1963, and composed experimental pieces, such as Ad libitum *(1969), which he defined as a "happening." Between 1965 and 1980, his works were published by Universal Edition. They include his* Souvenir *(1971) for violin and piano (or string orchestra), which was for several years on the repertoire of Gidon Kremer. It is no longer "new music" but a witty evocation of salon music fashionable in the Austro-Hungarian Empire. (Kupkovic also has a* K.u.K. Musik[33] *for orchestra written in 1978.)*

He left Slovakia for Germany in 1969 and was appointed professor of composition at the Hannover Academy in 1973. It was in Hannover that I met him some years later. By that time, he had turned his back on his avant-garde past. The pieces he played for me in his apartment were, if I remember correctly, in a mock-Handel style. A few years later, on another visit, he had gotten as far as Schumann.

It was all done impeccably but I could not help wondering if it had any raison d'être. Why write music à la Schumann and company, why should musicians play copies if they have access to the original? I could not convince the composer, of course, and I was quite depressed at the prospect that his oeuvre post-Bratislava would fall into oblivion. I wish I were wrong.

Ladislav Kupkovic is an extreme representative of a number of composers who early on in their careers deluded themselves that if they were to be noticed, if they wanted to be performed, they needed to adhere to the lingua franca of the international avant-garde. Eventually, some of them realized that they had voluntarily donned a straitjacket and they went out of their way to shed it—in many cases with the sad result that they surrendered instead to the straitjacket of bygone musical aesthetics without any relevance to our age. What they lacked was a strong personality which would have lent validity and, yes, a raison d'être to their compositions. Kurtág's bon mot comes to mind: "Was this piece worth getting up for?" You can, of course, easily substitute "day" for "piece" and you are faced with a fundamental existential question.

33. K.u.K. stands for "kaiserlich und königlich," that is, "imperial and royal," a description applied to institutions in the Austro-Hungarian monarchy. The emperor was also king of Hungary.

I.

Whatever we may hear or experience, enriches us.

We make use of numerous elements of historical experience directly, some indirectly and there are others which we merely arrange differently. We could hardly compose with the nothing we bring to the world at birth.

It follows that experiences similar to Lutosławski's with Cage occur in my life all the time. My style today would be unthinkable without hundreds of such impulses. An "alien" influence also helps me to avoid making mistakes: I can leave alone where others have failed.

The process whereby I eventually broke with atonal music was enhanced by my listening to innumerable such works by other composers. It is a human characteristic that it takes a certain quantity for you to realize how senseless a particular phenomenon is.

II.

No doubt about it: the sounding environment influences composers even if that influence cannot be pinpointed in any concrete fashion: the material that lends itself for use in a composition is only present in a highly stylized form. However, musical processes mirror the environment, otherwise audiences have no access to a composer's abstract manipulations. Whether consciously or instinctively, the composer works with all the various sound phenomena of the environment: car honks just as much as birdsong, the noises of a row, or various kinds of music broadcast on the radio. Everything. I can reveal to you that I am particularly fascinated by the sonorous world of large railway stations.

III.

A composer possesses an individual style if his works can be recognized without our being able to tell exactly how. This is important because we must be able to differentiate between individual style and individual hackwork.

Mozart had an individual style. The traits of that style add up to such a rich and complex unity as to make them impossible to analyze within the framework of music theory. (Musicologists who imagine they can do it, have no idea what they are talking about.)

An individual hackwork comes about—especially in new music—if the composer is writing the same thing all the time, in other words, he artificially narrows down the scope of his works, to create a similarity between them.

In order not to hurt the feelings of my colleagues, I am going to take an example from the fine arts: Anthes's figures between heads and legs or Hundertwasser's golden and silver rainbows are all hackworks. Indeed, the fine arts today are nothing but hackwork lacking in any personal style. I believe the same is true of much of new music.

A personal style can only evolve during the course of artistic work: concentrated aspects that constitute a style come about by themselves. On the other hand: a hackwork is always the outcome of conscious action. In other words, a composer can only acquire a personal style if he does not endeavor to have one; if he strives for it consciously, that is, artificially, it will end up as hackwork.

Our age which produces a great deal of worthless stuff, forces composers to create hackworks by demanding that they have a personal style.

1982

Thirty-One

GYÖRGY KURTÁG (1926)

The University of Rochester Press published my three interviews with the composer in 2009.[34] *In my introductions to the conversations, I poured out my love for his music in a rather effusive manner. What is there left for me to say?*

In the early 1980s when I was in the middle of collecting material for this book, I also approached him. I forget what his initial reaction was but it is a fact that one day he turned up in my office at Editio Musica Budapest and said he was ready to reply to my questions, as a kind of "hommage à Bálint." He, a composer of numerous musical homages (and two tributes in writing, in honor and in memory of his friend, György Ligeti) consented to give me what must have been his very first interview, in recognition of my promotional work on behalf of his music.

In the three years that followed, we worked on the text time and again. Kurtág or his wife would ring me to suggest a different phrase, a different order of paragraphs, the omission or addition of sections of the text. Their painstaking effort to chisel at the text to make sure it reflected exactly what the composer meant gave me an idea of the way he worked on his music. I carried out their wishes dutifully and initially with great pleasure—until one day in 1985, I felt I had reached the end of my tether. The Kurtágs gave in and accepted the interview in the form you will find below. This interview has been translated into several languages: for many years, it remained the only one of its kind, the only one to be quoted from if one needed an authentic statement by the composer. It has also been included in the University of Rochester Press Kurtág book of 2009.

By the nature of things, the manuscript had to be brought to a close at one point, but life, Kurtág's life, has gone on. It has done so with the lessons drawn from his breakdown in November 2007 conveniently (predictably? irresponsibly? happily? alarmingly?) forgotten. He and his wife Márta may have decided, shocked as they were by what had appeared to be a stroke, to cut down on their travels and ceaseless activity, but they have carried on nonetheless, in response to the many invitations for Kurtág to give master classes, attend rehearsals and performances. He has also been approached with offers of commissions and in some cases has expressed interest. The future will tell which of these plans will actually bear fruit.

For those who may have read the book, here is a short list of premieres which at its publication in September 2009 had not yet taken place:

The Colindă-Baladă, Op. 46, *for chorus and instrumental ensemble, one of the central compositions discussed in the book, was premiered on March 29, 2009, at the*

---

34. Bálint András Varga, *György Kurtág: Three Interviews and Ligeti Homages* (Rochester, NY: University of Rochester Press, 2009).

festival Cluj Modern at Cluj-Napoca in Romania, with Cornel Groza conducting the Transilvania Chorus and a group of instrumentalists.

Kurtág then succeeded in finishing Anna Akhmatova: Four Poems, Op. 41 *for soprano and chamber ensemble, in time for the first performance at New York's Carnegie Hall on January 31, 2009 (Nataliya Zagorinskaya, soprano, UMZE Chamber Ensemble conducted by Péter Eötvös).*

Finally, not only did he revise four of the six movements of New Messages, Op. 34A *for orchestra, he also added a* Double *to the one called* Schatten *(Shadows). The world premiere took place in Freiburg, Germany, on November 7, 2009 (SWR Symphony Orchestra Baden-Baden and Freiburg, conducted by Sylvain Cambreling).*

I was eleven or twelve years old when the experience that turned me into a musician occurred. Schubert's "Unfinished" Symphony was playing on the radio, and when my parents told me what it was we were listening to, I was amazed that adults could recognize classical music! Sometime after that, I was alone at home and again listening to music on the radio. I realized that they were playing the "Unfinished" Symphony. I asked for and was given the score, and I learned the two-hand arrangement of the piece. That is what decided that music would become highly important in my life.

Between the ages of five and seven I had piano lessons, and I was fond of serious music. At the age of seven I stopped the lessons and lost all interest in music. I sabotaged my piano lessons, practicing only five or ten minutes a week, because I derived no enjoyment at all from my own playing. The return to music was through dance music, tangos, waltzes and marches. I must have been around ten when I started dancing lessons, and later, when I went with my parents on our summer holiday to Herkulesfürdő,[35] I danced every evening with my mother in the public rooms at the spa. She was very young and very pretty at that time.

Dancing, then, was one of mother's enticements in the summer months, in winter it was playing piano duets. We played brief, crude transcriptions of passages from operas. It was fun dancing with her (and for me every tango and every waltz had its own individual character), and it was also fun playing duets. Once, all of a sudden, we had a go at the first movement of the *Eroica.* This was far beyond me—perhaps both of us—but we read right through to the end of the symphony, then went on to the First and later the Fifth. (Mother was never willing to play the *Funeral March.* At the time that seemed superstitious, but it may have been a presentiment: she died at the age of forty.)

Between the ages of five and six, incidentally, I also composed—two little piano pieces, I believe—and the Schubert symphony also led me back

35. Bâile Herculane in Romanian, Herkulesbad in German, a popular spa in Transylvania.

to composition. I wanted to write a Jewish symphony in E minor with the title "Eternal Hope." But I also wrote a lot of other things too at that time.

Music that was new to me had a big influence, though in general few compositions affected me at first hearing. For instance, I had read a lot about Beethoven's Ninth, but I was hugely disappointed when I first heard it because my picture of it from what I had read had led me to expect something quite different. On that basis I had imagined a Ninth Symphony for myself, and the reality was so totally different in comparison that I was simply unable to find my bearings in it.

Bartók's *Cantata Profana* and *Music for Strings, Percussion and Celesta* were elemental influences, though that does not mean that their influence came through in my own compositions. The Violin Concerto, which I heard once in a BBC broadcast from London during the war, had just as much of an impact on me. Mátyás Seiber[36] gave the introductory talk and analyzed the piece, but even then I wasn't really able to follow it. Having said that, the Violin Concerto was to become one of the decisive experiences in my life later on, in the second or third month after I got to Budapest, in 1946. I sat through all the rehearsals held by Doráti and Menuhin, and later on learned the répétiteur part myself (for years I was perhaps the only one who knew it) and played it for years with Ede Zathureczky.[37] Whichever other violinists learned the part, I had the chance to go through the piece with them.

That had a direct influence on the composition of my Viola Concerto. I even incorporated some musical materials, though the influence of the Concerto for Orchestra and other Bartók compositions is more obvious. The process of getting to know a work gradually has proved more important than the first encounter. On the whole, I have rarely heard something and instantly realized its importance.

One other piece of music that had a big impact on me: *Az embernek halála* (For each man his own death) section of *The Sayings of Péter Bornemisza*[38] is a direct response to Penderecki's *Threnody for the Victims of Hiroshima* (1959–60). The memory of a live performance directly influenced the structure of the piano part of that section.

Even Webern did not influence me through listening but through study, the "interrogation" of small details. But with Bartók, too, the encounter was such that I began to practice. . . . The first piece—around the age of fourteen, when I was preparing to become a musician and studying at Temesvár—was the second of the Bagatelles (1908). I didn't make much

36. Mátyás Seiber (1905–60), Hungarian composer, a pupil of Kodály. He moved to England in 1935.

37. Ede Zathureczky (1903–59), Hungarian violinist.

38. *The Sayings of Péter Bornemisza*, Op. 7 (1963, rev. 1976), concerto for soprano and piano.

sense of it. After that came *Song* from the *Nine Little Pieces* of 1926. I was boarding with the family of a grammar-school boy of my own age. He was a good musician; he played the classical repertoire on the piano and also, I think, sang in the choir when Kodály's *Psalmus Hungaricus* was performed in Temesvár. My practicing infuriated him so much that, as I recall, he even beat me up to stop me playing Bartók.

Bartók didn't appeal to me either; he was somehow so abominably good. Erich Kästner, in his children's book *The 35th of May*, writes about a bachelor uncle who invites his nephew round to the house every Thursday, and they lunch together on meat salad with raspberry syrup and similarly absurd dishes. Meanwhile they keep on saying, "Abominably good, isn't it?" To me, Bartók's music was abominably good in the same way. *Bluebeard* was also distinctly ugly to my ears, but it still excited me—and, of course, the fact that it met with resistance from the people around me only added to its attraction. I somehow discovered a taste for Bartók's music beyond my own taste and consciousness.

The first of my compositions, to which I am now more willing to admit, was the Suite for Piano. I myself don't know exactly when I wrote it, I must have been sixteen or seventeen. The first movement—*Mintha valaki jönne* (As if someone were coming)—is a response to my composition teacher Max Eisikovits's setting of a poem by Endre Ady.[39] Its basic experience—I am waiting and they are not coming—was painfully familiar to me, and that became the first movement of the Suite. (I didn't quite get as far as composition with Eisikovits; we only went through harmony and counterpoint, with much sweat and tears. In point of fact, I was never able to acquire a proper foundation in compositional technique. My instrumentalist fellow pupils, a cellist and the violinist Stefan Romaşcanu, completed our assignments much more adroitly.)

Interestingly enough, it so happened that I gave programs to the first movements of some of my later works as well. That was the case with my String Quartet, Op. 1. I'm not sure whether I attributed a program to the work retrospectively or was already conscious of it during the composition process. I was living in Paris, in a crisis that made it impossible for me to compose: in 1956, the world had literally collapsed around me—not just the external world but my inner world too. Numerous moral questions had also arisen in relation to the work I was doing with Marianne Stein;[40] my entire conduct as a human being had become highly questionable. I sank to terrible depths of despair.

---

39. Endre Ady (1877–1919), Hungarian poet.

40. Marianne Stein (1913–94), Hungarian psychologist who worked primarily with artists and musicians. During the year Kurtág spent in Paris, she helped him to find his way back to composition.

Previously I had shunted responsibility for many things onto others, but now, all at once, I was obliged to recognize that I had become disillusioned with my own self, my own character. I have only ever been able to compose when I was on fairly good terms with myself, when I was able to accept myself for what I am—when I was able to discern some sort of unity in my view of the world. In Paris I felt, to the point of desperation, that nothing in the world was true, that I had no grip on reality.

I was living at the place of another of Marianne Stein's pupils, an American actress, and in exchange for my room I would take her two children for walks in the park. That was the Parc de Montsouris, a marvelous wilderness with fantastic trees. The experience of trees in winter was perhaps the first reality. That carried on almost until spring, when birds appeared as a second reality. Only later did I establish that the blackbird was the "fundamental bird"; the argumentative chattering of sparrows makes an appearance in the quartet's fourth movement, the "bird scherzo." One night I was startled out of my sleep by birdsong I had never heard before. I later identified it as a nightingale. A very special marvel.

The year in Paris and the work with Marianne Stein virtually split my life in two. I lost twenty kilos in weight. I once accompanied the singer Pali Déry, who had heard during a visit to China that a person could get by on less than twenty grams of rice a day. From then on I, too, lived effectively on rice, half of it with a stock cube, the other half with something sweet, and I began to do regular physical training. I had always been terribly clumsy at gymnastics. To begin with, I repeated some exercises that I had seen my mother do (she had been dead for more than ten years by then), but later on I developed the thing in my own way. I made angular movements, almost like playing a pantomime. I even tried to alter my writing to an angular, crabbed style.

The next stage of that was my starting to make angular forms from matches. A whole symbolic world evolved. I perceived myself as in a worm-like state, totally diminished in humanity. The matchstick forms and balls of dust (I didn't clean my room every day), along with black stubs (I also smoked) represented me. I gave this matchstick composition the title "The cockroach seeks a way to the light" (I stuck a lamp shape made from silver foil at the end of the composition). That was also supposed to become the program for the string quartet's first movement. The overtone chord symbolized the light, and in between the dirt. . . . I almost inscribed as an epigraph at the start of the movement two lines by Tudor Arghezi:

Din mucegaiuri, bube şi noroi / Iscat-am frumuseţi şi preţuri noi (From mildew, suppurating wounds and ordure / I generated new beauties and values).

That was already going through my head at the time I was making the matchstick composition.

That quotation is associated with Felician Brînzeu, a teacher at the lycée in Lugos—the teacher in my life (Magda Kardos in Temesvár[41] was later to signify for me that same primeval experience in music). During my second year at grammar school, in three months he taught Romanian grammar to a class of fifty children, mostly from peasant families, never handing out marks and making us continually discuss the material; the whole thing was almost a collective game. We had great fun, and for me it brought alive, once and for all, what the structure of a language was. Besides that, he was a very strict taskmaster with a mildly sadistic streak; he was quite capable of clouting you with all his strength. It's with him that I associate that Arghezi quotation, though it's quite possible that it stuck in my head much later, during the Romanian lessons at the Piarist Fathers' lycée in Temesvár.

I failed in drawing at school. I didn't have any talent for it then and don't now: I can't draw the simplest of objects even today. But during my year in Paris (and again at the end of the period of paralysis, which preceded *Játékok*[42] (roughly a year beforehand), for months on end I only drew, set down signs. In Paris I made drawings of the matches to start with: the room became simply full of matches; I had to get rid of them when I wanted to tidy up. As a reminder, I therefore tried to make drawings of them, but all that emerged from that was nonsensical jumbles. After that I drew something: there were stars at the edges and in the middle something wriggling. I still have it to the present day, and that's what I attempted to set to music in the seventh of *Eight Piano Pieces,* Op. 3. Around 1973 I used notebooks, putting only a sign on each page by pressing the pencil or pen against the paper and shaking my hand. There wasn't much difference between the signs, but it's as if a bit of them passed over into *Játékok* . . .

Childhood again . . . Slow processes . . . During my time at Temesvár, when I was seriously learning the piano, I had a rather low opinion of my mother's playing. In my childhood, however, those pieces of music had had a very special truth for some reason. She played quite a few of the Beethoven sonatas—the "Appassionata," the *Pathétique,* the Sonata in A Flat, Op. 26, *Les adieux,* Op. 81a, no. 26 in E Flat, and the Sonata, Op. 2,

---

41. Timişoara in Romanian, Temeswar in German, a city in the Banat region of Romania.

42. *Játékok* (Games) (1975–) Eight volumes have appeared so far of these short piano pieces, most of them written for two hands, some for piano duet or two pianos. In the Preface to the first volume, the editor writes: "The idea of composing *Games* was suggested by children playing spontaneously, children for whom the piano still means a toy. They experiment with it, caress it, attack it, and run their fingers over it. They pile up seemingly disconnected sounds, and if this happens to arouse their musical instinct they look consciously for some of the harmonies found by chance and keep repeating them." Some of the pieces equally lend themselves to performance by beginners (such as the seven-tone *Flowers We Are* or *Perpetuum mobile*—both in Book I) and by concert artists.

no. 1 in F Minor. The last one is a particularly important memory. For me, the second subject in the first movement, or that in the last movement, stands for a primal musical comportment. Later on, in my teenage consciousness, music like that became indistinguishably uniform, but it seems that in my childhood I was good at identifying it.

All in all, I had much better hearing when I was a child than I do now. Then I could mimic everything in singing, every external noise. I don't remember when—it may have been when my voice broke, or perhaps even earlier—I was told at a chorus rehearsal to shut up because I was putting everyone else off. Ever since then, and maybe it is related to that, my sense of absolute pitch for the singing voice has gone—right up to the present day. And my acuity for other sounds too has rather tended to deteriorate.

When it comes down to it, I have the feeling that it's not necessarily my ears that do my hearing, or my eyes that do my seeing.

During my grammar-school years, the time when I was becoming conscious of myself, I read in Lützeler's history of art that architecture, to all intents and purposes, was the experiencing of space—something that envelops a person, like music, which also envelops you. I experienced it again in the cathedrals of Rheims or Chartres. Chartres Cathedral, for instance, is wonderfully human in scale, of precisely the size that you can take in, and there I had the experience that when I was not looking I could sense the space with my skin, with my very back. For me, it's very often like that with music too: it somehow comes across from sensibility to sensibility, I both hear and don't hear the thing. I have also come across something of that kind with people who have an extraordinarily finely developed sense of hearing: in searching for a quality, they fail at times to notice even inaccuracies of intonation. In the recordings of rehearsals by Toscanini and Casals it is noticeable that if something was of paramount importance to them, they let other, quite significant errors go by. Toscanini runs through the second act of *Traviata*, for example, and he is so delighted to be able to sing even the part of Violetta that he isn't in the least bothered by the fact that the orchestra is meanwhile all over the place.

I had a similar experience once during the recording of my Viola Concerto (1953–54). I considered that the strings were not airy enough. András Simor, the leader of the orchestra, told me afterwards that I was only satisfied with the recording when they weren't playing at all.

How important are the sounds of Nature to you?

We've already talked about that: birdsong—blackbirds above all. In Berlin, a blackbird would regularly sing on the roof of the house where I was living—a truly great artist. I was living near the botanical gardens, and the neighborhood was simply full of birds. The blackbirds would wake up at dawn, getting on for three o'clock, and respond to one another in chorus from far and wide. I'll never forget once, after a discussion with

Péter Eötvös that had stretched long into the night, we went out into the garden to listen to this concert. Birds and trees—they both remained important for a long time.

And forms?

Forms—I have such an odd relationship to them, because I'm not at all sure that . . . I can't see forms, or even recollect them, but I feel secure in their proximity. I can cling to the twists of gnarled boughs without being able to reproduce them. The twists also lend an inner need, a demand for structure in music.

Yes, an inner need . . . that's a recurrent motif in Thomas Mann's work. In his short story about Schiller, "Schwere Stunde" (A weary hour) and in one of his letters to his wife Katia he writes that talent is little more than a demand, a striving for quality and that talent is a very heavy burden. That is what the density of twists in a bough means to me. For me, a line from Attila József is both reality and a program:

> *Távol tar ágak szerkezetei / tartják az üres levegőt*
> (Far off, bare branches construct / delicate support for empty air).[43]

One of my elemental musical experiences was again not purely musical: László Vidovszky's *Autokoncert* (1972). From the very first moment, I experienced it as something of a Beckettian tragedy. I was deeply shaken by the tragedy and poetry of the objects that kept falling and emitting sounds every thirty seconds on the empty stage, and the extreme economy by which all that acquired strict musical form. The idiom of the New Musical Studio that was emerging at the time played a major role at the start of *Játékok:* it gave me courage to work with even fewer notes.

What about individual style and self-repetition?

My fundamental reflection here is how, at any given moment, I experience Bach. With him one is in the presence of a brain that functions like a computer, which quite simply, starting from one and the same point, runs through, over and over again, the entire range of variation possibilities of the given piece of material. If we listen to Bach's compositions in poor performances, where the sound material is not perfectly articulated/interpreted, we may think that one piece is just like another. What I mean by all that is that one has to be very careful about saying of someone, fifty or even a hundred years later, that he was doing the same thing, or that he went down certain avenues in the same manner.

There was a time when people were inclined to think that Stravinsky created a neo-Classical something or other and churned out pieces in that

43. Attila József, untitled fragment, in *Winter Night: Selected Poems of Attila József,* trans. John Batki (Budapest: Corvina, 1997).

style. From today's perspective it looks completely different. The intervening period has demonstrated that they are "uniform" only to a superficial listener: the pieces have acquired individuality.

Even of Bartók, people sometimes tend to say that he repeated things that he had already made use of, and that in *Contrasts*, even at times in the Concerto for Orchestra, signs of a certain fatigue can be discerned—that they are not pristinely new. I myself am not so fond of *Contrasts*, but I'm not sure that I am right, because it may also depend on whether I have learned it thoroughly enough, whether I can judge it from inside. At the same time, the C Major in Bartók's *Rondo* may have a radiant glow to it, simply because I am listening to that particular C Major and not the C Major in the Sonata for Two Pianos and Percussion or the one in *For Children*.

How important is the problem of self-repetition for you in your own works?

It's important, important. I often forget about pieces that have already been written, and it does happen that I discover the same thing all over again. When I look back after a lapse of time, the moments of fatigue also stand out more; it is clear to me today which elements in my Viola Concerto have worn thinnest. Interestingly enough, those elements struck me at the time as specifically new or bold, perhaps because the pieces around them were even less fresh or had recourse to other sources.

To stay with a recent experience: the Attila József Fragments *have many new things to say even in juxtaposition to* Messages of the Late R. V. Troussova.[44]

I am not sure if it is true. According to András Wilheim, for example, I am treading on well-trodden paths.[45] That is something that I, at the present moment, am unable to experience; maybe I will later. Undoubtedly, there is a bunch of things that, one way or another, negotiate avenues with excessive regularity that were, indeed, familiar to me long ago. It's terribly important for me, and that is how it had to be, but that might change in me. Nevertheless, the piece is full of gestures where I am simply uninterested in whether or not I am familiar with them. The *Lesz lágy hús mellé ifjú kalarábé* (There'll be tender meat with young kohlrabi) section [no. 15 from *Attila József Fragments*] is the same do-re-mi material, note for note, as that of the penultimate song of *S. K. Remembrance Noise*,[46] but it finds a new voice from the very fact that in the second half it emerges from a Gregorian or folk-song-like recitative (where the text too changes: *De ez már a mi porunkból fakad* [But all this grows from our dust now]).

44. *Attila József Fragments*, Op. 20 (1981), for soprano solo. *Messages of the Late R. V. Troussova*, Op. 17 (1976–80), to twenty-one poems by Rimma Dalos, for soprano and chamber ensemble.

45. András Wilheim (1949), Hungarian musicologist.

46. György Kurtág, *S. K. Remembrance Noise*, Op. 12 (1975). Seven songs to poems by Dezső Tandori, for soprano and violin.

With the *Attila József Fragments,* what I somehow wanted was for something to exist that I can distribute like a pamphlet. For instance, *Irgalom, édesanyám* . . . (Mercy, mother . . .) [No. 18].

One is always coming back to certain problems. Right now, for instance, I feel like returning to a major chord and repeating it over and over again. Like the F-major chord in the *Twelve Microludes* for string quartet,[47] which is always played by the two violins on three different strings. It also thrills me what materials I can find to contrast with this chord. Or there is the mouth-organ-like piece in *Játékok (Hommage à Borsody).* So one keeps on returning, from time to time, to an identical piece of material in order to map out new possibilities inherent in it. As to the point at which that wanders off into self-repetition . . . certain major-chord pieces did not come off and have remained in the drawer; others I have released, but they are not among the works recommended for concert performance.

We are innocent when something comes off, as we are when it doesn't. I sometimes return home from Budaliget[48] with the notion that I have found something quite marvelous—and it isn't. At other times, something is born within two minutes that never needs altering: *Mercy, mother* . . . , for instance. I wrote that down in pencil, and not a note has been changed since then. There are numerous versions of the other pieces, and I had to return to them many times over.

In other words, what is good I receive as a gift: I am innocent in the matter. When I am as if paralyzed for months or years on end, the very fact that I can write anything at all is, in itself, a great joy. That alone is a gift. I am also quite aware that the first couple of pieces are generally just a warming up, and they are discarded. Sometimes, I manage to make something good out of nothing quite by accident. But more often than not I don't.[49]

1982/85

47. György Kurtág, *Hommage à András Mihály—Twelve Microludes for String Quartet,* Op. 13 (1977–78).

48. Budaliget is a suburb of Budapest where Kurtág used to have a place for composing.

49. First publication in English in the *Hungarian Quarterly* 42 (Spring 2001): 127–34.

Thirty-Two

HELMUT LACHENMANN (1935)

After a number of reminders and keeping my fingers crossed over several years, Helmut Lachenmann eventually addressed himself to revising the text of our interview conducted at his house in 1983. The result is, I think, an important statement by an important composer of our times.

I am particularly struck by Lachenmann's detailed analysis of his response to Cage and Nono; he goes far beyond stating the fact of their influence. His is the *ideal reply I had hoped for from other composers as well.*

He also refers to a phenomenon that would justify a book all by itself: the moment of courage *which it evidently takes for a creator to make an artistic decision. This is a subject I addressed already in the preface to the Hungarian edition. A daring innovator like John Cage needed the encouragement provided by Rauschenberg's white paintings to release* 4'33" *and this piece in turn gave Lachenmann the courage to "explore the potential of each sound, including extramusical sounds." Goffredo Petrassi drew courage from Alberto Burri and I could well imagine that Kasimir Malevich, too, had to muster his courage to come out with his White on White series of suprematist paintings in 1917–18.*

This could be an indication of the existential loneliness of a creative artist who through a logical development of his ideas over a longer period of time or in a flash of inspiration comes face to face with a product of his imagination which he simply does not dare to present to the world. He needs evidence of at least one like-minded person to mitigate his sense of solitude.

I.

The leap that Lutosławski made had been prepared: Cage's Piano Concerto only served as an "ignition" to embark on something that was in actual fact already given. Indeed, a pure, radical experience like the music of Cage is something special. If performed without any trimmings, it meant for me, too, a purifying experience. This is true also on a more general level: the encounter with music which is pure in spirit and material puts my senses on alert, I listen intensively and there arise new visions.

I am endowed with a kind of creative mechanism which works all the time and acts like a sensor: it responds to everything which interests me—or rather, which provokes me.

A composer like Cage who has liberated the musical material of all its norms, has made me realize that I was in fact free to do *anything*. It is this realization that has encouraged me to undertake steps which ought to have been made a long time ago—steps at which I balked out of fear of who knows what.

I heard Cage in Donaueschingen in 1954, pieces like *Williams Mix*, *34.46.776* and *Variations*. Later also the Piano Concerto of 1958, but only on tape. In Munich, Josef Anton Riedl would play pieces by Cage every once in a while, rather authentically. That did not leave me indifferent either.

What did Cage encourage you to do?

For instance, to have recourse to alienated sound. To concrete sound. But that cannot be limited to Cage alone.

Were you influenced by Pierre Schaeffer at all?

No, he is much too organized for me, in a way academic. He used sounds in an exotic manner. I hear a melody—but I hear it in the rhythm of a puffing locomotive. What I was looking for was the liberated sound, released from any context so that it is nothing but itself. At the time, Cage was one of my most important experiences. There was also another one: Nono's *Varianti*, played in Donaueschingen in 1957. I think it was probably one of his least successful compositions. It provoked a scandal at the time. The piece was performed again in Munich and I traveled there to hear it once more.

Nono does have pieces which are more dramatic and make more of an impact. However, *Varianti* has always fascinated me, as if it had been composed just for me. It seemed to open up a new landscape which I was to discover for myself, while Nono, in his later works such as *La terra e la compagna* or *Cori di Didone* grew once again poetic in a more concrete manner.

To put it like this: while Cage was one of those who encouraged me to explore the acoustic potential of each sound, including extramusical ones, it was Nono (and not Stockhausen and not Boulez) who induced me to experience sounds as means, sounds as the articulation of time, sounds as *valeurs* in an open scale of values—in an abstract way, that is, as part of a radical play of thought.

Actually, the sounds in Nono's *Varianti* are in the main "normal" string sounds. The flageolets are sometimes coupled with *pizzicati* in an interesting manner but not in the sense of a timbre-construction like in electronic music or in Stockhausen's *Gruppen*. In actual fact, this music is "clumsy." I could understand why it was unfathomable for others: one does not know what to feel, one finds (luckily, by the way) no dramaturgy; it is an absolutely unique landscape without any basis for comparison. An open space with nothing in it: a kind of serially articulated vacuum. And still in contrast with what I had experienced with Cage. That kind of encounter, following upon one with Cage, was for me as a composer one of the most important experiences of all.

The same idea of purified time and empty surface in Cage's famous *4'33"* had a kinship with the way of thinking of his antagonist at the time, Luigi Nono, of which both were unaware. (Nono attacked Cage by pointing out "Your freedom is the freedom of people who have nailed a board in front of their heads and have given up their will, people who have let the material take care of itself. Whereas I, as a composer, act through taking decisions and express myself in this manner").

What pieces did you compose under the influence of Varianti*?*

At the time when I got to know *Varianti*—as I said before, that was in 1957—initially, I more or less stopped composing. The music I had written up to then was a mixture of styles between Bartók and Messiaen. I did know, of course, Cage and Stockhausen and others—they fascinated me but also made me feel wholly helpless. I could not find access to them, from whatever angle I may have tried. Needless to say, it was due in large part to the kind of musical education I had had. And: the Music Academy offered absolutely no possibility of delving deeper.

In 1957, when I first visited Darmstadt, I also became acquainted with Stockhausen, Nono, and Pousseur as thinkers. Then, on hearing *Varianti* in the fall, I knew immediately who it was I wanted to continue my studies with. The piece was haunting me ceaselessly. I analyzed it, that is, to begin with, I wrote it down as a particell, something which is in actual fact impossible with such a ramified score. I felt like a savage who has been given a ballpoint pen and he has to find out what it might be used for, he bites into it to see if it is edible, gives it a try as a weapon to stab with, and so on. I explored the piece without having any idea of the laws governing its structure, without understanding it in any way.

Later on in Venice where I was studying with Nono, I composed many studies and score fragments—also for orchestra—and then I wrote a kind of paraphrase on this piece. Today I call it *Souvenir.* It could be some sort of a "Supervarianti": *Varianti* is scored for three flutes, three clarinets, violin solo, and, I think, 12–(0)–10–8–6. *Souvenir,* on the other hand, for six flutes (all of them doubling piccolo), six clarinets (all doubling bass clarinets), piano, xylorimba, eleven violas, eight celli, and eight double-basses. I worked at that score for nearly one-third of the time I spent with Nono. But thereby I had my trauma out of my system.

For me, Nono was a composer of decisive significance. However, I can hardly imagine that anyone could mistake my music for his. It was his attitude that impressed itself on me: that is, on the one hand, to think structurally in a strict manner but at the same time also to want to communicate in an expressive way. The integration of the "human" aspect—his example was the first one that I found really convincing.

The "human" aspect has its dangers, of course, if one puts it like that. I would never claim that the music of our contemporaries was "not human" or even "inhuman." Perhaps it was rather "all too human." Composition around me appeared to me often to be frozen in a kind of mannerism while one was under the delusion that the processes were forward-looking. That is indeed the old reproach made against Darmstadt and to a certain extent it was justified, too, although it was overdone and was misused by its notorious enemies as a cheap argument.

There was at least one Darmstadt composer who could not be accused of mannerism, and that was Nono. His material was the strictest and the most consistent of all. He did not partake of the development whereby Boulez, Stockhausen, Pousseur, Maderna, or Berio loosened the pointillist approach of serial thinking. What they understood to be progress, opening up, relaxation, was for Nono a corrupt step backward. Nono was adamantly faithful to pointillism and it was much later that he overcame it through the means of collage and other carefully applied methods, through infinitely expanding it whereas the others had long indulged, once again, in a picturesque, figurative repertoire—until the secret regression turned into an open one, as we are experiencing it all around us today.

"Rigor" of the musical material (in reality, the courage to perceive new aspects of the material, so in actual fact, the "freedom" of the musical material) to which those in the cage of convention had returned on the one hand—and on the other, the expectation that behind such rigor there operated not just a structuralist game but a visionary expressive will: that is what makes Nono a paragon for me.

One should once again present *Varianti* in a carefully prepared performance. Incidentally, another work that Nono composed shortly afterward, one that has also been relatively unpopular, is the *Diario polacco I.* He composed it during my stay in Venice and I participated a tiny bit in its gestation. This is once again a piece where I feel: here I am at home.

II.

My work underwent a particular phase which began with *temA* (1968) and lasted roughly until 1978. The *Tanzsuite mit Deutschlandlied*, written in 1979, no longer belongs there really, although it does contain features (as indeed do all compositions composed since) which bear its imprint. *Air* (1969) and *Kontrakadenz* (1971) are typical examples.

Whenever I had a chance to talk about this, in music seminars for instance, I called the technique developed at the time *musique concrète instrumentale*. It has in common with Pierre Schaeffer's *musique concrète* that it incorporates everyday perceptions. I, however, apply this kind of perception to our traditional instruments and, through the rigor of its structure, keep it free of any surrealistic interpretation.

In everyday life, I hear the most diverse sounds without ever considering their acoustic qualities. If a china plate falls on a stone floor, we hear timbres, frequencies, even rhythms, but our senses do not react to them in a musical or aesthetic manner—we hear that or how a plate has been broken to pieces. Perception requires all the acoustic signals in order to be able to draw conclusions as to what has happened as a result of a mechanical event. It was that kind of hearing that I wanted to incorporate into my music—on a traditional musical instrument. If in *Pression* (1969) the string of a cello has been bowed, it happens primarily not in order to celebrate an A or an F# but to communicate a particular characteristic energetic experience: the pressure of the bow, the kind of friction, the resonance of the instrument which has been influenced accordingly, and so on. Each of these parameters—and there emerged ever new ones—was consciously controlled, graded, etc., and hearing became participation in a consciously governed physical power play. It is with that perspective in mind that I have written music which operates to a considerable extent (but not exclusively!) with alienated playing techniques.

Of course, this kind of experiencing sound had always played a certain role in listening, also in the case of traditional music. In Beethoven's music, we sense the sheer force of a timpani beat or a trumpet signal and it is no coincidence that these timbres have a military connotation. The beginning of the Ninth is a unique physical experience. Or think of the so-called Impressionists! Think of the mysterious flageolet—mysterious, because the sounds appear to be more penetrating than one would expect from the relatively pressure-free bowing of the strings. There are other relevant experiences as well, such as the one whereby one blows into a flute from a greater distance and for all the effort all you get is something like an air noise with pitch-coloring. Or you maltreat the deep wooden keys of a marimba with a very soft padded stick and the sounds you get are quite weak, however powerful your beats may be.

Those are no "new sonorities" or "new effects" but their perception has been shifted. In this environment, the "normal" instrumental sound works like a particularly artistic exception. For some time, I consistently included everyday objects but have strictly avoided any "Dadaist" effect. It was not my intention to play with cultural taboos but to break them in a very unspectacular manner, in connection with a particular music-idiomatic task. It proved more provocative than any cleverly staged aesthetic "shock" which briefly startled the public but in actual fact amused it.

To make sure that my students would correctly understand a paradigm shift like that, I would often invite them to sit together for five minutes and quietly listen. It was not all that easy. After all, it was no meditation or any other ritual; they were expected to overcome certain socially ingrained inhibitions so that they could record, through their perception, what was happening around them.

That was what Cage was after with his 4'33".

That's right. But with Cage there is another aspect as well which turns the exercise back into art: listening with him also means, at the same time, pondering over listening. If I hear *4'33"* "correctly," my attitude is basically different from listening at a concert: I perceive—also myself—in a momentarily insecure social situation, and that is in fact a revolution against the kind of listening that has been traditionally inculcated in us. Normally, we follow what we hear via our antennae which have been installed in us. But here they are more or less useless: we are naked. Alone in the desert of a barbarically over-bred civilization. We have to develop our means of orientation out of ourselves.

This situation is what I would call existentially creative. That was what we had in mind during the sessions with the students. We recorded the minutes of silence on tape and subsequently prepared a kind of "score" of what was to be heard: the barking of a dog, a clanging flagpole, a car driving up, the slamming of a door, the rumbling of a stomach . . .

The so-called silence . . .

The so-called silence, and we know how *loud* silence can suddenly become, and how thrilling. Of course, on the tape everything is different: we register the changed physical conditions, for instance, the noise of the tape or the effect of the recorded sound. We listened to some of the recordings ten times in a row and in the end, it was suddenly a *hit*, almost a piece of classical music which could not have had a different form: after the barking of a dog there had to come the *crescendo* of an approaching bus, as if the driver had only been waiting for his cue. And so on. This exercise leads to a sensitization in all directions.

I believe that Debussy who talked so much of the sounds of nature had a similar attitude and I would imagine that composers have always listened to their environment even if they put their experiences to different use than we do today.

As I have said before: in order to call the listener's attention to what I have termed *musique concrète instrumentale*, I incorporated extramusical elements in the orchestral pieces of the time. *Kontrakadenz* (1970–71): the title comes from *cadere* = to fall. The bows fall/spring on the strings, the stickheads fall on the skin of percussion instruments, ping-pong balls roll out on the floor and spring off from there, plates rotate on the parquet floor until they topple over and, hitting ever faster against the floor, come to a standstill. Or there is, for example, the idea of the diaphragm-accent stemming from a long-held-out tone: a radio switched on, with its volume turned down completely or nearly so, will be suddenly, *quasi sforzato*, turned up and down again and is thus part of a rhythm, together with the *sforzato* accents of long-held-out trumpet tones and a marimba which has been abruptly rubbed with a "friction-stick." The broadcast might concern a program about immigrant workers, it could be light music or snatches of a report about landing on the moon. The content of the broadcast is wholly immaterial—but whatever it may be, it is full of life and is in the long run not immaterial at all: a gift of everyday life, ennobled, as it were, through the structural context I have prepared for it. In the meantime, I have left that practice behind, via several stages in between, without ever forgetting it.

III.

I cannot give you a worldly wise answer to this question, *ex cathedra.* One senses the personal idiom of a composer. A fragmentary definition can be deduced from numerous details if they are related to one another in a dialectical manner. For instance: you cannot always easily differentiate Bach's harmony from Wagner's, if you leave out of account the other structural elements. A single sound, however characteristic it may be, does not give us reliable information about the composer. Strings pressed down: that is not necessarily Lachenmann by any means. One has first to consider the context in which it occurs.

In order to be able to describe a personal style, one has to observe the material in which it is articulated; also, its relationship to, say, tonality or to established categories of listening. And: musical material is not just sonorities but also ways of their combination and sets of rules with their living dynamic. After all, personal style is not a self-made drawer into which the composer squeezes himself.

Can you recognize Stravinsky when he writes à la Pergolesi? Can you recognize Schoenberg when he is composing tonal music? Can you recognize the music of Lachenmann when he is not using noise? Of course you can. But in order to interpret it properly, you have to concern yourself with living phenomena such as spirit, or "trademark" in a transcendental sense. There are no a priori checklists you can fall back upon, just as for observing a human character.

Or: how can you define the personal style of Mozart? You can make it a hobby—trying your hand at things like that. One would arrive at the observation that, for instance, certain conventional turns, ornamental flourishes that one usually refers to as the "gallant style," are, with Mozart, suddenly charged with novel features, they have a freshness and although used by him as a matter of course, they assume a special significance. How? Perhaps through unexpectedly potent thematic links, perhaps through a complementary rhythmic relationship to the other figures, perhaps through textural "boldness," perhaps through a personal kind of inconspicuousness. Perhaps through the dialectic of matter-of-course and surprise. Well, how then?

Sometimes, I imagine our Western civilization as a village where the stock of musical means (our musical practice including the tradition it embodies) is represented by a large, complex organ with many manuals. Composing would accordingly mean that one sits at this organ which is accessible for everyone and plays it in one's own way. Whoever happens to be playing it would make the instrument sound differently, he or she would treat it in his or her individual manner—in a way, they would make it for a moment their own organ. And the grateful villagers who have come to know and love their organists, let others play it as well—and are happy about how wonderfully it works.

That does not exclude surprises in any way—on the contrary. The rules that function even in such surprises are often not consciously known to the individual organists/composers. No doubt, certain mannerisms do emerge in the process: in keeping with our metaphor, preferences for particular register combinations. But once one has realized the presence of such mannerisms, one will immediately modify them. That is a requirement of spiritual hygiene and also the love of adventure.

In composing, you do not operate a self-made automaton, to mechanically tap its stocks; rather, you ceaselessly—and quasi-unconsciously—ponder your own creative apparatus, you develop and remodel it. All the great masters have done so. And where this applies, the question of "self-repetition" does not arise. Stockhausen could easily have stuck to his personal style evolved in *Kontra-Punkte, Zeitmasze,* or *Gruppen*—a style that could no longer be bettered in its conciseness. But the same creative impetus which had taken him that far, made him renounce his typical compositional practices in the next piece. And still: the concepts he subsequently developed, his aleatoric processes, the "momentary form" right up to his working with formulas are all part of an unmistakable "personal style"—his. Of course, inflection and phrases can be repeated and the conscious recourse to situations that had been produced before is legitimate if it springs not from sly laziness but an inner need.

And yet: "one does not step twice in the same river." A permanently innovative motivation is of decisive significance. If one were to raise the question how one can recognize it, one would once again arrive at the question about the criteria of a personal style. If it involves a dependence on recipes, you have spoiled it right at the start. In other words, you should not expect a diagnostic recipe for the "control" from outside.

How lucky we are that we cannot reduce everything to handy formulas!

1983/97

Thirty-Three

GYÖRGY LIGETI (1923–2006)

György Ligeti was not the only Hungarian composer to have fled to the West in 1956. However, he was the only one to have established himself as a major figure in contemporary music; indeed, international recognition came to him amazingly fast, with the electronic work Artikulation *(1958), and two works for orchestra,* Apparitions *(1958/59) as well as* Atmosphères *(1960).*

They were followed at regular intervals by further compositions which confirmed his position as a leader of the avant-garde. For his colleagues in Budapest, he became an authority, something of a guru whom they sent their scores for comments. "What did Ligeti say about the piece?" would be a recurring question. One of the composers has presented me with his correspondence with Ligeti, or rather, Ligeti's letters and cards, which he kept through half a century. They are marked by the endeavor—obvious for an outsider—to tone down the edge of critical remarks, rather to encourage and to find positive aspects he could praise.

Ligeti told me that one of the features that bothered him about the music of his friends in Hungary was that it was well-groomed, rather too beautifully combed, so to speak. He meant "academic" perhaps, where imagination was stymied by a close adherence to rules.

In our first interview recorded in 1970 in Budapest (he had not visited the city since 1956), he described a nocturnal walk near Buda Castle in 1950 when the idea of stationary music had first occurred to him. "I would rather call it a stationary sound combination," he added. "I did not dare to hope that it would ever become a real composition."

One wonders, of course, whether he would have written Atmosphères *if he had stayed in Budapest. I expect he would have—but he would probably have had to wait decades before hearing it performed. In the absence of a live performance of the music he imagined, his development would have taken a different course.*

I sent him the transcript of our interview and he returned it, with fifty-five numbered corrections and changes, almost by return post. This initial contact marked the beginning of a relationship (I dare not call it friendship) which lasted almost to the end of his life. We met whenever I happened to be in Hamburg and he could take time off from his work, also in Budapest (for instance, when he was one of the first recipients of the newly created Bartók-Pásztory Prize. I was there on behalf of Hungarian Radio and the first sentence he said was: "I used to be a Bartók epigone." I was struck by this relentlessly self-critical statement—in ensuing years, I was to hear many similar remarks).

I was deeply moved by the concern he showed for my well-being. In fact, he was anxious to find a job for me in the West and sent me letters and cards about his moves. I was grateful and incredulous at the same time—that he should have gone out of his way to help me, who was after all an unknown young man. Years later Ligeti was one of those who recommended me to Universal Edition in Vienna—I took up my job in the promotion department in 1992. One thing I am proud of: the King's Singers told me they would dearly love to have a piece from Ligeti. I rang him and conveyed the message. To my delight, he agreed without a moment's hesitation. Nonsense Madrigals *(1993) was born as result of my mediation—a fact he recorded in a copy of the score he gave me.*

I felt close to him, almost as to an elder relative. His death was a personal loss.

I.

Yes, I am familiar with that kind of experience. Let me give you a few examples.

I did not know the music of Charles Ives for many years because it was never played. The very first piece of his I encountered was the Symphony No. 4, on an LP conducted by Leopold Stokowski. I heard it in the early 60s and I remember it struck me as rather odd. The second movement, however, made a deep impression with its simultaneity of scraps of American marches, folksongs, and liturgical music in great abundance, each in a different meter. In a flash, I recognized the possibility of composing music with different layers being played simultaneously at different speeds.

Of course, it was nothing new. After all, you have different dances sounding at the same time in *Don Giovanni*, but they are still held together by a common harmonic frame. With Stockhausen, too, you have layers of differing speed in *Zeitmasze*, but it did not make any impact, it did not trigger my imagination into action.

Another feature of Ives's music that fascinated me was the fact that it is ordered and chaotic at the same time. I dislike complete order just as much as a total lack of it. You know my flat in Hamburg: it appears to be tidy, but there is chaos in the drawers.

In your program note on San Francisco Polyphony *you have used this description as a metaphor.*

Exactly. The idea occurred to me while listening to the second movement of Ives's Symphony No. 4. Musically, the two pieces have nothing to do with each other.

Yet another example: At the Budapest Academy of Music, we studied Palestrina counterpoint in great depth and it did us a world of good, too. However, it meant that we more or less ignored the Flemish school which preceded it. Both Jeppesen and Kodály happened to think more highly of Palestrina than they did of anybody else. We were aware of Josquin and Ockeghem but neglected them.

In the early 60s, then, it was a great experience for me not only to hear some Ockeghem but also to study his scores. I analyzed the counterpoint, which is considerably more intricate than Palestrina's, and was captivated by its continuous surge, its lack of any culmination or development. The moment a melody has reached its culmination, another one takes over, rather like sea waves, rolling in on top of one another. We hear this music not polyphonically but like an evenly rolling web.

It exerted a direct influence on the *Kyrie* movement of my *Requiem*. You find a lot of other things there, too, but traces of Ockeghem are also discernible. Not the technique because my counterpoint is completely different from his, but he showed me the possibility of writing music which seems to stand still and yet flows on.

A third example: Schubert and Schumann have been my hobbyhorses in the past few years—wonderful composers, both of them. In Schumann, I am captivated by the drive, the peculiar impulse of his fast movements—in *Kreisleriana* or the *Humoreske*. If you subject them to a formal or harmonic analysis, the explanation eludes you. They are marked by inner ornaments, a liana-like burgeoning of secondary voices which are all his own—nobody has followed up on them since. I have recently begun work on a piano concerto and while you will find no trace of Schumann, the inner burgeoning is nevertheless there, indirectly. Its style is akin to the Horn Trio, but it is more complex in its polyphony and polyrhythm. The Horn Trio, in turn, was influenced by the late Beethoven sonatas and string quartets (as well as countless other things . . .).

II.

Noises do not influence me directly, but neither do I cut myself off from them altogether. The outside world makes an indirect impact. Music works with acoustic material, no doubt, but I do not think that the sounds of live or dead nature would influence me in a decisive manner.

Various types of movement do. In my view, you see, music mirrors the processes of motion through sound. Machines play an important role—you will remember my pieces which bear the instruction *meccanico* (such as *Continuum* for harpsichord, the *meccanico pizzicato* Scherzo of the String Quartet No. 2, the *meccanico* "clock" in the Chamber Concerto). I have, after all, also written a piece for one hundred metronomes.

This, then, is a recurring feature. It is, however, not the noise of the machines but their movement that attracts me. There are similar traits with Haydn and Beethoven in that a motif would delineate a human gesture, an inflection, a facial expression.

It has also struck me that in the past one would hardly ever have encountered continuous, even motion (people would walk, travel on carts or ride—continuous motion first appeared with the invention of the train), whereas today, we experience flying, floating in the air. Although *Atmosphères* and *Apparitions* are not programmatic in character—I did not set out to render the sensation of flying in either piece—flying did have an indirect influence on their floating, on the continuous transformation of their musical patterns.

Without asking for my permission, Stanley Kubrick used extracts from *Atmosphères*, *Lux aeterna*, and the *Requiem* in the music of his science fiction film *2001*. I was angry with him but I did like his work (apart from the mystical beginning and ending). While composing, I did not think of anything "cosmic" (*Atmosphères* is meant to convey "atmosphere" rather than "air"), but the film made me aware of the possibility of associating infinity with my music.

As far as *Lux aeterna* is concerned, the words only served as a chance for me to compose music which is in fact *musica aeterna:* as if it has been sounding from time immemorial and would be going on forever—we only hear a part of it. It emerges from nowhere, it is here and slowly disappears. The beginning and ending of the Cello Concerto is like that too. You could also think of it as sounding continually and we are approaching it, passing by and moving away from it as if from an object or a planet. I did have associations like that but nothing like arriving on a satellite of Jupiter on board a spacecraft. And yet, when I saw the film, I realized that that association was also possible.

III.

Mozart occurs to me—the most wonderful composer. He was always himself and composed in a single style he had developed once and for all, yet, within that style, never repeated himself. He repeated certain patterns, certain formal types, but the essence was new with every piece.

In his last years, following his father's death, his music took a tremendous upswing—just think of the string quartets dedicated to Haydn, the late string quintets, the operas. If you take a closer look at the quartets, you will see how he combined the sonata form with contrapuntal techniques or how his very special chromatic part-writing loosened up the logic of functional harmony—in the introduction to the String Quartet in C Major, for example. For me, Mozart is the ideal of perfection.

As for my own music: my organ piece *Volumina* is closely related to *Atmosphères* but I turned in a different direction after that. The musical principle of thick polyphonic texture applies to the *Kyrie* of the *Requiem* or later also to *Lontano*, but it was not repetition. On the whole, having completed any particular piece, I feel I have solved certain problems and I move on to seek solutions to other compositional questions. This is not development but slow change, the transformation of musical thinking.

1979/97

Thirty-Four

WITOLD LUTOSŁAWSKI (1913–94)

I first met Witold Lutosławski briefly at the Warsaw Autumn Festival in 1972 and a few weeks later in Graz, at the world premiere of his Preludes and Fugue for Chamber String Orchestra. I was much taken with the work even though I was still very much a newcomer to contemporary music. Spontaneously, as if moved by an instinct, I went up to the composer and asked him if he would be willing to give me a book-length interview. I really had no business doing so, for I had never consulted with Editio Musica Budapest (EMB), the Hungarian music publisher I had joined the year before, about whether such a book would be published. I just went ahead and posed the question as if publication were a foregone conclusion.

Lutosławski's face assumed the expression I came to know so well in the years to come: he raised his eyebrows so that only the ends closest to his nose rose, the rest slanting downward toward his temples. The result was an expression of anxiety, of hesitation, which coupled with his slightly nasal and high voice augured ill for my request. But the reply that did eventually come was positive. It was only a question of timing: he was a busy man, dividing his time between composing and conducting.

EMB readily agreed to cover the costs of my travel to Warsaw and publish the book: my director, László Sarlós, not only had faith in me, he was also aware that releasing a book on a composer coming from a socialist country would be a feather in his cap in his dealings with the Ministry of Culture. (Indeed, the music critic of the communist party's daily was to welcome the interview on ideological and political grounds.)

When I eventually turned up at Lutosławski's beautiful villa in the ul. Śmiała 39 on March 12, 1973, there was tacit agreement between us that our interviews would be devoid of any political connotation.

Let me quote from my introduction to the English edition of the book, Lutosławski Profile, *published by Chester Music:*[50]

> *"Have you got some sort of plan? he asked when we had sat down in a corner of the big hall downstairs, in two armchairs facing each other, and I had checked for the third time that both tape-recorders were working properly. (I had two with me, to be on the safe side.) I outlined my conception and he nodded in agreement that we could begin. "It is up to you," he said.*

---

50. Bálint András Varga, *Lutosławski Profile* (London: Chester Music, 1976), v–vi.

We met on five consecutive afternoons and talked for one and a half or two hours on each occasion. Slowly, there developed certain recurring moments, "customs" that imparted intimacy to our sessions. He would answer the bell when I arrived and ask how I was. I, in turn, inquired about how he had got on with his work commissioned by the Concertgebouw Orchestra. His reply would be invariably evasive. Then, he would draw aside the curtain of a little cloakroom and we would have a brief "struggle" about who should put my coat on a hanger—in the end, I would give in. While waiting for coffee to arrive, we would have a "chat" on general subjects; having drunk our coffee, Lutosławski would ask "Where did we leave off?" I would briefly sum up the previous day's talk and switch on the tape-recorders; he would lean forward, elbows on knees, and start talking. He was often tired, the tiny little wrinkles on his face formed something like a mask. It may sound absurd, but I could not get rid of the idea that the thin skin would easily peel off leaving his face smooth and young.

Having finished his reply to a question, Lutosławski would glance at me, with an encouraging smile in his blue eyes, waiting for the next one.

By Friday evening, I ran out of questions. Lutosławski asked me to send him the English transcript of the finished text (we conversed in that language—he has a beautiful, to my ears at least, almost perfect accent) so that he could look through it, omit and amplify. I promised to do so and that marked the end of the "nine hours with Lutosławski" (to quote the title of the German version). But a "postlude" still remained: the farewell dinner when I also met Danuta, Lutosławski's delicate, pretty and friendly wife. Before taking our seats at the table, Lutosławski turned to me: "I have spoken so much about myself, you must be interested to see my study. Shall we go and take a look at it?"

We ascended the wooden staircase to the first floor and entered an L-shaped room. In the shorter arm of the L there stood a piano, in the longer one, right next to the window, stood the desk where he works. He opened the top drawer and produced a little parcel which bore the letters ZM. "Here I collect my ideas about a piece to be written for Zubin Mehta." On another parcel marked CW: "These are the sketches of the composition for the Concertgebouw Orchestra." And so on, everything spick and span, in perfect order. On the desk, beautifully sharpened pencils in a little holder. At the wall, a number of reference books and dictionaries. A small photograph shows Brahms—beard, paunch and all—as well as Karl Goldmark, moustached and wearing a wide-brimmed head, with his back turned towards Brahms. "They must have had a row," Lutosławski conjectured.

The most memorable experience: a cupboard was opened to bring to light large paper bags, the contents written in hand on each of them. Incredulously, I deciphered the titles: String Quartet, Symphony No. 2, Cello Concerto . . . *All the sketches, notes and the scores themselves, in manuscript.*

I wrote that introduction in September 1973 for the Hungarian edition while details of my visit were still fresh in my mind. What I cannot fathom is why I omitted to recall another memorable experience: before our leaving his study, the composer sat at the piano and played a few bars of Debussy. Never before or since have I heard such delicate touch—a piano sound the utter beauty of which I have no words to describe.

Nor can I fathom, in hindsight, why a composer of Lutosławski's standing had not been approached by a major international institution offering a secure home for his priceless manuscripts. Of course, Paul Sacher did not establish his foundation until the very year I interviewed the Polish composer, in 1973, but was there no other foundation of a similar kind elsewhere? Admittedly, an approach may well have been made in later years and the manuscripts are in good hands. (Actually, Lutosławski donated five of his orchestral scores to the Music Library of the University of Southern California in 1985, on the occasion of the opening of a Polish Music Center within the library. I fear he did not realize the significance of having his entire oeuvre under one roof. Indeed, he was extremely generous with his manuscripts. One day, upon returning home in Budapest, I saw a large envelope sticking out of my post box. It included twenty-three sketches of his Third Symphony, with a letter in hand. They are now in the Music Archives of the Berlin Academy of Arts, as part of my collection.)

We remained in close touch for the rest of Lutosławski's life. I succeeded in persuading the national concert organization to invite him to conduct in Budapest. The first concert was followed by several others and we would also meet privately: Witold and Danuta (as I was allowed to call them) came to my place for dinner or they would invite my wife and me to their hotel. They were unassuming, wonderful people, touchingly devoted to each other. On one occasion they said they could not imagine one of them dying before the other; ideally, they wanted to die together in an air crash. But it was not to be: Witold left Danuta in 1994 and I understand she practically starved herself to death, dying soon afterward.

Witold was concerned about how his music would fare after he was gone. Would it continue to be played fairly regularly, would any of his pieces make it into the repertoire? Sadly, I have the impression that the bulk of his work lies untouched on his publishers' shelves—that compositions that made such furore during his lifetime— Trois poèmes d'Henri Michaux *(1961/63),* Livre pour orchestre *(1968), Cello Concerto (1969/70),* Mi-Parti *(1975/76), Piano Concerto (1987/88), Symphonies Nos. 3 and 4 (1981/83 and 1988/92, respectively)—are slowly receding into oblivion. Could it be that Lutosławski was such a consummate interpreter of his own music that no generation of conductors was raised during his lifetime to take over the baton? Could this be a danger threatening all composer-conductors? Looking at those active today, I tend to answer that question in the affirmative.*

Lutosławski's description of how listening to John Cage's Piano Concerto had changed his musical thinking gave me the idea for the first question. You will find his reply of 1973 at the beginning of our interview.

As a postscript, I append two remarks of Witold's that I would like to pass on, so to speak, to those interested in his music.

One: he said, once in a while he derived no pleasure from listening to music of any kind, including his own. His way of ascertaining that his frame of mind rather than the music was to blame, was to listen to some Mozart. If he found he had no patience for that either, he knew that he had to wait until he was again in a receptive state.

Two: he said that even when he was not composing, he went on thinking in a creative manner, as he put it, to keep his brain in form.

Now over to our interview.

I.

After 1958 and the first performance of Funeral Music, the next key date is 1960 when you first heard John Cage's music.

It was in that year that I heard an excerpt from his Piano Concerto and those few minutes were to change my life decisively. It was a strange moment, but I can explain what happened.

Composers often do not hear the music that is being played; it only serves as an impulse for something quite different—for the creation of music that only lives in their imagination. It is a sort of schizophrenia: we are listening to something and at the same time creating something else.

That is how it happened with Cage's Piano Concerto. While listening to it, I suddenly realized that I could compose music differently from that of my past. That I could progress toward the whole not from the little detail but the other way round—I should start out from chaos and create order in it, gradually. That is when I started to compose *Jeux vénitiens.* If you compare it to Cage's work you will realize that the two compositions do not resemble each other in any way. And when a few years later I heard Cage's concerto again, the same effect failed to appear, it was as if I had been listening to a completely different piece of music. Perhaps because the first time I heard it I was not listening to it but to my own music.

You must have been ready to receive new ideas, the germs of the new were present in your imagination.

Yes, it was a stimulus, a spark to ignite the powder keg in me. I wrote all that to Cage who was in the process of publishing a collection of manuscripts and asked me to send him a score. I gave him the manuscript of *Jeux vénitiens* and wrote him a letter saying that that piece had opened up a new period in my life, and all that had been prepared by listening to his Piano Concerto.

Jeux vénitiens *was the first work in which controlled aleatory composition played a role. And the last work written in the "old style" was the* Three Postludes.

Yes. I had intended it to be cycle, but I left it off after the Cage incident. It was at that time that Andrzej Markowski asked me to write something for his ensemble, the Cracow Chamber Orchestra which was to appear at the Venice Festival the following year, 1961. That is why I appended the adjective *Vénitiens* to the title.

But to get back to Cage's influence: I would not say that I have taken over anything from him. In my music, chance plays a completely different role from that in his works. Yet, I owe Cage a lot because it was he who reintroduced chance into music. That element of composition had been known for a long time, but European composers had neglected it. It was Cage who reminded them of it.

II.

I do not use the sounds of nature consciously in my compositional work but they must exert a subconscious influence because, when looking through the finished score, I have in the past come upon traces of them in the themes of some of my pieces. For instance, in the third movement of *Jeux vénitiens*, the first phrases in the flute solo are reminiscent of birdsong [see fig. 6].

Figure 6. Birdsong as rendered by the flute solo in the third movement of Lutosławski's *Jeux vénitiens.*

They do not recall the song of any particular species, yet they do make the impression of birdsong. In the third "event" of *Novelette*, that is, in the fourth movement, I have recognized the blackbird in the rhythm of the main subject as played by the violin [see fig. 7]. That, too, took me by surprise—I never thought about it while composing. I then realized that I must have heard it through the open window of my house in Norway.

Birds are sometimes genuine artists commanding respect. Near Warsaw, around three o'clock one summer night, I heard one which possessed a breathtaking facility of variation. Alas, I did not have a tape recorder with me.

When people discuss what is "natural" in music and what is not, I often cite the example of birds. Some believe that whatever is outside the well-tempered twelve-tone scale is not natural. They hold that it contains the natural intervals such as the octave, the fifth, the fourth, and the rest. In fact, they are wrong. Only the octave can be described as natural, the fifth is an artificial creation, neither is it wholly accurate. The tone row, too, is less natural than other aspects of music.

As far as I am concerned, I feel it necessary to go beyond the twelve-tone row because it hampers the imagination of a composer living today. It is no accident that many of us endeavor to create sounds which have nothing to do with the well-tempered scale.

FORUM HOTEL
Budapest
Budapest V. Apáczai Csere J. u. 12-14.
P.O.Box 231. H-1368 Hungary
Telephone (361) 178-088 Telex 224178 forum h

My dear Balint,
Here is the "black bird" theme:

and thank you both again for a charming evening
as ever
Witold

Figure 7. Lutosławski was in Budapest to conduct a concert of his music and used the letterhead of his hotel to illustrate a point. Reproduced by kind permission of the Bálint András Varga Collection, Akademie der Künste, Berlin.

Birds, too, use a different kind of material—the most natural one imaginable. Some of their tones are much more complex than those we know in traditional music. They are made up of more frequencies and neither predominates, like in the oboe and the clarinet.

You have mentioned that in composing *Metastasis,* Xenakis was influenced by an early experience, that of hearing the sound of raindrops on his tent. That sound will have caught the attention of most composers. On one occasion, I heard extracts from traditional Chinese operas and the numerous percussion instruments which made up the orchestra produced the same rhythmic pattern. Such accelerating impulses are commonplace in Chinese music—in Europe, it probably appeared for the first time in Bartók's *Music for Strings, Percussion and Celesta.* In my view, this pattern conjures up the sound of starting rain. I do not know if I am right but that is my conjecture.

III.

Lutosławski replied to the second question in Budapest in 1982 when he was conducting a concert of his own music, with the Concerto for Orchestra, the Double Concerto for Oboe and Harp as well as Novelette *on the program. He also had a go at the third question but both of us decided it was not the real thing. The definitive reply was formulated in a letter he sent me from Oslo in July 1983.*

Still, an excerpt from the 1982 interview should be of interest. I had spotted a motif which occurred in the Concerto for Orchestra and cropped up again in Novelette *composed several years later. In the earlier piece, it appears in the percussion in the middle of the second movement, whereas the same rhythmic pattern opens and ends the later work.*

I never thought about that, but you are right. Interestingly enough, some patterns do seem to accompany you throughout your life. I hope I do not repeat myself too much because I have no desire to do so. Sometimes I am annoyed by motifs which keep coming back. I would like to get rid of them. In a new composition, everything must be new, but nothing can be *entirely* new, otherwise the integrity of the whole will be jeopardized. A piece of music which is new in every single aspect would be alien.

As a matter of fact, I am not against self-repetition, but, of course, on condition that the composer has created something worth repeating. After all, there were many great composers in the past (including the greatest!) who repeated themselves. Bach wrote hundreds of *da capo* arias whose form is absolutely the same. He must have been happy with it (and quite rightly so!) and probably did not need introducing any changes into it. His style, too, remained very much the same during his whole life and nobody would dare blame him for it.

The same goes for some other Baroque composers (Telemann, Vivaldi, and others) and also for some later composers, as for example Haydn, the author of dozens of symphonies and quartets belonging to the same family.

But in the course of time, a different attitude has developed and nowadays a strange mania of expecting new devices in each new work of a composer has become a principle for the professionals to judge the value of contemporary music by. To my mind, the cause of such an approach is the fact that the "message," the "content," or whatever we should call it, of many contemporary works is rather poor and the main reason for composing a new work lies in the demonstration of new devices, new elements of style or technique rather than conveying something important in a form created earlier.

So—a little paradoxically speaking—I envy those composers of the past who were able to successfully repeat themselves. It was, however, possible for them only because their repertoire of means of expression must have satisfied them well enough not to be anxious to look for new ones.

This is I am afraid not true of my own particular case. I have never been entirely happy with my repertoire of means of expression. I have been working for a very long time on a sound language that would better serve my purposes. What inclines me to do so is also the curiosity to investigate new, unexplored regions of the sound world. That is why each new work I compose is to a certain extent a new adventure.

1973/82/83

Thirty-Five

FRANÇOIS-BERNARD MÂCHE (1935)

Like Iannis Xenakis, who was a close friend, and numerous other composers, Mâche studied with Olivier Messiaen. Unlike any of his colleagues, however, he was the only one (as far as I know) to have obtained a degree in archaeology as well. In addition, he studied classical literature of which he was appointed a professor at the Lycée Louis-le-Grand in Paris. Mâche is also professor of musicology at the University of Strasbourg.

Perhaps under Messiaen's influence, he turned his attention, among many other things, to ornitho-musicology and has written a study which sets out to demonstrate that birdsongs are organized according to a repetition-transformation principle. As he puts it: One purpose of the book was to "begin to speak of animal musics other than with quotation marks."[51]

I.

I can report on two experiences which—while they did not have the dimension of Lutosławski's—have left deep traces.

One was my encounter with *musique concrète* in 1955. It was at that time that works by Pierre Henry were released on record. It was not any particular composition that interested me but the new sound world of concrete music.

The other experience occurred by chance: I heard Xenakis's *Metastasis* in a German radio broadcast. That will have been in 1957 or 1958. I was a young composer, still rather green, and while I could not yet offer an alternative to serial music with my own works, I felt an antipathy toward serialism which was similar to Xenakis's. His *Metastasis* proved for me that there existed a new musical language which had nothing to do with serialism. The significance of that encounter could be likened to that with concrete music.

Xenakis was working toward the same end as Varèse had done and I believe he succeeded in achieving many things where the older composer had failed. When I first heard *Metastasis,* I had not yet come across Varèse; years later, his ideas related to mass were to make a stronger impact than Xenakis's researches.

---

51. François Bernard Mâche, *Music, Myth and Nature, or The Dolphins of Arion*, trans. Susan Delaney (Chur, Switzerland: Harwood Academic, 1992), 114. Originally published as *Musique, Mythe, Nature* (Paris: Klincksieck, 1983).

In 1960, I composed a piece which I called *Volume*. It was scored for orchestra and included elements of concrete music. *Volume* merged both influences: the sound world of concrete music and the organization of orchestral sounds as suggested by Xenakis. It was no imitation of *Metastasis*—Xenakis's music rather served as encouragement to look for my own path.

II.

My work has centered primarily on sounds. As I told you earlier, I was initially fascinated by the new sonorities of *musique concrète*. Soon, however, I set myself the task of conquering reality. To begin with, in my tape music, I was happy manipulating unusual sounds, I then moved on to similarly unusual but real sounds with which I attempted to create a kind of fantastic reality.

In the beginning, I was steered by my instincts; later on, theoretical considerations connected with music history took over. I am increasingly convinced that the obsessive historical view that has put its stamp on twentieth-century music since 1912–13 has been losing its relevance. In judging musical compositions it is less and less possible to rely on notions such as past or future.

In my view, we are no longer supposed to seek novelty for novelty's sake (after all, the possibilities have more or less been exhausted). Instead, we have to focus our attention on the research of archetypes. Today, I am interested in the universal values of music. My methods include the comparison of musical systems and the study of musical structures used by animals. Their signals do not in my opinion serve purely as communicative functions but possess in the animal kingdom an aesthetic aspect as well. In my book[52] I set out to prove that there is no basic conflict between nature and culture. Consequently, in starting out from natural models in my own work, I merely draw on one of the characteristic features of music history.

III.

My reply to the second question is an indication that I attribute no importance to seeking novelty at any price. That tendency characterized the epoch ruled by the idée fixe of historicism.

52. François Bernard Mâche, *Musique au singulier* (Paris: Odile Jacob, 2001).

Nor am I afraid of repetition. It is no sin to use certain elements again, provided you do so not to make your job easier. I have in the past reused every aspect of an earlier composition, for I felt that at first go I had not succeeded in unfolding the possibilities inherent in it.

For me, repetition is one of the fundamental archetypes in music. It belongs to music making as a specific way of interpreting the world of nature, one of the possible replies we can give to the sounds surrounding us.

1983/2009

Thirty-Six

MICHIO MAMIYA (1929)

I accompanied a Hungarian orchestra to Japan in 1979 and was overwhelmed by the tremendous welcome accorded to the musicians by audiences all over the country. Concert halls were packed to capacity and while applause following each work was lukewarm, to say the least (something which initially appalled and unsettled the unsuspecting Hungarians), the last piece on the program would unleash a storm quite unprecedented in the careers of European musicians.

The reception of Occidental music brought home to me not only the tremendous prestige it was enjoying in the Land of the Rising Sun but also the plight of Japanese composers. If they succumb to Western idioms, they are bound to produce derivative pieces. If they draw their inspiration from Japanese traditions, they fall into the trap of provinciality. In combining the two, they will still be faced with the need to establish an unmistakable identity.

I believe this dilemma is apparent in Michio Mamiya's replies, as indeed in those of Tōru Takemitsu. Mamiya deplores what he regards as a fallacy that composers must develop an individual style, drawing as he does his inspiration from folk music.

He read the text in 2009 and decided it needed no change.

I.

When I was a student in the early 1950s, the music and thinking of Bartók exerted a strong influence. I was fascinated by his choruses rooted in Hungarian folk music, his piano sonata, his second sonata for violin and piano, his third and fourth string quartets as well as his study on Hungarian peasant songs. I understood that his music was nourished by folk traditions and that recognition induced me to turn toward Japanese folk traditions myself in order to find my own compositional idiom.

This effort had the result that music gradually talked to me differently than before. I drew the conclusion that the salient characteristic of folk music was its saturation with tenderness. Interestingly enough, that realization immediately brought me closer to Western music.

In Bartók's compositions, just as in the folk music of many nations, I discovered the same tenderness as in Japanese folk music. In other words, Bartók's works and his thinking influenced me indirectly.

II.

Silence is the composer's canvas. Before starting to compose, I imagine eternal silence as a canvas for the music I want to write. I love music, I love listening to music, most of all to pure folk music. And, in order to conjure it up, I need silence.

We are surrounded by many kinds of sounds, some of them beautiful. Sometimes even the ticking of a clock can suggest interesting musical ideas, although I do not believe that I need sounds of the outside world to inspire me. All that could serve as the subject of psychological research.

III.

In pondering this question, I grew very sad: it mirrors the poor state of our culture. In our century, the slogan "new is good" has tormented many creative personalities, including composers. It is as if most composers were forced, as an obligatory assignment, to seek an individual style. As a result, they cannot develop and chisel at their style, their way of expression, their musical tastes over a longer period of time. The new swiftly fades into old and vanishes.

The notion of idiom presupposes common rules, grammar, and vocabulary. In this sense it is silly to talk of an individual idiom.

In anonymous folk culture, performance is marked by a common style. No one seeks a personal one. That explains why folk culture has preserved its constancy and why it can serve as a basis for all urban culture. This is true also of the great Classical masters.

In the process of folk music's existence, some elements are repeated infinitely, they are handed down from generation to generation, all the while refining characteristic traits, the simple, beautiful forms.

Each performance differs somewhat from another one, even if the performer remains the same. This permanence and constant renewal of folk culture is reminiscent of processes in nature and the universe; such is also the stream of time and such is our life. Music, as a mirror of the universe, could become a wonderful creation in the hands of man.

If I find it necessary, I repeat what I achieved in earlier works. The value of a composition has nothing to do with its style, whether it is "old" or "new." What matters is the truth of expression—that it should be nourished by a spiritual hunger which finds an echo in the listener's heart.

1984/85, approved in 2009

Thirty-Seven

GIACOMO MANZONI (1932)

Like Luciano Berio, Manzoni studied composition at the Milan Conservatory where he was subsequently to teach harmony and counterpoint. In addition, he enrolled at Bocconi University in the same city to devote himself to foreign languages and literature.

It is no wonder, then, that so much of his oeuvre should comprise settings of texts by a wide variety of writers: one of his operas is based on Thomas Mann's Doktor Faustus *(1989) (premiered at La Scala, with Robert Wilson directing and Gianni Versace providing the setting and the costumes); for* Musica per Inferno di Dante *(1995) he engaged the services of a close collaborator of Berio, Edoardo Sanguineti, to write the libretto.*

His orchestral compositions, too, frequently employ vocal soloists, to sing words by Nietzsche, Hölderlin, Beckett, or Bruno Maderna. Apparently, Manzoni needs inspiration from the outside, so to speak, to set his creative imagination in train: his purely instrumental compositions are often homages to composers like Varèse or Nono. The same applies to chamber music with settings of Rilke or Emily Dickinson.

Manzoni has kept in close touch with languages on another level as well: he is a noted writer on music and has also translated works by Schoenberg and Adorno into Italian.

I.

I can only recall a few moments which could be likened to Lutosławski's Cage experience. However, they have not been associated exclusively with contemporary music. They have been evoked by Perotinus, Wagner, and Berg as much as by Ives or Xenakis.

Experiences like that cannot be confined to music alone. I for one have received stronger impulses from certain external and internal impulses of the environment. Most recently, for instance, it was the San Giovanni degli Eremiti church in Palermo which impressed me with its majestic and solemn nave: I could almost hear sounds streaming from the stones. My earliest experience is linked to the Baptistery in Pisa: Giovanni Pisano's enthralling, almost magical sculptures not only inspired me to hear sounds but also conjured up scenes of music theater.

Finally, many years ago, on a gorgeous autumn afternoon, on the Campidoglio, an intoxicated stupor came over me and it seemed as if the surrounding hills, the Roman palaces and churches were inundating me with sonorities which joined in a fantastic *sinfonia*, merging with light, colors, space, and movement.

II.

The all-encompassing change created by industrial civilization in our sounding world is bound to leave traces on everyone, not least on composers for whom sounds are the basic material they work with. As far as I am concerned, external sound events do exert an enriching influence but I have never transferred them into my music without transforming them. Composition for me is a highly complex, indirect and analytical process where any external influences are submerged in something which is through its nature quite "different."

III.

I would put this question to an aesthetician. You cannot expect a composer who grapples with the material, with creation itself, to reply coolly and objectively to a question which I believe has occupied the minds of critics and musicologists for centuries.

I can only say that self-repetition and well-worn clichés repel me. Composition is not a daily and peaceful activity as it may be for several of my colleagues luckier than I am. It is a path full of the hardships of searching and exploration, an attempt to master hurdles which face me anew in each new piece: composition is INVENTION.

1983/2009

Thirty-Eight

PAUL MÉFANO (1937)

It was in his capacity as conductor and founder-director of the new music ensemble 2E2M that I first made contact with Paul Méfano, in the vain hope that he would program some Hungarian music. Talking to him as a composer was more productive, as indicated by our interview below.

Méfano studied with Messiaen directly and also at one remove, his teachers having included Boulez and Stockhausen, in addition to Henri Pousseur. On a grant from the Harkness Foundation, he spent two years in the United States (1966–68) subsequently living in Berlin for a year.

Attending the Summer Courses in Darmstadt was a logical consequence of this background. Recognition of his achievement arrived when he was invited to teach at the Paris Conservatoire, a position he was to exchange later to become director of the Versaille Conservatoire (1996).

I.

I have also had crucial experiences of a relevant nature. The first one occurred at the Paris Conservatoire. One of Bach's *Brandenburg Concerti* was performed, led by a very inadequate conductor. I was not yet a musician at the time, but however poor the interpretation may have been, the music exerted an extraordinary influence. It moved me to tears and I decided to become a musician. I was sixteen and resolved to devote my time to musical studies after finishing secondary school two years later. My goal was to become a composer.

The fact that I strongly responded to music was proved by an earlier experience as well. I was born in Iraq, in the town of Basra (I was the first Frenchman to have been born there). There lived a milk-woman in our neighborhood. She would balance a huge vessel on her head and offer her goods chanting loudly. The curious melody which she repeated many times fascinated me and in later years I attempted to conjure it up in my own works.

Hearing [Boulez's] *Pli selon pi* for the first time in 1960 was of equally crucial significance. It represented a fundamentally new musical idiom compared to those I had come across until then and it stirred me up no end. On the whole, however, non-European folk music has been more important than European music. Gamelan of Bali, for instance, is of greater interest than new music which often strikes me as indifferent. Of course, I am fond of the brass froth of Messiaen's compositions, I am fascinated by Stockhausen's *Kreuzspiel*, and also by Morton Feldman who has so much to say with such economical means. It is as if he lit little sparks in the Void.

Witold Lutosławski's powerful creative vein has also been of significance, especially the colors, diversity, and liveliness of his Symphony No. 2. Sometimes I am gripped by the synthesizer, too, not in new music but in rock. However, rock music itself does not interest me in the least, it is not my world.

If he is played well, Maderna is the Schubert of contemporary music. I have no time for Nono, but interestingly enough, one of his orchestral pieces, *Per Bastiana—Tai-Yang Chen*, has influenced me a great deal.

As far as the first half of the twentieth century is concerned, Stravinsky and Bartók are of course important, I enjoy conducting them, too, together with Debussy and Ravel. Debussy lives in me constantly, just as Mozart and Schubert, but their music strikes me as if it had been written on another planet, I seek no direct contact with it.

II.

I respond to sounds of the environment extremely sensitively: to the noises of cafés and large department stores just as much as to those I come across in nature. Incidentally, it was Cage who called my attention to the latter.

Sometimes impressions of an aesthetic kind strike a chord. For instance, a miniature Chinese ivory figure of the seventh or eighth century may evoke sounds. Oddly enough, other handmade objects, too, may conjure up musical images.

A sound picture: in Bali, near a sanctuary, my attention was attracted by wild screeching. I went closer and shrank back: a cock-fight was going on and the odd noises were being made by men who, just like at the stock exchange, were calling out stakes—they were laying wagers on the cocks. Those sounds also affected me.

In my music, I seek perfection and would like to call up nature—at the same time dissolving it in the elements, in the sea. I have only banalities to say about the sea. It is simply wonderful. However, what tops everything: the Aeolian flutes I heard on Solomon Islands. Gouged out tree trunks are set up on the shore and when the wind blows they make a uniquely wonderful, glassy sound: it is supposed to be made by the souls of the dead. One does not know if it is produced by man or by nature. In my house, a similar sonority is sometimes produced by the water taps. I owe beautiful sound experiences also to fountains. Incredible natural phenomena also appear if Pierre-Yves Artaud's flute playing is recorded at close range. All of that is a circle where everything echoes answers to everything else.

I like listening briefly to the gliding of car tires on the highway or to the machines of airplanes. In hearing the sound of the planes, I also hear the wind. There is always some tie between nature and the culture to which I belong—also music as I conceive of it. Ever since my very first pieces, I have been looking for these sounds and I enjoy breaking them down to their microscopic ingredients. You learn a great deal of interest about the human organism if you examine it through the microscope. Sounds reveal even more fascinating things.

III.

I like diversity. As soon as I have completed a work which is marked by a particular style, a particular spirit, I turn in another direction. The elements that determine some of my compositions may appear heterogeneous to the outsider, but I am convinced that those who know my career, my musical idiom thoroughly, will find a unity in all that diversity. Basically, my music is characterized by permanence and fundamental identity. My old pieces, dating from the second half of the 1950s, contain traits which I developed further in later years. It can happen that an aspect of a composition which is but a germ, assumes greater significance elsewhere while features which had a transitory importance for a period, later wither and disappear.

I am not concerned by the danger of repeating my style. I seek my own truth and my truth is exploration, progressing further, ever further. Instead of exploiting an idiom I have found in fifty different compositions, I prefer to look for something new and pass on what I have found.

A personality, if there is one, should surface by itself. If there is none, to hell with it! That is the law of gladiators, the law of nature. A merciless law, but once we have joined the club of creators, we have to accept it.

The endeavor to create immortal works springs from absurd vanity. We have to give our best we are capable of at any given time—that is what counts. Later on, we shall see if there is any unity in what we have produced. For all the breathtaking diversity of his oeuvre, Charles Ives has left behind a unified lifework. The same is true of Berg. The same question has of course to be posed in contemporary music as well. In some cases, we find versatility in unity, in others unity is crystallized out of versatility. It is also my aim to be able to create a radical unity out of heterogeneous elements.

1983

Thirty-Nine

ANDRÁS MIHÁLY (1917–93)

I hope I am not being unjust to the memory of the composer András Mihály in saying that I believe he would now be largely forgotten if it were not for György Kurtág's Hommage à Mihály András. Twelve Microludes for String Quartet, Op. 13 *(1977/78), and several other homages. They include Kurtág's highly regarded orchestral work* Stele, Op. 33 *(1994/2006), which is based on a piano piece in memory of the composer in the sixth volume of the piano series* Játékok. *Also, a few notes from Mihály's early Cello Concerto helped Kurtág to find a fitting ending to* Stele.

However, after World War II, András Mihály was a highly respected and influential figure in Hungarian musical life—perhaps not so much as a composer but as founder-conductor of the Budapest New Music Ensemble, which (in addition to programming music by contemporary Hungarian composers) presented to Hungarian audiences whatever was new and important in the world of contemporary music on an international scale. He was a peerless professor of chamber music at the Budapest Academy, a successful director of the State Opera House, and his television programs in which he talked about and conducted some of the pivotal compositions of the past century had some of the quality of Leonard Bernstein's programs of a similar nature.

He was one of those Hungarian intellectuals who after the war engaged themselves in rebuilding cultural life in the country. He sincerely believed in the ideals of socialism and in the interests of its noble goals he was for a time ready to close his eyes to the malfunctioning of the system, indeed, to the crimes committed by the Stalinist puppet regime. Mihály was led by the idea that classical music should be brought to the people (the "masses" to use a term much in currency in the 1950s). That could only be achieved if new music being composed was simple and drew its inspiration from folk music. That is also why he wished to suppress Bartók's abstract, "modern" works and restrict performances to the composer's folk music arrangements. (Paradoxically enough, he referred in our interview to those very compositions as having been of particular significance in his development). The result was a plethora of pocket Kodály pieces produced in Hungary en masse.

By the time he founded the Budapest New Music Ensemble in the 1960s, Mihály had left those ideals behind and composed in an advanced idiom. However, when he discussed the chances of my promoting his works, the one piece he singled out was the Cello Concerto of 1953.

I.

I decided early on to become a composer. I studied composition and the cello simultaneously, so it was inevitable for my strongest impulses to come from traditional music.

I could not tell under whose influence I eventually found access to the realm of twentieth-century music. I had played quartets by Schoenberg, Berg, and Milhaud before the war, but none had exerted a strong enough influence which would have helped me to decide the direction of my orientation. It was not until the early 1950s that I began to evolve a style for myself even though the times were anything but conducive for that. I was past thirty—but as a composer, I was about twenty. During the war, as well as in the period prior to it or in the years of transition following it, it was impossible to concentrate on creative work.

I owed the greatest experience of the early 1950s to Bartók's late compositions: to the curious phenomenon that something sounds like modern music and is nevertheless popular. In my young years that would have been unthinkable. Modern music hardly ever met with success except for a branch of twentieth-century music which by then seemed distant to us. The works written in a popular style by great masters like Bartók were also well received.

Under the influence of those pieces, I also attempted to develop my own popular musical idiom. That is how the Cello Concerto came to be written in 1953. That experiment, however, soon lost its momentum.

I owed my next memorable experience to *Pierrot lunaire.* We studied it with my pupils at the Music Academy for a whole year (it so happened that my chamber music class consisted of young musicians suited for it and there appeared in Hungarian musical life Erika Sziklay who seemed to have been predestined for that very work). You cannot possibly study a composition more thoroughly than we did.

That process directed me toward very free composition. I attempted to evolve my own world which may have been stricter than *Pierrot lunaire,* but was far from the cerebral construction of melodies as recommended by a particular trend in twentieth-century music. I tried to create a melodic and harmonic idiom which was based on expansion and contraction. In other words, where in proportion to the expansion and contraction of the melodic line, a harmonic world would also expand and contract, almost like a mixture. My Third Symphony stands for those efforts.

To sum up: late Bartók was a positive experience, Schoenberg's world was more or less a negative one. (I never followed his principles of construction. I merely attempted to find a middle course between a completely free and a completely constructed method of composition.)

My third important encounter—once again, as a performing musician—was Kurtág's *Bornemisza Concerto.* It made a tremendous impact: traces of it are to be found in my Third String Quartet.

Next, I stopped composing, at least for the time being. My work at the Opera House was incompatible with composition.

What was it that impressed you so much in The Sayings of Péter Bornemisza*?*

It is difficult for me to talk about it. Kurtág has achieved something wonderful: he has invented a twentieth-century drama and has also invented its redeeming twentieth-century lyricism. That implies a great many technical solutions. It is roughly also what I sought to do in my Third String Quartet—creating an almost unbearable tension. With Kurtág, this tension is also unbearable and it has been created as a result of extraordinary compositional invention. It also brings its resolution which in our age is at least as much of a feat as its opposite, the creation of tension.

Similarly to the *Bornemisza Concerto,* my string quartet is also the depiction of a life story. Both of us resort to a dramatic stance in a Beethovenian sense: here I am, listen to me. The most characteristic example is the first movement of Beethoven's Fifth Symphony. A feature Kurtág and I have in common is the reinterpretation of *Scherzo* as a *danse macabre.* This is present in a number of movements with Kurtág and it also applies to the whole of my second movement, my *Scherzo.* And finally the lyrical resolution which in my piece appears at the end of the third movement and with Kurtág, too, appears in the last one.

If you do not mind, I am not going to tell you about the rest of the ideas I took from him.

II.

There are two types of composer. One did not appear until the twentieth century, really: the one who makes his living as a composer. I suppose I could call him a "professional composer."

The other type—and that's where I belong—is a musician who performs, teaches, and also writes music, in other words, is active in several fields. Obviously, the performer-composer has his head full of music, his inner ear is busy, while the other type of composer can listen to the world around him with a clear and music-less mind. What follows from this? That certain aspects of music become more crystallized in my head than with a "professional" composer, because I live my life with actually sounding music nourishing my inner hearing. Nearly forty years of teaching, playing in an orchestra, conducting, coaching, the time I have been spending with the chamber ensemble, my own instrumental practice—all that has added up to a sizable stock of sound experience and has been stored in my head just as in a computer. In this way, I have acquired an infallible inner hearing which would have been unimaginable without the storehouse of impressions I have amassed.

This way of life, however, has also meant that I have had to go without periods devoid of music, time for traveling in the world with rested ears, time to be devoted to absorbing and collecting sonorities. If I happen to be sitting in a tram, I cannot hear the ringing of its bell because I have in my head the music I taught a few minutes before or what I am going to conduct in the evening, or what I am composing.

Consequently, I am nourished by the sound experience drawn from music that already exists rather than the sound world on the border between music and nonmusic.

III.

Every composer repeats himself. After all: composition is writing your autobiography. In one piece there appears a darker face of the composer, in another one his lighter face, in one work he is aggressive, in another he is calmer, in one he is desperate, in another one he is optimistic. But all the while it is the same face!

Composers in the past did not bother about the question whether this self-portrait is being enriched with markedly new features. Vivaldi, for instance, who produced one work after another, only took care not to repeat exactly the same piece. But he wrote a great many compositions with the same brushstrokes, the same method, for his job was to supply new pieces day after day, say, for the orphanage where he found employment.

Ever since the emergence of a repertoire—in other words, since composers no longer have to meet an urgent demand—they have sought to lend unmistakably individual traits to their works in order to establish their claim to become part of the repertoire. The accent is no longer on quantity but on justifying your raison d'être, your presence. In this situation, you wait until you can present many interesting, new features of your personality, or your technical mastery or musical vision: only then do you write a new work.

That is how the type of composer has appeared who writes little. One example is Boulez, who is nevertheless an extremely significant figure. In other words: if you wait until you have something new to say, you will naturally repeat yourself less.

Some composers have a go again and again at a big work, that is, at the attempt to present the most authentic possible portrait of themselves. There are some who can envisage the form they will want to realize: they set about writing the work and complete it even if they find midway that the cell from which the work unfolded is unsuitable for shaping that very form.

As far as I am concerned, I work very slowly and discard a great deal in an effort to bring about what I set out to achieve. I am not sure that this method is any better. It is neither here nor there whether the composition you have been grappling with has come about through the birth and death of a number of abortive pieces. If you write a hundred symphonies and one of them turns out to be good, then it was worth writing the other ninety-nine. If you decide not to release the ninety-nine, just the one good symphony, the result is the same. To put it another way: you made the right decision, because in view of the demand for music today, only that one was needed.

At the beginning, when you are drawing up your plans and the first ideas crop up in your mind, the piece is something alien, something outside you, waiting to be born. Then, there comes a time when it has created its own laws and the piece sets about kneading the composer. It raises demands for which the composer has to rack his brains in an effort to find the right ideas. You must face the difficulties created by your material even if your head appears to be empty. This is often an excruciating process. You cannot fall back upon an older piece of yours to see if you found a solution to a similar problem. You can only concern yourself with the need to decide whether the solution you have arrived at is worthy of the piece. And, of course, you will only have a real overview after the piece has been completed.

1983

Forty

TRISTAN MURAIL (1947)

Music was no first choice for Tristan Murail: he opted for Arabic and economics before joining Messiaen's stable at the age of twenty. His horizons, however, extended well beyond Messiaen's class: Murail was very much aware of the presence in Paris of Iannis Xenakis and looked also to Giacinto Scelsi as well as György Ligeti for creative impulses.

Like many of his contemporaries in France, Britain, and elsewhere, Murail (together with his friends Gérard Grisey, Michaël Lévinas, Hugues Dufourt, and Philippe Hurel) founded an ensemble to perform their music: L'Itinéraire (1973). Perhaps even more important than performances was their mutual goal of developing a new aesthetic, which derived from their research of the overtone spectrum of sounds. Dufourt's article of 1979 (published in 1981), "Musique spectrale" gave the movement its name.[53]

In 1980, the group attended a course at IRCAM and Murail in particular engaged, with the help of the computer, in a thorough exploration of acoustic phenomena. Between 1991 and 1997, he taught composition at the same institution, lectured in Darmstadt and at the Centre Acanthes.

Tristan Murail lives in the United States, where he is a professor of composition at Columbia University.

I.

No doubt about it: during the course of his career, a composer's thinking undergoes changes, but they rarely occur from one moment to another.

I studied with Olivier Messiaen at the Conservatoire, together with Gérard Grisey, Didier Denis, and Michaël Lévinas. At that time, almost all my generation composed in a postserial style: the *Reihe* replaced the idiom of Gabriel Fauré. However, the institution itself did not change—it retained its conservative, academic spirit.

I felt I had reached an impasse. I wanted to start from scratch, to begin with point zero. I longed for clear harmonic structures, a sound world based on different principles. Even if that endeavor may have been basically intuitive, the example of Ligeti and Xenakis proved most helpful. It

53. Hugues Dufourt, "Musique spectrale: pour une pratique des formes de l'énergie," *Bicéphale*, no. 3 (1981): 85–89.

did not show me a particular direction of development but it confirmed my choice of path and liberated my thinking.

I owe a more radical change to my discovery of electronic tools and computers. They enabled me to evolve models of thinking which nourish my work to this day.

I have been working with IRCAM's equipment for two years now—an experience which has opened up new vistas. The possibilities are well-nigh infinite. I attended a course run by IRCAM and learned how to use the classical synthetic programs. They had been developed in the main by Americans, at Stanford University and elsewhere and soon enough it became clear to me within what narrow limits they were operating. I embarked on independent research at IRCAM and developed a program which is quite individual: I believe I have succeeded in realizing what Stockhausen had attempted to do at the Cologne Studio. He had failed to achieve his goal simply because the equipment was lacking in the tools we now have at our disposal. The computer has supplied me with the key. I applied what is called additive synthesis which is related to the solutions used in my instrumental music. I wrote a piece which merges instrumental and tape music almost completely: the tape supplements the spectrum and timbre of the instruments. I made use of the equipment called 4X by its inventor, Giuseppe di Giugno. It renders sound transformation in real time possible.

Once I was faced with the task of formulating my ideas for the computer, I realized that I had up until then lived in the prison of traditional patterns which had fettered my imagination. Patterns had lost their raison d'être. The computer prompts me to make use of the laws of mathematics, physics, and acoustics. Right now I am addressing myself to the problem of getting the machine to create form and sound simultaneously.

II.

A difficult question: how do sounds influence me? I listen not so much to the sounds of nature but rather to those of the city, just like Varèse did. For instance, I am interested in noises to do with the underground railway: the rolling of the carriages on the rails, the closing of doors. In Le Havre where I spent my young years, I was struck by the sounds produced by the dredgers working in the harbor. They actually appear in my first pieces.

Sounds created by instruments as well as electronic sounds are equally important: I regard them as materials which can give birth to musical forms. Sounds for me are more than timbres. They are in themselves microforms which you can analyze, break down to their constituents and put them together again, expand—just like a musical form. The structure of my compositions is often reminiscent of a single huge sonority regardless of whether it is of instrumental origin or not. Several pieces make use of the pealing of bells and I also have sounding aggregates based on a structure resembling the sound of bells.

III.

I am told that my works possess a recognizable individual style. The presence of an individual style entails the danger of self-repetition and while many of my friends have not been able to evade that trap, I believe I am too young to have to worry about it.

I feel I am developing all the time, I am making progress, I am making new discoveries all the time which I have to understand and try out. My development is so fast that I could almost say that my style is different at the beginning of a piece from my style at the end of the same work. That is what makes a composition dynamic. The question is whether I ought not to call a halt to making yet more discoveries and concentrate rather on digesting what I have found so far. It could be that I shall write a few pieces which draw on the results of all the experiments I have made up to now. I fear, though, that I shall not be able to withstand the urge to go on experimenting all the while.

I hope I can preserve this heightened spiritual state throughout my life. No composer can live without it: after all, each new piece is a risk—each new piece is a wager.

1983

Forty-One

MARLOS NOBRE (1939)

Marlos Nobre is probably the best-known Brazilian composer today. His biography, the range of his teachers, and the years he has devoted to studying his craft, tell of an insatiable thirst for knowledge and an unswerving dedication to his calling.

His professors have included Alberto Ginastera, Olivier Messiaen, Riccardo Malipiero, Aaron Copland, and Luigi Dallapiccola at the Latin American Center in Buenos Aires. Subsequently, Nobre worked at the Columbia-Princeton Electronic Music Center in New York, in addition to a stint at the Berkshire Music Center at Tanglewood, where he attended courses by Alexander Goehr and Gunther Schuller and met Leonard Bernstein.

Back in Brazil, Nobre was music director of the National Symphony Orchestra in Rio de Janeiro and of the radio run by the Ministry of Culture, but he retained his ties with the United States as visiting professor at Yale University in 1992. His international standing is indicated by his presidency of UNESCO's International Music Council in 1986–87.

As a conductor and pianist, Marlos Nobre has appeared widely in South America and Europe.

I.

I think I can perfectly understand the point made by Lutosławski, for I have had many similar experiences in listening to music by other composers. Normally, I have no problem concentrating on the works of my colleagues, I listen attentively and with interest. It does happen, however, that a particular musical idea (be it a rhythmic pattern or a special orchestral sonority) suddenly attracts my attention. Usually, it only occupies my mind for a very short time, perhaps just a few seconds and the rest of that particular composition may hold no more interest for me. It is like a flash or an electric shock that sets in train creative ideas in my mind and could even prove to have been the impulse for composing a new work.

I can remember such moments very clearly. For instance, some years ago I was on the jury of UNESCO's International Rostrum of Composers in Paris and in that capacity, listened to numerous new works. At some point, my attention was gripped by a passage of peculiar rhythmic interest. Sadly, I can no longer remember the composer's name or the title of the piece. I do know, however, that those few seconds served as inspiration, they gave me new ideas regarding my position as a composer.

I realized that there was a way after all of ridding myself of the doubts which were tormenting me at the time. It was a pointer how I could compose music that was more direct, more open and had less to do with serial and multiserial composition. An outcome was my *Sonancias III* for two pianos and two percussionists which opened a new period in my career. That piece is completely different from the one I had heard in Paris but possibly I would never have written it had it not been for the encounter with that composition.

Something similar happened in 1982 when I was sitting on the jury, together with Penderecki, Ginastera, and Taira, of the Caracas International Composers' Competition. I studied 170 scores, all of them orchestral pieces and my head was full of sounds. All of a sudden, an anonymous score attracted my attention like a magnet, with one of its rhythmic patterns becoming a starting point for my guitar work *Momentos IV.* I composed it onboard a plane between New York and Rio de Janeiro. My orchestral composition *Convergencias* received impulses from Ginastera's *Estancias*, likewise written for orchestra.

Last but not least, I would like to cite the example of Lutosławski's *Trois poèmes d'Henri Michaux* which I heard in 1970. While listening to that wonderful music, I discovered new possibilities in myself, in my own compositional work. Without having seen the score, Lutosławski's music liberated me, gave me courage and self-confidence. It confirmed my conviction that serial and multiserial composition had its limits and induced me to seek more "Latin" solutions (that is, ones that afforded more room for the imagination and the subconscious) in creating music. Lutosławski's masterpiece provided the ignition for composing the orchestral work *Mosaico* in that very year, 1970.

II.

I have had two different experiences in this connection. On the one hand, I believe that everyday sounds do have an influence on my work, indeed, they can serve as motivation. On the other hand, I need absolute quiet for composing; any outside noise disrupts my concentration and drives me to desperation.

Just as with music by other composers, where a particular aspect—lasting just a few seconds—can inspire me, the same is with sounds of the environment. For example: one day I was driving through a long tunnel and landed in a traffic jam. Soon enough, there arose a veritable symphony of car honks. It was bound to leave an impression and true enough, traces of it are to be found in my *Concerto breve* for piano and orchestra (1969). It appears in the trumpets and trombones without my actually meaning to imitate the "honk symphony." I wrote the concerto several years after the event, and apparently, the impression I had received in the tunnel was strong enough to influence me subconsciously.

The same is true of birdsong and other sounds of nature: I have always responded to them with heightened sensitivity so that they have become part of my subconscious and have influenced my creativity. Still, I never attempted to notate birdsong in the way Messiaen did. In my *Mosaico* of 1970, you can discern sonorities which sound as if they had come from nature without my being aware of it when writing the piece.

III.

In my view, individual style is the constant presence of a composer's "manias." It is never identical with self-repetition. Self-repetition signifies the death of a creative personality, it is the empire of routine.

What I call "individual style" could also be described as "personality." A truly creative composer will always be ready to integrate novel ideas, but even when he is working with new materials, there always remains something recognizably his own.

Lutosławski was impressed not so much by Cage's actual piece but by the American composer's freedom, his independence from Western musical traditions. Lutosławski absorbed this freedom, adapted it to his own personality and as a result composed such highly individual works as *Jeux vénitiens* or *Trois poèmes d'Henri Michaux*.

In my view, that is what style is about: the capability of a creative mind of developing its own world by integrating all sorts of impressions from the outside, selecting whatever is best for him but keeping his independence in the process.

1985

Forty-Two

LUIGI NONO (1924–90)

I met the composer in Graz, Budapest, and Amsterdam and was moved by his cordiality. I was also embarrassed by it: it seemed obvious to me that it was due to my coming from a communist country; he appeared to assume that I, too, was an ardent adherent of the faith. (Nono had joined the Italian Communist Party in 1952 and as far as I know remained a member all his life.) I hated to disappoint him, so I suppose I just smiled and did my best to reciprocate his friendliness.

Nono readily agreed to reply to my three questions and after transcribing the tape, I sent it to him for approval. I never heard from him, and my reminders remained unanswered. I comfort myself that it is nevertheless authentic: after all, those are his words.

I.

When listening to the music of a contemporary composer, I try to understand the way he created it and the ideas he set out to realize in the piece. In new acoustic phenomena, I examine the new elements as if under a magnifying glass.

Every composition is of course a manifestation of our time, it has a structure peculiar to its language and it has an ideal. It is important for me to become acquainted with everything that characterizes our age.

The music of Josquin, or Giovanni Gabrieli, or Beethoven is, however, much more important. Not because having studied it I will compose differently but in order to understand a composer's thinking in a given historical period, the kind of materials he worked with, his relationship to those materials, the compositional principles he developed, the sort of contact he established with his contemporaries and with the reality of his age.

II.

Nineteen sixty-eight was a significant year for the whole of Western Europe. The students' movement played an important role, however different it may have been in France, the Federal Republic of Germany, or Italy.

In Italy, this movement emerged as a consequence of the long and difficult struggle that workers had been waging since 1960. The students' movement then established a tight contact with the workers—a process which was not without its complications. It goes without saying that a great deal of debate was going on. Several demonstrations were organized in Venice, not only in 1968—but in that year, some one hundred students decided to boycott the Biennale. Venetians were joined by Germans (the followers of Rudi Dutschke) as well as French from Nanterre and Paris. Finally, about two hundred people demonstrated on St. Mark's Square, in the presence of five thousand policemen.

There followed a strike at Marghera, an industrial district of Venice, then workers of the chemical industry put on large-scale demonstrations, occupying the streets and the railway station.

I experienced all that on the spot, at close quarters. The noise of demonstrations, the discussions, the rhythmic pattern of slogans—all that exerted a profound influence on me, not merely their form or their rhythm. I realized that we were also having to do with an informational signal of our time. It was our own folklore. I drew on those experiences in my *Musica manifesto No. 1.* The first part is a setting of a poem by Pavese, for two female voices and electronics, in the second part I used recordings of demonstrations in Venice and Paris as well as of fighting with the police.

In that connection, I studied the characteristic features of human hearing—its development, its passive and active aspects, its response to contemporary environmental effects in big cities, in the country and in factories. I examined the way we talk—the way a worker would talk in an automated factory as well as at a farm (there is considerable difference between the two), how we talk in our private life from an acoustic and a psychological point of view, what is the difference between speaking habits of people in villages and in cities—not in general but in accordance with their social status.

I find it very important for us to further expand the rich possibilities inherent in the human voice, naturally not only in the sense of bel canto. That is why I study a wide range of singing styles—ritual, folk, or art song in Europe and outside of our continent, in the present and in the past, in different social strata. For instance, I compare the Andalusian style of singing with that in Southern Italy which had been influenced by Andalusian singing, or Gabrieli's choruses with similar compositions by Schoenberg, Dallapiccola, and others. It is my goal to understand the connection between intention, the acoustic material, and compositional principles—to better understand reality.

Actually, I find all sounds important. The sound of the sea in Venice, in the lagunas, is completely different from Sardinia where the sea is open. I look at these major differences also from an acoustic standpoint. It is primitive and banal to talk in a romantic or idealist manner of the rumbling of the sea. The truth is that the differences are huge not only acoustically but also on the level of knowledge and emotions. Also as far as the sounds of leaves or birds are concerned. In Venice where I live, I endeavor to observe and to hear precisely the simultaneous sounds of the sea, the trees, and also boats, bells (Venice has a lot of them!), and human speech.

III.

Perhaps we can talk of a personal style if the composer does not pay too much attention to it. Rather than worry about it, he should address himself to the renewal of musical idiom.

Self-repetition occurs if one lets oneself go, if one lacks the courage to embark on something new because it would entail a great deal of restlessness. If he sticks in his way of life or just in his thinking to his established habits. Then he would repeat himself.

I feel that restlessness can prove to be the spring of creative fantasy. The figure of the wanderer known from ancient Hasidic tradition and also from Nietzsche and Robert Walser, the great Swiss writer, is also present in music. That, too, is like the sea. There is water everywhere, one has to make way for oneself—but no trace is left, one has to start all over again. In his poem *Kolumbus*, Hölderlin gave a wonderful poetic expression to this. That we have to be on the move all the time, we have to wander, searching for the new. So that we can be surprised. Never sit comfortably.

This is an important question for me, especially nowadays, when conservatism is on the rise in the world. Not only in the field of culture. We have to find new paths, away from models, forms, dogmas. We have to arrive at new formulations in theory and in practice, to work out new means of analysis, to address problems in their entirety rather than reduce them as it suits us. We should further expand our capacity of the fantastic and the rational! Wittgenstein attributed considerable significance to the scientific and the imaginary moment.

We have to find new bases, new values. Many mythological values belong to the past. The ancient Greek gods have sunk and their places have not yet been taken by others. In our lives, in culture, and in politics, there are values and gods that have grown well-worn.

As a composer and as an Italian I feel I must wander.

1978/80

Forty-Three

KRZYSZTOF PENDERECKI (1933)

For a few years early on in his career, Krzysztof Penderecki was a symbol of pioneering new music, with composers in the so-called socialist countries avidly listening to his music and studying his scores. György Kurtág, for one, acknowledges to this day his indebtedness to Threnody for the Victims of Hiroshima *(1959/60) for 52 strings—the lessons he drew from the piece were put to use in his* The Sayings of Péter Bornemisza, Op. 7, *a "concerto" for soprano and piano of 1963/68.*

To quote from Baker's Biographical Dictionary of Twentieth-Century Classical Musicians: *"After a few works of an academic nature, he developed a hyper-modern technique of composition in a highly individual style, in which no demarcation line is drawn between consonances and dissonances, tonal or atonal melody, traditional or innovative instrumentation, an egalitarian attitude prevails toward all available resources of sound."*[54]

Like Kupkovic but far less drastically, Penderecki at one point turned his back on his avant-garde past and set out instead on a path which seems to run parallel to (or cross) that of Gustav Mahler. I must have been the umpteenth interviewer to have pried into the background of his volte-face, nevertheless, the composer replied without any sign of impatience. Sadly, however, he never responded to my request that he look again at the text of our conversation for the purposes of this book.

There is an episode I would like to record here which throws light on his tremendous popularity in the 1970s when his name seemed to stand for new music as such. Actually, it concerns Witold Lutosławski and his wife Danuta, who spent some time in Budapest in the late 1970s, Witold conducting a concert of his music. He had a day off and I wanted to show him a beautiful Romanesque chapel in Northern Hungary. I drove him to the village of Nagybörzsöny, which in the Middle Ages had been quite prominent as a rich mining settlement. We drove some of the way along the Danube, in a countryside of idyllic beauty. I had been there a number of times but was still as taken with it as on the first occasion. Rather to my disappointment, Witold was immersed in a topic he was expounding on and only spared the most fleeting look at the river and the forest when I pointed them out.

On arriving at the village, we made straight for the vicarage: the key to the gate of the thick medieval wall that enclosed the chapel was with the priest. He answered the door and I introduced Witold and his wife. "This is Mr. Witold Lutosławski, the Polish composer."

---

54. *Baker's Biographical Dictionary of Twentieth-Century Classical Musicians* (New York: Schirmer Books, 1997), 1032.

"Oh," the priest replied, "A Polish composer! I know Penderecki!" That is what I would call world fame.

I.

My case was different.

I started composing in 1959, a year after finishing my studies. I was brought up on the classics, with practically no idea of the Second Viennese School: we heard absolutely no music from the West until 1956. It was in that year that I first heard *Sacre* in a live performance. Bartók and Schoenberg came later.

Do you mean that before 1956 Bartók was missing from concert programs altogether?

His music was practically absent. For instance, none of his string quartets was played.

I completed my studies in 1958. I was an aggressive young composer who rejected the tradition that had been presented to me at the Academy. I wanted to annihilate the past. I was waiting for the occasion to demonstrate something *different.*

I turned toward Schoenberg and Webern with interest but I suppose it was too late for them to play any role in my development: I was already firmly established on my own way, I was experimenting with string instruments and, from 1957, was working in an electronic music studio. That work meant more to me than anything else. It opened my ears, it acquainted me with a kind of music I had never even dreamed existed.

Electronic music also came from the West. I find it remarkable that you had a studio nevertheless.

It was only set up in 1957; 1956 had been a turning point in the history of Polish culture. Gomułka's appearance marked the end of Stalinism—everything became more open.

In my case, then, it was not a single composition that changed my way of thinking—it is to the electronic studio that I owe a great deal.

The equipment at your disposal must have been rather rudimentary compared to today's standards.

Just like in a manufactory, we worked exclusively with our hands. Today, one just presses a button and the music is there. In the fifties it was much more complicated.

Well then, I was firmly resolved to annihilate the past, to break with everything to do with it: form, instrumental technique, and above all, the traditional way of playing string instruments. Just look at my pieces written at the time: *Threnody, Polymorphia, Canon* for strings, the first string quartet.

I composed *against* the nature of instruments, I treated string instruments like percussion.

In the past several years, you have radically changed your style and turned toward the past.

I shouldn't think so. I remained faithful to the style developed in the late fifties for many years—but then I arrived at a point where I felt I had reached an impasse. In the *Magnificat*, forty-eight parts make up the texture of the piece—no one could possibly perform it without making mistakes. There was more theory to it than practical considerations. Next, I composed *Canticum Canticorum Salomonis* for sixteen voices and small orchestra and suddenly I felt I could not go on like that.

So far, I have reached a deadlock on two occasions in my career. First in 1962, after completing *Fluorescences* for orchestra. It wholly dismantles the framework of the medium, there is not a single normal tone in it. The *Stabat Mater* was written right afterward where I returned to sixteenth-century Flemish polyphony. The *Stabat Mater* prepared the ground for the *Lukas Passion;* it also draws on my experiments with instruments and electronics and there appears, too, a very simple polyphony (in actual fact not all that simple, only against the background of that era).

Secondly, as I mentioned before, I reached a cul de sac after completing the *Magnificat* and *Canticum Canticorum Salomonis.* It was at that time that I began to conduct my own works. I remember how often it came to a struggle with orchestral musicians who protested against unorthodox ways of playing their instruments. Those experiences confirmed my decision to change course.

I joined an important current in music history: I took up where Mahler had left off. I was not the only one to do so: Shostakovich also followed in Mahler's footsteps. After all, Schoenberg's is not the exclusive truth—in our century, we sometimes delude ourselves that only one path is possible. It's wrong. You can set out in different directions.

In my Second Symphony and my Violin Concerto which are perhaps the first products of the new style, I returned to my own early pieces, the style which characterized the years preceding the *Threnody.* There is a real kinship, then, between compositions written in 1954–55 and around 1975.

Do you accept your avant-garde period today? Do you regard the works you wrote then as justified and necessary?

Absolutely. Eventually, however, the avant-garde appeared to me suspect because it stopped changing for a long time. If a composer always writes the same thing, you wonder whether he lacks fresh ideas.

I was always afraid of repeating myself. I may be interested in a particular kind of music over a period of several years, I write a number of pieces within a given style but then I have to change. My neo-Romantic style has been left behind by now. It lasted exactly ten years: it ended with the *Requiem* of 1984.

Where are you turning next?

It is difficult to describe. Oddly enough, I am returning to my style of the 1960s—new sonorities, to a certain extent to the cluster technique. Of course, there is more to it than that.

Have you written anything in this manner?

I have not finished anything yet. Right now I am composing an opera for Salzburg. It won't be new in every way; after all, you cannot radically break with the past. However, I have parted company with tonality or quasi-tonality.

II.

Has the idea for a new work ever sprung from a single tone?

I remember, I was commissioned to write a short orchestral piece for Monte Carlo and I simply could not get started. No ideas came to me, neither did I feel like writing a short work. It happened in 1974 that I was holidaying with my family at the Baltic Sea and one misty evening the sirens were sounded. They had an incredible impact on me. They reminded me of horns but they were somehow different. The sirens set something in train in my imagination.

In the piece, I tried to conjure them up with a muted horn, surrounded by the "mist" of twelve ocarinas.

What is the title of the piece?

Jacob's Awakening.

III.

If you take a look at the history of twentieth-century painting, you will see that—especially in the first decades of the century—stylistic periods followed one another in quick succession. Of course, some painters of modest talent did the same thing all their lives. Those artists were of decisive significance, who created something new, something fresh all the time. This does not mean, of course, that they ceaselessly set out on uncharted territory, their ideas may very well have focused on the past every now and again. You cannot go forward all the time—that solution would be far too easy.

Having arrived at his mature style, Chagall had recourse in all his paintings to a circumscribed repertoire of motifs.

Yes, of course. There are two kinds of painter—and perhaps composer as well. While Chagall was painting the same picture, Picasso invented something new every other year. It is similar with composers. Some remain within the bounds of a single style—but in the second half of the century it would be difficult to find a genuinely important composer who would have stuck to one direction.

If we were to listen to your Violin Concerto and compare it to an early piece, would we be able to identify the same composer?

I think so, yes.

Are there features to which you have remained faithful?

The expression, the culminations, the structure, the form, the development are always the same, irrespective of the idiom I have chosen.

1985

Forty-Four

GOFFREDO PETRASSI (1904–2003)

Next to Ferenc Farkas, Goffredo Petrassi was probably the most influential teacher of composition for two generations of Hungarian composers between the 1940s and 1960s. For one thing, he helped them shed the stifling influence of Bartók, which, as an outsider, he was probably in a better position to identify than his colleagues at the Budapest Academy. Zsolt Durkó (1934–97) related how he had been given the assignment of composing little pieces for each lesson and invariably, Petrassi would point to phrases which were "come Bartók" *(like Bartók). In the end, Durkó could bear it no longer and decided to take revenge: he took a closer look at Petrassi's own scores and triumphantly presented his professor with a list of passages which also showed Bartókian traces. Petrassi calmly explained that he, having found his own voice in music, could afford to borrow from the Hungarian master, but young composers who had yet to arrive at their own musical individuality, did well to consciously excise influences of figures of the past.*

I.

I can tell you about two similar experiences. One was linked to Stravinsky's *Symphony of Psalms.* I was gripped by its novelty and felt close to it in a spiritual sense as well. It may not have led to a fundamental change—that has never been the case—but it has left a trace on my style. It helped me to take a step forward. Incidentally, that happened in 1933.

The other experience occurred around 1957. It was a composition by Bruno Maderna that induced me, so to speak, to "change places." I must add, however, that these changes cannot be likened to the revelation experienced by St. Paul on the road to Damascus. I had been prepared for those changes, for I felt the need to compose differently from before.

What was it in the Symphony of Psalms *that fascinated you?*

The composition as a whole. It called my attention to a new approach to sacred texts, to the text of the Bible. I had had a traditional upbringing rooted in the Italian Renaissance, Palestrina, and the great polyphonic music that came later. In the *Symphony of Psalms,* however, I was confronted with a concept of polyphony which no longer respected the laws that had governed music ever since the Renaissance. That concept was fundamentally new, much drier, much more harmonious and less contrapuntal.

Have any of your works been directly influenced by Stravinsky?

I shouldn't say that. Stravinsky's influence was present in my music over a period of several years—but it was not the presence of any one of his compositions. It was the poetry of his music which I absorbed to the extent that served my goals. Naturally, I kept a distance from his style.

Still, which of your pieces represents that period in your life?

The *Ninth Psalm* for chorus and orchestra.

The other composer you mentioned was Bruno Maderna.

I first heard his music around 1957—I think his style had matured by then and his personality had grown independent from Darmstadt. The encounter with Maderna's art helped me a great deal—it gave me courage to make a big leap forward. I was ready for it intuitively but lacked self-confidence.

A few years before, a painter had influenced me in a similar manner. I was insecure, I did not know how to master the serial technique. One day, I came face to face with pictures by Alberto Burri—I bought two on the spot. Burri is a great artist of international standing. He had broken with the traditional means of expression and experimented with new techniques and new materials: instead of brush and paint, he worked with tar, sackcloth, and a wide range of other, very simple materials. For all that, his pictures made a strong impact on me. I thought I ought to have the courage, too, to turn my back on my earlier concept of music, make a leap and confront my own personality, my scale with serial techniques.

I met Burri around 1951 and Maderna in 1957 or so. The works I composed after that have nothing to do with Maderna's style but they do demonstrate that I had bidden farewell to my clichés and was able to compose more freely, with broader inner horizons. The first such piece was the *Serenata* (1958) for five instruments.

Can you remember which of Maderna's compositions you heard?

The second *Serenata* (1957) for eleven instruments. That was the work that to a certain extent determined the subsequent changes in my music.

The change was not complete, neither did it happen from one day to the next: traces of it are to be found in my string quartet begun in 1957 and completed the year after. Experiences like the encounter with the second *Serenata* help to focus on and realize something that is vaguely present in our head but we lack the courage to take the decisive step toward what is "different"—to try out new possibilities which are not alien to our makeup.

It was not the pointillistic technique that attracted me, rather the fact that Maderna had liberated himself from the schemata dictated by Darmstadt—that he was free to heed his imagination and test his invention through continually changing instrumental combinations. Maderna's vitality was reborn in every single new work.

The critic Massimo Mila described Maderna as an anarchist stone mason who knew how to build houses. As for me, I consider myself to be a Utopian rather than an anarchist—in other words, a close kinsman of the latter. And I like to remember what Maderna once said in an interview: "Consistency is the vilest thing imaginable in the world. I hate consistency because it equals death." I subscribe to that to 90 percent.

With regard to my *Serenata:* the very instrumentation indicates that I veered from the traditional path. It is no simple thing to bring together a viola, a double bass, a flute, a harpsichord, and some percussion. By their very nature, they are heterogeneous instruments. But I set myself similar tasks in almost every work: I select heterogeneous instruments to see what I can do with them.

II.

Sounds do not influence me in any way: anything to do with music must come from within. This does not mean, of course, that a sound, a noise, or even a title in a newspaper cannot attract my attention.

Such was the case with *Coro di morti* (1941). It was a literary phenomenon, the title of a poem by Giacomo Leopardi that set the idea for the piece in motion. Even a chance encounter in the street can evoke interest because it can release emotions which had been slumbering in us. I do not believe that an impulse like that would work like lightning without the initially unconscious emergence of a state of readiness. I cannot recall any such experience—or, if I had one, it was of an intellectual nature or reached me through the mediation of culture.

My guitar piece *Suoni notturni* (1959) is not meant to conjure up a nocturnal mood. All I had in mind was the fact that the sound of the guitar was best audible in the stillness of the night. Landscapes, the sounds or the atmosphere of nature have never had any influence on me. I may have been inspired by events of an autobiographical nature—but those were events that took place in me, never extraneously. As a human being, I am interested in natural phenomena—being an artist, I am sensitive—but they have never influenced my work as a composer directly.

III.

Personal style is self-repetition.

To begin with, the composer, the artist should know what he may do and what he must steer clear of. However, the artist who is well aware of his own style and keeps on repeating himself is no true artist. To use a favorite metaphor of mine: self-repetition is as if we were living off dividends—that is, passively, sponging on our own past achievements. This is not the right path for an artist.

Repeating myself was always alien to me. I have written eight concertos, each with its own instrumentation. Why? Because if we have created a work of a particular timbre and a particular sound structure, and we are pleased with the result, why should we want to do it again? We no longer live in an age where one could churn out with impunity fifteen symphonies and eight string quartets, repeating the same cliché. Shostakovich could do that, but under specific artistic and social conditions. However, he cannot be an example for us. For musicians in the West, self-repetition is wrong; in a certain sense it is immoral.

1982

Forty-Five

EMIL PETROVICS (1930–2011)

I would like to refer you to Emil Petrovics's comments in the following interview on the music of his younger colleague, László Vidovszky. There you have one aspect of the composer's personality in a nutshell. He does not mince words, never mind the sensibilities he might be hurting. He may have indirectly been addressing his words to Vidovszky spurred by his pedagogical instincts—Petrovics was for many years a respected professor of composition at the Budapest Academy of Music—but it might just as well have been an expression of his irascible character. Recently, he published a two-volume autobiography, which beyond demonstrating his flair for writing (in his youth, he had planned on making fiction his profession) has also managed to enrage many people in the music profession, including those of the generation of his erstwhile pupils.

Emil Petrovics has been a major figure in Hungary, both as a composer and as a public figure. He is credited with two successful operas, both of which count as significant achievements of postwar Hungarian music: C'est la guerre, *1961 (with influences of Puccini and Alban Berg), and* Crime and Punishment, *1969 (where he takes a step further along the thorny path of adapting the inflection of spoken Hungarian with its accents on the first syllable to the requirements of music that had departed from the idiom developed by Zoltán Kodály: in his vocal works, such as* Psalmus hungaricus *or his a cappella choruses, Kodály proved a master of prosody, he had found an ideal solution to setting Hungarian texts to music. That solution, however, could no longer be applied to a more advanced musical style).*

In addition to teaching at the Academy, Petrovics also directed the Hungarian State Opera House and was a leading light of Artisjus, the national copyright agency.

In 2009, he looked at our interview and decided it needed no change.

I.

I have had no experience of a similar nature.

Let us examine this question from a wider angle. You see, I did not decide to become a composer from one moment to the next: the decision was the outcome of a slow process. And, unlike most of my colleagues, I did not approach music through Beethoven, Mozart, Bach, or Tchaikovsky. My first musical experience which really shook me was Bartók's *Divertimento:* I heard it on the radio when I was sixteen years old or so. It was followed by

Bluebeard's Castle and later by *Psalmus Hungaricus.* I discovered "music history" later, going backward, as it were.

It was also in my teens that I strolled into the concert hall of the Music Academy during a rehearsal of Beethoven's Ninth Symphony. Erich Kleiber was the conductor, I believe. I arrived in between two movements, or perhaps they had stopped playing briefly. All of a sudden, they started to sing the theme which you know in every imaginable arrangement from musical clocks to light music and I felt I was going to cry. That has been the way music has affected me ever since: it goes right to my heart, it touches my emotions, it enthralls me. My brain is involved least of all.

When I was young, I often regretted not to have written a particular work. For a long time, my heart ached because I had not composed *Boris Godunov.*

Summing up: I have received crucial impulses from works composed by others—they showed me the power of music and the path awaiting me.

That emotional approach was probably replaced or supplemented later by conscious analysis: when you wanted to find out through what compositional means those impulses had been achieved.

Of course. However, it took me a long time to have a clear notion of how to respond to a new work by my colleagues or even to a lesser known composition by Stravinsky. (At the Music Academy, I knew precious little of his oeuvre; I tried to find my bearings in it with Ligeti's help. For instance, he treated us to a detailed analysis of *Rake's Progress.* It was a great experience and raised my interest without actually enabling me to become fond of it. I find the opera entertaining to this day but cannot find all that many attractive features in it.)

At that time, we were anxious to learn as much as possible; my younger and older colleagues felt they had missed out on something and did their best to catch up fast. An effort like that is rarely rewarded by great experiences, it deprives one of surprises, of the chance of an unexpected encounter with something extraordinary—the chance to admire, to succumb.

In 1960, in Paris, I attended a concert of the Domaine Musicale, conducted by Pierre Boulez. One of his pieces was on the program, together with Stockhausen and Varèse. Perhaps *Ionisation,* I forget which one. A gentleman in tails sounded a siren once in a while; the happening was quite amusing but musically it did not make much of an impression.

In 1964, I visited Hamburg and heard a number of works in the opera house which at that time was directed by Rolf Liebermann. They included Krenek's *Jonny spielt auf.* It made a foul noise. My acquaintance with Adorno dates from the same period and it became increasingly clear to me that I had absolutely no truck with Central-West-European German music, philosophy and aestheticism. Today, I am no longer interested in Schoenberg, Krenek, Dessau, or even Stockhausen. For me they are all the same, because—through a wide variety of means—they provoke the same thing in me: protest. Thanks to my instincts I have been saved (or have deprived myself of) any danger that such compositional means could exert a revelatory influence on me.

In 1983, at the Palazzo Medici in Rome, I attended a festival organized by the French Academy. They played contemporary music for a whole week—works by French and Italian composers. With the exception of Berio whom I like and respect, I heard nothing but aggressive misuse of musical means and cramped efforts to bring about something never heard before. I had never heard so many poor pieces, at concerts publicized at great expense and only attended by thirty people. I sat there, astounded, and thought: does this make any sense? I felt I had nothing to do with all that. Not only did it fail to give me any new ideas—I knew that as far I as was concerned, it was all wholly superfluous. I also knew that it was nonsensical to look for the "totally new."

Those three experiences (1960, 1964, 1983) and of course others like that made me realize that I was not attracted by unusual or interesting means of expression but was only concerned whether the music made any effect on me. I may be conservative or perhaps such is my makeup. My composer colleagues I mentioned earlier also showed me what *not* to do, what to steer clear of.

True, in the 1960s I also strove to create something new, to try out new tools. When I looked back at those endeavors in the 1970s, I realized that those novel features had no natural place in many of my compositions, I had put them in arbitrarily, for novelty's sake.

For instance?

My String Symphony was played recently three times in succession—quite decently, too. I know I need to revise it by eliminating precisely those features of which I thought at the time: "Well, I have had the courage to compose it this way."

Under whose influence?

The Polish school, primarily Penderecki. For example, string clusters and various effects which I had employed sparingly, of course. I felt I had leapt over my own shadow. It did not make me happy and it is clear to me today that my path led in a different direction.

For the past decade, I have no longer been willing to "rape myself," so to speak; I seek what I really am. Music I have heard in the world has confirmed this resolve. I have the courage to accept that, now and then, I enjoy writing major triads in 4/4, without any inferiority complex. It has nothing to do with neoromanticism which has recently become fashionable. I started teaching at the Music Academy sixteen years ago and foretold then that the time would come when Stockhausen and company would triumphantly discover the triad. Then that would be the fad to follow.

The triad and other things do make sense. It is important that one should compose true to what one thinks about music. It is possible, it is indeed imperative to go beyond what has gone wrong in this century (I am thinking not only of music, but the other arts as well, all our lives). We have to go beyond what has driven the arts under its yoke, in the name of human freedom. It is my belief that mankind will be able to do so, at least I hope that it will, because I could not live without that hope. It is my belief that music can only justify its existence if it can create some sort of harmony in both the listener and the performer.

Harmony—with harmony?

With harmony! *Don Giovanni* is at least as ruthless and tough as *Wozzeck*. I appreciate *Wozzeck*, too, but I could not listen to it as much as to Mozart. It tramples on my life, my ears, my heart so aggressively that I am unable to follow its musical and thematic bitterness. It never for a moment creates the harmony from which I could step toward disharmony.

How about Berg's Violin Concerto?

That's different, it is perhaps his most harmonious work. The thing has been deteriorating ever since and most of what is being presented as contemporary music today, even on the radio, I tend to reject—I switch it off. They should leave me in peace. Radio producers, critics, and aestheticians are all out to explain that today's music is ugly because it mirrors the ugliness of our lives today. Ugliness can be depicted in a "non-ugly" fashion!

The situation around me is schizophrenic. For instance, László Vidovszky has written an opera, *Narcissus and Echo*, which does not wholly convince me, but he has composed a chorus to end it which proves that he is an excellent musician. He could be a wonderful composer if he had faith in music and if he did not believe that he had to write pieces which no one else does. I have known all along that he has good ideas. *Autokoncert* or *Schroeder's Death* are based on extremely amusing ideas even if they have little to do with music. The chorus, however, has shown me that he could be an outstanding composer if only he wanted to. Since then, I have had more respect for him but I am also more angry with him. He can do it! Lots of people can't—and can easily get away with life, without the struggle and torment that go hand in hand with the creative process.

II.

To my mind, the sounding world has not got more to do with music than the seen world. What makes music a specific phenomenon is that it has a form, that it goes from somewhere to somewhere, it reaches a particular point and lasts a given time frame. Any noise is amorphous, that is, it is an acoustic phenomenon without context. When birdsong is speeded up or slowed down or manipulated in any other way, it makes no musical sense to me. It only sounds like music.

The noises of modern times simply disturb me—I am disturbed by the sound of cars and planes, although I accept their existence and make good use of them. I do not believe they can give you any musical ideas. I try to devise Balkan rhythms to the rattling of the train, I see if it can be turned into a 5/8 meter—but that has nothing to do with music.

III.

This is the most essential question for a responsible composer.

I believe it is very difficult to talk of style. We have rather to do with a biological phenomenon. Everyone moves, eats, and looks in his own fashion. In music, too, one has one's own specific facial expressions and range of gestures. A series of sonorities, a particular passage of music is different with Balassa, Soproni, Lutosławski, or Xenakis. My late mother used to say, "My son, I always recognize what you have written." She was biased of course, but others have also told me that my music has a taste, a flavor all its own. I could not define what it is, just as I am not conscious of the way I sit down.

In my opinion, a musical idea, a musical conduct or gesture has a place in the works of a composer throughout his life. There are lots and lots of recurring moments with Beethoven or Puccini; with Verdi, it is actually ludicrous how many times he wrote practically the same thing—but in a different context, it always meant something different.

Even if I do not think I am conservative, I am one of the preservers. It would give me no pleasure to be a pioneer, I do not rummage in places which are outside my competence. You can devise new means, I have also devised some if I am not mistaken, but that kind of spiritual effort does not amuse me. It would bore me if I had to find something new all the time.

Rather than find out—you have to find. You have to find the tones. As to which ones, will be determined by your biological makeup. You have to find—that's the secret.

1984

Forty-Six

HENRI POUSSEUR (1929–2009)

I wrote the Belgian composer early in January 2009, expressing the hope that he would take a look at his replies of 1983. The letter was returned: the address was apparently incomplete. I then found out his e-mail address and sent the letter again, on January 29. He replied early in February, with his message inserted after my first paragraph. In red letters, it said: "Thank you, dear Mr. Varga. I am very ill, irrevocably. All best wishes, hp."

Pousseur died a month later, on March 6.

I am deeply moved by the very fact that he took the trouble to reply. We had a friendly relationship even though I achieved precious little for those of his compositions which are part of the UE catalogue. I concentrated my efforts on his pioneering music theater piece Votre Faust *(1969) based on a libretto by Michel Butor. It is not easy to realize: the singers and the instrumentalists have to learn the music of several strands of the score and the text because it is for the audience to decide what course the action should take—that is, to choose one from among the possibilities offered by the composer and the librettist. The performers must be able to continue whatever the outcome of the vote was, without a moment's hesitation. I had hoped that at least Pousseur's eightieth birthday would break the ice, but projected productions were cancelled. He took it all philosophically.*

It was always a great pleasure to talk to Pousseur (mainly on the telephone; we only met once, at the railway station in Waterloo, a small town near Brussels, where he lived). I was struck by his intelligence and immense culture: he was a great man. The future will decide whether he was also a great composer.

I.

I have had no experience comparable to Lutosławski's, but there is no doubt about it: the impressions we receive from music—particular compositions, musicians, or schools of thought—exert a continuing influence on the creative process and nurture it. We may receive such impressions while studying a score but it is live music that makes the strongest impact. It has happened to me as well that in listening to some compositions, including contemporary pieces, I concentrated on what they might contribute to my own work. It was not a question of a decision taken beforehand—it was the music that turned my attention in that direction.

For instance, I would think—let's see, perhaps I could do something similar, in a different context. Or: this could be done better or in a different fashion. You can also find models, especially in older music or music coming from different cultural backgrounds—they might even provide you with guidance as to the solution of a problem you have been grappling with. An experience like that might help us approach the goal which until then was but a murky dream. The result can often be very far from the source of inspiration since it was born out of a composite of diverse elements.

II.

Yes. The sounds of nature, the human environment, the city and industry can play an important role in my music. Not only in electro-acoustic pieces—that would be obvious or at least likely—but also, indirectly, in my whole oeuvre. Any artistic activity would strive to condense, to concentrate, to unify, that is, to create a balanced form. Reality hardly ever serves it ready-made.

At the most, you may encounter an extraordinary moment or a unique view which possess a considerable power of persuasion. In such rare instances, the world outside exerts the most intensive influence. In the main, however, it is the general experience that we crystallize and synthesize in a novel manner.

III.

My reply to the first question is also true in part of the third one. I feel that a personal style is fed by a multitude of collective currents; we are the focus, the crossing point of intersecting trends, of colliding waves. Our own work, then, is a mirror of a great deal that hails from somewhere else.

I believe I do not go out of my way to cultivate my personality, my independence. My personality is the result of my work—it is a product of my range of interests, my convictions as well as of the solutions I apply for problems which appear to me to be the most encompassing ones or those shared by most of us. In any case, everyone has a personality and it leaves its mark on whatever one produces in one's workshop.

With regard to self-repetition, it comes about, perhaps, precisely when we try to prove how individual we are. It does entail the risk of becoming increasingly stale and what is worse, actually turning sterile.

1983

Forty-Seven

STEVE REICH (1936)

In my mind's eye, I can see the composer on stage, participating in a performance of his Clapping Music *(1972). The piece is performed by two, facing each other, clapping increasingly intricate rhythmic patterns which appear to require the highest degree of concentration. What could be more basic to music than two people clapping? And yet it is immensely thrilling, you respond to it with your body as well as with your mind and the tension in you leaves you perhaps nearly as exhausted as the two performers must be feeling, even though the exercise only lasts for five minutes at the most.*

At the other extreme, there is Tehillim *(1981) for voices and ensemble. I have not heard it for decades but its majesty still haunts me. It is a setting in Hebrew of Psalms 19, 34, 18, and 150; whether or not it is an expression of Reich's faith is immaterial. If it is true that "beauty is in the eyes of the beholder," I suppose you can also claim that the "message" of music is in the mind of the listener.*

I.

I have had no experience that is the same as Lutosławski's, but I have had a number of experiences with music that may be somewhat similar.

A. When I was fourteen years old, I heard a recording of *Le Sacre du Printemps* for the first time. I had never heard anything like it. (In fact, at that time I had not heard *any* Stravinsky, Bartók, Schoenberg, Berg, or Webern.) It made an enormous impression on me and I believe that the seeds of my desire to become a composer were planted at that moment.

B. In the same year—when I was fourteen—I also heard my first jazz recording. It was by Charlie Parker, Miles Davis, Kenny Clarke, and others. It also made a huge impression on me and I decided to begin studying snare drum with Roland Kohloff (formerly timpanist with the New York Philharmonic) that same year. I would say that my drumming studies and the rhythmic impulse in me that was touched by Stravinsky, jazz and, later that same year, by my first hearing of the *Brandenburg Concerto No. 5* formed the basic musical energy in me which is still at work in my own compositions.

C. In 1957 I studied composition privately with Hall Overton in New York City and he had me return to playing simple music at the piano, in particular, the first two books of Bartók's *Mikrokosmos.* In these pieces I first clearly understood the different modes beyond major and minor. Even more importantly I became clear about the nature of canons as a basic compositional technique. Canons at the unison have since formed the basis of almost all my music. The entire "phasing" technique discovered with tape loops in *It's Gonna Rain* (1965) and then transferred to musical instruments with *Piano Phase* of 1967 can be correctly seen as a form of canonic procedure where the subject is short and the rhythmic distance between the two or more voices is constantly changing.

D. In 1962, via a talk by Gunther Schuller, I examined A. M. Jones's book *Studies in African Music* which, together with my work with tape loops in 1963, made me aware of the repetition of short patterns with their downbeats in different places as a new and radically different compositional technique. A few years later I encountered another book, *Music in Bali* by Colin MacPhee, which showed me, in notation, music made of repeating patterns played simultaneously in different note values so that one could hear rapid interlocking eighth notes, slower moving quarters, still slower half notes, and one huge gong which played only once per cycle of 64 beats.

E. While a composition student at Juilliard and later while studying with Berio at Mills College in California in the early 1960s, I used to spend many evenings at jazz clubs listening to John Coltrane. I also listened frequently to many of his recordings. One recording in particular, *Africa Brass,* capsulizes what I and many others learned from Coltrane: over one single harmony, maintained for as long as half an hour, many notes or even noises can be played. On *Africa Brass* the entire harmony stays rooted on the low E of the double bass, yet over it Coltrane, Eric Dolphy, and others play notes inside or outside the key of E minor as well as french horn glissandos, and shrieks on their saxophones.

F. In 1964 I helped Terry Riley put together the first performance of his *In C.* I suggested that he put a "pulse" in the piece to keep the players together, which he did using drummed out high Cs on the piano. The piece showed me one way that repetition of short patterns could function as a compositional building block. The influence Riley's piece had on me was similar to the influence La Monte Young had on Riley several years earlier in Berkeley and was also similar to the influence I had on Phil Glass in 1967 when he heard and studied my music for the first time in New York. Still later my *Drumming,* plus Riley and Glass had a formative effect on John Adams, Louis Andriessen, Michael Nyman, Gavin Bryars, and eventually many others, some in the world of pop music.

II.

Your question strikes me as very European. You say that everyday sounds either "inspire" a composer or they leave him "completely cold." My answer is: neither of the above. I find some natural sounds—particularly rain on a roof, and nearby running streams or ocean surf, cicadas or crickets, and birdsongs among others, to be—at one time or another—comforting, fascinating, or mysterious. City sounds I find generally irritating—especially if I am trying to sleep. When I first did tape music in the early 1960s, I found natural and machine sounds interesting, but not nearly as interesting as human speech, which I used to make my early *It's Gonna Rain* and *Come Out.* Basically, I get musical inspiration not from "sounds" but from music—notes, rhythms, and timbres. I should add that in *Different Trains* of 1988 I was inspired to combine the speech melody I had discovered in *It's Gonna Rain* and *Come Out* with real musical instruments, namely the strings in the Kronos Quartet.

In *City Life* of 1995 I did use sounds I recorded in New York including car horns, boat horns, subway chimes, door slams, and many others including human voices. My primary idea was to "marry" the sounds to an appropriate instrument. Bass drum and door slam, car horn and amplified oboe, air brakes and cymbal, voices and strings, etc. After pieces using sampling like *Different Trains, City Life, The Cave,* and *Three Tales* I felt a need to return to instrumental music from 2002 until 2009 when I am now, once again, turning to sampled speech to match with the Kronos Quartet.

III.

Individual style is the revealing of one's musical intelligence and emotions in concrete works. This revelation continues, and hopefully develops, throughout one's lifetime. Self-repetition begins when musical intelligence and emotions cease to develop and one nevertheless continues to grind out music. Such self-repetition is earmarked by techniques which appear in earlier works and reappear in new works with no further significant development in terms of harmony, counterpoint, rhythmic structure, orchestration, etc.

One can find poor works within an oeuvre where self-repetition begins, only to find them followed by a fine work that breaks new ground. Breaking new ground should not be confused with mere novelty, and developing a preexistent style should not be confused with self-repetition. Bartók's String Quartet No. 5 develops the new ground broken by his String Quartet No. 4, and he then goes on to break further new ground in his (paradoxically more "conservative") String Quartet No. 6.

The distinction between novelty and radical development on the one hand and self-repetition and development within a style on the other is difficult to make, but a composer must be able to make such distinctions in his own work—or suffer the consequences.

1983/2009

Forty-Eight

WOLFGANG RIHM (1952)

I worked for and with Wolfgang Rihm between 1992 and 2007, the fifteen and a half years I spent in the promotion department of Universal Edition, Vienna. I got to know him in a wide range of situations: visiting him in his spacious apartment in Karlsruhe, where he showed me the score he was currently working on, comparing it to the previous one, which was derived from the same root; listening to some of his earlier pieces he himself had not heard for some time (he was pleasantly surprised by one and was sensitive enough to detect my uneasiness caused by the other, stopping the machine without a moment's hesitation). On another occasion, he attended a performance of his La lugubre gondola/Das Eismeer, *a work for two pianos and orchestra. The title is of course a reference to Franz Liszt's eponymous piano piece and the painting by Caspar David Friedrich. He was visibly moved, even upset by the piece. If I remember correctly at a distance of seventeen years, he described it as a requiem; walking with him in the streets near the Salzburg Festspielhaus prior to the world premiere of a cello concerto (he was extremely nervous and worried, for the conductor did not seem to have an antenna for his music—in the end, the performance was a triumph. However, I experienced at the closest possible range the extent to which a composer is helpless once he has dispatched his score on its way); addressing a public before a concert (Rihm is a superb speaker, his mastery of the German language and of course his tremendous intellect make sure he puts his message across lucidly), giving an interview (we only did one, at the very beginning of our work together—his sentences were print-ready); at the prize-giving ceremony in Munich where the prestigious Ernst von Siemens Music Prize was awarded to Wolfgang Rihm (in his tribute, the speaker addressed a question that is raised time and again in connection with the composer: his awe- and suspicion-inspiring prolificacy. The speaker recalled Luigi Nono's admonition: "Wolfgang, you need a crisis!" When it was Rihm's turn to reply and express his thanks for the prize, his towering figure faced the public, which was of course made up of friends, colleagues, and people he knew or people who knew him, and said in an unusually high, almost plaintive voice: "But I have crises all the time!"); a chapter all to itself: Wolfgang Rihm in the restaurant (his knowledge of food and wine is encyclopedic. Studying the menu and the wine list takes some time and is done in consultation with the waiter who is invariably happy to have at last met someone who knows his business. "Why should I eat poorly if I can eat well?" he replied to a silly remark of mine. Sitting in a small room in one of Berlin's several Cafés Einstein surrounded by old-style cupboards filled with glasses, he even picked the matching glass for our wine. Of course, smelling and tasting wine is by no means a formality. I have witnessed him sending it back, and the waiter, rather less self-assured, returning with another bottle which then passed* muster); bumping into him in the Brussels Musée des Beaux Arts as he was studying the painting *La Chute d'Icare* by Pieter Brueghel (1558) (he launched into a lecture on the picture, pointing out details. I took on the role of listener/pupil as I would do whenever we were together); Rihm reciting a text (I bought the volume that included Botho Strauß's *Schlußchor*, a play the last section of which bears the title "Das Gehege." Rihm decided to set it and turn it into a one-act opera. I had had rather a hard time grasping what it was that appealed to him and told him so. We were sitting in my hotel in Basel on the eve of the world premiere of a work for tenor and orchestra, and Rihm took the book from me, opened it randomly and started to read it out loud. It was a revelation: the text came to life, the way he modulated his voice and inserted pauses, accenting certain words, lent sense to the text); Wolfgang Rihm, the public figure (as a major representative of German musical life and a former pupil of Stockhausen, he was called upon to comment on the latter's statement that the terrorist attack against the Twin Towers in New York City on September 11, 2001, had been a formidable artistic achievement. Rihm told me how he had suffered agonies in formulating a text which would not condone Stockhausen's words but would find a credible explanation for them). The only role in which I did not experience him was as committee member. He sits on several public bodies, anxious to represent the cause of composers of classical music.

Wolfgang Rihm has a large frame. He is tall and walks at a dignified pace; when he has his black overcoat on, he looks rather like a Protestant pastor. He is fully aware of the impression he makes: "I am big and I am German, so I must be careful not to put people off. That is why I speak quietly and bend my back a bit so that I am not too tall."

His German birth also has a bearing on his choice of text. When the Bach Academy in Stuttgart commissioned a Passion from him, he selected Lukas "because he is the least anti-Semitic of them all." I heard the Austrian premiere in Salzburg soon after the first performance in Germany and was rather depressed. I could not see the point of a new Passion—especially in a style reminiscent of Johann Sebastian—when Bach had had his say centuries ago. I was wrong, not for the first and certainly not for the last time: *Deus Passus* has since been performed many times; a Hamburg church has introduced what should become a tradition of programming it every other year.

I also erred when Rihm reported to me on the telephone that he had been commissioned to write short orchestral interludes to be interspersed with movements of Brahms's *German Requiem*. "Why rape Brahms?" was my first reaction. Wrong. I was tremendously impressed by what has come to be known as *Das Lesen der Schrift* (The Reading of the Script): the music with its somber colors seemed to be rising out of the bowels of the Earth, it sounded as though hailing from ancient times—and it was amazingly at one with Brahms. I have since heard of people who could not tell which section was by Brahms and which was by Rihm, also of others who were not even aware that music by Rihm was also being performed.

When I approached him with my three questions in 1982, he was just thirty years old and was well-enough known for me to have heard of him in Budapest. He replied almost by return post and in hand: the computer or the typewriter are not for him. When I asked him to amplify some aspect, he did so readily. Over twenty years later when I wondered if he wished to add or change anything, he said he was quite happy with the text as it was.

I.

Listening to a work by another composer and all of a sudden sensing in it my own possibilities: it is an experience I know well. By and large, that is what happens each time I listen to music. It would be difficult to name a single composition which would have had a more powerful influence on me than any other. There was one, however, which gave me the very first impetus: *Arcana* (1925–27) by Edgard Varèse. I heard it around 1970 and almost shuddered with the recognition illuminating my goal in a flash: creating music out of a "big bang," to help with its birth out of some kind of a percussive raw state, without any avant-garde constraints. *Arcana* awoke in me a desire for freedom.

What other music has influenced me? There has been a lot but none has had the impact of Varèse's composition. When I was a child, Mussorgsky's *A Night on the Bare Mountain* (1866–67) inspired me to write a mass. It was never performed, of course: I was only ten years old. Two years later, I heard Florent Schmitt's *Psaume XLVII* (1904) on the radio—monumental, odd, blaring—which at that time taught me that music could assume the form of a giant torrent of sound. Today I find it rather academic but at the age of twelve I felt something similar to listening to the pealing of bells on Sundays to which I loved surrendering myself.

As a member of a chorus, I sang Berlioz's *Requiem* (1837) and a rarely heard piece by Debussy: *Le Martyre de Saint-Sébastien* (1911). The latter is still present in me—and when singing it, I remember enjoying the fact that I was standing right in the middle of the sound. Bruckner's *Te Deum* (1881–84) and Verdi's *Requiem* (1874) were also unique experiences. I also came under the influence of Stockhausen's *Momente* (1961–64). I was studying with him in 1972 when he rehearsed and performed the definitive version in Bonn.

There are times when I listen to a particular composer with an almost encyclopedic dedication—possibly followed by a long abstinence (perhaps satiety). Right now, it is the music of Arnold Schoenberg I am feeling closest to—the pieces he wrote between 1907 and 1920. Who knows how many times I have studied the scores, how many circles I have made round them. However, the basic experience continues to be, again and again, that first encounter with *Arcana.*

II.

I do not consciously draw on the acoustic reality that surrounds us but I am aware of the extent to which it does influence my music.

Nowadays, any sound produced by an orchestra echoes, whether the composer wants it or not, the industrial environment which in its turn is marked by rumbling and speed. And soft music mirrors the longing for stillness which, in "softer" times, did not need to be so forceful.

Furthermore, the way we think of form is influenced by the possibility of swift switches, of cuts (film technique as optical-acoustic reality), of dissolve; a productive form of fragmentariness is set against academic processes (against music invented, so to speak, from start to finish, from beginning to ending) and leads to a way of thinking which is no longer dualistically centered but vibrates in many shapes.

III.

I question the very notion of personal style: in my view, "personal" is the antithesis of "style." "Style"—it is something artificial, it is a trademark. "Personal"—it is surging, it is freedom, at least it ought to be. In any case, you cannot coerce anyone to be individual—least of all an artist.

Self-repetition is basically the same thing as style. It excludes the personal—something which in music we can still only characterize through sound. It is terrible but true that an individual sound cannot be created artificially—you either have it or you do not. An artist cannot calculate it. The more he potters away at it, the farther he gets from his goal. The only way for an artist is to guard the freedom of anarchy, that is, working in a dialectic state of compulsion and eruption.

1982

Forty-Nine

PETER RUZICKA (1948)

In my professional life, I met Peter Ruzicka in his various capacities as intendant and artistic director: of the Radio-Symphonie-Orchester Berlin (it must have been soon after his appointment in 1979, at the age of thirty-one), of the Hamburg State Opera House, the Munich Biennale, and the Salzburg Festival.

He is the most reserved person I have ever met, a characteristic which made promotion not exactly easy. However, Ruzicka is also one of the most important patrons of new music; in all his positions, he has commissioned (he is still artistic director of the Munich Biennale) a large number of new compositions. What particularly impressed me and filled me with gratitude was the tremendous support he gave to his colleagues, especially the younger ones who were writing chamber operas for his festival in Munich. I read several of his e-mails, which are paragons of empathy: he could put composers at ease, who may have been having a minor crisis delaying the delivery of the score on time, by saying how wonderful he found their music and how much faith he put in the opera in gestation. At the party following the world premiere, he would extol the composer and the production team with words of heart-warming praise. All of this was tremendously admirable and in striking contrast to the shield he would hold up to protect himself in private communication.

In 2009, Peter Ruzicka reread the text he had written in answer to my three questions. He remarked it was now rather distant but he accepted it as a document of his views as expressed nearly thirty years ago.

I.

I have also had a similar spontaneous revelation. It happened in the autumn of 1971: in a late-night radio broadcast, I heard a new orchestral work by Helmut Lachenmann and it became clear to me straight away that it represented a new aesthetic ideal which would have a bearing on my work as well. That composition was *Kontrakadenz*, one of the major (and least-known) works of new music.

In that piece, Lachenmann had rid himself of the paraphernalia and expressive residues of "tonal hearing" in the broadest sense of the word. Tonality here means the traditional aesthetic middle course, an unencumbered and unencumbering protected position in the middle of a highly differentiated field of tension. From that point of view, Penderecki and Ligeti also write "tonal" music because it flirts with the habits of tonal hearing. Lachenmann rejects the established norms of communication and treats musical material from the standpoint of a radical aesthetic. His music sets freedom against the customary process of marketing and undiscriminating utilization.

Naturally, "countertonal" composition is only possible with a material which is devoid of all traces of "tonality." That is why this material has been arranged from what one might call energetic points of view with the accent placed on the ways of sound production rather than on the sounding result. All that comes up against taboos and it is precisely on this count that the limits of genuine traditional emancipation are shown up.

The significance of Lachenmann's music lies in the fact that it advocates the spirit of discovery, research, query, sniffing and observing, it mirrors a never-ending process of learning of which listeners—members of society—also partake.

II.

I can answer this question with a definite "yes." I have indeed written a number of pieces which would never have been born without the inspiration of "sound" in the broadest sense of the word. *Metastrofe* (1971), *Sinfonia* (1970–71), and *Feed Back* (1972) are manifestations of the vision of an integrated orchestral sonority. That vision was uppermost on my mind in the early 1970s and it came about under the influence of complex sound fields which I had filtered from some musical event or "concrete" sonorities.

III.

My first attempts at writing what I called critical music go back to 1972 or so. You can call it a style, if you like; I have little time for that notion today. Instead of letting music be, music would have to make itself the object of scrutiny, it would need to listen to itself, perhaps question itself; music would need to be written about music. In my view, that is the logical consequence of the development of new music after World War II. The musical material which had a pioneering, innovatory significance and which brought music forward for decades, had by then (1972 at the latest) grown exhausted. I reacted to that recognition in my own way, by writing compositions for orchestra: *Befragung, Feed Back, Torso,* and *Abbrüche,* all between 1973 and 1978.

It goes without saying that critical music does not necessarily avoid the trap of self-repetition. I must confess I tend to feel today that you can only compose music which ponders the impossible. Perhaps all that remains in the end is silence.

1981

Fifty

LÁSZLÓ SÁRY (1940)

For Hungarians who have taken any interest in the home contemporary music scene over the past several decades, the name of László Sáry is closely linked with the names of Zoltán Jeney, László Vidovszky, Péter Eötvös, Zoltán Kocsis, György Kurtág Jr., and some others who between them founded the Budapest New Music Studio in 1970. Just fourteen years after the Hungarian uprising and nearly twenty before the communist system collapsed, the ideological climate was anything but conducive to the formation of a group of composers and instrumentalists with the goal of presenting music from the East and West which was otherwise unavailable for the Hungarian public. They also played their own compositions, which had more to do with John Cage or Christian Wolff than what they had studied at the Academy of Music or heard at new music concerts in Budapest.

Looking back, one remembers—or rather, I remember—mainly the American contributions to the Studio's programs. But László Sáry has been kind enough to supply me with the entire repertoire between 1970 and 1990, when the Studio ceased to exist as a closely knit group and its members got together only occasionally, once or twice a year.

Looking at the list of composers featured on the concerts, one realizes just how varied the repertoire was. Here are those played with some regularity: Pierre Boulez, Earle Brown, Morton Feldman, Charles Ives, Olivier Messiaen, Goffredo Petrassi, Steve Reich, Frederic Rzewski, Erik Satie, Tomasz Sikorski, Karlheinz Stockhausen, Edgar Varèse, Christian Wolff, and Iannis Xenakis.

It was of course all terribly suspect and the music critic of the socialist party's daily newspaper actually contacted the Ministry of Culture warning the powers that be that a perilous ideology, Zen Buddhism, was being propagated at the Studio's concerts. Ironically, the group worked under the auspices and on the premises of the Young Communist League. In any case, the concerts were allowed to take place and some of those who attended them did so as a sign of opposition to the regime.

Through his son, György Kurtág followed the Studio's activities with interest, attended some of their concerts, and was actually influenced in his own work by some of the pieces he heard and saw there (Vidovszky's Autokoncert, *in particular). More than twenty years older than the group's members, he became something of a father figure. His fiftieth birthday in 1976 was celebrated by a joint composition, one of 662 works performed by the Budapest New Music Studio between 1970 and 1990.*

László Sáry has reread our interview and has asked me to add a few sentences to his reply to the third question. Otherwise, he saw no need for change.

I.

I attended the Darmstadt Summer Courses in 1972 and heard a lecture there by the American composer Christian Wolff on the possibilities inherent in using chance operations. Some of his compositions were also performed (*Burdocks*, String Quartet,[55] and *Stones* from *Prose Collection*). It all confirmed the realization (which had matured in me since the late 1960s) that there were other ways of compositional thinking and practice than our classical ways in Europe. I wrote *Sounds for . . .* at the time which focuses on the most extensive possible exploitation of the parameters of a sound. There was a close kinship between the piece and Christian Wolff's thinking. The exploration of the many ways a tone can sound produced new interrelationships between time, intensity, and timbre which could never have been achieved through traditional compositional means. Utilizing the laws of chance has continued to play a central role in my compositional practice to this day.

It should be remembered, though, that you can only grasp and absorb an idea if its germs have been in gestation in your mind ready to be born. An outside influence can only serve as encouragement or as recognition which helps the germ to come to the surface.

II.

I have always been fond of the sounds of nature, of the outside world in general. I have observed that natural sounds (of animals, the wind, water, or even that of a saw) could serve as an example for producing sounds on an instrument. Natural sounds occur almost "by themselves." That observation has been helpful not only in instrumental practice but has also shed light on the essence of the workings of the creative process. Sounds, colors, and movements in nature appear to be unequivocal and evident because there lies no *intention* behind them. That is why consciously produced effects are limited. If we observe the way a ripe fruit falls from the tree or a mass of snow slides from the roof (without any intention!), you will find the above statement justified.

III.

Before replying to the third question, I would like to mention some important musical and spiritual influences which have had a decisive influence on my thinking and compositional practice.

---

55. This may have been *Lines for String Quartet*, composed in 1972.

One is the poetry and writings of Sándor Weöres,[56] another is the works and writings of John Cage, and a third one is the teachings of Oriental philosophy. Let me quote the words of Bodhidharma, the first teacher of Zen: "What is the deepest sense of holy truth?" asked the Emperor. The master replied: "Open and wide—not holy."

I have never been concerned with individual style. In composing most of my pieces I have always been moved by some outside influence, impression, or experience. I am not even aware of having a style or voice of my own. Artistic practice is in my opinion a process of cognition. Getting to know the world and ourselves. In that process, the role of the individual is more of a barrier than anything else which isolates, narrows down, and does not let me identify with other sounds, concepts, or cultures. My goal is not so much ridding myself of my personality but to expand and open it to such an extent as to allow it to absorb the widest range of impressions.

1984/2009

56. Sándor Weöres (1913–89), Hungarian poet. A child prodigy, his poem "The Old Ones," written when he was fourteen, was set by Zoltán Kodály in one of his major choral works. The remarkable musical qualities of Weöres's poetry have inspired a great many other composers, including György Ligeti.

Fifty-One

PIERRE SCHAEFFER (1910–95)

During the hour or so we spent together, Pierre Schaeffer struck me as a bitter, disillusioned, and relentlessly objective man.

He was disillusioned with the world around him and he was bitter that his fame was based on an achievement he more or less regarded as a by-product: musique concrète *had been but an adventure. What really counted for him was a treatise, a summary of his research into the phenomenon of noise—and the book had not been translated into English, so that it could not exert the influence that was its due.*

On the other hand, Schaeffer considered that his real calling was fiction writing. His oeuvre as a writer, however, appears to have been quite slim: some essays, biographies, short novels and plays. Perhaps that is why the international encyclopedias of literature that I have consulted take no notice of him. Making an effort to take an objective look at his life, one may conclude that he may well have been disappointed. Nevertheless, he is considered today one of the most influential experimental, electroacoustic musicians, the first composer to utilize a number of contemporary recording and sampling techniques that are now used worldwide by nearly all record production companies. His collective endeavors are considered milestones in the histories of electronic and experimental music.

In answer to your first question I can briefly say that for me, Bach has been the only composer of any interest, ever since I was twelve years old: it was at that age that I first came across his music. No one else exists for me. As for your second question: noise has been the subject of my research. I did not examine it as a musician; I attempted to find out what was noise all about, what was its interrelationship with music. On a more general level, the relationship between music and all other aural phenomena. And finally: I am quite certain that I do not repeat myself, since I gave up composition some twelve years ago.

Now let us take a look at the three questions once again.

I.

My father was a violinist, my mother was a singer. I have heard music ever since I was a baby. As a child, I played the cello and the piano and was quite successful in solfeggio as well. And yet, it was not until I was twelve years old that I discovered music for the first time. Perhaps I was fourteen—I cannot remember.

This peculiar encounter did not occur in the conservatory but during a class at secondary school. A teacher brought home to me what a Bach fugue was: within a certain system, a particular arrangement of tones makes a proposal which is answered by a counter-proposal. Two dimensions merge here: melody and simultaneously with it, its harmonic opposite. I do not think music has ever gone beyond that. As far as I am concerned, nothing written since is of any interest.

In my view, music has followed the history of society. It reached its culmination in the eighteenth century at the time of the flowering of European civilization. Music's decline began already in the nineteenth century and ours is a mad, criminal, and bloodthirsty era which may well be preparing the end of the world. Music is part of that process in that it mirrors the cataclysms of our future. Most composers take part in that folly—out of vanity or careerism—and believe that they are capable of constantly turning out something new.

Nowadays, everything is "new": music, painting—even the art of cooking. New politics—sadly, there is no such thing, it only gets worse all the time. Nor is there new music—that is my opinion. And now let us turn to the second question.

II.

I am going to tell you why, at a particular moment in my life, I embarked on an adventure which I called *concrete music.*

I am not a composer. I have a degree in engineering but I have always regarded writing as my calling. As for my profession: I was one of the pioneers of broadcasting. I set up an experimental studio during the German occupation (today, they would call it an *atelier*) with the aim of developing the bases of radio art. Is it possible to create art devoid of the visual aspect? Is blind art viable?

Those were great years even though we had to work clandestinely during the occupation. We also participated in preparing the liberation of Paris. The first broadcasts went on the air a few days before the withdrawal of the Germans: it was rather a perilous undertaking.

It was after the war that the development of radio art really got under way. We wanted to find out all the possibilities inherent in this genre based only on text, background noise, and music—a genre that freed the imagination.

Logically enough, I attempted on one occasion to create an experimental work in which I set out to explore at what point background sound, the condensing of noise turns into music. (In other words, *musique concrète* was the outcome of an accident, just as most other innovations. One stumbles on something one was not looking for.)

There followed some hard years. In contrast to my contemporaries, I hate noise. I was not attracted by composition; I was out to examine what noise was, how the ear functions, what is the transition between music and sounds called noise. I summarized my research in a bulky volume (*Traité des objets musicaux. Essai interdisciplinaire* [Edition Seuil, 1966]). In the book, I point out: just as musical sounds—even the purest ones—have their own regular structure, so does noise. It is free of anything accidental and is based exclusively on the laws of physics. Noise is present in the sound of the violin or in the human voice.

I set up a well-based theory which provides answers to all relevant questions. I can claim that without any vanity. People do not know my theory and if they teach it, they distort it. The book has not been translated even into English—yet another proof of human stupidity.

The book's subtitle indicates the fact that I examine the subject from the standpoint of physics, acoustics, psychology, philosophy, and musicology. Apparently, this multifarious approach makes people feel uncomfortable. Although music unifies within it everything! I reproach my contemporaries primarily for their lack of courage to think in an interdisciplinary manner. They talk a lot of nonsense when they hold forth on acoustics, psychology, or music.

The only excuse for concrete music—for it did have its shortcomings—was the fact that it attempted to break out of the prison erected by serial music, this Austrian innovation. I can claim to have been the first one to drive a hole in the wall of that prison, however rudimentary the tools at my disposal may have been. These initiatives had a positive feedback all over the world, with the widespread establishment of studios of concrete (and in particular) electronic music.

There is a basic difference between concrete, electronic, and computer-generated music, but I am sure they will merge sometime in the future. Concrete music preserves the relationship between the ear and natural sound phenomena—that is its essence. Owing to their origin, natural sounds are pleasant to our ears, we like them, just as natural materials, like trees, stones, marble: we have grown used to them over millions of years.

What I was after was to find out how we could identify the musical element within the sound structure and how we could, based on the outcome of our research, determine the aesthetics of sound.

I realized that contrary to general belief, we have dual hearing because we hear the sound and music simultaneously. This duality has a philosophical aspect as well which goes against today's fashionable linear thinking. This rejects contradiction and duality. It is my conviction that in any sound we can hear two different things: the physical or instrumental processes which create it and man's will to communicate something musical via sounds. My conclusion: every music whenever and wherever it may have been created is based on a natural foundation, since the human ear is the same everywhere. Due to the nature of sounds, all music is similar with differences which spring from historical and cultural choices, as a result of varying systems and functions.

III.

I cannot answer this question because I am not a composer. Why did I stop writing music which I had always regarded as an experiment? It had a positive and a negative reason.

The positive reason has nothing to do with music. I used to work a great deal in radio and television—but after all, we only have one life and for me, writing was my actual vocation. I only have a few years left to write my books: philosophical works, novels, and other things. For me, music was an accident. An unfortunate accident.

The negative reason: music today is in a crisis. My contemporaries try to flee from their all-encompassing metaphysical fear in that they seek an impossible sort of music: stochastic or repetitive music, Stockhausenian blah-blah, Cageian clownery. I do not wish to become the victim of new simplicity—I prefer to reject it all.

After a fantastic century crammed with discovery we have arrived at a point where we are up against limits. Acceleration cannot be increased indefinitely. One can still invent something new, production can still be increased, but man remains the same. Man does not develop—rather the opposite.

The problem of music is the relationship between man and a fantastic means of expression: sound. Sound is nothing but the oscillation of the world. That's all. It is wonderful that through the use of sounds with their different frequencies we can create something entirely mysterious which is music. My contemporaries, however, treat this extraordinary phenomenon in a rude manner—out of mere vanity. They pose superficial questions, even though it would be their task to seek serious, profound, and functional contact between the means of expression and the internal content with which they can make an impact on people.

It could be that the twenty-first century will set itself the goal of calling a halt rather than to develop further. So that we can inhabit this globe and accept our human condition. Because if we maintain this speed and crash against a barrier, we shall smash ourselves to pieces.

1983

Fifty-Two

DIETER SCHNEBEL (1930)

Dieter Schnebel may well be the only composer today who is also an active preacher: he continues to exercise his vocation as a Lutheran theologian on a regular basis at the Johann-Sebastian-Bach Church at Berlin-Lichterfelde. His studies of theology went side by side with those of philosophy and musicology (at Tübingen), and he graduated from the Music Academy at Freiburg im Breisgau in 1952.

It was natural for the young composer to visit Darmstadt and to address himself to experiments with serial music. As he says in his contribution to this book, it was thanks to an encounter with John Cage that he turned in another direction and explored new possibilities inherent in the human voice, texts, and the stage. His works in the field of experimental music theater (which he also taught as a professor at the Berlin Academy of Arts between 1976 and 1995) have established him as a leading figure in German musical life. Foremost among them is Glossolalie *(1959/60). I saw a performance of it some time in the 1990s at the Witten Festival and was much impressed by the total unpredictability, originality, and madness of it. After the performance, Schnebel appeared on stage, stocky and priest-like, with a jovial smile on his face, as if to say "Wasn't it fun? Glad you enjoyed it."*

He is also known as a writer on music, with books on Schubert, Verdi, Wagner, and Webern.

I.

The encounter with Cage's piano concerto around 1958 and acquaintance with his ideas led, in my case as well, to fundamental changes in my thinking. I owe similar impulses to Luigi Nono (*Variazioni canoniche*) and Stockhausen (Piano Pieces I–V). And, of course, to Webern, Varèse, and Ives.

II.

Sounds of the environment play a role in several of my compositions (*Choralvorspiele I/II* 1966/69, *Hörfunk/Radiophonium I–V* 1969/70). The same is true of nonmusical, "concrete" sounds, in works like *Thanatos-Eros* (1979/82) for orchestra and human voices or *Jowaegerli* (1982/83), Alemannian words and pictures after Johann Peter Hebel,[57] for vocal and instrumental sounds and percussion. I believe that the sounds of our world—the friendly ones just as much as the hostile ones—constantly affect our music, including my own

57. Johann Peter Hebel (1760–1826), German poet.

compositional work. In my view, composers are always open to whatever they may be hearing day by day—to sounds around them.

III.

Perhaps you posed the question in the wrong way: style is the result of self-repetition. I surely possess an individual way of expression—but whether I have a style? I hope I don't. I would like my pieces to have been born each in its own manner—for each to have a style of its own. In other words, I am for "stylelessness." I do my best to avoid repeating myself. Whether I succeed?

1983

Fifty-Three

ALFRED SCHNITTKE (1934–98)

This interview changed the title of this book literally at the last minute. I had more or less despaired of ever finding the cassette on which I had recorded our conversation, until—as it happens sometimes, mysteriously, inexplicably—it turned up out of the blue when I least expected it. The title reads from now on: Three Questions for Sixty-Five Composers.

I met Schnittke at the Aldeburgh Festival in June 1988, that is, two years after *the publication of the Hungarian edition of this book. There was no question in my mind, I simply had to grab that unique opportunity. Twenty-two years on, it has now found its place in the American edition.*

We conversed in German, which Schnittke spoke fluently, if sometimes haltingly, with perhaps just a trace of Russian accent. Born to a father who came from Frankfurt am Main, Schnittke had spent the years between 1946 and 1948 in Austria, where he began his music education. Hence his command of the language. He remembered those years fondly, with their unforgettable musical experiences, such as Beethoven's Ninth Symphony under Josef Krips, Bruckner's Eighth under Klemperer, or the Abduction from the Seraglio *under Knappertsbusch. He wrote: "I recall a basic music tone, a certain Mozart-Schubert sound, which I carried within me for decades and which was confirmed upon my stay in Austria some thirty years later."*

I remember his slight figure, which even then, ten years before his death, struck me as emaciated, all the more highlighting his eyes, deep-set with an intense glow that radiated his genius as much as it may have mirrored his physical weakness.

I believe I first heard music by Schnittke in the late 1980s at the Prague Spring Festival: his Concert for Chorus *(1984/85) with its sumptuous sound took my breath away. It was timeless music of the kind Schnittke talked about in our interview, perhaps music that he "received as a gift," to quote his own words. Some time later I heard his* Moz-Art à la Haydn *(1977) for two violins and eleven strings—a haunting experience with gestures of the Baroque conjured up out of context, following a logic I could not quite fathom.*

Even more disturbing is his (K)ein Sommernachtstraum *[(Not) a Midsummer Night's Dream] composed for Salzburg in 1984/85. He calls it a "Mozart-Schubert-related rondo," and adds: "I did not steal all the 'antiquities' in this piece; I faked them." The fakes do work very well, with the first few minutes sounding like genuine Mozart. As the piece progresses, however, the Mozartian music is put in inverted commas, becomes increasingly alienated, and finally turns absolutely crazy. It is unsettling, Schnittke's "polystylistic" at its frightening best. His polystylistic at its entertaining but no less spooky best is his* Faust Cantata *of 1982 (which was to be incorporated in his opera* Historia of D. Johann Fausten *of 1990). You listen incredulously as the initial heroic tone, the solemn recitative imperceptibly morphs into a genuine musical, Mephistopheles being sung by a countertenor, uttering hysterical, high-pitched shrieks while a contralto is singing a melody which ought to have become a hit years ago. And then there is the Viola Concerto (1985), which Yuri Bashmet and Valery Gergiev have played the world over. I heard them in Rotterdam and was bowled over by the intensity of this music, and yes, by its timelessness.*

I am thrilled to be able to make public for the first time a transcript of my conversation with Alfred Schnittke.

I.

I cannot recall an extreme case which would have led to a sudden change in my musical thinking. I can, however, report on two contrasting experiences which surface in my work every now and again.

One is the sudden emergence of something which comes as a complete surprise—it is just there. In other words, I write a composition which appears out of nowhere, free of any influence by music that came before. The piece that is going to be played tonight, the Symphony No. 4 (1984), belongs to this category. I cannot trace any outside influence in it, it was born simply as it is.

At the other extreme, I have works which show a marked influence of music by other composers, especially by composers who lived a long time ago. I am receptive not just to music which was written today; for me, time is not limited to any particular period in music history. There exists a time span within which I can move freely. I can go 600 years back and I can also try and move forward. And yet, I stay within the same circle.

That explains why some of my pieces sound as if they have been around for a long time. It is quasi-old music. Such is my *Requiem* (1974/75) which could be described as old music, but not of any particular period in history. It is music of a different time, I do not know which one. Arvo Pärt comes to mind. He composes music which could have been written in the sixteenth century. You cannot explain how a composer who lives in the twentieth century writes music in a style which dates from 400 years ago. And yet, there is nothing artificial about it, it does not sound as if it had been restored, so to speak. It is genuine. There is, then, a new approach to the notion of time which characterizes some of the music being written today.

Can you name a piece of yours which, as you put it, "moves forward" in time?

Yes. Much of what I wrote twenty years ago sounds as if it were music that does not yet exist. Such is my orchestral work *Pianissimo* (1967/68). It is a field of many tones which influence one another. The music is not from this reality. It is from another reality.

There is yet another group of works where you cite music by other composers.

Yes, there are numerous quotations, pseudo-quotations, stylizations, and innumerable nuances of styles mutually influencing one another. There is a particular technique whereby one tries to say what has already been said in the past, in a different manner. I feel as if I were ceaselessly torn between these various extremes. On the one hand, one receives a gift—the music is all of a sudden there—and on the other, I write something which appears to be a quotation of something. I cannot make up my mind between them.

Does the question of originality come up at all?

It does not concern me much. Of course, I think of it sometimes but to my mind, however much one might make an effort to be original, there will always be an aspect which turns out to have occurred to someone else before. In other words, striving for originality does not really make much sense.

II.

Sounds of the environment are terribly important, even though they can also be unbearable: there are simply too many of them, they can be too loud. Still, I can recall particular cases where musical solutions were suggested by the sounds of nature. They can serve as a subconscious prop: nature comes to our aid. For instance, you hear a noise which seems to consist of the overtone scale. This occurs quite often, one experiences this at various spots. One never knows quite what it is but one hears it, and it becomes absorbed in the music. You hear muffled, deep tones which you cannot identify. You put them in your music with the bass trombones producing sounds recalling those tones. You also hear very high pitches which can be reproduced by flutes or piccolos. The sounds they produce appear to be coming from elsewhere, not from the orchestra.

III.

This is a question to which there is no unequivocal reply. Let us consider the life of Frédéric Chopin. If I were a contemporary of his, I might well have the impression that he did not develop—that he wrote the same piece all the time. As someone living today, however, it is precisely the absence of development that I consider to be one of the most attractive features of his music.

Is a composer supposed to be developing all through his life? He has created his own world and there is no reason why he should not stay there; he ought not to be taken by his ears and pulled up high, forcing him to "develop" artificially.

1988

Fifty-Four

GUNTHER SCHULLER (1925)

I am grateful for all the thought and time Gunther Schuller invested in revising the transcript of our interview, recorded at his house at Newton Centre, Massachusetts, sometime in the early 1980s.

Here is an excerpt from the composer's letter of April 15, 1985:

"The interview is now in quite good shape, and represents my views and thoughts on your questions accurately. I had to amplify some answers a little, because as I answered them 'live' to you, they were not entirely clear. I have also answered your additional questions in your January 7 letter. All best wishes for your project."

I feel that Gunther Schuller's text is an important historical document, an eye- and ear-witness account of a pivotal phase in postwar music history. Beyond its immediate autobiographical significance, it sheds light on the way an American composer would respond to the spirit of the Darmstadt Summer Courses in the 1950s, a kind of witches' kitchen of new music in the making. As a European, I personally find his comments on the American scene of tremendous interest. For one thing, he looks at Aaron Copland from a different angle than I who had met him in Budapest in 1973, having translated his book The New Music *into Hungarian. I found him a jovial and friendly old man; nothing hinted at the dictator he appears to have been considered by some people back home.*

While American composers had no ready access to scores of the Second Viennese School because of historical circumstances, their Hungarian counterparts were deprived of them for ideological reasons (which were of course also rooted in history: the division of the world after 1945), whereas in Austria after the Anschluss, *ideological considerations of a different color banished Arnold Schoenberg and his pupils from public musical consciousness (see the interview with Gerhard Wimberger).*

With regard to the plates of the scores of the twelve-tone composers that Schuller mentions: they were not hidden by Universal Edition during the war, since the publisher had been taken over by the Nazis who installed one Johannes Petschull as its director. It was Alfred Schlee (1901–98) who buried the plates in his garden, thereby saving them for the future. (He had joined the firm in 1927, only to retire as its director some sixty years later.)

I.

The major influences on my music came from Schoenberg and Stravinsky. My first encounter with the music of Schoenberg could perhaps be likened to Lutosławski's Cage experience: it served as something of a watershed in my development.

However, I am basically a self-taught composer. I learned about composition not from teachers, but from the music itself, i.e., from studying the scores and listening to music. I became an avid record collector (both jazz and classical) already in my young teens, and have always listened to a great variety of music. Also, I grew up in New York and there were even then—in the late 1930s and 1940s—three radio stations that played good music day and night. I left high school when I was sixteen, working as a professional horn player—I have no diplomas or degrees; I am what we call in America a high school "dropout." So I never had a chance to study composing at a conservatory or a university.

At first I made my living as a horn player in the Ballet Theatre Orchestra with Antal Doráti, then with Eugene Goossens in the Cincinnati Symphony, and later with the New York Philharmonic, and for fifteen years as principal horn of the Metropolitan Opera. Goossens did a lot of then-new music, and, of course, Mitropoulos introduced all of us to Schoenberg, Berg, and Webern when he was music director of the New York Philharmonic. Unlike some orchestra musicians, I did not sit in these orchestras bored and unlistening. I was listening hard and learning from the actual acoustical experience of the great masterpieces, past and present.

As I have said, I owe my most decisive musical influence to both Schoenberg and Stravinsky. To appreciate that, you have to know that in the early forties American musical life was divided into two camps: one was that of Stravinsky and Copland, that is, the neoclassical style; the other opted for Schoenberg and his pupils. The latter camp was very much in the minority. I was soon to realize that as a result of my interest in Schoenberg I was ostracized by the Copland camp. Composing dodecaphonic music in 1945 in New York took courage. Why? Frankly, because Copland and his school completely dominated the musical scene. William Schuman, Peter Mennin, and David Diamond and most other American composers belonged to that group.

The scores of the Second Viennese School were very hard to come by in the United States. During the Second World War they were simply not on sale in the shops, and in the libraries one had to look hard to find them. I later learned why: when the Nazis took over in Vienna, Universal Edition hid many of the plates of the Viennese twelve-tone composers. In this way many compositions survived the war. Nevertheless, some also were lost, such as *Royal Palace* by Kurt Weill.

In one respect I was very lucky: my wife studied piano with Eduard Steuermann, the man for whom Schoenberg wrote all his works for piano. He became a very sought-after piano teacher in America, and I attended every one of my wife's piano lessons. I learned a lot from Steuermann. He also was in possession of all the Schoenberg scores, all of them at that time extremely rare. For example, he had *Erwartung* (of which he had also made the piano reduction). I get goose pimples even today—forty years later—when I think of the effect seeing that score for the first time had on me. I had known of it, of course, having seen excerpts from it in books; but now I had the full score in front of me. Through this circumstance, then, I got to know this score and much of Schoenberg's music better than most Americans, who either were not interested or had no access to it.

I was also one of the first in America who knew of Messiaen during or even before the war. As a young boy I was a soprano in the choir of St. Thomas Church at Fifth Avenue and Fifty-Third Street in New York. The church had an excellent choir master and organist in British-born Thomas Tertius Noble. He was, incidentally, also my first teacher of harmony and music theory. Even though he was already in his sixties, he was open to new music. He had in his repertory the Hindemith organ sonatas, for example, new at that time; also the modern Flemish school, and also the organ works of Messiaen from the 1930s. Many musicians I met and even my father (who played violin in the New York Philharmonic for forty-two years) had at that time never heard of Messiaen.

In those years I absorbed every possible musical experience like a sponge. I came under Messiaen's influence; around the same time I became deeply attracted to Scriabin (those with sharp ears can discern his influence on my music to this day). Debussy and Ravel also played a role in my development. When I first heard *La Mer,* I almost fainted with ecstasy.

I went to Cincinnati in 1943. It was in that year that the record of the Berg Violin Concerto was released, in the performance by Louis Krasner and the Cleveland Symphony conducted by Artur Rodzinsky. Krasner had commissioned the concerto in 1934 and premiered it at the ISCM Festival in Barcelona in 1936. He is also credited with the first performance of the Schoenberg Violin Concerto. Rudolf Kolisch was supposed to premiere it, but he put it off because of other commitments for so long that Schoenberg agreed that Krasner could play it. Incidentally, I brought both Krasner and Kolisch to Boston when I was president of the New England Conservatory. They are both great men, of the caliber of Steuermann.

I was immediately fascinated by Berg's music. The score of the Violin Concerto was, of course, not to be had. So I decided to do something quite extraordinary: I copied the last two sides—eight minutes of music—from the recording. I wrote it out in *particell.* I still have it. You see, for me it was not enough to hear the music: I needed to see it in score form. When the score became available again after the war I compared it with my own transcription. It was remarkably close; the notes were all correct; but, of course, I did not know the exact instrumentation: whether, for example, it was a second clarinet or a third playing a certain note. I even mistook the saxophone for a horn. It took me a few months to complete because at the same time I was playing in the Cincinnati Orchestra; I did not have endless hours all day to do it.

What was it that took my breath away? The work's rich harmonic idiom which was new and atonal, but somehow still built on a tonal basis. And young as I was, I appreciated that link between the worlds of atonality and tonality. That is how I then quickly came to the music of Schoenberg and Webern: through Berg's Violin Concerto.

The Pro Arte Quartet, led by Rudolf Kolisch, played the four Schoenberg quartets—they were much later picked up by the Juilliard. We practically never heard Webern in New York until 1948. It was, I think, the young New Music Quartet that first included in its repertoire Webern's late Op. 28 String Quartet. Of course, later everyone discovered and played Webern, especially when Stravinsky in 1955 induced Columbia Records to make recordings under Robert Craft of all of Webern's works. Of course, Darmstadt also caught up with Webern in the early 1950s and the Age of Webern had set in.

At first Webern was a harder nut for me to crack than Berg. His is a different aesthetic world. But hearing a beautiful performance of Webern's Symphony, Op. 21 by Mitropoulos and the New York Philharmonic really revealed the beauty of that music to me.

I was one of the first Americans to visit Darmstadt and Donaueschingen. I made my "debut" at the *Ferienkurse* in 1953, a few years after Boulez and Stockhausen first attended it. Initially, I was quite impressed by what I heard there, especially the music of Luigi Nono—and the early work of Stockhausen and some of Henze. Also other visiting composers like Alexander Goehr and Bruno Maderna. But in a few years Darmstadt became so narrow, so egocentric, so dominated by a small clique of composers, that I lost my appetite for the place. Also they completely ignored the work of composers like Milton Babbitt and Roger Sessions, the former having written outstanding serial compositions long *before* Boulez and Stockhausen.

I admire the early work of Stockhausen. I regard *Gruppen* as a masterpiece, and I was the first to conduct *Zeitmasze* in the United States. But after a while, especially after his conversion to Cage, he became too obsessive, a would-be dictator of music, making a new *pronunciamento* every year as to how we were all to compose.[58] I think I made a big mistake: in the course

58. Here is an extract from my television interview with Stockhausen in Budapest, on October 7, 1984: "It appears as though there is a schematic image of Stockhausen who was born into a particular situation in history, simultaneously with the explosion-like development of technology—one who had to play the role of writing pieces, each of which was to become a model for other composers. I had to play the role of a pioneer. I was also predestined for that by my character: I am adventurous but at the same time pedantic too. In other words, my character combines the artist and the scientist, a type which did not emerge in music for a long time." In Karlheinz Stockhausen, *Texte zur Musik: 1977–1984* (Cologne: DuMont Dokumente, DuMont Buchverlag), 6:432.

of dinner one night in Darmstadt, I told him about Cage. He listened very fascinatedly, and next year proclaimed John Cage to be the greatest American composer. (For me, incidentally, Cage is more a philosopher than a musician. He is a kind of interesting creative dilettante.)

I took more to the music of Luigi Nono. We became close friends. I introduced his *Canto sospeso* and *Polifonica-monodia-ritmica* to the United States. I like his early works up to this day. Later, after *Canto sospeso,* he turned for a while toward a kind of mechanical serialism, which deprived much of his music of its original lyricism and beauty and content. But he is still a very important composer to me.

To get back to Darmstadt: in the early fifties there came about an alliance between the German radio stations, composers, publishers, modern music journals, and festivals. Radios, as you know, are subsidized by the state and can broadcast new music without any great risk. A political/business linkup developed: a festival premiered a new work, it was recorded or taped by a radio station, and then the tape was broadcast throughout Europe. And everybody became richer and more famous. As a result of a terrific publicity machinery, everything was made to sound bigger and better than it really was. That is how lesser composers, like Pousseur or Kagel, became touted as "great" composers. We were told in Darmstadt that they and Boulez and Stockhausen were the masters of our time, and we should all compose like them.

There were three composers in Darmstadt in those early years who thought this was all pretty silly: Alexander Goehr, Harrison Birtwistle, and me. We were young and fairly cocky, and didn't necessarily swallow Stockhausen's line. I am proud of that. In the end—around 1957—I left Darmstadt, never to return.

II.

We cannot gauge precisely—because we do not know enough about the creative process—what it is that we absorb, and how, and what changes these influences produce in us. I am sure that the years I spent in New York (I grew up there), the sound world of that city has in some way indirectly, subconsciously, left its mark on my music. I must have been influenced by New York life, most directly, of course, by New York's incredible music life, the concerts, the programs on the radio, and recordings. The rhythm and freedom of jazz, too, for I have spent half of my life in jazz, as you know. I might have composed differently had I grown up in North Dakota, like my wife.

I have good and curious ears; and so I listen to every sound—and in different periods of my life different kinds of sounds have been important to me. But obviously, there had been a certain selectivity which has determined what I feel I can use creatively, and what I cannot use. I am by nature primarily a harmonic-thinking composer, like Wagner, Schoenberg, Berg, Scriabin, Delius, or Rachmaninov. Because of that, nonharmonic sounds, such as the wind—however beautiful it may be—or a lawn mower or other extraneous sounds do not appeal to me creatively—as they obviously do to Cage, for example. I can accept Cage's undifferentiated sound world as a listener, but not necessarily and completely as a composer. The idea of preparing the piano also shows that his is a different kind of musicality. This is no evaluative judgment, only a simple statement of fact. Cage is light years away from Berg; and I belong to the Wagner-Mahler-Schoenberg-Berg school, along with large, profound influences of Stravinsky, especially *Le Sacre.* But I admit that Cage's tabula-rasa influence and the rejection of some encrusted traditions can lead to fruitful musical/creative experiments.

I have not mentioned much about Stravinsky. But his sound world, his clarity of form, his precision of detail, all had a profound effect on me. There is, of course, hardly a composer of today who has not been overwhelmed by *Le Sacre* and *Petrushka* and later, *L'Histoire du soldat.* Stravinsky has been such a powerful influence that we almost don't talk about him; we take him sometimes for granted. He is like air and water. Stravinsky was for me a most important counterbalance to the Schoenberg School, especially in the realm of rhythm and meter, and continuity. What form lessons *The Rite of Spring* can teach us—still today! It is through Stravinsky and some French composers (Milhaud, for example) that I learned not to become a twelve-tone fanatic.

When I was a young composer in New York, I was told I had to choose between Stravinsky and Schoenberg. I and my generation of composers said: "Nonsense! They are both great masters. We can learn from both."

I respond perhaps more to the visual arts, to painting than to external sounds. I initially wanted to become a painter. Later I wrote my first major orchestral work at the age of nineteen, inspired by the picture *Vertige d'Eros* by the Chilean painter, Echurren Matta, perhaps an appropriate subject for an exuberant young man. . . . Then there is my most famous orchestral piece, *Seven Studies on Themes of Paul Klee.* Although I knew much of Klee's work, I once encountered a whole series of his pictures at the house of the cellist, László Varga. I used to be a guest at his house every week and would admire the wonderful reproductions in the books on Klee in the library of Varga's painter-sculptor wife. (In those years such books were a rarity.) That is how I came upon some of the paintings by Klee which are visual representations of musical forms, revealing the strong influence of music—especially Bach—upon his work. So I conceived the idea of translating some of Klee's "musical" paintings back into music.

Other nonmusical influences? At the age of nineteen, I had a transcendental experience, to use Joyce's phrase: an epiphany, a revelation. I was staying at my father's house in the country, working on a cello sonata. To have a rest and to think a little, I went for a walk and lay down by a brook under a big tree. As I looked up, I saw the branches of the tree above me, its incredibly complex and "perfect" leaves against the blue sky. It was such a pure experience—suddenly so intimately in touch with nature. I shall never forget it. Everybody probably has some experience like it—but the vision of those leaves and the rays of the sun coming through them has become a permanent part of my life, etched into my brain to this day. I think in some subtle, intimate, indefinable way it profoundly influenced my work for weeks and months and years.

It showed me something of nature that I had not previously been aware of in such an intense way. I had always been close to nature, for I used to draw and paint flowers for days on end. But that was some kind of a *revelatory* experience. What I saw above me taught me more about form and structure and beauty, formal relationships than many a composition. I had found the same perfection in that vision as in Mozart operas, or in Beethoven's great forms, or in Strauss's *Till Eulenspiegel* (which is an almost "*perfect*" piece). Geniuses are in some ways the expressions of nature—after all, man is part of nature, lest we forget.

III.

Your question refers to a critical problem in new music. So many musical compositions I have heard since the mid-1950s have consisted of not much more than the repetitions of clichés: the same ideas coming back again and again and again. They had bored me probably the first time—and *certainly* the tenth time. But I have had to listen to them hundreds of times since. Of course, I know that in *every* age there have been more bad composers than good ones and the current situation, seen in perspective, is no different. But the musical-political alliances I spoke of earlier have also contributed to the emergence of a kind of "professional avant-gardism." If the critics, publishers, radio stations, and propagandists and others with a vested interest pronounce this or that piece "a masterpiece," and Boulez and Ligeti bless and sanctify it, then young people tend to believe that that is the way they have to compose, too; they will be successful, fashionable.

As far as I am concerned, I do my best to avoid self-repetition. It happens sometimes that my instincts tell me that I have not yet exhausted all the possibilities inherent in a particular idea. Then, of course, I try to realize it more completely or in a different way in the next work. There are, in other words, borderline cases where it is not a question of self-repetition but rather the desire to more fully realize a larger idea.

There are many examples of that in music history. Composers have returned to the same device five, six, seven, or more times, until they have exhausted it, and only then turned to something else.

I have also sometimes gone back to pieces I wrote in my youth. I find that I poured out a great many ideas, but not always with their possibilities fully explored—simply because I was not completely aware of them and their full implications. In this way, there is a continuity in my music, as old ideas live on in a renewed form. I think this happens to most composers.

1984/85

Fifty-Five

JOHANNES MARIA STAUD (1974)

"I've now reached nine minutes fifty-seven seconds," Johannes tells me on the telephone. He keeps me posted on the progress of whatever he is writing, true to what he told me some years ago about the way he keeps track: "Like a bookkeeper."

What really impressed me about his music when I first heard it some time in 2000, was the sensitivity and musicality of it: the delicacy of the sounds he imagined for the few instruments accompanying the soprano, in his Vielleicht zunächst wirklich nur *[To start with, perhaps really not more than] (1999), premiered in Vienna by the Ensemble Modern. The music touched a chord in me; I responded with my instincts.*

The piece made me happy, for I felt that I was visiting a landscape I had never seen before and yet where I was at home. It was wonderfully reassuring to find a young man of such talent: creating new within the familiar. It was sheer pleasure to hear tiny details within the overall soundscape, so that you sat up and savored, say, the sound of a harp, like the glint of light on a painting—tiny but absolutely essential.

For Staud, the idea for a piece is more often than not suggested by extramusical impulses: the writings of the ancient Greek philosopher Anaximander as well as Leonardo da Vinci inspired Apeiron *(2004/5) for large orchestra (a commission of the Berlin Philharmonic), a work by the American artist Bruce Nauman (1941) produced* Violent Incidents *(2005/6) for saxophone solo, winds, and percussion, the incomparable atmosphere of the novels of Bruno Schulz (1892–1942) captured the young composer's imagination to create two large-scale orchestral pieces which attempt to conjure up Schulz's world:* On Comparative Meteorology *(2008/9) for the Cleveland Orchestra and* Über trügerische Stadtpläne und die Versuchungen der Winternächte *[On Deceptive City Maps and the Temptations of Winter Nights] (2009) for string quartet and orchestra. The titles are taken from Schulz, a remarkable Polish-Jewish writer shot dead by the Gestapo in the middle of a street in Drohobycz, a small town in Galicia.*

Literature, philosophy, the arts—Johannes Maria Staud is remarkably well-versed in all, but he is just as sensitive to natural beauty, coming as he does from the most mountainous region of Austria, Tyrol. The Alps are his second home, skis his second pair of legs. In between two compositions he disappears from Vienna and gives vent to his tremendous pent-up energy on long and physically demanding tours. Tall, slim, blond, with a permanent three-day stubble, he is the picture-book Austrian youth. In fact, Johannes is a healthy young man in every sense of the word, he is not averse to sowing his wild oats every now and then and has no truck with the ivory tower. The two sides of his character—the creative and the down-to-earth—complement each other in perfect harmony.

He is a passionately political person. The formation of a coalition government in Austria, which included the extreme right-wing FPÖ, incensed him to such an extent that he poured all his protest into the orchestral work . . . gleichsam als ob *. . . [As it were] (1999/2000). He does not hesitate to take drivers of SUVs to task for polluting the environment and deplores the way the tourist industry ruins the slopes of the Alps.*

Johannes has a restlessness which is only suspended when he bends over the score of a new piece. Talking to him is like receiving a rejuvenating injection, his enthusiasm and optimism are infectious—unless you happen to ring him when he is composing: then he is "away," as he puts it, and has to force himself to come back to earth. You quickly hang up to let him return to his private tilting yard where his pencil leads him to states of frustration and the rewards of euphoria.

I.

By far the most decisive, indeed the most radical experience in a composer's life—at least in mine—is getting down to composing for the very first time. It is a mysterious moment: the play instinct, the pleasure over sounds, the keenness to imitate and the fascination with the unknown are suddenly short-circuited and evoke an irresistible urge to invent one's own music instead of being content with the contemplation, performance, or adoration (like in a museum) of already existing masterpieces.

Whatever may come afterward, such as the emancipation from musical idols, the unsettling encounter with great pieces in great performances (something that has come my way not infrequently), a critical examination of one's own idiom and setting out toward a new musical language—sometimes just a plan, at others something one (half-) succeeds in carrying out—all that is part of the daily life of a composer. The experience of being deeply moved is, however, just as unpredictable as is the influence of particular works on one's own musical horizon. It can even happen that one is inspired by compositions one actually rejects, the idiom and musical interests of which are diametrically opposed to one's own.

There is one point on which I fully agree with Lutosławski, even if he was not the first and only one to have formulated it: as a composer, one is *always* in a schizophrenic state of mind when listening to (and reading) music, because any music, independently from its style, will be filtered by one's own preferences and aversions. The insatiable hunger for "exterior impulses" is, however, not restricted to music. I never succeed in "switching off" when visiting an exhibition, reading a book, or seeing a film, I cannot dissociate myself from my own artistic work and existence. Is this something to deplore, is the loss of naiveté something to lament? I do not think so, for I have never known otherwise, I have never experienced it differently.

II.

Noises, sounds or music only disturb me while I am working—then they upset me in such an extreme manner as to drive an amiable, enlightened, tolerant, and good-humored person to utter despair, spluttering hatred, muttering curses, and entertaining the wildest fantasies of vengeance. To begin with, there are the cars with their engines running outside my window. Then the TV set next door whether roaring or softly chirping (particularly perfidious!). There is the maniacal darabuka-player practicing in the apartment overhead or a mandolin being subtly plucked in the one underneath. Try as I might to stuff my ears with whatever I have to hand, sounds still reach my inner ear. I may relent when birds visit the trees outside (I usually keep the window open while working), unless it is a stubborn blackbird that has made up its mind to annoy me with the relentless repetition of the silliest patterns. (Perhaps that explains my antipathy toward minimal music . . .) I do not mind insects buzzing around me but I do draw the line at clumsy autumn flies taking it into their heads to hum round my desk lamp, ending up—just to provoke me—on my manuscript paper to demonstrate their independence from the world of affects. I can put up with the general murmur and rumble of the city from afar (nowadays it is called *ambients*—or was that yesterday?), indeed, it actually helps concentration up to a point. The only sounds that I am really fond of while composing are the howling of the wind, the rain beating against the window pane, and the soft falling of snow (to make sure poetry also gets its fair share).

However, away from my desk, I am the most tolerant person imaginable with regard to noises and sounds, to an extent that is in a way unworthy of a composer. Soft (much better: loud!) background music in bars, lively muzak in elevators and department stores—normally, the evil incarnate—meet with my unreserved welcome. Also, noises far more preferred by my colleagues, such as the (Babylonian) babble of voices, the squeaking of shunting trains, the din of factories or the sighing of doors, the roaring of the ocean, and galloping horses inspire me immensely and provide me with raw material for my work with all its amiability and aimlessness, evoking as a result far more than my disinterested satisfaction.

III.

This is the trickiest question of all, one that cannot very well be answered by a composer who lacks the necessary distance to himself, to his obsessions and his work. If I did have that distance, I might make a good music theoretician, a poor composer, or both at the same time. In the opposite case, that is, the absence of the necessary distance (which applies to me),

I might still be a bad or maybe a good composer; I would, however, certainly make a miserable music theoretician. I will nevertheless try and reply to the best of my ability. This inconsistency goes to show, I believe, that I would never have made a music theoretician, or, in any case, I would have been a wretched one. (Lack of distance, incidentally, is not to be mistaken for the absence of self-criticism.)

Personal style and self-repetition are divided by a thin line. An assessment is made difficult by the fact that one's obsessions, "primal musical situations" concentrated in a dramatic form, accompany a composer over the years like a shadow. If in each new work the "primal musical situations" are moved further away from their starting points (in the sense of evolving variations), one might come close to what is called a personal style. The richer the range of such "primal situations" is, the more imaginatively the composer handles their combination and further development, the more open-minded he is to generate new "primal situations" through synthesis or autonomous implementation, the less he will run the risk of repeating himself.

However, I am not that sure that self-repetition is necessarily a bad thing, as suggested by the question. To my mind, in the right hands and motivated by good intentions (that is, not generated by composing way too much), it can very well have its own charm, fascination, and distinction. The visual arts, incidentally, have had a much more relaxed approach to this question (or was that twenty or thirty years ago?).

2010

Fifty-Six

KARLHEINZ STOCKHAUSEN (1928–2007)

The interview took place in October 1984 in Budapest where Stockhausen was a guest of the new-music festival. Twenty-six years on, I can vividly remember the intensity of the composer's presence as well as my delight that my questions met with such a ready response. I sensed a thrill at hearing Stockhausen relate his encounter with Messiaen's Mode de valeurs et d'intensités *(1949), for it brought me, I thought, in direct contact with music history.*

There also came an unexpected meeting some twenty years later in a hotel restaurant near Donaueschingen where I was a guest of Wolfgang Rihm. Stockhausen, dressed in white, went past our table and stopped to greet his former pupil. I also stood up to shake his hand and mentioned my name. He did not seem to be able to place me and appeared to be convinced that I was someone else. It is a measure of the intensity of his personality and the quiet strength of his conviction that I found myself almost embarrassed not *to be the one he took me for. It was but a brief duel—he left and I returned to my chair, rather dizzy.*

A couple of years later, the festival Musica in Strasbourg featured an extract from Stockhausen's monumental music theater work Licht *(1977–2002), the complete performance of which takes a whole week. I heard and saw a rather odd ceremony based on a concept I could not quite grasp. It was perplexing more than anything else and a sense of boredom enveloped the hall. Nevertheless, Stockhausen was heartily applauded when it ended and he, once again dressed in what looked like a costume specially designed for him, looked pleased.*

I wanted to make sure my translation of the German interview was faithful to the original, so I sent the script to Suzanne Stephens, the American clarinetist who worked with the composer for several decades and is now chair of the Board of Directors of the Stockhausen Foundation for Music. I am grateful to Ms. Stephens for revising the manuscript. (The titles of Stockhausen's compositions are rendered in block capitals, in accordance with the style adhered to in his books published by DuMont.)

I.

Something like that happened once in my life. In Darmstadt, in 1951, at the Summer Courses for New Music, a French music critic played a record of Messiaen's *Quatre études de rythme.* One of the etudes is entitled *Mode de valeurs et d'intensités.* I asked him there and then to play the piece again and again and a whole new world opened up before me—an inner world—in listening to this "point music," this "star music," as I called it at the time. After the Darmstadt Summer Courses were over, I returned to Cologne and told a music critic of this experience. He asked: "What does this music sound like?" And I repeated: "It sounds like the stars in the sky."

At these Summer Courses I also met a Belgian pupil of Messiaen's, Goeyvaerts, and he explained how Messiaen had composed the piece. It clarified many things for me, because I had written twelve-tone music before but it had never occurred to me that rhythm could be just as nonperiodic as pitches could be nontonal or that the intensities of the pitches could also be so different.

Later on when I heard it again, the piece did not have such a strong effect on me. However, it was thanks to that experience that four months later, in January 1952, I moved to Paris because I was determined to study with Messiaen. I attended his courses on aesthetics and rhythm for a whole year.

What piece did you compose as a result of that experience—perhaps Mosaik*?*

Already as I hitchhiked back from Darmstadt, at a motorway service area, I jotted down sketches for *KREUZSPIEL* (1951). I then traveled to Hamburg and composed the piece there. It was published, is played often, and is considered as my first so-called "point music."

Would you agree with Lutosławski that when listening to a work by another composer, sometimes one switches off and involuntarily hears one's own music inspired by the one being played?

Surely, Messiaen's piece evoked an inner world within me which was not Messiaen—but of course there was a connection. I had a similar experience later in Japan when I heard Gagaku music for the first time. I did not compose any Gagaku music afterward but did innerly hear a new, spatial music.

There are also natural phenomena which can evoke something like that. For instance, in Yosemite Valley in the United States, I had a remarkable experience which led to a whole section in *HYMNEN, electronic and concrete music with soloists and orchestra* (1967). The following happened: in Yosemite Valley, there are almost vertical walls of rock on both sides of the valley. At a particular spot, water falls from an altitude of nearly a thousand meters. The deeper it falls, the more it sprays until it turns into fog at the bottom. The mountain face has veins which run through the stone like horizontal fever curves. As I was staring at the waterfall for several minutes, all these horizontal lines began to move upward. I found the effect absolutely unique, because I always followed particular masses of the water as it fell and after three or four minutes had the impression that the whole mountain was rising. After this experience, I came to the electronic music studio in Cologne and spent several weeks searching for a way of doing something similar with sound.

In the fourth region of my composition *HYMNEN*, there is a passage lasting circa three minutes in which slow glissandi constantly fall downward, starting extremely high. Since they directly follow one another, the entire hearing range is always filled with slowly falling glissandi. From this glissando wall, I let very clear lines of pure tones emerge. When the glissandi are over, the sine tones remain as a clear line, and one has the impression its pitch slowly rises, although in reality it does not. This results from the unusual effect caused by the preceding length and prominence of the slowly descending glissandi. That is how experiencing nature can lead to a new music.

II.

Ever since *GESANG DER JÜNGLINGE, electronic music with a boy's voice* (1956), I have become more and more interested in ensuring that particular sounds can be recognized in abstract sound worlds. In the electronic music *KONTAKTE* (1960), of which there is also a second version with piano and percussion, there are clearly recognizable marimba tones, drum sounds, certain cowbell sounds, high bell sounds, etc., all produced electronically. I had analyzed natural sounds for several months, afterward producing some synthetically: I had discovered the natural law of how these natural sounds were formed, i.e., what kinds of oscillatory forms they have. And once you have recognized this law, you can also transform one known sound into another known sound. You study the laws of acoustic alchemy and as a result become a composer capable of composing sound syntheses and sound transformations.

MOMENTE (1962–64/69) came after that. It is a work which occupied me for nearly ten years, one which also integrates the reactions of the audience. For instance, sometimes the chorus claps rhythmically until it turns into statistic clapping which sounds like normal audience applause. Indeed, it is composed to directly connect with the initial applause of the audience when the soloists and the conductor enter—as the answer of the chorus to the audience.

The chorus claps against the audience, the clapping becomes more and more rhythmic and gradually turns into music. In addition, there are also calls like "stop," "disgraceful," "yes," "bravo," "no"—calls that I had heard from the audience in concerts of my music.

The solo soprano uses every imaginable onomatopoeic expression, singing, shouting, whispering, giggling, and laughing. Entire cascades of laughter have been composed with rhythms and pitches.

MOMENTE was followed by *MIKROPHONIE II* (1965) where typical slang expressions or slang phrases are sung by the chorus. Through an electronic process these are transformed and distorted so that the female singers sometimes sound like witches. Calls that people address to each other in everyday life—some of them erotic or vulgar—are reflected in a curious fashion, like through a distorting sonic mirror.

Finally, in HYMNEN there appear national anthems, that is, completely banal material as well as numerous other situations (recordings made in a Chinese shop, at a student protest demonstration in Aachen, at a ship's christening in Hamburg, at a soccer match with crowds of people shouting, the squawking of birds, and boys shouting in a school yard). Linked to the American national anthem, you hear odd short-wave sounds (Morse signals, whistling, shrill screeching), as if someone has turned on a radio station at night, with distorted broadcasts. In the context of the "International" the words of a croupier: "*rien ne va plus Messieurs Dames,*" "*faites vos jeux Messieurs Dames,*" etc., are heard. Out of the "*Rouge*" called by a croupier in a roulette hall emerges a four-part fugue in four different languages on the word *rouge*, with all the different variations of the color red as listed in the color catalogue of a London paint company.

So, there are many examples (I cannot list them all here) in *HYMNEN* for the way identifiable sound events are integrated in the world of unidentifiable music. They open up like little windows to a world which we know and which we call the "concrete" world (the French speak of *musique concrète*). What this means, really, is that in a music one makes use of sound objects, also sound complexes or phrases which have a wholly concrete meaning in life, which have a name. Sounds or sound events with names are used by me at particular places where most of the sounds do not have names—they are new sounds. The composition *TELEMUSIK* (1966) is an example of how I have inserted many short windows in the music history of mankind. A piece of music recorded among Vietnamese mountaineers or a moment of a tribe in North Africa, yet another one with the voice of a Kraho-Indian woman (a mother singing to her baby), a recording made at a temple in Nara, a Chinese orchestra with flute solo, a moment of Hungarian music, or of Flamenco—all connected with my electronically produced sounds through mutual modulation (I call it "intermodulation").

My compositions have brought forth processes which can be used by others as well: how an *objet trouvé* (as the French call it in painting) can be related to another *objet trouvé*, that is, transform one into the other. Or, how one can modulate the rhythm of one "objet trouvé" with the melody of another "objet trouvé" and can then modulate the result with the harmonic structure of a self-made "objet nouveau."

A completely special concept, "parametric intermodulation," has become very important for me. The old word "modulate" has acquired an entirely new meaning, like in electroacoustics: one can modulate an oscillation form with another oscillation form through electronic operations and both can "intermodulate" with each other, so that what emerges is more than the sum of the two. Like in the case of genetic syntheses or with particular chemical syntheses, the components of a new substance can no longer be analyzed. This has become important in music. That is why I sometimes use the words "musical alchemy" and "intermodulation."

III.

All of music—as a human statement—consists of gestures. One could rewrite the whole of music history as one of gestural styles. Although one would not simply describe the way rhythms are formed, melodic and harmonic laws, and which instruments are used, and how particular formal mechanisms of repetition or variation occur; instead, one could rewrite the whole of music history as the history of a "gesticology" (a new word which I now simply invent).

By that I mean that in the future, the personal style of a composer would not simply be identifiable through his use of instruments, what his preferences are as far as rhythmic, melodic, harmonic, and color combinations are concerned, what dynamic forms (envelope curves) or what formal divisions he applies—rather, one recognizes a composer through the kind of gesture which characterizes him—from being quiet to being extremely impulsive (with all the degrees in between). To this belongs a personal scale of the degrees of changes within which someone moves in accordance with his temperament: how fast or slow something changes, how much time it takes; how condensed the changes at particular spots are and how still and extremely void it is elsewhere. All those are traits which describe the characteristics of a creative spirit in an abstract manner.

A "metastylistic composer" let us say, can less easily be recognized by the facade (as in the previous generation one could identify Debussy or Stravinsky or Bartók or Hindemith or Schoenberg), but more likely through his intensity gestures, his temporal gestures, his spatial gestures (that is, in which direction of space something is placed, something shoots or moves slowly, when it stops, how often it moves to another point in space): all those are criteria of a composer's uniqueness. Such criteria could also serve as examples for all other criteria.

One can take over gestural criteria without producing stylistic clichés, because the uniqueness of the musical gestures of the composer are innovations of general validity and are also extensions of the musical idiom. I believe it is important in the future to observe what sort of original gestures a composer actually has in his treatment of space and time, what are his degrees of change, his processes. I find that more important than his use of instruments or colors. Such orientation will be important because today, the traditional stylistic material is at the disposal of everyone. In the future, every composer will have access to the whole of music history, all the styles that have ever existed as his material and added to that will be many new musical styles that have been developed by the composer himself.

One has to imagine the entire material of music as a museum housing recordings of all folk musics and art music styles of all times on this planet. My "pieces" are also there as well as the "pieces" of all other composers. They are all musical "photographs" which one can link together to make new musical compositions.

What impulse, what characteristics of composition does then a composer have in comparison with those of another composer? That is why a composer will principally be judged on the basis of his gestures, energetics, his sense of time, his sense of space. It is, for instance, a characteristic mark of a composer if the duration of his works keeps on getting longer, until in the end—as I see it in a kind of Utopia—they become a single lifework for each composer; I mean, a composer will be working on a single work all his life, integrating in it whatever he is doing.

To return for a moment to the question of self-repetition: you have mentioned that a part of HYMNEN is like a section of GESANG DER JÜNGLINGE. During the process of composition, how important is it for you to create something you never did before?

It is always important that as far as possible, everything that I do was never done by me before. And if you say that a part of *HYMNEN* is like *GESANG DER JÜNGLINGE*, then I must reply "no," because if you could show me such a section, I would immediately delete it, even today.

You said yourself: "By the way, I did that already in GESANG DER JÜNGLINGE . . ."

Yes, but what I mean by that is that I used something in *HYMNEN* that one knows already. That has, I think, nothing to do with a particular piece. The abstract method of using something in a composition that others know already, is different from being the copy of a work. For instance, in *GESANG DER JÜNGLINGE*, one recognizes children's voices, in *HYMNEN* one recognizes national anthems—that's what I mean. If you can show me that in a piece I have done something in the same way as in another work, then I believe I ought not to have done that. To my mind, there must always be a reason for creating something and the reason can only be, to try out something that oneself, nor anyone else, has ever tried out before.

1984

Fifty-Seven

ANDRÁS SZŐLLŐSY (1921–2007)

It was quite an effort to put the date of death after that of András Szőllősy's birth. Ever since we met in 1972 or so, when I started promoting his music in the world, I would ring him on February 27, to wish him many happy returns on his birthday. The last time we met I visited him in his tiny apartment filled with books, Etruscan objects, and some remarkable paintings by Hungarian artists, and found him with the glow gone from his eyes. His beloved Irish setter had died shortly before (his wife had departed several years earlier when the composer himself was becoming physically too weak to look after her) and I saw on his face that he had given up. He was sitting in his armchair, fully dressed with jacket and tie, his feet on a low stool and waited for Death to fetch him. That would have been in October 2007; he died in December, two days after Stockhausen.

When I was introduced to Szőllősy, he was fifty-one years old. An explosive personality, he would easily fly off the handle, get worked up about anomalies in Hungarian or world politics, about intrigues among his fellow-composers, whatever. He was also emotional. His eyes would fill with tears on hearing a piece of music that moved him—and that piece of music could be by himself. What moved him would be an empathetic performance—for instance, of his Pro somno Igoris Stravinsky quieto *(1978), a kind of requiem in memory of the Russian composer who was one of his idols (others being Mozart and Bartók above everybody else). I attended the rehearsals by the Dutch ensemble that had commissioned it. The instrumentalists had to recite the Latin words of the Requiem—and tears would roll down Szőllősy's cheeks. He also cried when the King's Singers premiered one of the pieces he had written for them. The atmosphere in the church at Brighton in the South of England was absolutely unique and so was the perfection of the ensemble's rendition. I can still see the composer's stocky figure rise at the end of the performance and move with both arms outstretched, head leaned sideways, to thank the singers.*

Szőllősy was for many decades professor of music history at the Budapest Academy. He also wrote some books, but most important, he drew up a catalogue of Bartók's oeuvre. The "Sz" you see after a Bartókian title are the first two letters of his name.

He readily granted me an interview to reply to my three questions but was not satisfied with the result. The text below was written by András Szőllősy. Now that he is gone, it strikes me as his testament.

I.

I belong to the generation born early enough to be present at the world premieres of some of Bartók's or Kodály's works. Those premieres were among the most important musical experiences of my youth. The generations coming after us probably cannot even assess the effect those premieres exercised on us. I saw Bartók and Kodály as twin stars and therefore sought in their works what they had in common rather than what kept them apart. As a result, I did not reach below the surface. Instead of analyzing the inner structure of the musical material, I put the accent on the composers' stance that lent itself to be celebrated in festive newspaper articles. I looked for moral and national paragons in those masters.

Later, when I would have been mature enough to explore the deeper layers of music, the war and the years of reconstruction made serious work impossible. It was not until the mid-50s that it began to dawn on me and some of my friends that the world of music was broader than what we had believed it to be, that it encompassed a variety of trends, some of which made us stop to think even if they did not necessarily recruit us to be their followers.

The year I spent in Goffredo Petrassi's master class in Rome in 1947–48 proved tremendously helpful in broadening my horizons. It was not until much later that I actually learned to appreciate what he had taught us. He did his best to open doors for me that led to a deeper understanding of new music but I found it difficult at the time to pass through them. In each door there stood watch the spirits of Bartók and Kodály.

I think I first visited the Warsaw Autumn Festival in 1957. By then I had become much more open to absorbing new ways of thinking about music. That was my first encounter with representatives of the new Polish school and also with works by composers from the West. The magic of hearing the music live, the fact that scores which had looked so complex to the eye could actually be performed, meant a great deal. I heard a piece by Lutosławski at the very first concert: it was the *Trois poèmes d'Henri Michaux*. It made a deep impression. In contrast with the stringency I had found in the music of Bartók and Stravinsky (I had kept my admiration for him, first conceived as a student at the Budapest Academy) I came face to face with incredible freedom in the treatment of orchestra and chorus, also in the fact that a composition could be led by two totally independent conductors and that the two ensembles met through chance—but the chance was, nevertheless, somehow organized. I thought that compositions which possessed such a high degree of freedom would obviously be different each time they were performed but such changes did not go beyond those experienced by a Beethoven sonata in different interpretations. I was intrigued by that sound world and when, around the age of fifty, I got down to serious composition, I could not rid myself of its fascination for a long time. I would not say that I attempted to follow it; I had always wanted my music to be much more organized but I did endeavor to give it a rich and varied sonority similar to the Polish composer's music which lacked organization or was at any rate organized in a way which differed from anything I had heard before. Perhaps that was one reason why I wrote so many orchestral works at the beginning.

II.

Sounds of the environment hold no interest for me whatsoever. I believe that it is the composer's job to create his sound material. He must not copy. Of course, certain sonorities are bound to be soaked up by his consciousness (or his subconscious) and in imagining a sonority, those memories are involuntarily conjured up. Stravinsky's definition of the composer's task is the most precise one I know of. He said composers had to create order among tones in time. Once that has been achieved, the composer has done his job. It should not concern him that each listener interprets his music in his own fashion, through his subjective associations.

How do you then explain the pealing of bells that marks a group of your pieces? The bell makes a physical appearance at the end of your Concerto No. 3 (1968), while in Trasfigurazioni *(1972) and a number of other compositions you create a bell sound through instrumentation.*

I believe I do not contradict the truth of the above if I accept that any sonority is allied to a certain range of associations. I have been attracted to bells ever since my childhood because of the images they evoke in me. When composing the Concerto No. 3, I wished to create a surprise effect similar to the one made by the trumpet which is sounded perfectly unexpectedly in Honegger's String Symphony (1941). I decided in favor of the bell. Soon, though, I felt that an actual bell made a much too direct effect. Perhaps that is why I resorted to bringing about its sound through the instruments at my disposal, thereby perhaps expanding its range of associations. That effort has incidentally taught me a great deal about the analysis of sonorities. I made the same analysis (using a less scientific method and perhaps less consciously) as some of my contemporaries who explore the laws of certain sounds with calculations supported by machines.

III.

I wonder if there is such a thing as a personal style. It is our job "to create order among the tones." There are obviously umpteen ways of doing that, yet it is quite likely that all methods that make any sense have been tried out already. Historical periods and prevalent tastes do impose their limits on the way composers define "order" for themselves. The same is true of what they regard as chaos.

I believe personality does not lie in a composer's capacity to devise something radically new. If we were to delude ourselves that someone has succeeded in doing so, it suffices to study the history of music in any depth to realize that ideas that may appear to be totally new have emerged in the past (often centuries ago). For some reason they went unnoticed at the time and were not absorbed in the "order" as understood by composers.

Originality manifests itself in the rearrangement of musical phenomena based on an individual approach to interrelationships of the existing constituents of music. Stravinsky is an obvious example. He is widely regarded as an innovator—but if you examine the elements he worked with, practically each one turns out to have existed before. The manner, however, in which he created order among those elements and brought them into relationships with one another, was certainly his alone.

In other words, he had an individual style.

I am not sure whether you need to call it an individual style: he had after all three or four distinct stylistic periods.

But those periods were all marked by his unmistakable personality.

That is true, but I would rather say that he had a personality which shone through his stylistic periods, even when he was playfully donning musical masks. What I admire in Mozart, Bach, and Stravinsky—to name three peak achievements of the human spirit—is the fact that they were able to create a unity out of the well-known sound phenomena of their times and thereby lent them a significance which they did not possess before.

You ask: what is personal style and where does self-repetition begin? In my view, a personal style can only be defined with any precision fifty or a hundred years after the composer's death. As long as he is active in a living musical environment, musical ideas are in permanent flow. To put it in a simplified manner: composers influence one another.

A mature, late piece in a composer's oeuvre can shed light on areas of his earlier works which, at the time of their emergence, seemed negligible even for the most painstaking analyst. Perhaps because the latter did not yet have the knowledge and the methods to integrate unusual phenomena in an order developed out of well-known stylistic features. Just think of Schoenberg: until he evolved the rules of composing with twelve equal chromatic tones, nobody realized that relevant passages had existed in works by Bach, Mozart, Liszt, and others.

No doubt about it: if you write the same music all your life, you may create the impression as though you had a personality. This occurs if a composer has found (or thinks he has found) a procedure which sets him off from his colleagues. If, however, that is all that procedure is meant to achieve, it is bound to lead to self-repetition. What is fascinating about a genuine personality is the way he changes from work to work and has the courage to stake the frontiers of his imagination ever wider, enriching the world he can call his own.

1982/85

Fifty-Eight

TŌRU TAKEMITSU (1930–96)

Trying to interview Takemitsu was a tantalizing experience: his ideas were within immediate reach and yet hopelessly unattainable. Their richness and originality shone through his inability to express them: his English vocabulary was simply too limited. I have omitted all my innumerable groping questions. After all, ours was no dialogue—rather, we were comrades in a frustrating struggle for expression.

Rereading the interview after thirty years, I can still hear Takemitsu's quiet voice and see his face, which remained expressionless (or showed the same expression) throughout—only his eyes were alive with the effort to find the right words. Despite his poor English, this monologue had a very special, a very Japanese atmosphere. For me, the figure of the shakuhachi master is like a painting or the subject of a haiku. So is Takemitsu's lakeside house surrounded by thousands of cherry trees in full blossom.

I.

I am interested in all kinds of music: the widest range of folk music, jazz, or rock.

I am an autodidact as a composer, I learned directly from Bach, Beethoven, Debussy, Cage, Stockhausen, Schoenberg, Bartók, and many others. I absorbed all these influences in an open and sincere manner.

Debussy exerted the strongest influence. Whenever I am about to write a new piece, I go back to him and study his scores carefully. Why? This would be difficult to explain. Perhaps it is a question of taste. Or perhaps because I am Japanese.

Debussy's colors awake my musical fantasy. I have mastered the secrets of instrumentation, I know how to achieve beautiful sonorities. However, that is not sufficient. In the initial stages of work, when I imagine the music I am going to write, it is always colors that first emerge—colors in space, colors in time. For me, timbres are in close relationship with the perception of time and space. It is difficult for me to talk about this: I still have a lot to learn, I have not yet been able to mix enough colors. Each work is an attempt in that direction. Debussy was a master of colors—I am still only groping.

Apart from western music, I am also interested in traditional Japanese music and sometimes I compose for Japanese instruments. For the past two or three years, I have been studying the biwa.[59]

---

59. The biwa is a flat Japanese lute.

In our traditional music, a single note can be extremely complex. (Some composers in the West, such as LaMonte Young, show a similar way of musical thinking.) In the West, each tone has a function of its own. In Japan, it is different. Some Zen Buddhist shakuhachi[60] players concentrate on producing a single tone. I have an old friend—he is past seventy—who is a master of the shakuhachi. He rises early, at four o'clock, and plays around with a tone selected at random for three hours, finding an infinite number of colors in it.

For me, it is also important to discover as many aspects of a single tone as possible. In *Waves* (1976) I explore the possibilities inherent in the clarinet, that is, I examine how much variety lies in a single tone of the clarinet. The most important element of music is change. Perhaps this notion has a different meaning in the West than in Japan; in our country, it is linked to Japanese philosophy. My poor English makes it very difficult for me to talk about this.

II.

The pieces I wrote during the past several years have had a great deal to do with water. I love the sea. It has many faces. Numerous currents are whirling in it, each with a tempo, a color, and a temperature of its own. This phenomenon reminds me of the structure of music.

Twenty-five years ago when I started composing, I carried out concrete musical experiments with water. During a visit to France I was surprised to find that Pierre Schaeffer was working in the same direction. In my *Water Music* (1960) I use the sound of dripping water. I collected material from rivers, wells, and the sea and in the process of concentrating my attention on these sonorities, I grew fond of water.

Nature is important for my music in other ways as well. All four seasons are beautiful in Japan. I live on the shore of a lake and forty thousand cherry trees blossom in the neighborhood. Still, I prefer the autumn when trees, the grass—nature as a whole—change from day to day. One cannot catch the actual moment of change, only its result is tangible. It is a phenomenon that is of interest for me also as a composer.

III.

Each time I sit down to compose a new work, I am determined to write something different from before. Still, my friends tell me: "Your music never changes." As a musician, I am led by the desire not to repeat myself. After all, every day is different, and I myself change as well, I grow older.

I would like to compose whatever happens to be my own present. Sadly, it is very difficult.

1979

---

60. The shakuhachi is a Japanese flute of Chinese origin.

Fifty-Nine

DIMITRI TERZAKIS (1938)

Composers who hail from countries with a strong indigenous music tradition are often faced with the challenge of integrating their heritage in an idiom that takes account of contemporary means of expression, in an endeavor to develop a style they can call their own.

*The Hungarian composer Rudolf Maros (1917–82), for instance, embedded a Hungarian folk lament in its original form in a twelve-tone context (*Siratό [Lament] 1969, for soprano and chamber ensemble*) and attracted some attention with it at a Warsaw Autumn Festival. It was to remain a one-off experiment.*

Iannis Xenakis, who was very much aware of his Greek heritage and was not ashamed of a folk tune bringing tears to his eyes, turned his back, with a conscious effort, on that heritage in creating his own music.

His compatriot Dimitri Terzakis has taken a course rather like Michio Mamiya and has turned to the music traditions of his native country (including the music he has heard on his regular visits to Mount Athos) in his search for an idiom of his own.

The very first sentence of our interview puts me in mind of a remark by Xenakis: apparently, when Greeks go west, they say they are "going to Europe." The country which is regarded as the cradle of Western civilization considers itself outside of the continent.

I.

I was born in a country where music is part of a different sphere of culture than in Western Europe. When I moved to Cologne in 1965, I came in touch with new tendencies and it became clear to me that my musical mother tongue differed from that of my colleagues. Their compositions helped me to distance myself from their idiom and find my own.

Greek musical tradition is closely related to Oriental music and it has put its stamp on my thinking. I was gripped by the art of medieval Byzantine composers: Koukouzeles, Kladas, Glikis, and among eighteenth-century composers Petros Lambadarios, Bereketis, and Balassios.

I do not imitate them but make use of those of their technical means which seem to me suitable for further development: their nontempered intervals (after all, they employed micro- and macrointervals), their way of thinking, their specific melodic lines.

I started my experiments with one of new music's taboos, melody, in 1968. In my opinion, the horizontal, melodic layer awaits rehabilitation; non-European tradition which has so far remained unexploited, could lend the music of our times a new face.

My long conversations with monks on Mount Athos have taught me what genuine simplicity is about and I have realized how much more difficult it is to write simply than to compose complex music. I believe in simple music's power of expression. That is why I respect Verdi: he composed with a limited range of means and created works of genius.

II.

Sounds of the outside world do not affect me directly but they may well influence me subconsciously. While at work I try to isolate myself from everyday noises and become absorbed in myself, if you like.

During my visits to Athos, I am fascinated by the unique atmosphere of nocturnal liturgies. At the pale candlelight of the ancient churches, the figures of the monks are like moving shadows and when I leave the hour-long ceremony and briefly step outside, I am surrounded by the perfect silence of untainted nature. That experience may well be unique anywhere else in Europe and it has left its impact on my music. Its relationship with Oriental mysticism (which exerted an influence on Byzantine music) is undeniable. When I talked of a different musical thinking earlier on, I also had that in mind.

III.

There is no such thing as absolute individuality: every composer is more or less indebted to other composers. This is a concatenation where the borders cannot be drawn with any precision.

As far as self-repetition goes, here, too, the borders are vague. You can only establish at the end of a composer's life or after his death whether or not he repeated himself. I know composers who do something different in each new work but in each one they borrow at second or third hand. I prefer those who have developed a style of their own even if their contemporaries may detect self-repetition in their pieces.

You need repetition if you are to develop your technique—this is a process which takes time. Possibilities must be tried out in a range of compositions. It is only for the composer to decide when it is time to move on.

The selection of technique is no matter of free decision: it depends on the composer's personality. As far as my own technical development between 1968 and 1983 is concerned, I can differentiate between three periods: (1) My melodies moved freely but within a narrow range; I often used micro-intervals. (2) Later on, I ordered my material according to tetrachords, following Byzantine examples and enriched them further with my own invention. Tetrachords became melody-creating elements. (3) In this phase I took the *isson*, this bourdon tone of Byzantine music and developed it further. In my music, it becomes much more complex (incidentally, this mystical element of music also comes from the Orient). In the wake of thirteenth–fourteenth-century melismas, I developed my own.

The three phases are clearly delineated but their sound worlds are interrelated, something I regard as important. As I have mentioned, I intend to exploit fresh, untapped musical material and find the relevant technical means. This is something which takes more than just one or two compositions to accomplish.

1983

Sixty

SIR MICHAEL TIPPETT (1905–98)

After a concert at London's South Bank where Sir Charles Groves conducted a symphony by Michael Tippett, I was rather embarrassed to find the composer standing next to the conductor in the artist's room. I cannot now see why I should have been surprised but my embarrassment was due to the fact that the symphony had made no impression on me whatsoever. On entering the room, both of them looked at me expectantly and I was rather hard put to know what to say. Luckily, I had recently read Tippett's introduction to a volume of Bartók's selected correspondence in English translation and rather than say something polite about the symphony, I congratulated the composer on his piece of writing.

A few years later, at the Bath Festival, I was genuinely taken with his opera, The Knot Garden *(1966/69) and was happy to tell him so afterward. He must have been in his eighties, but had a boyish air about him, slim as he was, with a naughty smile in his eyes.*

For many years, I used to receive a newsletter in the post devoted entirely to performances of Tippett's music. At one point, the flow came to an abrupt stop, I fear because there was not enough material to fill it. Unlike Benjamin Britten, Tippett seems to have remained a national rather than an international figure.

I.

In the sense which you describe what Lutosławski told you concerning a piece of John Cage, I had something almost exactly the same when I was listening to a concert of modern music of some kind at the Edinburgh Festival and my vague recollection, not absolutely accurate, is that I heard a piano sonata played by some pianist that was Boulez. I am not dead sure this is correct—it would be very difficult to find out exactly what it was—nevertheless, what happened was a sudden understanding of something of this kind of piece which was extremely static, seemed to me to mean: start this process of invention by polarity. That is, I realized I could only use such a technique if I was able to put against it something very energetic and rapid. From this came the usage of two words which I got in fact from some book on painting in Crete and Egypt—which was *arrest* (which would obviously be the static) and *movement* (which would be the energy).

At that, I turned to my neighbor whoever he or she was and said: "The Third Symphony has begun." In fact, it had.

II.

Sounds of the outside world, whatever they may be, do not affect me very much. Except insofar as those very sounds could cut off the outside world in some way, by a murmuring sound. For example, I used to have this experience quite a lot in walking out into the woods outside my house, where if there were a wind in the tree leaves, and this would produce an effect of an interior world within which things could begin. Otherwise, the only sounds which would operate in the way you describe the outside world are the accidental sounds that generally come from music itself—radio, whatever—these do affect me.

But when it comes to the deliberate act of invention, of composition, apart from cogitation as to what the structure of the piece might be, then I need and always have needed, to cut off the outside sounds with an aura of sound which I physically make myself, generally at the piano. This is complete, quite absolute, and I am hardly aware of what happens. If anybody comes into the room, I am very startled and disturbed as if I am forced suddenly to come out of it. Without that kind of world made from interior sounds, I could not do the actual final operation of finding the invented sounds that I myself want for the composition.

III.

This also, I think, is in fact two questions. What is individual style? This, I think, is extremely difficult to define and in fact, both my biographers have had a great difficulty in discerning as it were where this comes from. Especially Professor Kemp looked back very carefully at all the unpublished works when I was learning my job to see if it was possible to discover where this style came from.

It is not easy because at some point one imagines that a personal style must be personal and although it is based on a tradition of many kinds, the personality is something very special. To define it is almost impossible. I certainly cannot define my own.

The second part of the question ("at what point does self-repetition begin?"): again, this is quite individual. I can't answer it quite in the terms of the question. What seems to me, in my own life, is that there have been points at which a certain kind of style, generally produced from functional needs—the need to be dramatic in an opera, or the need to be contemplative in some other work—these have effected, or forced, a change of general style, and this produces an accumulation of techniques and abilities to do what you want in this form. If the demands do not produce another step in a different direction then obviously you would repeat yourself if you went on writing. I have never had this experience very much because I find it rather boring to do so.

The other element which is much more difficult to explain is that there seems to be a drive even in fairly late old age to experience anew this inventive proclivity and to see where it takes you. I think if I were sure, either by my own sensibilities or by the outside critical world that I was repeating myself in any literal term of repetition—then I would stop.

1983, read and approved in 1996

Sixty-One

LÁSZLÓ VIDOVSZKY (1944)

A cofounder of the Budapest New Music Studio in 1970, László Vidovszky's decision to leave the capital and move to the city of Pécs in the south of the country where he was appointed professor at the university may have contributed to the petering out of the group's regular activities around 1990.

Vidovszky was a composer in the EMB stable and I met him early on: when I joined the company, I was rather green as far as new music was concerned and I asked if there was anyone who could give me a crash course so that I had some idea of what it was all about.

Someone suggested Vidovszky, twenty-eight years old at the time (I am three years his senior) and he came to my place. The conversation proceeded haltingly and ended without my becoming any wiser. As it turned out in the years to come, not only is Vidovszky an extremely private person, he also has difficulty in expressing his ideas by the spoken word. I remember an occasion in Finland at a press conference arranged by the Kuhmo Festival where I ended up as his mouthpiece, so to speak, for I knew the answers he was unable to articulate.

I cannot claim to have developed any close relationship with László Vidovszky, perhaps I do not even know him to any reasonable degree. But I do admire his music, which has always impressed me with its stunning originality. A Hungarian Satie perhaps? I do not know. In any case, it is no accident that Kurtág should have been influenced by his Autokoncert *(1972), a haunting piece of music theater with instruments dropping from the rope on which they were precariously suspended and in doing so, producing a sound. I never heard or saw it but understand it creates an eerie experience.*

Living in the provinces and with very little contact outside Hungary, Vidovszky appears to have accepted his isolation. He has performances every now and again in Budapest and Pécs and he is happy with that. A great pity: his music ought to be part of the international consciousness.

I.

For me, an existing composition represents a *possibility* just as much as music that has yet to be written or pieces that will never be born. It is therefore natural for me to integrate any work which strikes me as genuine music in the music that lives in me. I cannot, however, undertake to explore and register these influences; they are at least as diverse as the works themselves.

It may occur that a single turn of phrase heard at a concert calls for further development. It may also happen that I have an impulse to write existing compositions again, changing only minor details.

Those are simple and fleeting influences. Much more significant is the presence of composers whose work has accompanied me all my life. However, precisely because of their permanent and persistent presence, it would be difficult to pinpoint any particular, uniquely circumscribed influence. It is as if I were to define the influence of a threshold I step over day by day.

(*László Vidovszky provided the above in 1983. I found it rather vague at the time and asked for more details. He did send me an additional paragraph in 1985, which in 2009 he replaced with a page and a half of new text:*)

I cannot report on any musical encounter which could be likened to Lutosławski's but I find his case exemplary. It represents after all an extreme situation of discovering one's heritage where the circumstances (a message from heaven in the form of a radio broadcast) are at least as important as the music itself. Cage has also had a liberating influence on me, but in a much slower and piecemeal fashion. I first met him at the Warsaw Autumn in 1965, at a performance of Merce Cunningham's ensemble. Works by a range of American composers were performed, including *Variations II* (1961) by John Cage, played by him together with David Tudor. Only the choreography and the stage have left a lasting impression, as a puritanical and ascetic but also dreamlike visual and gestural world. I have kept hardly any musical memory of that evening although in retrospect it was indeed a brilliant program.

Five years later in Paris the same music made a huge impression (the *Song Books* [1970] with Cathy Berberian, the simultaneous performance of the Piano Concerto and *Rozart Mix* [1965], followed by *Musicircus* [1967] in the empty halls of Les Halles due to be demolished). It was probably a perception of more than purely musical nature. In Western European culture which was still self-confident and strong at the time, the gestures which had been unfathomable for me in the pseudo-Empire style theater of the *Pałac Kultury i Nauki im. Józefa Stalina*[61] struck me as a revelation.

That was not the only occasion I had a hard time coming to terms with the oeuvre of a composer. At high school, I bought a score of Webern's piano *Variations* Op. 27 (1936) almost by chance and then decided to play it at a school concert. I could not count on any help from my teachers, the most I could hope for was that they would not forbid the performance. I set about learning the piece which offered absolutely nothing to hang on

61. Joseph Stalin Palace of Culture and Sciences.

to—I proceeded from bar to bar literally at a cost of physical pain. I cannot of course judge today my performance at the concert, but little music has remained anchored in me as deeply as Webern's. Although I have not written dodecaphonic or serial works, Webern's music has remained a basic point of reference ever since.

There is little to say about any musical impressions in my childhood. Rather, I remember sounds and sonorities (like those of trains or domestic animals, the noise of the beach or the schoolyard). In the absence of concerts and records, my main musical experience at the time was linked to the piece I was currently studying. Luckily, my teachers encouraged me to address myself to the books of *Mikrokosmos* which were being published in those years. I am still filled with admiration by the fact that I should have been able to learn so much from those pieces beyond Bartók's music.

It is perhaps no accident that initially I gave an evasive answer to this question. I find it difficult to describe and define the mechanism through which I absorb musical heritage. Recently, I lighted upon a recording I had last heard fifty years ago but later forgot about completely (an LP recorded jointly by Chet Baker and Gerry Mulligan) and was astonished by its kinship (at least for me) with the last movement of my *Páros* (2007) written a few years ago. Sometimes, music I had never heard before can immediately appear to be evident to such an extent that the encounter evokes hardly any emotional impact (for instance, slowed-down birdsong, Conlon Nancarrow, or even Olivier Messiaen). There are, on the other hand, oeuvres which remain inaccessible for me (Richard Strauss, Schoenberg). There are some which attract and repel me at the same time, like Berlioz and Wagner. My relationship with musical heritage tends to change in any case: a composer may vanish from my sphere of interest for a long time, only to return later that much stronger. This is true also of the greatest ones. However, there is a composer whom I have felt close to all the time, ever since I first met him: Franz Peter Schubert.

II.

With me, it is a conscious effort not to close my ears to the sounds of the environment but this is in no way synonymous with any wish to "use" or "integrate" those sounds. The kind of sonority which impels me, as a composer, to act, is rather to be found in unknown landscapes rather than in the street or the meadow. I do not deny, however, that given sufficient humility and sharp attention, you can discover in the latter events, too, a world specific to music. This has been borne out by the example of a number of composers.

III.

On the surface, there might be a similarity between individual style and self-repetition. If, however, we define a work not on the basis of formal criteria, it will be easy to realize that the two are diametrically opposed. A personal style presupposes the profound identity of a composer and his means *as well as* a constantly novel way of utilizing those means. It is precisely the novel way that leads to a deeper exploration of the means. Self-repetition, on the other hand, is the outcome of a lack of sufficient conviction and the absence (or inadequate assessment) of the creative power necessary to produce a work. In both cases, the composer starts out of himself and returns there, but individual style means the enrichment of expression and musical possibilities (while the traits remain the same), whereas self-repetition is at the same time the manifestation of an interior disintegration. The curious listener will want to know, of course, how he could "recognize" which of the two possibilities he is witnessing. That requires, however, a great deal of musical sensitivity and experience.

1983/85/2009

Sixty-Two

WLADIMIR VOGEL (1896–1984)

I am indebted to Wladimir Vogel for the trouble he took to reply to my questions. Surely, he must have been in poor health: he passed away a few months after posting the envelope.

Easily the oldest of the composers in this book, he represents a generation that heard Scriabin play the piano and had Busoni for a teacher. His was a searching and adventurous spirit as demonstrated, among other things, by his works for speaking chorus.

A summary of his idiom is offered by Baker's Biographical Dictionary of Twentieth-Century Classical Musicians:

"Gradually, he approached the method of composition in 12 tones as promulgated by Schoenberg, while Busoni's precepts of neo-Classical structures governed Vogel's own works as far as formal design was concerned; many of his polyphonic compositions adhered to the Classical harmonic structures in 4 parts, which he maintained even in choral pieces using the Sprechstimme. *Serial procedures were adumbrated in Vogel's music through the astute organization of melodic and rhythmic elements."*[62]

Alone among the composers contributing to this book, Wladimir Vogel decided to reply to all three questions in one continuous block.

The first major experience of my youth was linked to Alexander Scriabin. Both his music and his personality made a deep impression. I attended his piano recitals in Moscow between 1912 and 1914 where he played some of his own compositions as well. I was also influenced by his ideas regarding the background to his works, especially those of his last sonatas and orchestral pieces, because I was close to the Russian Symbolists.

Scriabin's influence was felt also in my first years in Berlin. The pieces I composed then bear traces of his piano technique. Later, when I became acquainted with Schoenberg's music of his middle period, I amalgamated his musical idiom with Scriabin's style and technique.

Meanwhile I became a pupil of Ferruccio Busoni. It was not so much his music that impressed me but his broad cultural horizon, his aesthetic and his stance as a composer. I was convinced that I could learn from him more about the cultural heritage of the West (I had serious gaps there) than I would if I joined the new German school.

---

62. *Baker's Biographical Dictionary of Twentieth-Century Classical Musicians*, 1452.

It was at that time, in 1923, that I wrote my large-scale piano composition which I entitled *Komposition auszuführen auf einem und zwei Klavieren.*[63] The first part is a *Sonata* to be played on one piano and its accent is on the personal, the subjective. In it, I unified the piano techniques of Scriabin and Schoenberg; I responded to the terseness of the latter's *Six Little Piano Pieces,* Op. 19 (1911) but it was also my goal to overcome the spasmodic character of the music of late Scriabin, with the help of continuous forms of motion. With the appearance of the second piano, the material turns spotty, and I studded it with ever denser rhythms which rendered the music more objective. It also helped the formal intensification. This work was influenced by Busoni's *Fantasia contrappuntistica* (1910).

It was at that time that I turned away from the structure of Scriabin's late compositions: they were based on a single chord which resulted in monotony of sound. Since then, my creative effort has been marked by the endeavor to absorb as many means of expression in new music as possible.

However, I was never influenced by Stravinsky, Prokofiev, Hindemith, and Bartók. (With regard to Bartók: the Amar-Hindemith Quartet played the world premiere of my first string quartet at the ISCM Festival in Frankfurt in 1927. The second movement is based entirely on glissandi. Bartók's letter addressed to Annie Müller-Widman is proof of his presence at that concert. The lessons he drew from my work were implemented in his own third and fourth string quartets.)

In 1936, Willi Reich delivered a lecture on composing with twelve mutually related tones. Under the influence of that lecture, I once again turned toward Schoenberg. Characteristically enough, my first dodecaphonic composition was the a cappella chorus *Madrigale:* I wanted to try out the technique first on vocal material. The work is based on a melodic row.

I recognize the principle of permanent development—one that also determined the work of Scriabin and Schoenberg—as compulsory in my own composition. The same is true of Busoni's conviction "not to repeat what we have succeeded in solving in the past." Still, I do return to what I invented before, to develop it further, to make it more mature. That is what ensures the continuity of my compositions.

The genre of reciting chorus is important in my work; the relationship between music and word is also of primary significance. I use the reciting chorus in both large-scale and smaller compositions as an independent element of heightened expression and effect. The chorus does not speak in unison but—similarly to singing choirs—it is divided into four sections clearly differentiated both with regard to the pitch and the timbre of the speaking voice. I notate the parts on three staves without specifying the pitches. They are either united in natural, expressive speech or appear in spoken soli.

---

63. Composition to be performed on one and two pianos.

With regard to a recognizable style of my music, I cannot comment. It has occurred that my pieces broadcast on the radio were identified as mine by those who missed the announcement so that they had to go by the style of the music.

In recent years, my music has been marked by the economy of means and the transparency of the material. I strive to make the listeners' job easier: through hearing the individual voices clearer, they can participate in the musical events. As well as becoming simpler, my music has acquired more pronounced emotional elements.

From the sounding environment, I have often used the pealing of bells—a sound that has accompanied me ever since my youth. This has nothing to do with impressionism—rather, with atmosphere.

To sum up: I have always been an outsider, from the earliest times to the present day. I do not belong to any school or trend of modern music (the word "modern" also includes "Mode"—that is, fashion)—a feature that has helped me little in the conditions of today's music industry.

1984

Sixty-Three

GERHARD WIMBERGER (1923)

When we met in Budapest in 1980, Gerhard Wimberger was a prominent figure in Austrian musical life: a professor of conducting and composition at the Mozarteum in Salzburg, he was also associated with the festival, sat on important committees, received major prizes, and was elected a member of the Munich Academy of Fine Arts. His music was also broadcast regularly on Austrian Radio; I remember in particular his Ausstrahlungen W. A. Mozart'scher Themen *(1978)—in English: Radiations of W. A. Mozartian Themes—under his baton.*

In the three decades that have passed since, Wimberger has more or less disappeared from public life and concert programs. He is not the only composer to have been forgotten in his lifetime but of course one never knows: we may just be experiencing a lull to be followed by a renaissance of his music.

I.

I belong to the ill-fated generation whose youth was overshadowed by Hitler's *Reich.* My musical development was likewise determined by history. I remember, around 1940, my piano teacher locked the door of his studio and under promise of secrecy produced a score from his cupboard: it was a viola piece by Paul Hindemith who had been blacklisted by the Nazis. Another teacher told me of Stravinsky: it was as if he had evoked a mirage—distant and unattainable.

After the war when traveling was free, I was not yet in a position to do so. That is why Ernst Krenek made such a deep impression: in 1952 or 1953, in the Salzburg Mozarteum, he delivered a lecture on twelve-tone music. I had until then composed in an angular Hindemith style, tonal music with many fourths and fifths; it was Krenek who made me realize that there was another way of selecting tones as well. By the time I visited Darmstadt in 1955 (that was the only time I attended the Summer Courses), the music I heard there did not hold much interest, since I was also composing with twelve tones.

After a time I bade farewell to that technique but I owe it to Krenek that he liberated me from the world in which I had lived until then. Under the influence of that experience I composed differently in a harmonic and melodic sense—the rhythmic aspect of my thinking, however, remained unchanged. My development toward a freer, more complex and multilayered rhythm took place gradually.

II.

My reply to this question is a definite yes. The world of sounds and noises is of great significance for me. Not so much those brought about by machines or by nature, much rather acoustic phenomena produced by people. For instance, I am fascinated by the statistic accumulation of applause in a concert hall: the way individual clapping grows denser and eventually adds up to continuous noise. The duration of this process depends of course on the size of the audience. My attention is also riveted by the rhythmic diversion of sounds of varying intensity in a room—like right now. (*We were talking in the crowded foyer of the Hotel Intercontinental in Budapest.*)

I have endeavored to exploit those impressions in my choruses. It is not a question of imitation, rather of stylization, abstraction.

A few years ago I turned toward electronic music. One of my first electronic pieces, *Naturmusik* (1975), used sounds recorded in nature which I transformed electronically: the chirping of cicadas and crickets which morphed into the croaking of frogs followed by the murmur of sea waves with their varied rhythms, then distant cries of seabirds. The piece ended with the return of crickets and cicadas. Of course, I attempted to give it all a musical form.

I mentioned applause a while ago, the statistic accumulation of individual strata: more and more layers are placed on top of one another until you can no longer differentiate them and they acquire a musical dimension. I carried out relevant experiments in my home. I recorded a musical structure on tape, I doubled it or recorded another layer, then a third one and there eventually emerged a complexity which could no longer be followed by the human ear—still, if I did my job well, the end result made musical sense.

III.

It is embarrassing to talk of my personal style. It is as if I had to comment on my own face or the color of my eyes—I am not vain enough for that. The presence or otherwise of a personal style is recognized by others, mostly after the composer's death. Only very few speak a musical language which is characteristic enough to be identified while the composer is alive. Nowadays, however, it is often distorted into mannerism.

I endeavor to use a wide range of musical means. I never restrict work on the musical material to a single method. I have written merry pieces but bitter and serious ones as well.

I hope I still possess sufficient fantasy to go on discovering new things. In this way, I can steer clear of the danger of repeating myself.

It could happen, of course, that certain aspects of my music occurred in earlier works as well. I try to forestall that by setting myself new tasks. Once I have completed a composition for chorus, I next address myself to an instrumental work. In this fashion, I am forced to seek different solutions from a technical point of view.

If anyone could nevertheless discover characteristic features in my works, it would make me very happy.

1980

Sixty-Four

CHRISTIAN WOLFF (1934)

Before meeting Christian Wolff in person, some time after 2000, at the Donaueschingen Festival, I had heard his voice. I was visiting György and Márta Kurtág in Berlin in March 1999; they were guests of the Wissenschaftskolleg (Science College)—something of a privilege also accorded to people like Walter Levin of the LaSalle Quartet or Gérard Mortier, director of major opera houses and festivals, whom I was also to meet there on other occasions.

Kurtág told me how Christian Wolff had, at his request, recorded on tape extracts from the Iliad *in Ancient Greek, and proceeded to play a few minutes. It was quite an experience to hear the American composer's voice, imbued with emotion, reciting the text with its many diphthongs and sibilants. Kurtág could follow every word and Márta also understood most of it. The composer said: "I have just written another* Hommage à Wolff.*"*

Like some of his contemporaries, Christian Wolff was fascinated by the classics as much as by music. At Harvard, he pursued a training in classical literature and went to Florence to study Italian and classical literature. On returning to Harvard, he obtained his PhD in comparative literature, teaching there, and later at Dartmouth College, music, the classics, and comparative literature.

He was a pupil of Grete Sultan in piano and of John Cage in composition, later to become a member of the New York Group. ("I have a wonderful pupil. He is sixteen and his favorite composer is Webern. He has great intelligence and sensitivity. What's more, he was born in France. His name is Christian Wolff.")[64]

In Donaueschingen, we happened to be staying at the same hotel. He was checking in when I arrived and I introduced myself straightaway. My enthusiasm was dampened by his reserve (in the ensuing correspondence he claimed he had not been aware of any aloofness on his part) and sadly it never came to a proper conversation.

I was all the more impressed by his music. The rehearsal gave me an idea of Wolff's total dedication to his work and the importance he attributed to every detail in performance; the concert opened a window onto his world—one that was closed after a tantalizingly short time.

---

64. Letter from John Cage to Pierre Boulez, before April 1950, in *The Boulez–Cage Correspondence*, trans. Robert Samuels, ed. Jean-Jacques Nattiez (Cambridge: Cambridge University Press, 1993), 57.

I.

I've not had one, single converting experience like the one described by Lutosławski. A continuing series of meetings with other musics and musicians has affected me, directly and indirectly, so that I've wanted to respond or have felt more free to proceed to do what I did. Probably my own lack of formal and institutionalized training in music has left me open to a variety and a number of such meetings.

The slow movement of Bach's *Fifth Brandenburg Concerto*, I think, first caused me to want to try to write music. I actually began trying to write after hearing the quartet music of the Viennese school and Bartók, with the idea that what I did should be unlike anything known to me, which is how that music has struck me.

Meeting Varèse and hearing some of his music reinforced that notion. At about this time (I was still in school) we went regularly to hear Dixieland and Chicago jazz—Sidney Bechet, James P. Johnson, Peewee Russell, among others. I was very taken by the idiomatic virtuosity of the players, by the rhythmic propulsion, by the free heterophony of the ensemble playing, and by the alternating expressive world: lyrical-blues and the wildly manic. I didn't know how to respond in my own work—couldn't see or find the means—but hoped somewhere, in the back of my mind, sometime to find them.

My last piano teacher was Grete Sultan, completely unwavering, though gentle, in her seriousness about music, and quite selfless. In 1950 she introduced me to John Cage. He and his work—all of it—and his way of working have of course made an extraordinary difference, too pervasive to describe in detail (I tried summarily in an article called "Under the Influence," in *Tri-Quarterly* 54 [1982], and in *A John Cage Reader*, ed. Peter Gena and Jonathan Brent [New York, 1982]). Above all there has been encouragement, freeing up, and a strong example of discipline, cheerful discipline.

Cage immediately introduced me to Satie's work, Webern's Symphony, Op. 21 (1928), then Morton Feldman, Merce Cunningham, David Tudor, Pierre Boulez, and Earle Brown. What can I say? Abstraction, sound for its own sake, and poetry. Simplicity, transparency with mysteriousness, selfless yet expressive (cf. Satie, Webern). Intricate, violent, and cool complexity (cf. Boulez, *Music of Changes*, 1951). Inventive, quiet, precise virtuosity, and open pleasure in the new and difficult (Tudor). Final, intuitive confidence in every sound written, with no system whatever to support it (Feldman). Graphics open to the widest use (cf. Brown). Theatrical presence, fluid, exact, and surprising (Cunningham, Tudor).

In passing I should mention playing early keyboard music, especially Frescobaldi with his discontinuous blocks of music (like Satie) and his suggestion that sections of pieces (toccatas, I think) could be omitted at the choice of the performer. After a while rock and roll, and rock, then Terry Riley and Philip Glass: full sounding, clear, modal, with pulse, though its effect didn't seem square, a kind of temporary clearing of murk. But there was also the tangled Ives, and his bits of tunes.

While staying in London in 1967 and 1968, I saw a good bit of Cornelius Cardew and joined in performances of his *The Tiger's Mind* (1967) and *Schooltime Compositions* (1967), as well as performances with AMM, the improvisation group of Lou Gare, Eddie Prévost, and Keith Rowe, whom Cornelius had joined. Our work was collaborative in nature and based on group improvisation. Apart from the presence of the players themselves and the sound making materials available, nothing at all was prearranged. Those pieces based on verbal texts or schematic, graphic notations—mostly clear and simple in themselves—were unexplained and ambivalent or even multivalent in their use for performance.

The Scratch Orchestra, founded in 1969 by Cardew, Michael Parsons, and Howard Skempton, was a model of large-scale collaborative and variously improvised music making. Around the time I first learned about this orchestra, I heard a recording of music by the Ba-Benzele Pygmies, performed by an entire community—women, men, and children. The music was improvised, polyphonic, and unhierarchical in texture, and I imagined this to be a realization of what the Scratch Orchestra might sound like. Not long after, the piece *Burdocks* (1970–71) resulted, which was wonderfully performed by the Scratch. A few years later, hearing a performance of the thirteenth-century *Cantigas di Santa Maria* confirmed a way of writing I had been trying in order to produce a music both melodic and heterophonic, economically notated (one or two voices on one stave), and flexible in instrumental realizations.

By the early 1970s I was moved, like many others, including close musical friends, by a strong sense of political issues, and questions of how this might involve musical work. Revealing and encouraging was the surprise of Cornelius Cardew's tonal arrangement of traditional political songs, mostly Chinese and Irish, and Frederic Rzewski's use of minimal procedures (such as those of Riley, Reich, and Glass) joined with political texts, especially in *Coming Together* (1972). At this time I also first heard Hanns Eisler's mass songs, *Solidaritätslied* (1929–30), *Heimlicher Aufmarsch* (1930, rev. 1938), and the *Kominternlied* (1928) in particular. Soon after, I started going to performances by politically oriented songwriters and singers: Pete Seeger, Peggy Seeger and Ewan McColl, Holly Near, Charlie King, the Chilean group Inti-Illimani.

This account is incomplete—more of Frederic Rzewski's work has affected me, his connections to jazz, for instance. Coltrane's *Alabama*, paradoxically meditative political music. Some of Eric Dolphy's bass clarinet playing. Ornette Coleman. Sam Rivers. And I hope it doesn't stop there.

II.

Everyday sounds, especially in the countryside, natural mixed with machine—cars, trucks, airplanes, tractors, chainsaws—do, I expect, affect my work. I don't particularly try to shut them out. My earlier work in particular was made in a way that ambient sounds would not be felt as interruptions; sometimes they could serve as cues with which the players might coordinate. It's worth noting that a considerable amount of ambient sound is some sort of music—radio, tapes, TV, etc.

III.

Individual style could be taken as what—given a measure of technical competence—the musician cannot really do much about, as one cannot do much about one's physical and temperamental makeup; the reach of one's hands, the timbre of the voice, for instance. To be sure, one may exercise, develop somewhat, clarify or obscure these given elements, but apart from deliberate refusal of their use, the notion of repetition doesn't seem relevant here. (This view of style takes its example from nonindividualistic, traditional kinds of music making.) Or one might, stressing "individual," take style as that to which self-repetition is relevant when the self becomes a problem—when you lose confidence in your material, when you no longer feel that it and its expressive possibilities can be changed. (This is more like the "high" art, and romantic, view.)

1984

Sixty-Five

IANNIS XENAKIS (1922–2001)

We met at the twenty-second Warsaw Autumn Festival in 1978. Five years had passed since the interview with Witold Lutosławski which had given me the idea of inviting composers to an imaginary roundtable and putting to them the first question. Xenakis's unexpected presence in Warsaw provided me with a welcome opportunity for an interview. In answering, or rather, evading my first question, Xenakis reported on an experience that gave me the idea for the second one:

Metastasis, that starting point of my life as a composer, was inspired not by music but rather by the impression gained during the Nazi occupation of Greece. The Germans tried to take Greek workers to the Third Reich—and we staged huge demonstrations against this and managed to prevent it. I listened to the sound of the masses marching toward the center of Athens, the shouting of slogans and then, when they came upon Nazi tanks, the intermittent shooting of the machine guns, the chaos. I shall never forget the transformation of the regular, rhythmic noise of a hundred thousand people into some fantastic disorder . . . I would never have thought that one day all that would surface again and become music: *Metastasis*. I composed it in 1953–54 and called it a starting point because that was when I introduced into music the notion of mass . . . Almost everybody in the orchestra is a soloist, I used complete divisi in the strings which play large masses of *pizzicati* and *glissandi*. In other words, I do not use the term "mass" in a sociological sense.

Another experience of my youth dates from the time immediately preceding the war. I used to make outings to the countryside near Athens. I would take my bicycle, select a spot to erect my tent and listen to the sounds of nature. Crickets, for instance: their chirping was coming from every direction and was changing all the time. Those are also mass sounds, you see? But I also liked listening to the wind and the sea or the rain as it was lashing at the side of the tent.

How about birds?

No, I do not think so. I like them but birds sing melodic patterns and they do not interest me.

The first question touched upon a concern that was of vital significance for Iannis Xenakis's work. It was absolutely essential for him to have severed all contact with musical tradition and to produce works that would be in the literal sense new, both in music history and in his own oeuvre. He realized that this was hardly possible and was frustrated by it.

In our book-length conversation published by Faber and Faber in 1996, he said:

> I don't want to have roots. Of course, I had some; I also had my influences, but luckily there were so many that none proved decisive. I've mentioned them before: Romanian and Greek folk music, Byzantine chant, Western music, non-European music. I've tried to understand them; I liked some and disliked others, but I have let each one come close to me, not remaining outside any of them or saying about any of them that it was not music. In this way, I succeeded in becoming free, and that's why I have no roots.[65]

In 1980 when I saw Xenakis in Paris for a set of interviews which was published in time for his portrait concert in Budapest in November that year, he added:

I want to tell you about Debussy, and Ravel also; they wrote their music in modes, or harmonies, that differ from the traditional tonal harmonies of the German school. Ravel's piano suite, for instance, *Le tombeau de Couperin* (1914/15), and also the orchestral version, is one of his best pieces, and several passages reminded me of ancient music. It's not dominated by tonic-dominant thinking, which is inseparably linked to German and Central European music in general. Bartók is an exception. He also moved away from tradition—for instance in *Mikrokosmos* (1926/39) in which he obviously wanted to do something different.

What considerations led to your writing the article on Schoenberg and serial music for Gravesaner Blätter, *which was to become famous later on?*

I suddenly realized what it was that Schoenberg wanted to achieve with the twelve notes. That was one of the starting points of my article. The other: that I didn't like his music, nor that of the serialists. I felt they were continuing the pathos of German music and had carried it to an extreme. It was only later that I learned to appreciate Schoenberg's compositions, especially his piano works. They are witness to an immense power of imagination. Imagination is, of course, something intuitive, but I could understand those pieces by separating them from the theory. As far as Webern's music is concerned, it reminds me of the film music of that time.

How is that?

Yes, it *is* like film music. Especially the early little pieces—perhaps because they are realistic. The later ones are much more dull. But the early music is colorful.

Berg?

A romantic old chap. I like his Violin Concerto.

In your article you point out that serial music became so complex that it was impossible to keep track of the compositional thought, the line.

---

65. Bálint András Varga, *Conversations with Iannis Xenakis* (London: Faber and Faber, 1996), 51.

Serial music is based on the row. You can't do much with twelve notes, they have to be repeated, and meanwhile the tempo, the distances between the notes, change. There are two methods: they transpose the row, that is, play it higher or lower, and also use the inversion of the row, its retrograde and retrograde inversion. (Years later I identified all that as the "four group" structure, or the "Klein group," named after the German mathematician Felix Klein.)

Schoenberg's invention was of extraordinary significance at the time. He conceived of melodic patterns in a geometrical manner. If you think of the row as a jagged line and look at it in two mirrors, one horizontal and one vertical, you get the four basic versions which I mentioned just now. Schoenberg turned to this solution because the tonal wealth had been exhausted, there was no other way, he had to find something new. One feature of his method was the negation of the octave as a self-standing interval. In this way, however, the continuity of the row was weakened. In the case of several rows (polyphony) it's difficult to identify each one. Another characteristic feature was that each note was played by a different instrument (*Klangfarbenmelodie*) so that the timbre was also changing continuously. In the case of many rows (in the music of the Darmstadt epigones—Stockhausen, Boulez, and others) it was obvious that the rules of serialism couldn't be fully observed. The composers thought they were orthodox serialists but that was only true on paper. In reality they had mass events which they should have listened to in an unbiased manner. On the level of conscious thinking they should have introduced such notions as average density, average duration, colors, and so on. I tried to point that out in my article. All that, however, would have led to a radical way of thinking which could result in only one thing: instead of serial music, stochastic music, probabilities.

How was your article received? Did they try to refute it or did they ignore your conclusions?

On the surface they pretended not to notice it but in fact they were furious. A few months later they suddenly did something similar but on a poor scientific basis: that was aleatoric music.

In other words, the appearance of aleatoric music was a kind of reply to your article?

It was a consequence of the fact that they had reached an impasse. My article, and primarily my music, may well have evoked some reaction, but instead of thinking about it and considering the possibility that I might be right they started something which they thought was new and found a name for it. I had not yet employed the term "stochastic music." They hit upon the expression "alea," "aleatoric," the meaning of which was close to their aims—but the definition was nevertheless false. In science, aleatoric is used to mean "probable." In mathematics, an aleatoric variable is an exactly circumscribed notion. The serialists, however, loosened up its meaning and identified it with improvisation. They continued to write rows, because that was what they were used to, but gave the interpreter the choice of playing this or that, here or there. The interpreter could choose according to instinct. However, that is not aleatorism but improvisation on a given material computed according to the serial system. Stockhausen did that, then Boulez in his piano sonatas and finally it became improvisation. It has failed to produce any enduring theory in musical composition, although the written parts—not the improvised ones—are often quite interesting. It was a fashion, like jazz. Like fashion, that music didn't last.

Xenakis was not the only composer to distance himself from serial music, nor was he the only one to have been ostracized, mainly in Germany, for his critical stance. It took many years for his music to find acceptance and he was deeply hurt by this. He carried wounds on his face—he had lost an eye and his cheekbone had been blown off during the fighting against the invaders of his country—and he also carried wounds in his psyche. He welcomed allies and I felt he regarded me as such. I was immensely honored to have been called a friend in one of his letters and when I asked him to draw his music, not only did he praise me for having an "interesting new idea," he also signed the drawing with the words "je t'embrasse" *(hugs).*

Having an interesting new idea, or as he put it in reference to Bartók, "to want to do something different" was, as I pointed out above, veritably a question of life and death for him. He saw no reason for composing unless he was convinced that the new work would bring something basically new. Toward the end of his life, the Gods meted out the cruelest possible punishment to Iannis Xenakis: they deprived his brain of the faculty of creativity.

By the time we met in Paris in 1980, the third question had been added to the other two. His extempore reply failed to satisfy us. Instead of trying to rephrase it at a later date (as Lutosławski did), he sent me an essay he wrote in 1981, "Music and Originality," first published in the Italian journal Spirali *in 1982 and then in the French magazine* Phréatique *in 1984. In his letter, he pointed out that the ideas expressed there were linked to the fundamental problems he had first expounded in 1958 in Nos. 11/12 of* Gravesaner Blätter, *edited by Hermann Scherchen (In* Search of a Stochastic Music*).*

Xenakis asked me to introduce his reply to the third question with a quotation from that article followed by the essay of 1981 translated into English almost in full and end it with an extract from an article by Alan H. Guth and Paul J. Steinhardt which appeared in the May 1984 issue of Scientific American *(90–102). In his opinion, there was a connection between the conclusions reached by the American authors and his own views.*

An extract from Iannis Xenakis's study "In Search of a Stochastic Music," Gravesaner Blätter, *nos. 11/12 (1958): 112–13.*

Ταυτόν Γὰϱ νοεῖν τε χαί εἶναι
Ταυτόν Γὰϱ εἶναι τε χαί ούχ εἶναι.

"Because it is the same thing, to think and to be" (Parmenides)
And my way of paraphrasing it:
"Because it is the same thing, to be and not to be."

Ontology

In a Universe of Emptiness. A brief wave train whose beginning and end coincide (Time zero), disengaging itself endlessly.

Nothingness resorbs, Nothingness creates.

It is the generator of Being.

Time, Causality

Music and Originality
by
Iannis Xenakis

The average man as concerns intelligence improvises at times in whistling, in singing, or even abstractly in his imagination. Then he puts notes, sounds, noises end-to-end independently of any visual thought associated or not to these sound events. The fact is that he invents events often intuitively, without thinking, unconsciously or for pleasure. Even when he sings while shaving, he juxtaposes known melodies with small or large variations because he does not remember them always exactly. This sort of exercise or rather this loose combinatory power of the average man is in fact a form of creativity on a lower level but creativity all the same because he makes, starting from known things, different and other things. This is a good definition, on the first approach, of creativity. And creativity, even in this primitive form, of rearranging already arranged objects, is a primordial faculty of living matter, *a fortiori* of man.

Let us suppose now that the man observes his improvisation—as if he could split himself in two, as it were, with one of his selves acting and making choices and the other self observing the result of the successive choices and decisions. This talent of self-observation is also a property of living things and especially of man, and is the conscience.[66] This power of observation is not a simple, isolated activity. It is accompanied by comparisons of facts, forms, thoughts, etc., all stored in one's memory. From these comparisons are born judgments in similarity, in likeness, in difference on the most elementary level, and higher up, are born judgments in value, indeed, aesthetic. On the most elementary level, judgments made on similarities, likenesses, and differences are accompanied by countings, that is a sort of statistical judgment or valuation that defines the frequency of such-and-such a similarity, likeness, difference. He categorizes these frequencies which in the case of space correspond to symmetries and in the case of time to recurrences and to renewals.

66. Xenakis may have meant "consciousness."

And he forms the notion of a rule, of a law that is the archetype of the symmetries and temporal repetitions of a same category.

Here our man can make a leap upward and ask himself the following question: if in what he observes in these actions (choice-decisions) in music (also in fine arts, etc.) he deducts the notion of a rule, of a law, which represents the first mould in a series of similarities, then why not try to define a rule or law which is not in his memory stock? That is, to define a rule that is new and that does not come from observation. It is this that will give rise to a higher form of creativity. To create, therefore, amounts to his making something original, that is, having no similarity or resemblance to anything already observed. To give birth to something from nothing. To engender the unengendered.

But then another question, immediate and of a higher order, suddenly arises: is this possible for man or, by extension, in the universe? Of course, the Gods, who were invented by man and in his image, know how to and are able to engender the unengendered. This shows to what extent this question is joined to the mental spiral of man, amalgamated to it, blended and merged into it, in the progress of civilization throughout history. If, consequently, the rule seems to be a repetitive manifestation of a more profound essence which is the universal principle of the least effort, then to engender the unengendered means a high effort, and more and more high.

To get at this problem from a more precise point of view, let us examine the definition of the degree of complexity in computer science of a set of events. Let us suppose we take a series from the set of ten symbols 0, 1, 2, . . . , 9. Example 0. 333 . . . In order to communicate this series, it suffices to give the *0*, the decimal point, the 3, then the one instruction "repeat the *3*." A rational number therefore has a finite list of instructions which ends invariably with the instruction "repeat the second part of the list indefinitely" since it is periodic with a definite period. On the other hand, an irrational number also has a list of instructions. Its length is infinite since it is not periodic. Likewise a decimal number of digits drawn at random has also an infinite list of instructions. It is for this reason that the number π or any irrational number transmitted solely by the list of its digits has the same complexity as a number whose digits are drawn at random with a probability distribution, for example the uniform distribution. The two lists will have the same length. In the same way, a construction coming from nothing, therefore totally engendered, totally original, calls for an infinite mass of rules duly entangled, a mass such that it covers the laws of a universe different from ours. To give an example: we construct the rules of a tonal composition. This composition supposes therefore a priori "tonal functions." It supposes also a combinatory conception since it acts upon entities and sounds defined by instruments. To go beyond this low level of originality, it is necessary to fabricate other functions or no functions at all. One is therefore obliged to conceive forms of thoughts foreign to the preceding ones, thoughts unlimited by forms and without end. Here we are thus in the obligation to weave progressively an endless cloth of entangled rules and this just in the combinatory domain, which excludes already and by definition the possible continuums of sounds.

Now the inclusion of the notion of continuity will increase as much the length and breadth of the cloth as its compacity.[67] Moreover, if one wanted to engender the unengendered in the domain of sound, it would then be necessary to give rules other than those of sound-machines such as pipes, strings, membranes, which is possible today thanks to the computer and related technology. Technology is only a simulacrum of thought and its materialization. It is therefore only an epiphenomenon in this discussion. Indeed, rules of sound synthesis such as those ensuing from the Fourier series must not be taken as a basis for construction.[68] Other rules have to be formulated, rules that have to be different—this is what is critical.

So, when all is said and done, the demand, the necessity of originality obliges, indeed forces us to conceive a universe different from ours, in its totality as well as in its detail. Perhaps a superhuman task.

Finally, because of this demand, we are confronted with all manifestations of thought in all sciences, pure or social, by overlappings, coverings, or identifications. Thus musical composition in the profound sense of the term is engaged in questions of theoretical or experimental physics, of astrophysics, of genetics, of psychology, of pure and applied mathematics, etc.

So if genetics is a tremendous combinatory factory, both deterministic and stochastic, it stands to reason that construction in music must devote itself to penetrating there each time that the discrete case is considered in order to free itself. In the same way for quantum mechanics: can one imagine and make sound-corpuscles having spin or which are defined only by group structures? Not in order to imitate it but in order not to make the same thing, to free itself.

Now another perspective. We have seen that construction goes through originality which is defined by the creation of rules and laws outside of the memory of the individual and even of that of the human species. Up to now, we have left aside the notion of rule, of law. The time has come to discuss it. "Rule" or "law" signifies a procedure, finite or infinite, always the same, applied to continuous or discrete elements. This definition implies the notion of repetition, of recurrence in time or of symmetry outside-time. So in order for a rule to exist, it must be applied several times. Several times only? Without doubt an infinity of times in the eternity of time and space. Because if a rule only exists for one time, it will be engulfed in this immensity and reduced to one point and therefore unobservable and nonexistent.

---

67. Here Xenakis crossed out the word "density" and wrote "compacity" above it.

68. "In mathematics, an infinite series used to solve special types of differential equations. It consists of an infinite sum of sines and cosines, and because it is periodic (i.e., its values repeat over fixed intervals), it is a useful tool in analyzing periodic functions. Though investigated by Leonhard Euler, among others, the idea was named for Joseph Fourier, who fully explored its consequences, including important applications in engineering, particularly in heat conduction." *Britannica Concise Encyclopaedia* (Chicago: Encyclopaedia Britannica, Inc., 2003), 684.

Therefore, in order for it to be observable, it must repeat itself an infinity of times.

We have accepted the idea of originality, of creation starting from nothingness. A rule must be absolutely new. This is clear. But a rule is a procedure applied to elements. These elements must also be engendered from nothing. If we conceive the elements, whatever they may be, as tiny procedures, therefore as tiny rules, then we see that the notion of rule-procedure can be applied indefinitely in the two senses—in the microcosmic sense and in the macrocosmic sense, by nesting, by levels. Thus the same notion of rule-procedure is sufficient. Example: sounds which have a pitch are elements that have been submitted to a rule-procedure which form a melody. But the pitch of the sound in turn may be considered as the result of a rule-procedure of the repetition of a wave-form at a frequency corresponding to the pitch. The wave-form itself, which is nothing but a line, may be engendered by a rule which is stochastic or of another nature. We have already now 3 levels of nested rules: the level of the melody, of the sound, and of the wave-form. We could continue likewise in both senses, toward the smallest as toward the largest.

But the fact remains that the universe: (a) is made up of rule-procedures, and (b) these rule-procedures are recurrent. It is a little as if the Being, in order to continue to exist, had to die, and once dead, had to begin again his cycle. Existence therefore is a dotted stream.

Can we imagine at last an infinitesimal microscopic rule created from nothing? Even if physics has not yet found anything like that, in spite of "Lamb's Shift" which says that every point in space in our universe bubbles in virtual pairs of particles and antiparticles, we could imagine such an eventuality which besides would be of the same nature as the fact of pure randomness, detached from any causality.

It is necessary to maintain such a conclusion of a Universe open to originality which forms or disappears without respite in a whirling which is really creating starting from nothingness and disappearing into nothingness. The same goes for the foundation of art as for the destiny of man.

Music is but one path among others for man, that is, his species, to imagine, first of all, then, after long generations, to drive the existing universe into another universe, created entirely by man. Moreover, if man, his species, is made in the image of the Universe, then by virtue of the principle, that one is forced to state, that creation is starting from nothingness and disappearing into nothingness, then man, in turn, will be able to redefine his universe as an environment that he would grant himself in harmony with his creative spirit.

Paris, 1981

"The Inflationary Universe"
Alan H. Guth and Paul J. Steinhardt

Recently there has been some serious speculation that the actual creation of the universe is describable by physical laws. In this view the universe would originate as a quantum fluctuation, starting from absolutely nothing. The idea was first proposed by Edward P. Tryon of Hunter College of the City University of New York in 1973, and it was put forward again in the context of the inflationary model of Alexander Vilenkin of Tufts University in 1982. In this context "nothing" might refer to empty space, but Vilenkin uses it to describe a state devoid of space, time and matter. Quantum fluctuations of the structure of space-time can be discussed only in the context of quantum gravity, and so these ideas must be considered highly speculative until a working theory of quantum gravity is formulated. Nevertheless, it is fascinating to contemplate that physical laws may determine not only the evolution of a given state of the universe but also the initial conditions of the observable universe. . . .

From a historical point of view probably the most revolutionary aspect of the inflationary model is the notion that all the matter and energy in the observable universe may have emerged from almost nothing. This claim stands in marked contrast to centuries of scientific tradition in which it was believed that something cannot come from nothing. The tradition, dating back at least as far as the Greek philosopher Parmenides in the fifth century BC, has manifested itself in modern times in the formulation of a number of conservation laws, which state that certain physical quantities cannot be changed by any physical process.

A decade or so ago the list of quantities thought to be conserved included energy, linear momentum, electric charge and baryon number. . . .

If grand unified theories are correct in their prediction that baryon number is not conserved, there is no known conservation law that prevents the observed universe from evolving out of nothing. The inflationary model of the universe provides a possible mechanism by which the observed universe could have evolved from an infinitesimal region. It is then tempting to go one step further and speculate that the entire universe evolved from literally nothing. (102)

ENCORE

> "Es ist vielleicht ungemein bezeichnend, daß der Musiker für die bildende Kunst nur ein geringes Interesse aufzuweisen hat; er ist geartet, den Dingen auf den Grund zu gehen—durch die äußere Erscheinung hindurch."
>
> —Gustav Mahler, in a letter to the composer and critic Max Marschalk, December 4, 1896[69]

The "encore" to the three questions—indeed, the fourth question—takes its origin in the random look I took, some time in 1995, at page 108 of the first volume of Igor Stravinsky's conversations with Robert Craft.[70] For some reason, I got the volume off my shelf one day and opened it where Craft poses the question "Would you 'draw' your recent music?" illustrating his point with graphic images of his own invention of Bach, Wagner, Webern, and others. Stravinsky responded by drawing a diagram with the comment "This is *my* music." That exchange, those drawings gave me the idea of approaching composers with the same question. Can they think of a graphic image which would represent, rather than any particular piece, their music as such?

My goal was to provide a survey of contemporary composition in visual terms. The initial response was encouraging but I had to realize right at the start that few composers would be able to meet the condition of providing a single drawing: Wolfgang Rihm sent three, in keeping with his conviction that his view of his own music was in a permanent state of flux; Arvo Pärt went so far as to "illustrate" a number of his works each with a different image; Cristóbal Halffter and Henri Pousseur appeared to have produced a new work of which they sent a graphic score. György Ligeti, too, provided four drawings rather than one but he opted for a thrilling solution in that he distinguished between four stylistic periods in his compositional development and found a corresponding image for each.

Karlheinz Stockhausen and Steve Reich were of the opinion that the graphic image of music was in fact the score and could not see the point of my project. Boulez, Lachenmann, and others rejected it out of hand, whereas Milton Babbitt admitted he had no talent for drawing and engaged an artist to do it for him. Elliott Carter sent a postcard with a reproduction

69. "It is perhaps uncommonly characteristic that musicians take but slight interest in the arts; it is in their nature to delve to the depth of things—right through the outside appearance." Quoted from letter no. 137 in Gustav Mahler, *Briefe* (Leipzig: Universal Bibliothek Reclam, 1981).

70. Igor Stravinsky and Robert Craft, *Conversations with Igor Stravinsky* (London: Faber and Faber, 1958), 108.

of a painting by Willem de Kooning, writing on the margin that to his mind, that picture faithfully reflected his view of his music.

Luciano Berio, Mauricio Kagel, and Harrison Birtwistle promised to contribute to the project but in the end failed to do so. It was late in 2009 that the German publisher Peter Mischung presented me with a thin volume of drawings by Kagel.[71] Dedicated to his wife Ursula, the first drawing bears the inscription *para mi amor* with a tiny heart in red, dated July 2008. The composer died on September 18 of that year and the book appeared soon after. The drawings, dating from the decades between 1970 and 2008, are all in color, all but one are of faces and, to my mind, have a rather French air about them, reminiscent in part of Jean Cocteau. They demonstrate that the composer's sense of humor (some sketches look like caricatures) extended to his graphic works as well but, as far as I can judge, they have nothing to do with his music.

In the end, I had to admit defeat. The collection ended up too slim to match my goal but it is perhaps varied enough to confirm the assumption that music can very well be rendered in visual terms.

While some composers have no natural inclination to draw and only did so at my request, others find a more or less regular outlet for their talents in the graphic arts. For Kurtág, filling one book after another with blotches of India ink was a vital means of channeling his pent-up impulses at a time, in the early 1970s, when he was unable to compose. The Sacher Foundation in Basel has something like a thousand such products. They were put to paper with the composer's conscious will switched off and represent an aesthetic value which merited the choice of a selection for an exhibition.

Every now and again, one's talent is like an embryo: its potentialities at birth are undefined and only develop in an unequivocal direction at a later stage. Even then, the decision in favor of one and against another direction can be extremely hard to take and the only workable solution proves to be to remain faithful to more than one.

This dilemma has dogged creative artists in many fields. Victor Hugo could easily have stuck to his painting brush and his pencil; Alfred Kubin—on the strength of his one novel—could have made a remarkable writer; the unique world that Bruno Schulz conjured up in his novels was equally present in his pictures; whether Ingres might have made a good violinist is, in the absence of recordings, hard to judge.

But, to return once again to composers, Schoenberg may not have been a professional painter but his pictures have an unmistakable individuality, an almost scorching intensity. Hindemith was a superb draftsman, as testified to by a book published by the foundation carrying his name. My visit to John Cage's apartment in New York brought me face to face with his works of art, hanging properly framed, on his walls. Friedrich Cerha has created an impressive body of work in the way of *objets* and drawings, some of which have been

71. Mauricio Kagel, *Hochzeitstagebuch* (Wolke Verlag Hofheim, 2008).

presented at an exhibition. Next to his country house, he has built a chapel all by himself and inserted among the stone blocks some medieval carvings which are perfectly integrated with the rest of the architecture. Talent—genius—is the presence in the mind of an initially inchoate urge to express, to communicate something, whether in sounds and/or words and/or colors and forms.

Interestingly enough, of the composers who have contributed to my project, only Louis Andriessen has felt the need to fall back on colors, all of the other pictures are in black and white. Whether one can draw any conclusion from that, I cannot say. The drawings could perhaps be interpreted as diagrams rendering structure or direction or depicting music as an object in space. All that makes color irrelevant. This is certainly true of Johannes Maria Staud's contribution, which the composer himself describes as a product of his unconscious. The restlessness of the lines with their differing density and direction enclosed within the boundaries of the piece of paper is a reflection, beyond the music, of the young composer's vibrant personality. Iannis Xenakis, too, indicated that his drawing was a mirror of the way his thinking was functioning during composition.

I trust this "Encore" to the three questions sheds further light on the psychology of creativity, an aspect of the book that I did not envisage at the time of planning it but which appears to have emerged unintentionally as a sum total of the interviews and the drawings.[72]

72. The drawings, unless otherwise indicated, are reproduced by kind permission of the Bálint András Varga Collection, Akademie der Künste, Berlin.

Louis Andriessen (1939)

Amsterdam, November 26, 1996

Dear Mr. Varga,

The design (which I liked very much, seeing it back—I did not have another copy) concerns my composing *as a whole.*

In the first place, it is a consequence of the famous Stravinsky drawing: basically the same but more *rude, unreliable,* more *differences,* more *improvisation,* more *anarchy.*

Don't even try to interpret details.
My music is about gesture, movement.
Not about language. That's why you can't read what is "written."

Much success with your book. Keep me informed.

With best wishes,
Louis Andriessen

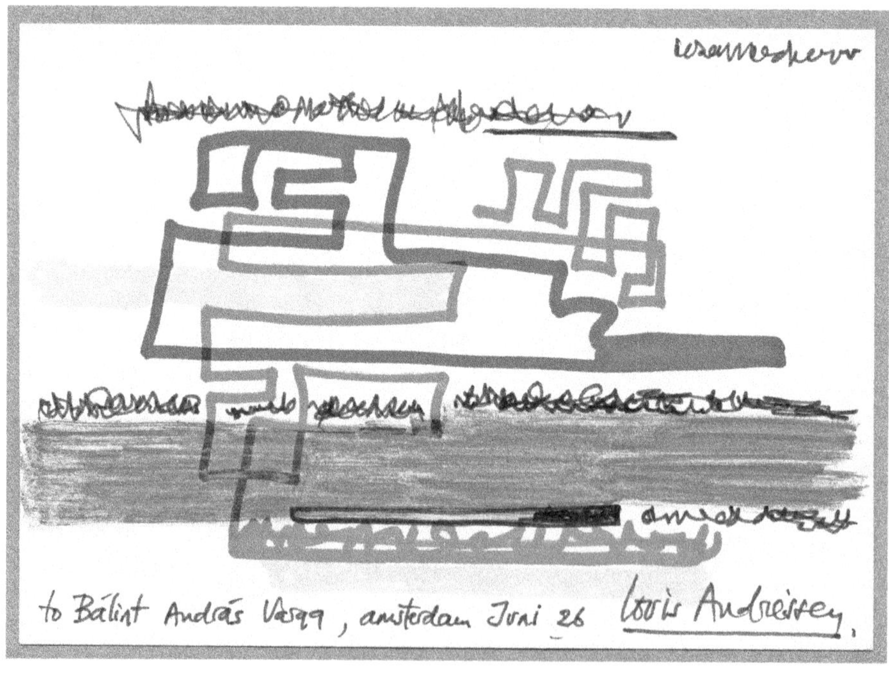

Milton Babbitt (1916–2011)

Princeton, July 19, 1996

Dear Mr. Varga,

I am delighted to learn that there is renewed interest in your project. After bringing myself to face my responses, I see no reason to alter them, but thank you for having given me the opportunity to renew my acquaintance with them.

I am pleased to enclose the visual expression of my music which I have never considered before, since my relation to my music has never been visual, but only aural. To accomplish the enclosed visualization I have secured the services of a distinguished graphic artist.

I look forward to the success of all your projects, and look forward to meeting you.

Very truly yours,
Milton Babbitt

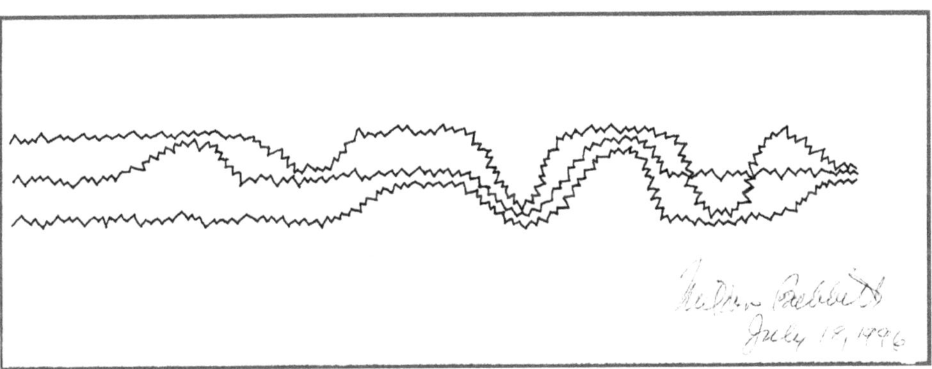

George Benjamin (1960)

London, 30th September 1997

Dear Bálint,

Many thanks for those scores of Wolfgang's orchestral works which I was delighted to receive. It was such a pleasure to see him in Lucerne last month.

I enclose the requested "Picture" of my music. I really have no idea if it represents my work in any real way at all . . . still I hope it's better than nothing. (I'm far from convinced, in fact!)

Hoping to see you here, or somewhere else, in the very near future.

All the best wishes, as ever,
George

"Wolfgang" in George Benjamin's letter is Wolfgang Rihm, whose works he conducts at regular intervals, mainly at his concerts in Britain.

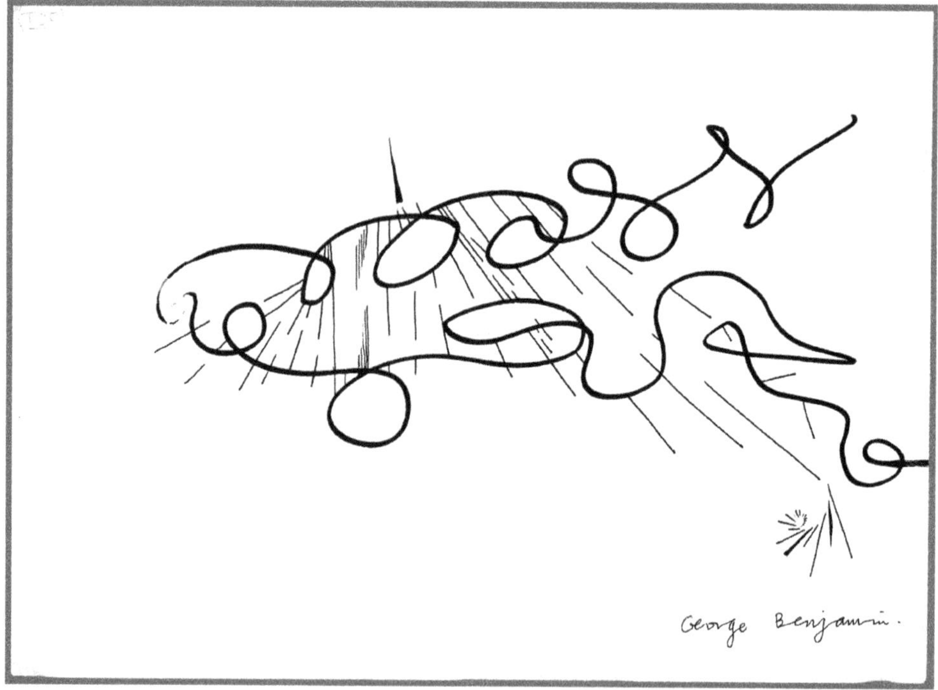

Earle Brown (1926–2002)

March 1995

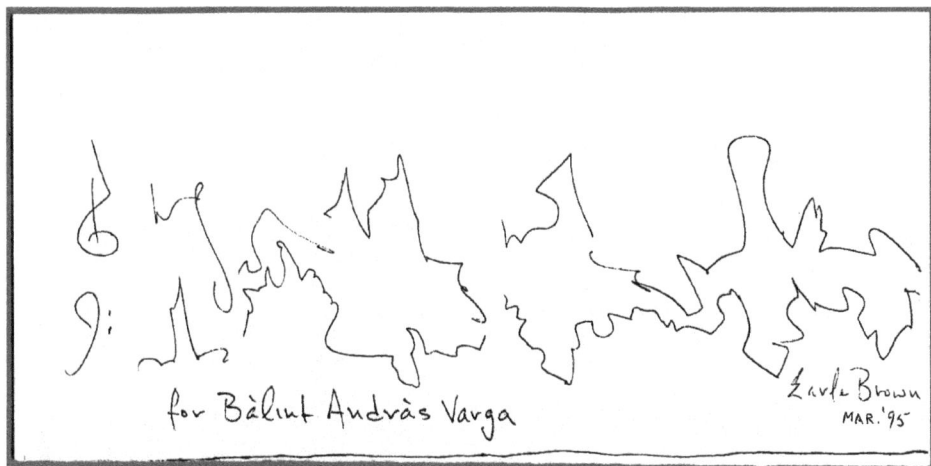

For Bálint András Varga

for Bàlint Andràs Varga

Earle Brown
MAR. '95

Elliott Carter (1908–2012)

Painting, 1948. Oil and enamel on canvas. 42 5/8 x 56 1/8 inches. Collection: The Museum of Modern Art, New York. © The Willem de Kooning Foundation/VBK, Vienna 2011.

Friedrich Cerha (1926)

I have had in my music and in my stone sculptures recourse to fundamental lapidary forms on the basis of which variously complex events could be developed. This drawing came about in the late 1970s, almost as a by-product of trying out my India ink brush. Perhaps it had the function of triggering something off, or perhaps that of evening out.

George Crumb (1929)

Philadelphia, June 17, 1996

Dear Mr. Varga:

I feel that the figure of a circle best represents the essential meaning of my music. In fact, many of my pieces contain examples of what I call "symbolic notations" which are very frequently representations of circles! In some cases the players must go around the circle many times (as in *Musica Mundana 1*). Even when I write music in the conventional linear manner, the sense of the music is often "circular"—i.e., there are elements which recur like cyclic elements (refrains, etc.).

Most cordially,
George Crumb

Here is a graphic representation of my music!
—George Crumb
[June 17, 1996]

Marc-André Dalbavie (1961)

"The technical Universe fails to supply that which my generation aspires for"—writes the composer who is regarded as a representative of the spectralist school in France.

Marc-André Dalbavie studied composition in Paris with Michel Philippot, analysis with Betsy Jolas and Claude Ballif, electroacoustics with Guy Rebel, orchestration with Marius Constant, musical computing science with Tristan Murail, and conducting with Pierre Boulez. Since 1996, he has been professor of orchestration at the Paris Conservatoire.

Franco Donatoni (1927–2000)

Milano, 2. 11. 1995

Dear Mr. Varga,

I enclose what you want.

Sincerely yours,
Franco Donatoni

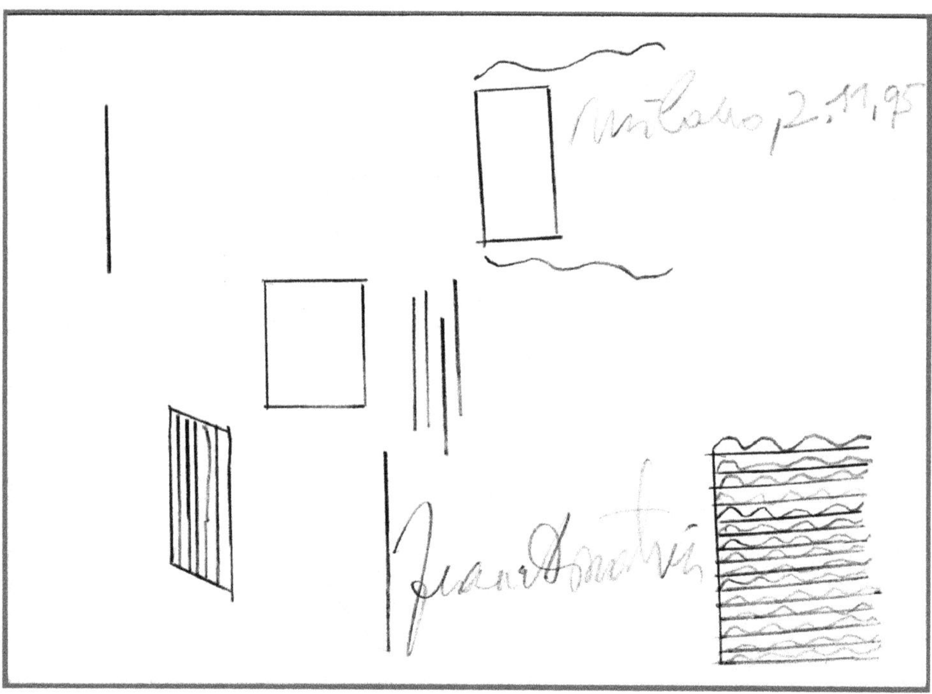

Pascal Dusapin (1955)

Paris, May 21st, 2001

Dear Mr. Varga,

I received your so enthusiastic phone message and I thank you very much for it! And now your letter which I'm answering so late. . . . But this month of May was devoted to completing my opera on which I have been working for 3 years for the Bastille Opera: . . . Phew! It is finished now! . . .

Regarding my drawings, I devote a little time to them almost every day. They relax me and above all they allow me to think about music without composing music which is often so useful. . . . These drawings have been sent several times. Today I am giving priority to "mixed exhibition" in order to avoid any confusion. On one side the drawings, on the other side the *real* musical manuscripts. Would you enjoy seeing some more? In the meantime, I am very happy about your project.

Best wishes,
Pascal Dusapin

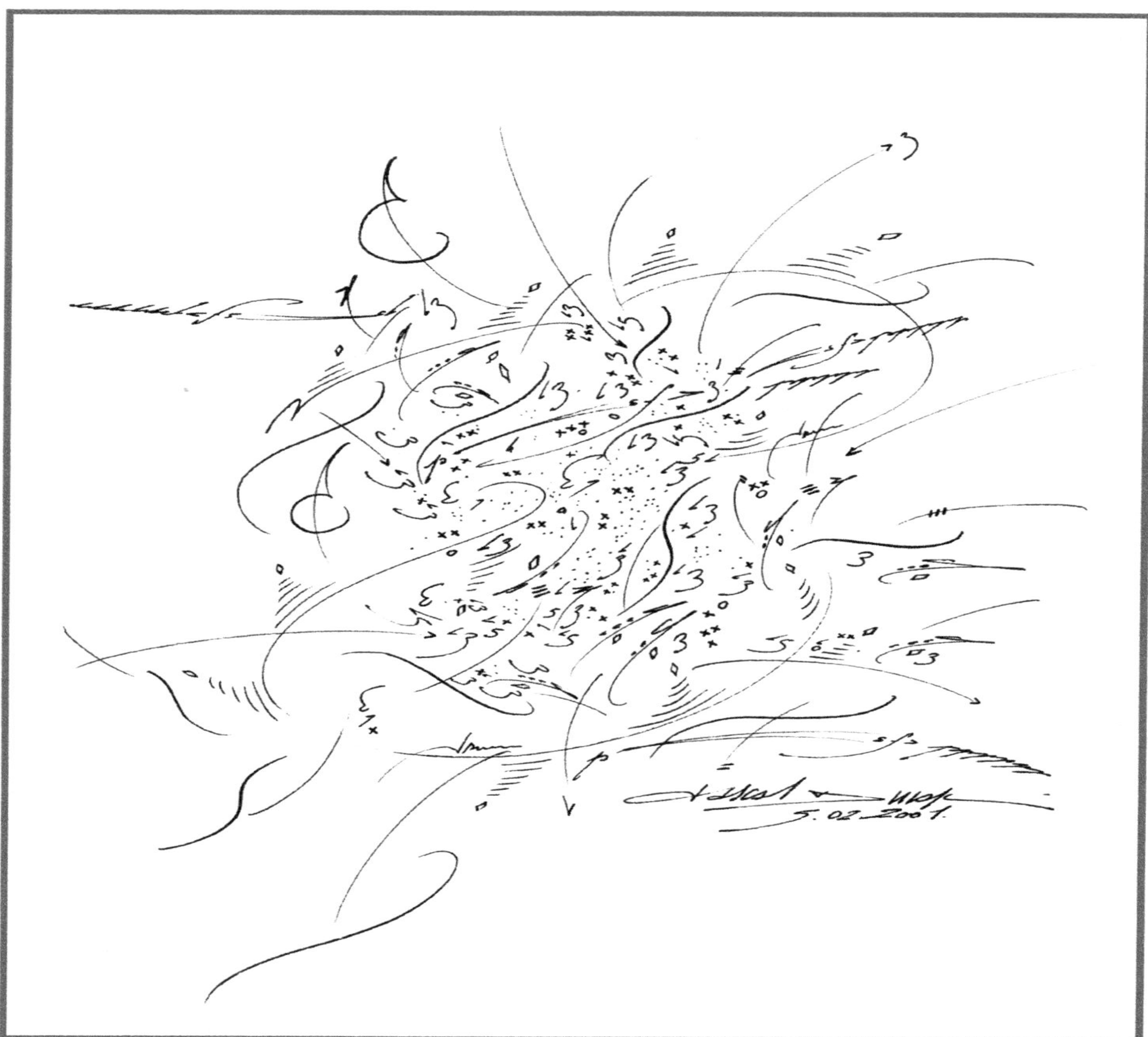
5. 02. 2001.

Henri Dutilleux (1916–2013)

Paris, le 15/XI/1996

I hope the fax with the interview has reached you safely (albeit very belatedly). I want to apologise again for my tardiness. I am sending you this little sketch to reply—if possible!—to your request.

Above all, I wish you much success for your work and yourself now that the year is coming to its close.

Sincerely yours,
Henri Dutilleux

Paris, décembre 1996

I realise I did not sign the drawing, neither did I date it even though you asked for it.

So here is another one! . . .

HDX

Sylvia Fómina (1962)

Micropolyphony or timbral pointillism

The Argentine composer of Russian parentage studied with György Ligeti. Her life, her thinking, and her music are marked by her experiences during the years of military dictatorship in her native country. Fómina dedicated the first work she composed after settling down in Germany, Expulsion. Désagrégation. Dispersion *(1992) for violoncello and tape to the "absent generation": thirty thousand victims of the regime who vanished without a trace between 1976 and 1983.*

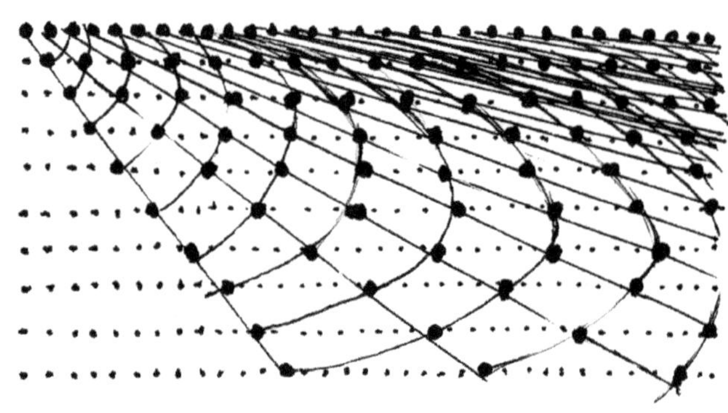

Beat Furrer (1954)

14. 2. 1995

For Bálint Varga

Very sincerely,
B. F.

Beat Furrer was born in Switzerland and moved to Vienna in 1975. To all intents and purposes, he is now an Austrian composer. In 1985, he founded the new music ensemble Klangforum, which he led until 1992. He has established himself as a major composer of his generation and is also sought after as a conductor.

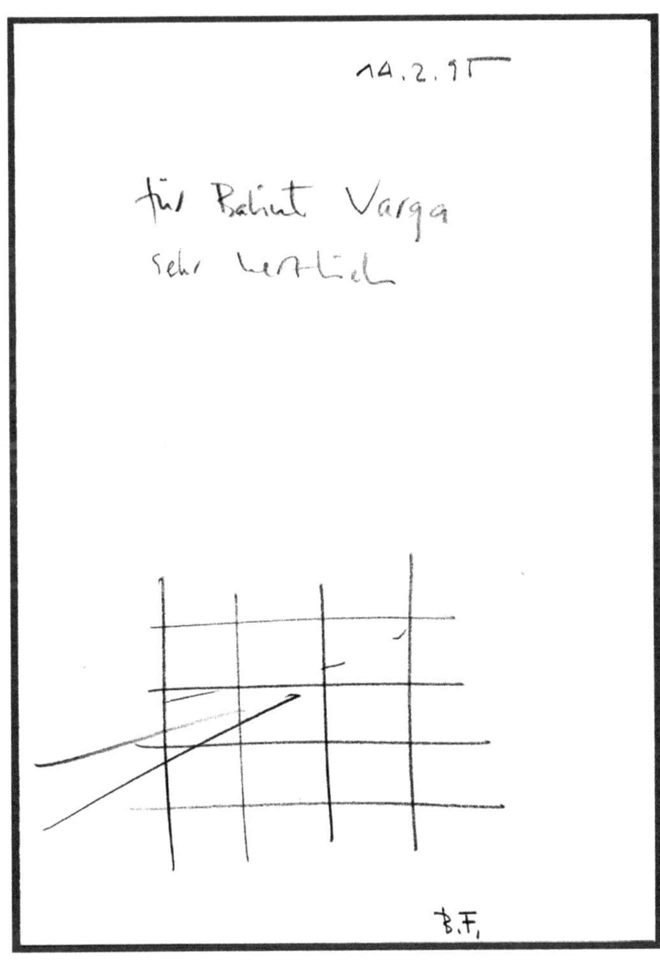

Cristóbal Halffter (1930)

Villafranca del Bierzo, 27. 2. 1995

Dear Mr. Varga,

Is this what you had in mind? We shall talk about it in Vienna.

With friendly greetings
from your
Cristóbal Halffter

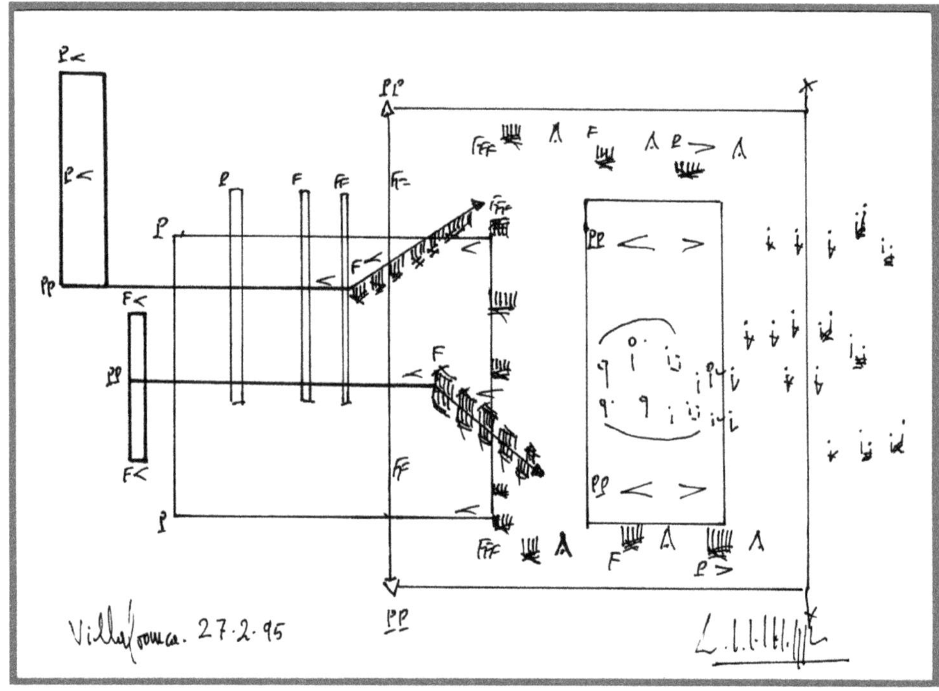

Jonathan Harvey (1939–2012)

Sussex, 19. 4. 2004

Dear Bálint Varga,

Here is the drawing you requested!
I hope to meet you again . . .

Best wishes,
Jonathan Harvey

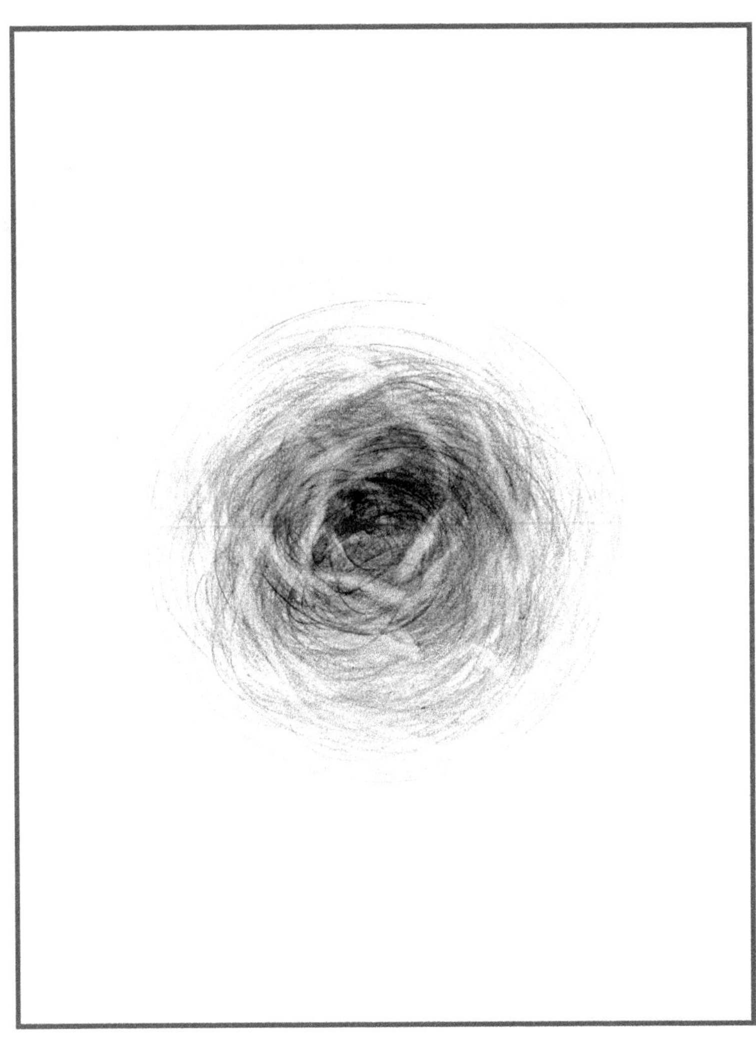

Toshio Hosokawa (1955)

Hiroshima, 10. April 1996

Dear Mr. Varga,

Herewith I am sending you "This is my music." It is a Japanese word: *Kokoro* (it means soul, heart . . .). My music is calligraphy in the air.

With kindest regards,
Toshio Hosokawa

György Kurtág (1926)

24. I. 1955

Dear Bálint—

Well, that's what I can do—although Márta says it is no longer valid. Still, that's my ideal.

With great love,
Gyuri

Kurtág sent me three drawings. Two of them are alike but one is rather smaller than the other. He insists that the smaller one mirrors his music more faithfully than the slightly larger one. Underneath the three figures he wrote: "A group of dancers like that—or puppet theatre?—has also cropped up once in a while." The reference to his wife, Márta, reflects the very special relationship between the two of them, one that spans over sixty years. The pianist Márta Kurtág is present in the composer's life on several levels, including as performer of his works and critic of his pieces in gestation. She is Kurtág's "projected ego," as he puts it; he consults her on everything he undertakes.

A few years later, I asked the great Austrian sculptor and graphic artist Alfred Hrdlicka (1928–2009) to take a look at the composers' images: I wondered how they would strike him, unaware as he was of the senders' identities. Hrdlicka examined them one by one and pronounced Kurtág's two "insects" to be of greatest interest: he sensed an element of concentration in them which he found missing in all the others.

Kurtág György 1995 I 24

Kurtág György 1995 I 24

egy ilyen tánccsoport – vagy bábszín-
ház – is előjött néha –

György Ligeti (1923–2006)

It took a little bit of persuasion for György Ligeti to give in, come to my office at Universal Edition, ask for a piece of paper, and "draw his music." I admit I was so excited that I felt my heart throb right in my throat. I left the room to let him get on with it in peace and was thrilled, on returning, to find four images, each bearing a date, representing his music in four different creative periods.

Several months before, when I gave him a white postcard-size piece of paper to draw on, he wrote on it in English: "Don't ask the old man: he will give you what he wants to give. (Shona proverb, Zimbabwe, Africa)."

Well, the "old man" did relent, thankfully, and gave me what I wanted.

I knew, of course, that drawing came to Ligeti quite naturally. He did not pretend to possess any talent in the professional sense of the word, but he would doodle if bored and the result could be quite fascinating. In 1948 or 1949, he presented his wife Vera with a drawing in color of The Last Judgement *(it hangs in his Vienna house); he also gave his son Lucas, then a little boy, two quite large-scale pictures, in the way of imaginative fairy tales. Almost all of his pictures had a recurring motif: a spider. It was an insect that had instilled fear in him ever since he was a child and perhaps he tried to exorcise it by placing it in his pictures.*

Ligeti would also give drawings as presents to people he liked. There is a rather well-known one, for instance, which he gave to his composition teacher Sándor Veress as a birthday present. The one reproduced here was executed on a postcard in Cologne, on August 1, 1957. The addressee was a lady in Vienna who had helped him and his wife after their flight from Hungary earlier that year. According to Vera Ligeti it has never been printed before.

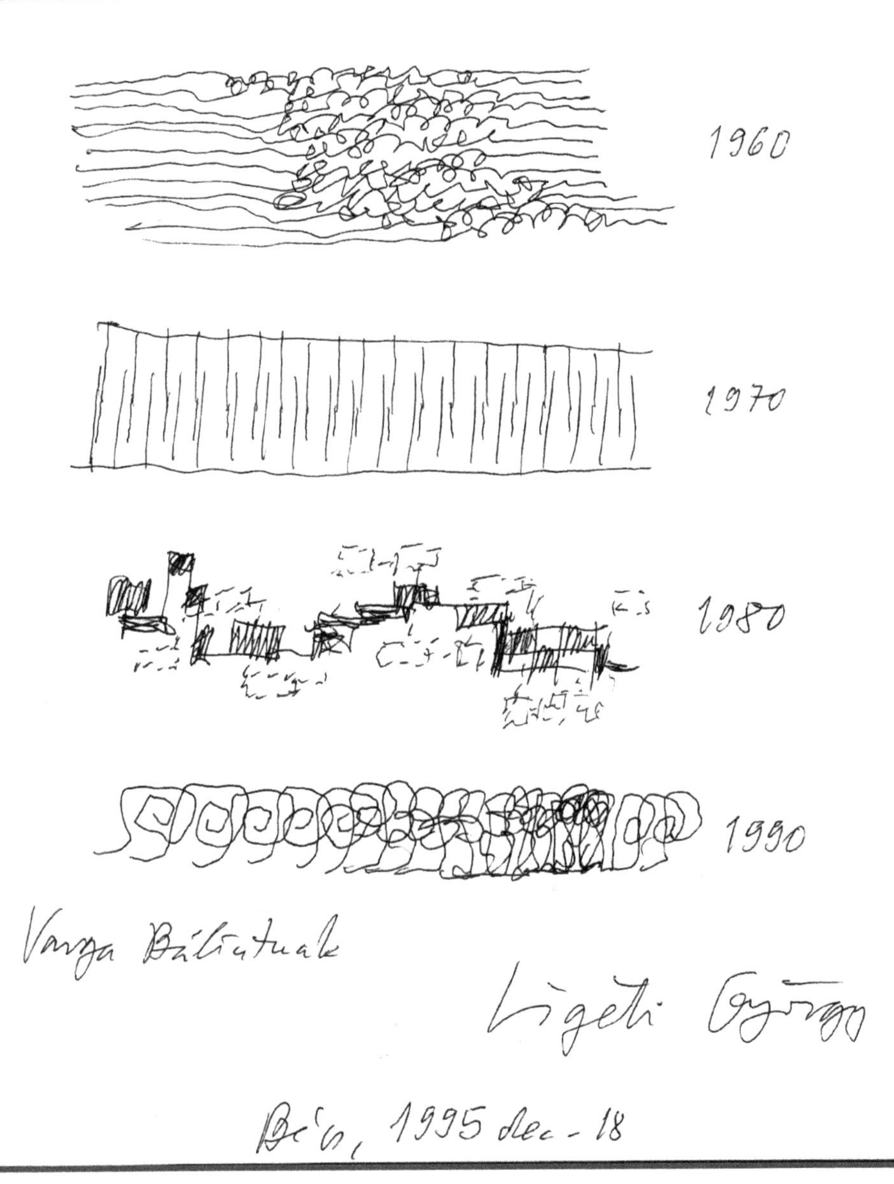
1960
1970
1980
1990
Varga Bálintnak
Ligeti György
Bécs, 1995 dec. 18

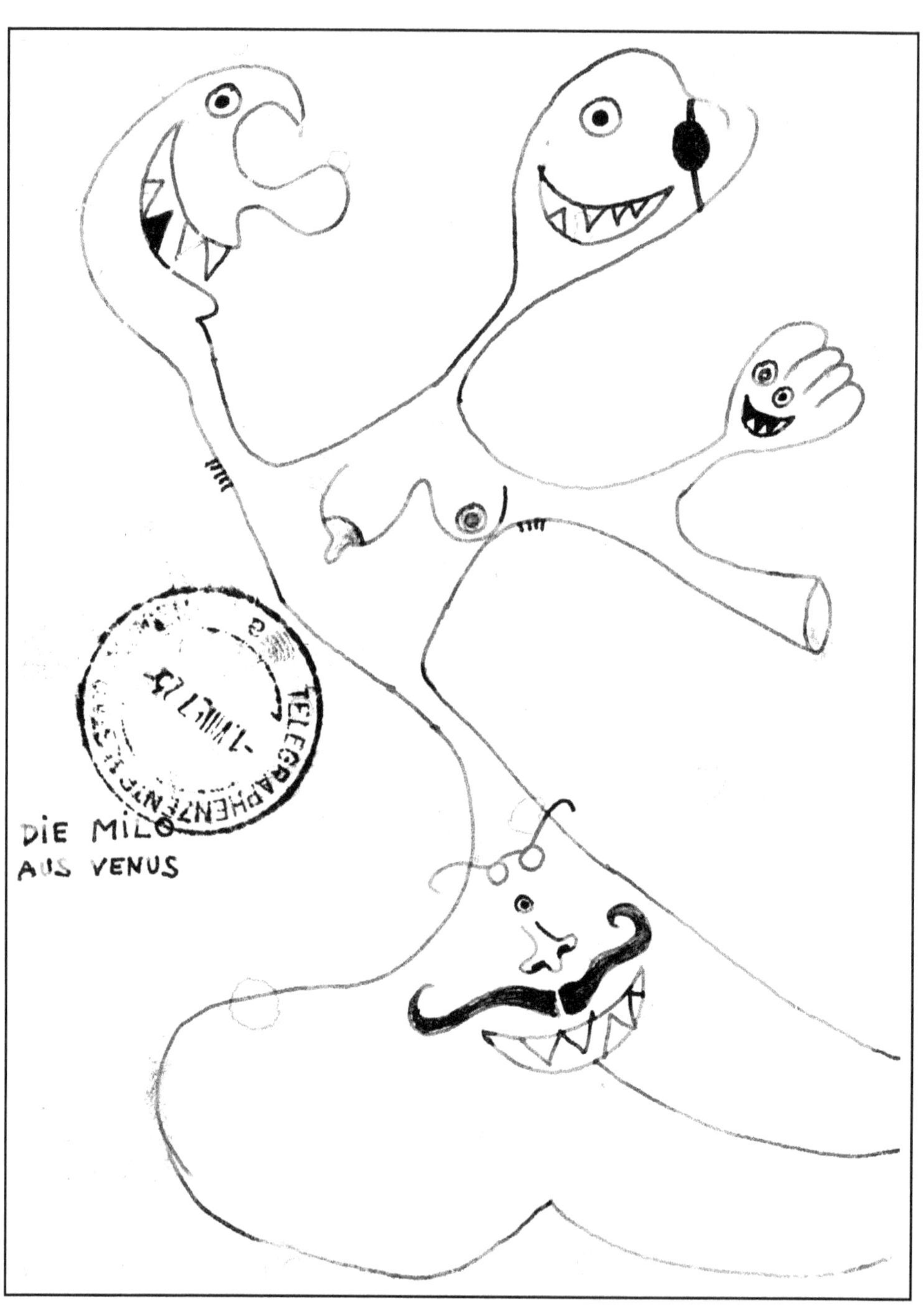
DIE MILO
AUS VENUS

Arvo Pärt (1935)

The card enclosed with the drawing bears the date Berlin, 4. 07. 1995, and the greeting "Kind regards—A. + N. Pärt"—that is, Arvo and Nora Pärt.

The composer ignored my request for a single drawing which would represent his music as such, but it is just as well: the pictures are fascinating in their imaginative variety. Also, Pärt "sees" his Tabula rasa *of 1977, a double concerto for two violins (or violin and viola), string orchestra, and prepared piano, almost identically with Robert Craft's image of Webern's music in his first book of conversations with Stravinsky. This goes to show the extent to which any visual representation of music is subjective.*

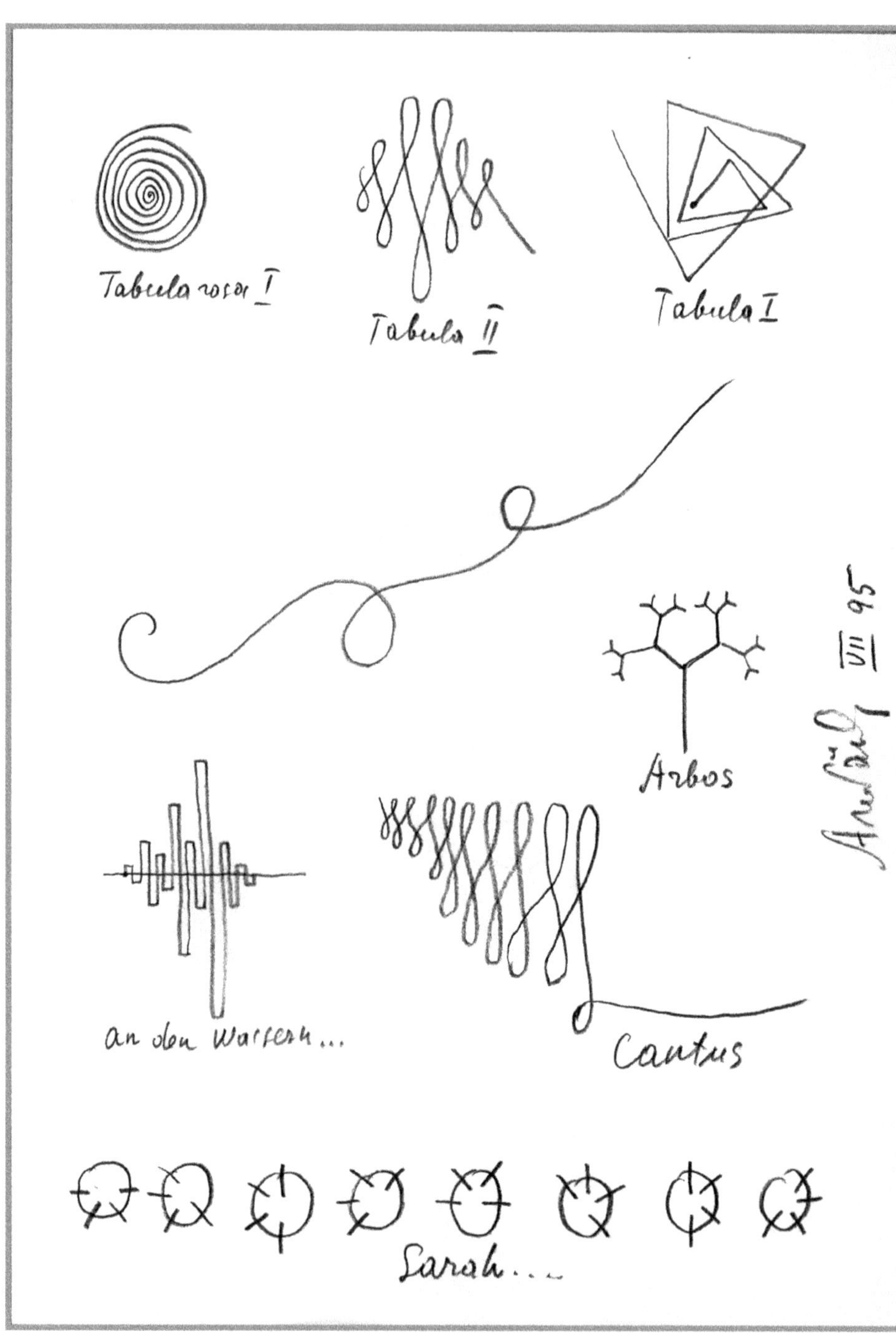
Tabula rasa I
Tabula II
Tabula I
Arbos
an den Wassern...
Cantus
Sarah...
VIII 95

Henri Pousseur (1929–2009)

Waterloo, 30 March 1995

Dear Mr. Varga,

What do you make of the enclosed little drawing? Not too complicated? (Should that be the case, please send another card so that the size is the right one.)

With best wishes for today,
Pousseur

An afterthought, Waterloo, 14 July 2005

To begin with, this is a two-dimensional space (to symbolize multidimensionality).

On the one hand, it represents the four directions of the wind, and also (at least) the entire globe on which I try to move (mostly mentally) as much as possible, in order to contribute to the so difficult and lengthy process of creating harmony among its inhabitants.

On the other hand, it comprises, as the X-axis (perhaps:?) the frequencies (pitches, timbres and other qualities of sound) and, as the Y-axis, *time* (once again, a summary of multiparameters), which means that, for the first-mentioned purpose, I treat not only all the elementary dimensions of sound but also all its forms of stylistic and grammatical organisation as available.

The south-west quarter provides a highly concise, coded, "patamatic" illustration of the "way" (Tao) where the extremely contrasting aspects can dynamically unite. The north-east one shows rather the flow of music from its (written, in any case innerly conscious) conception through vocal-instrumental (also electronic) realisation towards the aural consciousness of the (actively participating) listeners. Something that can be perceived as a turning wheel (the arrows encompassing the picture).

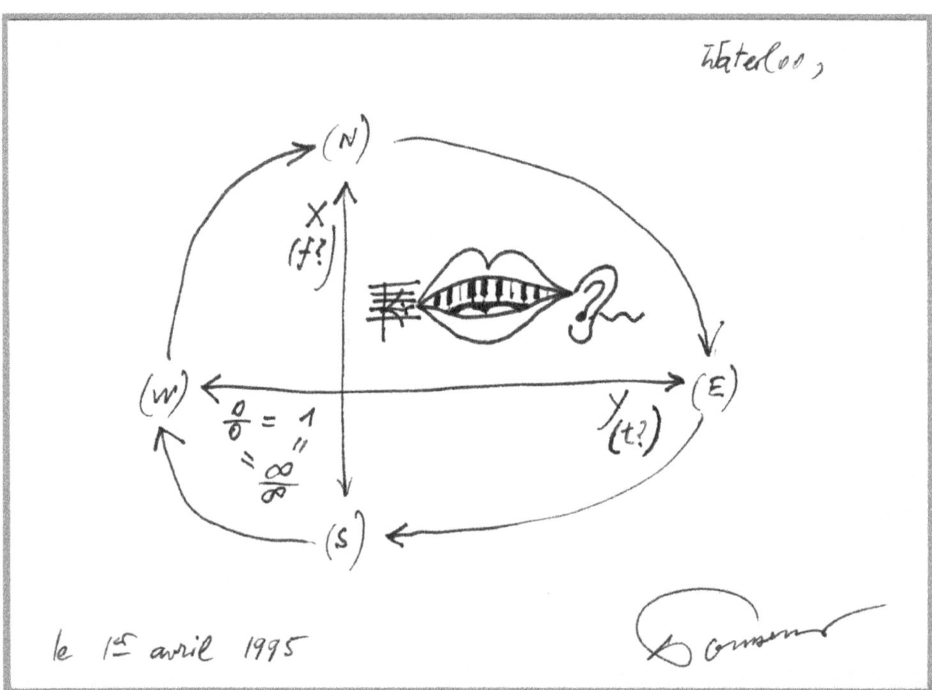

Waterloo,
(N)
X
(f?)
(W)
(E)
Y
(t?)
0/0 = 1
= ∞/∞
(S)
le 1er avril 1995

Steve Reich (1936)

[March 1995]

I understand the first 3 drawings but none of the others.
Here is my drawing of Bar 2 of *Clapping Music.*

Steve Reich

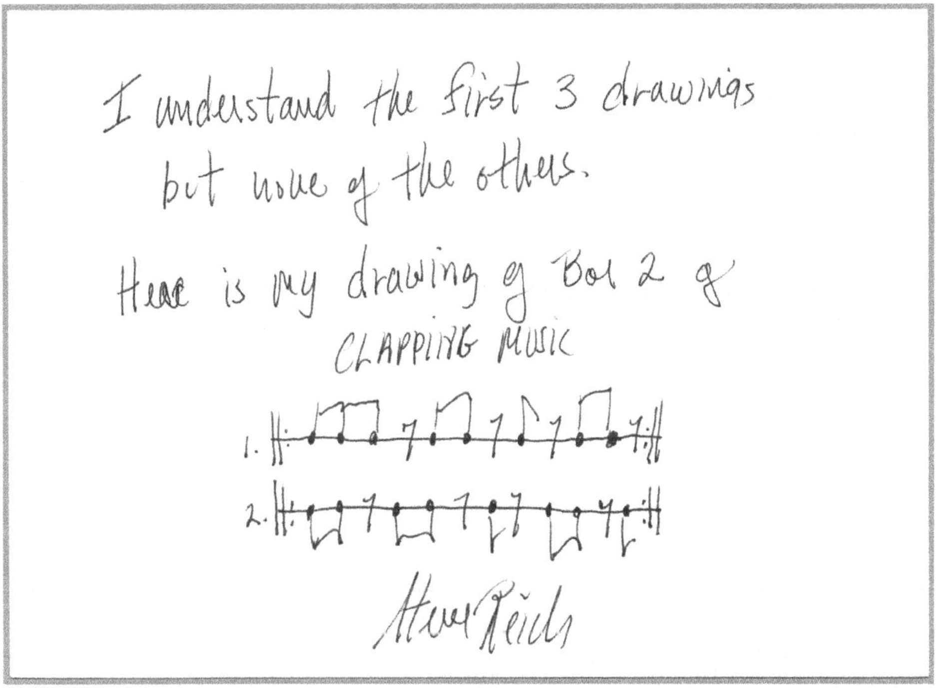

I understand the first 3 drawings
but none of the others.
Here is my drawing of Bar 2 of
CLAPPING MUSIC

1.

2.

Steve Reich

Wolfgang Rihm (1952)

I set the ball rolling early in January 1995 by sending a copy of the relevant page from the Stravinsky/Craft book with the drawings, a blank white card the size of a postcard, and a letter explaining what I was after, suggesting that the composers draw on the enclosed piece of paper. (This is the "regulation-size card" referred to by Rihm.)

By the end of the month, a large envelope with his drawings arrived in Vienna and so did three drawings by Kurtág. It looked very promising and I was optimistic that my plan of presenting a comprehensive survey of contemporary music in graphic images could be brought off. Sadly, it was not to be.

24. I. 95

Dear Bálint,

Naturally I cannot say (and draw!), like I.S. "*This* is my music."* However, I can today, on 24.I.95, pretend to be someone who pretends to be able to present his music as a pictogram. Here is the result. Always, only, and always always complete with date. Because tomorrow it might "look" like this: [ ] or like this: [ ] or like this: [ ] . . . or like this: !

But always yours
Wolfgang

*He only meant to comply with Robert Craft's request who presented him with the limited range of his ideas as little appetizers: the other picturelets are not by St. Igor but by Craft . . .

In the upper right-hand corner:

P.S. ". . . the fact that I am not replying on the regulation-size card could fit the picture of my music." I have picked up this sentence *en passant.*
W.

In the upper left-hand corner:

. . . it has all added up to a folder. But that should be no problem. In this way we have made sure that the projected publication has footnotes and an appendix.

HOWEVER:

This is a fake! My music has *never* looked like *this:*

This signature has also been faked. Watch out!

Here is the genuine one:
(repeated once again, as proof)

In the lower right-hand corner:
The date is *false!* On that day, no music could have looked in any way. See the decree of the Office of Musiclooks and Pictureprohibition of the day before.

Well, what did I say? Today, (25.I) my music looks like this:

Lieber Bálint,

natürlich kann ich nicht wie I. S. sagen (und zeichnen!) "This is my music" * Aber ich kann heute – am 24. I. 95 – so tun, als wäre ich jemand, der so tun könnte als könne er seine Musik piktogrammatikalisch in den Griff bekommen. Ergebnis anbei. Immer, nur und immimmimmer mit Datum. Denn morgen "sieht" sie vielleicht so aus:
oder so: … oder so: … oder so: !

Immer aber — Dein

Ligeti

* Er hat es ja auch nur Robert Craft zuliebe getan, der ihm seine begrenzten Vorstellungen als Appetizerchen vorzeichnete, denn die anderen Bildlein sind ja nicht von St. Igor sondern von Craft …

P.S. "… daß sich nicht auf die Vorschriftsmäßigkeit Karte antworten kommt, möge zum Bild meiner Musik passen" Diesen Satz habe ich einpassend aufgeschrieben W.

… Nun ist es doch ein Dossier geworden. Aber das macht nichts; so haben wir Fußnoten und Anhang der geplanten Publikation beide vorliegen. W.

JEDOCH:

Dies ist eine Fälschung! So hat meine Musik nie ausgesehen:

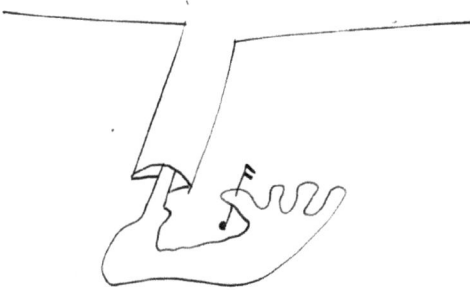

Georg Bößner

auch diese Unterschrift ist gefälscht! Vorsicht!

28. Januar 1888

Datum ist falsch! An diesem Tag kann gar keine Musik irgendwie ausgesehen haben: Vgl. Erlaß des Amtes für Musikanblick und Bildverbot vom Tag davor!

Hier echt:

György Ligeti

[nochmal bestätigt, zum Beweis:
György Ligeti]

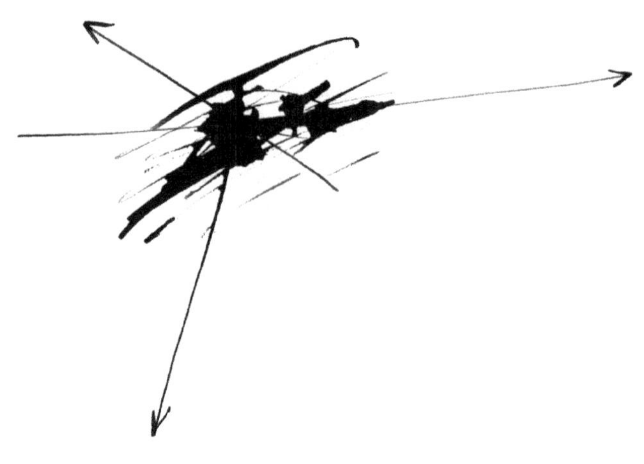

Wolfgang Rihm

24. I. 1995

na, was habe ich
gesagt!? Heute (25.1.)
sieht meine Musik
so aus:

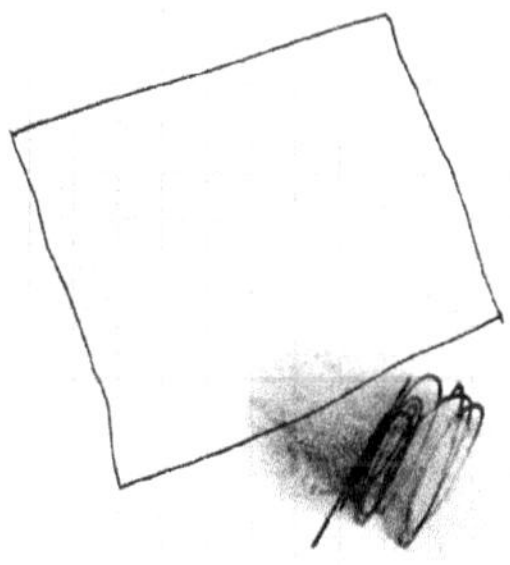

Wolfgang Rihm

25. I. 95

Peter Ruzicka (1948)

Hamburg, 16 November 1995

Dear Mr. Varga,

I am very sorry it has taken such a long time for me to find a solution to the assignment you gave me: to attempt a graphic image that corresponds to my music.

In the hope that it is not too late, I am sending you herewith an experiment. According to Ludwig Wittgenstein "If you cannot talk about something, you should remain silent." Let me add: one may at least draw.

With best wishes,
Peter Ruzicka

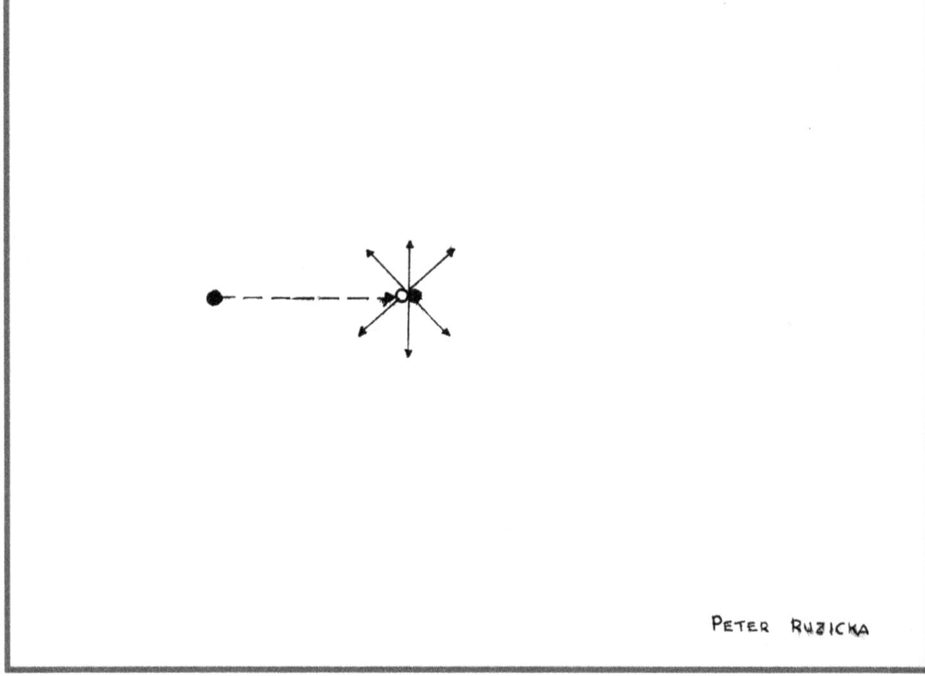

Johannes Maria Staud (1974)

24. 4. 2004

This drawing was made at the time of preparing the score of my opera *Berenice* in 2003/2004. Writing the fair copy always goes hand in hand with a second compositional process where all the decisions are weighed once again and one takes time to ponder questions a second time.

Before applying the pencil (always 2B in 0.5, 0.7 or 1.0) to paper, I draw circles and wave-shaped lines in order to arrive at the suitable position of the tip, that is, sharp for ties or stems, and blunt for cross-bars or dynamic signs.

The resulting drawing symbolizes my music, although—or rather: because—made unconsciously, better than any graphic image could do. Also, while these by-products may look somewhat alike, they correspond to the character of the music being composed.

András Szőllősy (1921–2007)

That is how I picture my music.

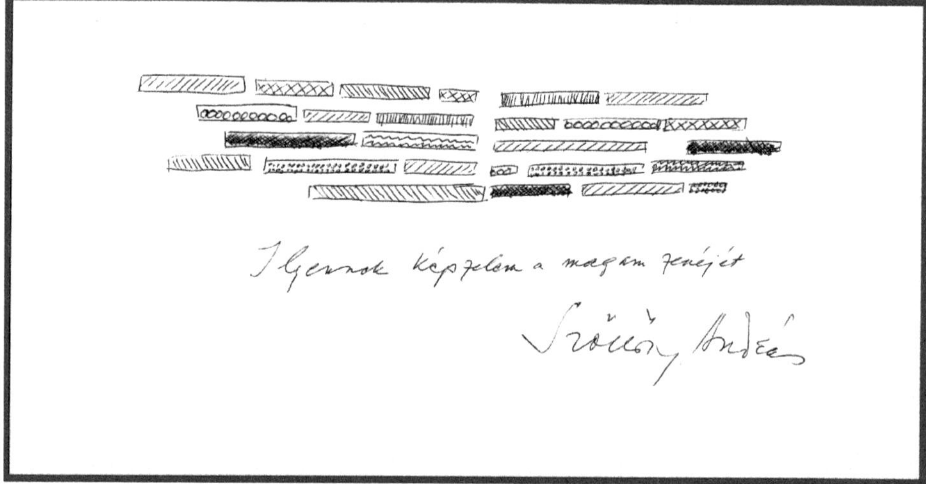

Iannis Xenakis (1922–2001)

Paris, May 1997

Dear Bálint,

This is a representation, a diagram, nothing real, a drawing of outlines, islets, of the idea or ideas that go into the composition!

Embracing you,
Xenakis

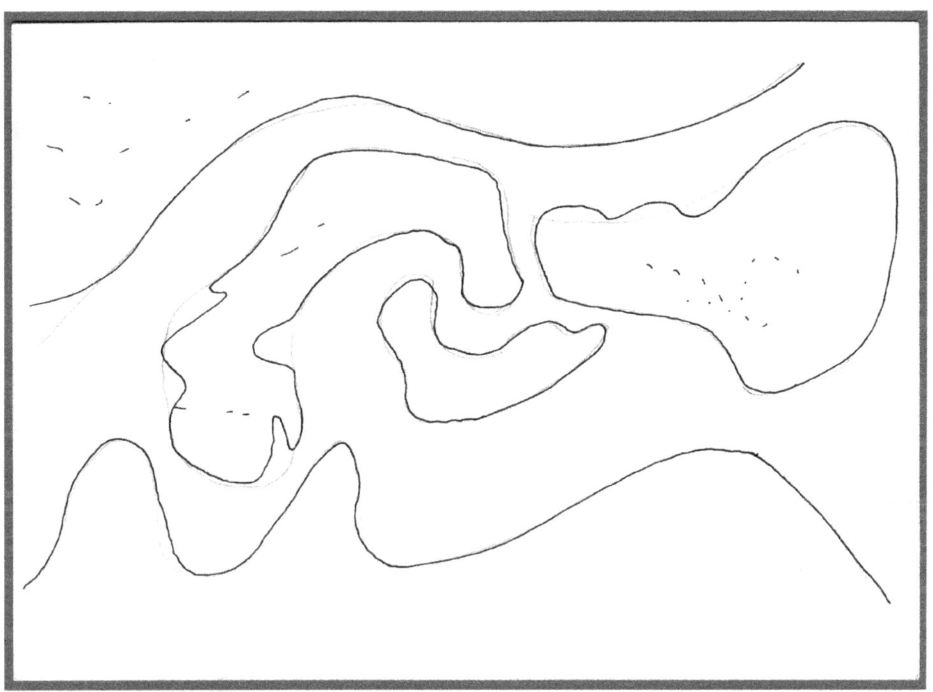

4

Dear Balint, is <u>this</u> what you want? I try to turn out memories so, I think, I become virgin again!

The Best to you

~

I. X.

<u>I</u> can try again if you dont like it!

INDEX

Eastman Studies in Music

Ralph P. Locke, Senior Editor
Eastman School of Music

Additional Titles of Interest

Analyzing Atonal Music: Pitch-Class Set Theory and Its Contexts
Michiel Schuijer

CageTalk: Dialogues with and about John Cage
Edited by Peter Dickinson

Composing for Japanese Instruments
Minoru Miki
Translated by Marty Regan
Edited by Philip Flavin

Concert Music, Rock, and Jazz since 1945: Essays and Analytic Studies
Edited by Elizabeth West Marvin and Richard Hermann

Dane Rudhyar: His Music, Thought, and Art
Deniz Ertan

Elliott Carter: Collected Essays and Lectures, 1937–1995
Edited by Jonathan W. Bernard

György Kurtág: Three Interviews and Ligeti Homages
Compiled and edited by Bálint András Varga

Intimate Voices: The Twentieth-Century String Quartet, Volumes 1 and 2
Edited by Evan Jones

The Music of Luigi Dallapiccola
Raymond Fearn

Music Speaks: On the Language of Opera, Dance, and Song
Daniel Albright

Music Theory and Mathematics: Chords, Collections, and Transformations
Edited by Jack Douthett, Martha M. Hyde, and Charles J. Smith

The Pleasure of Modernist Music: Listening, Meaning, Intention, Ideology
Edited by Arved Ashby

Ruth Crawford Seeger's Worlds: Innovation and Tradition in Twentieth-Century American Music
Edited by Ray Allen and Ellie M. Hisama

Samuel Barber Remembered: A Centenary Tribute
Peter Dickinson

The Sea on Fire: Jean Barraqué
Paul Griffiths

The Twelve-Tone Music of Luigi Dallapiccola
Brian Alegant

Variations on the Canon: Essays on Music from Bach to Boulez in Honor of Charles Rosen on His Eightieth Birthday
Edited by Robert Curry, David Gable, and Robert L. Marshall

A complete list of titles in the Eastman Studies in Music series may be found on the University of Rochester Press website, www.urpress.com.

Do today's composers draw inspiration from life experiences or from, say, the natural world?

What influences, past and present, have influenced recent composers?

How essential is it for a composer to develop a personal style, and when does this degenerate into self-repetition?

These are questions about which some of the most important composers of the late twentieth and early twenty-first century often have quite strong feelings—but have seldom been asked.

In this pathbreaking book, Bálint András Varga puts these three questions to such renowned composers as Luciano Berio, Pierre Boulez, Alberto Ginastera, Sofia Gubaidulina, Hans Werner Henze, Helmut Lachenmann, György Ligeti, Witold Lutosławski, Luigi Nono, Krzysztof Penderecki, Wolfgang Rihm, Karlheinz Stockhausen, Tōru Takemitsu, and Iannis Xenakis. Varga's sensitive English renderings capture the subtleties of their sometimes confident, sometimes hesitant, answers.

All statements from English-speaking composers—such as Milton Babbitt, John Cage, Elliott Carter, Sir Peter Maxwell Davies, Morton Feldman, Lukas Foss, Steve Reich, Gunther Schuller, and Sir Michael Tippett—consist of the composers' own carefully chosen words.

Three Questions for Sixty-Five Composers is vital reading for anybody interested in the current state of music and the arts.

The Hungarian music publisher Bálint András Varga has spent nearly forty years working for and with composers. He has published several books, including extensive interviews with Lutosławski, Berio, and Xenakis. His previous book for the University of Rochester Press is *György Kurtág: Three Interviews and Ligeti Homages.*

"In this rich book conceived by Bálint András Varga, eminent composers of different generations converse with each other through their highly distinctive answers to three recurring, probing questions. Each page of this book is haunted by questions of memory—not least, how a composer's specific style develops through time."

—Frank Madlener, general director,
IRCAM (Centre Pompidou, Paris)

"Typical of Bálint András Varga, the most civilized and intelligent of publishers, to elicit such a multiplicity of responses to three deceptively simple questions. Necessary reading for all who care about the music of our time."

—Sir Simon Rattle, principal conductor of the
Berlin Philharmonic Orchestra and artistic
director of the Berlin Philharmonie

"This book presents a rich collection of personal statements by our most famous recent composers. Their distinct responses to Varga's three questions offer the reader an insider's view of the ways each composer developed a musical style, situated in the tension between tradition and individual artistic experience. A fascinating compendium of an important chapter in contemporary cultural history."

—Franz Welser-Möst, general music director,
Vienna State Opera

www.ingramcontent.com/pod-product-compliance
Lightning Source LLC
Chambersburg PA
CBHW070403100426
42812CB00005B/1612

* 9 7 8 1 5 8 0 4 6 3 7 9 9 *